GLOBAL ISSUES

HUMAN TRAFFICKING

Kathryn Cullen-DuPont

Foreword by Jessica Neuwirth and Taina Bien-Aimé
President and Executive Director, Equality Now

Facts On File
An imprint of Infobase Publishing

GLOBAL ISSUES: HUMAN TRAFFICKING

Copyright © 2009 by Infobase Publishing

Facts On File, Inc.
An imprint of Infobase Publishing
132 West 31st Street
New York NY 10001

Library of Congress Cataloging-in-Publication Data
Cullen-DuPont, Kathryn.
    Human trafficking / Kathryn Cullen-DuPont; foreword authors, Jessica Neuwirth and Taina Bien-Aimé.
        p. cm.—(Global issues)
    Includes bibliographical references and index.
    ISBN 978-0-8160-7545-4
    1. Human trafficking. 2. Forced labor. 3. Child labor. 4. Slavery. I. Title.
    HQ281.C85 2009
    364.15—dc22   2008055931

Facts On File books are available at special discounts when purchased in bulk quantities for businesses, associations, institutions, or sales promotions. Please call our Special Sales Department in New York at (212) 967-8800 or (800) 322-8755.

You can find Facts On File on the World Wide Web at http://www.factsonfile.com

Text design by Erika K. Arroyo
Cover design by Alicia Post
Illustrations by Patricia Meschino

Printed in the United States of America

MP MSRF 10 9 8 7 6 5 4 3 2 1

This book is printed on acid-free paper and contains 30 percent postconsumer recycled content.

For Melissa Cullen-DuPont,
daughter, friend, colleague

CONTENTS

PART II: Primary Sources

PART III: Research Tools

List of Maps and Tables

Foreword

As we enter the 21st century, we continue to grapple with a plethora of ills plaguing the world, such as poverty, hunger, a fragile environment, widespread discrimination, and war. Fundamental human rights are too often denied by those in control, whether in governments, communities, or in the home. The list of these human rights violations is long, but one of the most heinous crimes has in recent years recaptured our attention: the selling and buying of people for profit, otherwise known as human trafficking.

Trafficking in human beings has existed since the beginning of civilization, but in recent years the scourge of trafficking, or what many people call modern-day slavery, has exponentially increased due to globalization, the magnitude of poverty, organized crime, government corruption, and (as it relates to sex trafficking) the growth of the global commercial sex industry. Indeed, throughout history, various societies have managed to incorporate slavery, or elements thereof, into their fabric, where human beings were invariably defined in law and in practice as objects. The city-states of Sparta, Athens, and Rome were built on forced labor. From the Babylonian era through the Middle Ages, up until a few centuries ago, governments allowed and profited from a thriving slave trade that contributed immensely to the growth of powerful hegemonies. Nothing, however, compared to the slave trade from Africa into the Americas, from the beginning of the 15th century to the Emancipation Proclamation in 1863, when slavery legally ended in the United States. While a number of writings and testimonies depict the intense brutality of slavery under which men, women, and children were legally owned as chattel, it is close to impossible for those outside of these experiences to fully grasp the suffering perpetuated by such unspeakable crimes.

As Professor Cullen-DuPont lays out in her book, today enslavement bears myriad faces. Millions of people are bought and sold every year around the globe either for labor or sexual servitude. Looking at a world map, every country in the world, except perhaps the continent of Antarctica, is affected by human trafficking. Countries are either a source, transit, or destination country, meaning that traffickers obtain their supply of human beings—generally from a developing country—transport and harbor them through a variety of places, to ultimately sell them into servitude in a final destination, most likely an industrialized nation. In addition, many trafficking victims never leave their countries of origin or are sold from one poor country to another. Finally, many countries are themselves a combination of source, transit, and ultimate destination.

Examples of modern-day slavery include small boys enslaved as camel jockeys. Men eager to find work are forced to leave their countries to pick fruit or work in factories under horrific circumstances from morning to night seven days a week with little or no pay. Young women seeking a better life are lured into the devastating commercial sex trade or to work as domestic servants under great abuse. Children are captured or recruited as soldiers; babies inherit a lifetime of debt bondage. Under the cloak of gender inequality, female infants are sold at birth, girls and young women are forced into early marriage or purchased by sex tourists, and women are sold, through mail order, as brides. People are trafficked for greed, to satisfy the demand for cheap goods and services, and to quench the demand for prostitution.

The complexities of human trafficking are staggering; complicated further with the rise of the Internet, they overwhelm governments. Official statistics assessing the number of trafficked individuals around the world are sketchy, but the numbers we have to date are frightening. The United Nations estimates that more than 4 million people are trafficked every year and the U.S. Department of State estimates that 14,500 to 17,500 individuals are trafficked into the United States from foreign countries. People are also trafficked within their own countries, as transport across international borders is not a defining characteristic of human trafficking. One statistic on which international agencies and governments all agree is that 80 percent of trafficked persons are women and children, and that the majority of that population is trafficked for commercial sexual exploitation. Some studies indicate that up to 800,000 United States–born children are at risk of exploitation in the sex trade.

Traffickers procure their victims in many ways. They kidnap targeted individuals or prey on vulnerable communities where desperation to flee poverty or support their families allows traffickers to deceive with sham offers of legitimate work in another country. Some traffickers purchase children and young women from destitute parents or promise them a better life only to sell them into sexual or domestic servitude. Other traffickers, in the form of pimps, lure vulnerable girls into the commercial sex trade. Regardless of how they are propelled into the web of trafficking—whether through force, deception, or coercion—the victims suffer unimaginable human rights violations, more often than not with no means of exit.

Reading this book will give you an excellent overview of the breadth and depth of trafficking and how this illegal industry affects our lives in ways that are not always apparent. Trafficked people often blend into our society. You may not realize that the man who sweeps your favorite restaurant or your neighbor's live-in maid may be victims of labor trafficking. Similarly, women and girls in the multibillion dollar commercial sex industry are also hidden in plain sight in massage parlors, brothels, on the streets, in strip clubs, or advertised blatantly on the Internet by sex tour operators or bloggers.

With the antebellum era behind us, one may ask why trafficked human beings do not leave their captors, seek help from law enforcement, try to return home, or run to a shelter. Chains on feet or locked doors are not needed for an exploited person to remain enslaved. Traffickers and their accomplices threaten their victims or their families with death or severe injury, coerce their victims psychologically and physically into believing they are not worthy of a life of dignity and escape is impossible. Foreign victims of trafficking may not be able to navigate the destination country because of language barriers or fear of the police. Also, while governments around the world officially condemn slavery and human trafficking, they grapple with ways to address human trafficking effectively, often leading to a culture of impunity, because of inadequate legislation, weak enforcement tools, or lack of political will to address the problem.

The economics of human trafficking also plays a significant role in the perpetuation of this human rights violation. As Cullen-DuPont indicates, the total dollar value of human trafficking is estimated at $32 billion. Hand in hand with arms and drug trafficking, criminal networks and individuals acting independently reap billions of dollars every year from the selling and reselling of human beings. Sex trafficking, in particular, contributes to entire national economies. The International Labour Organization, for example, estimates that the revenues generated from the commercial sex industry in Southeast Asia can be anywhere between 2 and 14 percent of gross domestic products. The demand for commercial sex, facilitated in countries where the industry of prostitution is legalized or normalized, is the engine that drives and contributes directly and fundamentally to the growth and perpetuation of sex trafficking.

Professor Cullen-DuPont also underlines the good news about national and international efforts and tools in place to address human trafficking, including the Protocol to Prevent, Suppress and Punish Trafficking in Persons, Especially Women and Children, adopted by the United Nations in December 2003. In the United States the Trafficking Victims Protection Act, enacted in 2000 was reauthorized in December 2008 as the William Wilberforce Trafficking Victims Protection Reauthorization Act, which inches closer to a strong national trafficking instrument that can effectively prosecute traffickers, address demand, and protect all trafficking victims. In addition, a number of other countries around the world are enacting comprehensive anti-trafficking laws that, if properly enforced, can act as valuable tools to address the issue.

While laws are essential first steps to address human trafficking both nationally and internationally, they are not enough. Governments must exercise political will to prevent trafficking by establishing programs that provide education and economic opportunities to their most vulnerable citizens, directly or through the United Nations and its agencies. Cullen-DuPont lists a number of advocacy and other nongovernmental organizations that have stepped in to fill these unmet needs by providing social, legal, medical, and educational services to trafficking survivors and those who are at risk. However, these organizations' respective capacities remain limited in light of the magnitude of the problem.

Still, there is a role for everyone in this struggle. We must, individually and as a society, examine and curb our insatiable need for cheap goods and services by asking the chain stores where we shop, our political representatives, and ourselves who picks our coffee beans or stitches the jeans we wear. Securing equality for women and girls is fundamental to ending sex trafficking. As the sex trade flourishes at the cruel expense of the most vulnerable and voiceless, we must shift the paradigm of normalizing the exploitation of women in the sex trade by educating the public and our families that women are not for sale. Raising awareness about human trafficking is the first step toward action. In countries and states where there are no anti-trafficking laws, or weak ones, we can work together to pass strong legislation by simply writing a letter or starting a campaign. The media is also a key tool in exposing stories and asking governments tough questions about law enforcement and policies to help trafficking victims, as well as amplifying the voices of survivors.

Eleanor Roosevelt, the architect of the Universal Declaration of Human Rights, once said that the destiny of human rights is in the hands of all our citizens in all our communities. The candles are lit to end human trafficking—we now need to spread a fire for its abolition.

—Jessica Neuwirth, president
— Taina Bien-Aimé, executive director
Equality Now

Acknowledgments

I would like to thank the many people who offered help and support during the writing of this book. At Facts On File, that list includes Editorial Director Laurie Likoff, for the inclusion of this difficult but extremely important topic in the Global Issues series; Executive Editor Claudia Schaab, for entrusting her series' topic of human trafficking to me and whose questions, suggestions, and thoughtful editing have greatly added to this book; Assistant Editor Alexandra Lo Re, who added to this book with questions of her own; Chief Copy Editor Michael G. Laraque and Copy Editor Alexandra Simon, who reviewed every word of this book with exacting care; Production Associate Brigid Duffy, for her work on this book; Art Director for Book Interiors Erika Arroyo, for the text design; Patricia Meschino, for the design of the various maps, tables, and graphs I have included in this book; and Alicia Post, for a cover design that conveys the horrific nature of modern-day slavery without exploiting its victims.

I would also like to thank those who took time from their daily work against human trafficking to provide me with information and, in some cases, to read the manuscript in its entirety. That list includes Paul Donohoe of Slavery International, Sarah Jakiel of the Polaris Project, Jessica Neuwirth and Taina Bien-Aimé of Equality Now, and John R. Miller, the former U.S. ambassador-at-large for modern slavery and former director of the U.S. State Department's Office to Monitor and Combat Trafficking in Persons. Particular thanks go to Ambassador Miller for his thorough and thoughtful review of my manuscript and to Ms. Neuwirth and Ms. Bien-Aimé for their foreword, which clearly outlines the need for greater public awareness of human trafficking.

My family has also offered help and support throughout the writing of this book. My husband, Joe DuPont, did everything he could to free my time for research and writing; my son, Jesse Cullen-DuPont, and my son-in-law, Karl Luecht, offered their own support; and my parents and three of my sisters—Martin and Arlene Cullen, Jeanne Jimenez, Eileen Ramirez, and Denise Paccione—acted as proofreaders. To the rest of my family, my friends, and the many colleagues at Pratt Institute and Goddard College who generously entered the years-long discussion of human trafficking that surrounded this book, I also extend my thanks.

Finally, there is one person whose help and presence during the writing of this book transcend categorization: my daughter, Melissa Cullen-DuPont, who as an associate editor at Facts On File first brought the Global Issues series to my attention and whose reading of my work was—as it has been for some time now—its final reading before leaving my hands. It is an enormous pleasure to dedicate this book to her.

I am grateful for all the assistance I have received during my writing of *Human Trafficking;* if my book contains errors despite such help, those errors are most certainly my own.

List of Acronyms

AASG	American Anti-Slavery Group
ACLU	American Civil Liberties Union
AFRUCA	Africans Unite Against Child Abuse
AID	Agency for International Development (U.S.)
ASI	Anti-Slavery International
BLinN	Bonded Labour in the Netherlands
BNRM	Bureau Nationaal Rapporteur Mensenhandel (National Reporter on Human Trafficking)
BTIA	Belize Tourism Industry Association
CATW	Coalition Against Trafficking in Women
CDPO	Chief Dowry Prevention Officer (India)
CEDAW	1979 Convention on the Elimination of All Forms of Discrimination against Women (UN)
CIA	Central Intelligence Agency (U.S.)
CIW	Coalition of Immokalee Workers
COMENSHA	COördinatiecentrum MENSenHAndel (see STV)
CRA	Child Rights Act (Nigeria)
CRS	Congressional Reporting Service (U.S.)
CSI	Christian Solidarity International
CST	child sex tourism
CSW	Commission on the Status of Women (UN)
DHS	Demographic and Health Survey (Nigeria)
DPKO	Department of Peacekeeping Operations (UN)
ECOWAS	Economic Community of West African States
ECPAT	End Child Prostitution, Child Pornography and Trafficking of Children for Sexual Purposes
EU	European Union
Europol	European Police Office
FBI	Federal Bureau of Investigation (U.S.)
FGM	female genital mutilation

FLSA	Fair Labor Standards Act
FTF	Fair Trade Federation
FTS	Free the Slaves
GAATW	Global Alliance Against Traffic in Women
GDP	gross domestic product
GPAT	Global Programme against Trafficking in Human Beings (UN)
GPI	Girls' Power Initiative (Nigeria)
HHS	Department of Health and Human Services (U.S.)
HIV/AIDS	human immunodeficiency virus/acquired immunodeficiency syndrome
HRW	Human Rights Watch
ICC	International Criminal Court
ICE	Immigration and Customs Enforcement (U.S.)
IFAD	International Fund for Agricultural Development (UN)
IFAT	International Fair Trade Association
IJM	International Justice Mission
ILO	International Labour Organization (UN)
IOM	International Organization for Migration
IPEC	ILO/International Programme on the Elimination of Child Labour (UN)
IRIN	Integrated Regional Information Networks (part of the UN Office for the Coordination of Humanitarian Affairs)
LRA	Lord's Resistance Army
MDG Report(s)	Millennium Development Goal Report(s) (by country)
MDGs	Millennium Development Goals
MHA	Ministry of Home Affairs (India)
MSPA	Migrant and Seasonal Agricultural Worker Protection Act (U.S.)
NAHTIWA	Network Against Human Trafficking In West Africa
NAPTIP	National Agency for the Prohibition of Trafficking in Persons and Other Related Matters (Nigeria)
NAPTIP Act	Trafficking in Persons Law Enforcement and Administration Act (Nigeria)
NCMEC	National Center for Missing and Exploited Children (U.S.)
1956 Supplementary Convention	1956 Supplementary Convention on the Abolition of Slavery, the Slave Trade, and Institutions and Practices Similar to Slavery
NGOs	nongovernmental organizations

List of Acronyms

NHRC	National Human Rights Commission of India
NLRA	National Labor Relations Act (U.S.)
NLRB	National Labor Relations Board (U.S.)
NPS	National Park Service (U.S.)
OVC	Department of Justice's Office for Victims of Crime (U.S.)
PHR	Physicians for Human Rights
PNDT	Pre-natal Diagnostic Techniques Act of 1994 (India)
PROTECT Act of 2003	Prosecutorial Remedies and Other Tools to end the Exploitation of Children Today Act (U.S.)
RUFARM	Roots and Fruits Women's Farmers Society of Nigeria
SAARC	South Asian Association for Regional Cooperation
SACCS	South Asian Coalition on Child Servitude (India)
SAGE	Standing Against Global Exploitation Project (U.S.)
SC	scheduled castes (India)
SPOs	special police officers (Salwa Judum, India)
ST	scheduled tribes (India)
STCI	Save the Children India
STDs	sexually transmitted diseases
STV	Stichting Tegen Vrouwenhandel (Foundation against Trafficking in Women, Netherlands). See COMENSHA
TIP Office	Office to Monitor and Combat Trafficking in Persons (U.S.)
TIP Report	State Department's Trafficking in Persons Reports (U.S.)
TVPA	Trafficking Victims Protection Act of 2000 (U.S.)
TVPA Reauthorization of 2003	Trafficking Victims Protection Reauthorization Act of 2003 (U.S.)
TVPA Reauthorization of 2005	Trafficking Victims Protection Reauthorization Act of 2005 (U.S.)
UM	unaccompanied minors
UN	United Nations
UNAIDS	Joint United Nations Programme on HIV/AIDS
UNESCO	United Nations Educational, Scientific and Cultural Organization
UN.GIFT	United Nations Global Initiative to Fight Human Trafficking
UNICEF	United Nations Children's Fund
UNODC	United Nations Office on Drugs and Crime
UN Protocol	United Nations Protocol to Prevent, Suppress and Punish Trafficking in Persons, Especially Women and Children
USAID	U.S. Agency for International Development

WISE	Women's Institute for Social Education
WOCON	Women's Consortium of Nigeria
WOTCLEF	Women Trafficking and Child Labour Eradication Foundation (Nigeria)

PART I

At Issue

1

⌒

Introduction

HUMAN TRAFFICKING

Two hundred years after the abolition of the transatlantic slave trade and more than 60 years after the General Assembly of the United Nations (UN) proclaimed that "slavery and the slave trade shall be prohibited in all their forms,"[1] millions of human beings are living in slavery. In Mauritania—despite the country's third official abolition of slavery in 1980—up to 20 percent of the country's population is born into an inherited slavery that began in ancient times.[2] In India, it is possible for children to be born into a debt-bondage enslavement that began generations, or even centuries, before they were born.[3] Most currently enslaved people, however, were born into freedom. These victims of human trafficking, as modern-day slavery is officially termed, lose their freedom when they are illegally, and often forcibly, transported across or within their countries' borders. If they possess passports or other official documents when they are trafficked to another region or country, these papers are often taken from them, leaving them without proof of identity or the ability to travel. Human trafficking's victims are then held in conditions similar to those imposed on enslaved people in earlier centuries: They are given no choice as to what work they will perform, paid little or nothing for that work, and confined under threat of violence or even death.[4]

Scope and Magnitude

As with any illegal activity, it is difficult to assess precisely the scope and magnitude of human trafficking. Different countries and different nongovernmental organizations (NGOs) have published such varying statistics that the United Nations Educational, Scientific and Cultural Organization (UNESCO) has established a Trafficking Statistics Project simply to collect and compare the published estimates. UNESCO acknowledges that data from the various sources are contradictory,[5] and the United Nations Office on Drugs and Crime (UNODC) also points out that any available trafficking statistics reflect only the activity that has been detected and reported by governments and NGOs.[6] Even with these limitations and contradictions, however, the available data expose an indisputable fact: Human trafficking is a global problem of enormous—and growing—proportions.

According to research cited in 2008 by the U.S. Department of State, approximately 800,000 people are trafficked across national borders each year, and millions more are trafficked within their own countries' borders.[7] The United Nations Children's Fund (UNICEF), in contrast, estimates that 1.2 million *children* become trafficking victims every year.[8] There is even greater disagreement as to how many already-trafficked people are presently living in modern-day enslavement. The International Labour Organization (ILO), a United Nations agency, estimates that there are 12.3 million trafficked people,[9] while NGOs Free the Slaves (FTS),[10] the American Anti-Slavery Group (AASG)[11] and others estimate that there are 27 million victims. The United States does not make its own estimate of currently enslaved people, but does note that credible estimates range from 4 to 27 million.[12] Depending upon which organization's statistics are cited, the number of people enslaved today may rival or surpass the 13 million people transported during the entire period of the transatlantic slave trade.[13]

It is possible to examine the scope of human trafficking through another means, however: through a survey of the wide range of products and industries that bear evidence of modern slave labor. Cocoa farmed in West African countries,[14] sugar from the Dominican Republic,[15] carpets woven in northern India,[16] luxury handbags and leather goods counterfeited in China,[17] fish caught from any of the world's oceans, [18] steel produced in Brazil,[19] oranges picked in the United States,[20] and work performed in Iraq by U.S. Department of Defense contractors or subcontractors[21] have all been linked to human trafficking. A closer examination of these examples only increases one's sense of just how pervasive trafficked labor may be in a given industry. According to the New York–based NGO Human Rights Watch (HRW), for example, in 2002 "nearly half the chocolate produced in the United States was linked to cocoa beans harvested by child laborers in Côte d'Ivoire. Many of these children had been trafficked from neighboring countries such as Mali and Burkina Faso."[22] In 2006, Brazilian steel used by automakers Ford Motor Company, General Motors Corp., Nissan Motor Co., Toyota Motor Corporation, household appliance manufacturer Whirlpool Corporation, and the sink and bathtub manufacturer Kohler Co. was traced back through various production stages to slave labor.[23]

If production of many of the world's goods is tainted with slave labor, so is the filling of many of the world's lowest-paid, most dangerous, and/or illegal service occupations. People are trafficked within and across national borders to perform involuntary domestic servitude, to be forced into prostitution, to engage in forced drug smuggling, to perform forced manual labor, to become child soldiers, to be forced into marriage, and to have their organs harvested.

Since there are financial calculations associated with all of the examples provided above, it is also possible to examine the scope and magnitude of human trafficking through its economic impact. The United Nations estimates that every year, worldwide,

> the total market value of illicit human trafficking [is] $32 billion, about $10 billion derived from the initial "sale" of individuals, with the remainder representing the estimated profits from the activities or goods produced by the victims of this barbaric crime.[24]

The estimate of $10 billion from the direct "sale" of human beings speaks, again, to large numbers of trafficked persons. Recently cited prices for the purchase of human beings include $600 for illegal Mexicans purchased for farmwork in the United States, $40 for young men purchased to become laborers in Mali,[25] and $800 for young girls purchased for prostitution in Thailand.[26] One need not complete all possible divisions to realize that at such prices $10 billion represents a crime of vast magnitude.

Finally, it is also possible to measure human trafficking in terms of its geographic spread. As UNODC executive director Antonio Maria Costa described it when introducing the UNODC's 2006 Trafficking in Persons: Global Patterns report, the list of countries associated with human trafficking creates a "map ... from one painful spot on the globe to the next."[27] As the report details, human beings are trafficked from at least 127 known "countries of origin," that is, countries that have citizens or noncitizen residents who have been enslaved or trafficked; these include Cameroon, Egypt, India, Jamaica, Ukraine, Laos, Rwanda, and Zimbabwe. They are trafficked through at least 98 known "transit countries," which are countries through which slave traders smuggle their victims en route to a final location, including Albania, Bulgaria, Hungary, Italy, Poland, and Thailand. They are then trafficked to final destinations in any one of 137 known "destination countries," including Belgium, Germany, Greece, Israel, Italy, Japan, the Netherlands, Thailand, Turkey, and the United States. Some participants in human trafficking travel to origin countries, as when sex tourists exploit minor girls or trafficked women, or even, as was brought to light in 2004, when a number of UN peacekeepers in Congo were found to use trafficked persons for sexual and other purposes.[28] As director of UNODC, Costa, summarized the geographic extent of modern slavery, "The traffickers' web spans the whole planet."[29]

HISTORICAL OVERVIEW
Earlier Forms of Slavery

The depictions of slavery in the Judeo-Christian Old and New Testaments, in the Muslim Koran (Qur'an), and in the classical texts of ancient Greece and Rome accurately reflect the existence of chattel slavery in early societies. Indeed, chattel slavery—the outright, legally recognized ownership of persons on the same basis as other property—"existed in all the ancient civilizations of Asia, Africa, Europe and pre-Columbian America."[30] Most slaves in these societies were captives of war and their descendants.[31] Free people could also be enslaved as a consequence of their own financial insolvency or for failing to satisfy a pledge they had entered into on behalf of another person. Additionally, they could be enslaved in punishment for lawbreaking[32] or, in times of destitution, they could sell themselves or their children into slavery as a means of survival.[33] In all these cases, a person's enslavement was viewed as a recognized, public fact.

In medieval times chattel slavery remained a publicly acknowledged and codified category for human beings. Commercial slave trading networks extended west from the Caspian Sea to London from the eighth to 11th centuries,[34] for example, while an expansive trans-Saharan slave trading network existed from the seventh to the 20th centuries.[35] The most notorious of the pre–20th century networks, however, was the transatlantic slave trade that took place among Europe, the Americas, and Africa from the early 1500s to the early 1800s, transporting approximately 13 million people from Africa to Europe and the Americas as chattel slaves.[36] The transatlantic slave trade, targeting people of one continent for delivery to two other continents, is considered not only the biggest deportation in history, but one of the cruelest episodes in human history. Many of its victims died in transit, and those who survived toiled under race-based laws that recognized neither an enslaved person's right to self-determination nor the legitimacy of his or her family ties.

There were variations in the personal and/or regional behavior of chattel slaveholders toward the enslaved, but—whether we speak of people enslaved in ancient Rome, medieval Europe, or 18th-century America—there were also many commonalities. First, a slaveholder was expected to provide for the most basic needs of the people he or she enslaved. Second, a slaveholder had the ability to exercise absolute control over the people he or she enslaved, including the ability to demand labor, sell away family members, and dictate living locations and conditions. Third, slavery was practiced openly, and one person's ownership of another could be enforced by law or publicly acknowledged custom.

The transatlantic slave trade ended in 1807, when Great Britain outlawed the slave trade throughout its empire. Legally recognized slavery within countries was not abolished until later and in stages: Britain abolished slavery within its borders in 1833, the United States in 1865, and Brazil—the last of the countries in the Americas to act—in 1888. While an international convention calling for a progressive but quick end to slavery was adopted by the League of Nations in 1926 and a proclamation prohibiting slavery was adopted by the UN in 1948, legally recognized chattel slavery continued during the last quarter of the 20th century. Among the last countries to sign documents abolishing legal slavery in their countries were Qatar (1952), Oman (1970), and, as noted above, Mauritania (1980).

Modern-Day Slavery

Modern-day slavery—or human trafficking, as it is officially termed—is quite similar to traditional slavery: The slaveholder exercises complete or nearly complete control over the people he or she has enslaved, and the enslaved person lives and works as ordered by the slaveholder.

There are, however, several important differences. First, since slavery is no longer a legally recognized institution, enslaved people are often hidden from sight or closely monitored to prevent disclosure of their situation. Second, slaveholders can no longer rely on property law to keep enslaved persons in their possession: Coercion, force, and the threat of force (including threats of violence against family back home) are the only remaining—and all too routinely used—means of control. Third, people enslaved today are generally expected to repay the costs of their own trafficking and ongoing living expenses, in a system known as debt bondage. That is, enslaved people may be paid for their labor or services, only to have a payment toward their travel costs—and even the slaveholder's cost of purchasing them from a trafficker—deducted from their earnings. Additional ongoing charges for food, lodging, and other maintenance expenses—frequently calculated in private by the slaveholder—are deducted as well. Debt bondage has existed since classical times, but the original form (which can still be found today) generally involves a debt or debts that the bonded person, to at least some degree, acknowledged. The modern-day version of debt bondage differs in that it frequently involves abduction or the deceitful abduction of persons into a servitude, for which imprisonment they are then forced to pay.

Regardless of whether bonded persons—or their families—are complicit in assuming the debts associated with their servitude, Kevin Bales would argue that those held in modern-day slavery are viewed as expendable in a way that those held in traditional slavery were not. Bales, director of the

Washington D.C.–based FTS and professor of sociology at Roehampton University in London, England, sees the fact that the human trafficker no longer absorbs the cost of enslaving and holding a person, but rather shifts those expenses to the victim, as central to the change in an enslaved person's value to the enslaver. As he explains it,

> [b]uying a slave is no longer a major investment, like buying a car or a house (as it was in the old slavery); it is more like buying an inexpensive bicycle or a cheap computer. Slaveholders get all the work they can out of their slaves, and then throw them away.[37]

The decision to throw away slaves is not to be confused with a slaveholder's decision to emancipate one's slaves and cease enslavement. Instead, it is a decision to extract all labor and service possible, without sustaining the health and lives of these people, who are viewed as easily replaceable. In Thailand, for example, girls as young as 12 are purchased into debt bondage for approximately $800, then prostituted daily in a brothel—often without condoms and often with shared needles to inject the contraceptive Depo-Provera. When girls eventually test positive for HIV, they are thrown out of the brothels to develop AIDS and die on their own.[38]

DEFINING THE VICTIMS OF HUMAN TRAFFICKING

The term *trafficking* was first used in the mid-20th century in phrases such as "white slave traffic" and "the trafficking in women and children" to refer to forcing women and children into prostitution. By the late 1990s, it was clear that the definition of human trafficking had to be expanded if it was to reflect accurately the broader reality of modern-day slavery. What was not immediately clear, however, was how very broad an accurate definition would need to be.

The definition adopted by Europol (European Police Office) in 1998 continued to define trafficking as referring especially to forced entry into the sex trades, but it began to expand the definition by leaving room for other, undefined, forms of forced labor. The following January, the Global Alliance Against Traffic in Women (GAATW), an alliance of NGOs from various parts of the world, arrived at a definition of trafficking that reflected their members' collective experience with human trafficking victims. That definition, set forth in GAATW's Human Rights Standards for the Treatment of Trafficked Persons (1999), specifically included forced labor alongside sexual exploitation. It also included the possibility that a person might be paid for work done involuntarily. The International Organization for Migration (IOM), an intergovernmental organization with 120 member states, adopted its own far-reaching definition in May 1999. Rather than refer specifically to forced prostitution, this definition is silent—and, therefore, completely inclusive—on the type of labor a trafficked person might be forced to undertake.[39]

In 2000, the General Assembly, as part of its United Nations Protocol to Prevent, Suppress and Punish Trafficking in Persons, Especially Women and Children (UN Protocol), adopted its own detailed and broad definition of human trafficking. It is the one most frequently cited today:

(a) "Trafficking in persons" shall mean the recruitment, transportation, transfer, harbouring or receipt of persons, by means of the threat or use of force or other forms of coercion, of abduction, of fraud, of deception, of the abuse of power or of a position of vulnerability or of the giving or receiving of payments or benefits to achieve the consent of a person having control over another person, for the purpose of exploitation. Exploitation shall include, at a minimum, the exploitation of the prostitution of others or other forms of sexual exploitation, forced labour or services, slavery or practices similar to slavery, servitude or the removal of organs.

(b) The consent of a victim of trafficking in persons to the intended exploitation set forth in subparagraph (a) of this article shall be irrelevant where any of the means set forth in subparagraph (a) have been used.

(c) The recruitment, transportation, transfer, harbouring or receipt of a child for the purpose of exploitation shall be considered "trafficking in persons" even if this does not involve any of the means set forth in subparagraph (a) of this article.

(d) "Child" shall mean any person under 18 years of age.[40]

This definition, which appears in a protocol whose very title places special emphasis on the trafficking of women and children, clearly signals a continued concern for the sexual exploitation aspects of human trafficking. By specifying "forced labor or services, slavery or practices similar to slavery, servitude or the removal of organs," however, the UN Protocol clearly acknowledged that human trafficking would no longer be defined exclusively by forced participation in the sex trades.

The UN Protocol has 117 signatories (member states that have signed the Protocol) and 124 parties (member states that have approved, ratified, accepted, or acceded to the Protocol) as of September 2008.[41] Nonetheless, the criminal codes of individual United Nations member countries continue to reflect variations in the definition—or even the existence of a definition—of human trafficking. Some countries have no specific human trafficking legislation and, thus, no official definition of human trafficking. Afghanistan, for example, has neither signed nor ratified the Protocol. It prosecutes some instances of human trafficking under kidnapping and other such laws, but it has no law specifically defining or prohibiting human trafficking itself. A number of other countries also continue to define human trafficking exclusively in terms of sex trafficking. Algeria is both a signatory and a party to the Protocol but its only law specifically concerning trafficking merely "prohibits the trafficking of minors for commercial sex exploitation."[42] (Algeria has, however, prosecuted some instances of sex trafficking in adults under its laws prohibiting pimping.) In contrast, other countries have adopted definitions that broaden the UN Protocol's list of specific trafficking offenses. Belgium, a signatory and party to the Protocol, for example, specifically includes the abduction of children for forced begging as a form of human trafficking in its anti-trafficking statute.[43]

The law enforcement agencies of parties to the Protocol are required to establish methods to investigate and prevent trafficking and to cooperate with the law enforcement agencies of other party countries to identify traffickers, and their victims.

THE INTERNATIONAL EXPLOITATION OF TRAFFICKED PERSONS

Prostitution and the Sex Trades

There is wide agreement among governments and NGOs that 80 percent of transnational trafficking victims are female and that 50 percent are minor children. There is also wide, if not unanimous, agreement that the majority of the approximately 800,000 victims taken across national borders each year are females trafficked into the sex trades.[44]

ADULT WOMEN

According to the UNODC, "adult women are the most frequent victims [of trafficking] followed by girls, boys, and men."[45] Certainly, adult women are abducted by threat of violence. A large number of these adult women, however, are trafficked—as the UN and many other governmental and organizational definitions recognize—by means of fraud or deception. These women are offered housekeeping, restaurant, modeling, or other jobs abroad or they are taken on "vacation" by so-called boyfriends (called "lover boys" by police and other authorities) who have worked to earn their trust and affection. Their global travel routes are often circuitous and difficult to trace. At the 2006 Conference on Human Trafficking in Canada, a representative of the

Royal Canadian Mounted Police cited a trafficking route from Fujan (China) to Vietnam to Egypt to South America to Europe to Mexico to the United States as one example.[46] Once in the destination country, these trafficked women are generally deprived of their passports and/or other identifying documents and then held captive. They are usually raped or beaten[47] into submission, and threats may also be made against their lives or the lives of family members back home.[48] Ultimately, they are forced into prostitution.

In most modern-day slavery cases, a woman trafficked into prostitution is placed into debt bondage. In this system, she is paid part of what she is forced to earn for the brothel or pimp, but she is also expected to repay the costs of her food, lodging, and clothing, plus the costs of her own trafficking. If all these monies are repaid, the implication is that the woman will be released. Trafficked women prostituted in this manner, however, rarely manage to pay off the debt bondage. As a Scotland Yard detective inspector summarized the debt-bondage prostitution of East European women in London:

> Some [women] have sex with as many as 40 men a day. It's very rare [for her] to get to keep any of the money she earns. We've seen places where £300 pounds ($580) a day goes to the brothel pimp or "madam," and that's even before the woman begins to try and pay off the "debt bondage" of thousands of pounds charged to bring her here.[49]

The Canadian conference also described paying off one's debt bondage as an insurmountable task. It was estimated that a prostituted woman would have to service between 500 and 700 men just to pay her travel debt.[50] Even if that travel debt is eventually repaid, bondage debt continues. As the U.S. Department of State's 2007 Trafficking in Persons Report summarized the plight of trafficked women who are prostituted and held in debt bondage, "often the [total] debt can never be repaid because the costs for food, rent, medicines and condoms are added every day."[51]

In cases without debt bondage, a prostituted woman receives none of the money she earns for the brothel owner or pimp, and her only hope of returning to freedom is to escape or be rescued. (In actuality, many a prostituted woman who escapes or is discovered by the authorities finds herself arrested as a criminal illegal alien, since she has no papers authorizing her presence in the country and since she has been engaged—albeit against her will—in illegal activity.)[52]

The women are held to the terms of these unilaterally imposed arrangements by the methods common to most human trafficking situations: coercion, force, and the threats of force or violence against them or their family members. In the case of prostituted women, however, blackmail is also used as a means of deterring victims from escape.[53]

MINOR CHILDREN

Minor children are also trafficked into prostitution. While some children are abducted by strangers for prostitution, many children are placed into prostitution by someone they know.

As is the case with adult women, young girls are sometimes trafficked into prostitution by "lover boys," young men who profess to love them. These young men enter into seemingly romantic relationships with young women they have selected as potential trafficking victims. Lover boys then stage day trips, vacations, or even runaway marriages to remove the girls from their families, then place the girls in prostitution.[54] While violence is ordinarily used as an induction into prostitution, these cases often rely on emotional coercion or manipulation of the girls' desire to believe they are loved. As Socialstyrelsen, the Swedish National Board of Health and Welfare, described it in a 2003 report:

> *Young women may, in retrospect, note that their first prostitution activity took place within the context of something like a romantic relationship, but that they did not define it at the time as prostitution. These can be girls under age 18 who have "love relationships" with men up to age 45, and who allow themselves to be sexually exploited in exchange for drugs or other compensation.*[55]

Girls are also trafficked into prostitution, wittingly or not, by their families. In many of these cases, a recruiter approaches rural parents living in extreme poverty, extending what appears to be an opportunity for a better life for one or more of the parents' children. The opportunity may be described as domestic or entry-level employment abroad (the U.S. 2007 Trafficking in Persons Report, for example, cites a girl from Kazakhstan whose parents accepted $300 to allow their daughter to go to Russia, supposedly to accept a job as a shop assistant).[56] The opportunity may also be described more grandly, as one that includes a vocational apprenticeship or even a formal education. What the girls find at the end of their journeys, however, is a life of prostitution.

In some cases, recruiters need not lie to the girls' families. In Thailand, for example, conservative estimates are that there are approximately 35,000 minor girls enslaved in prostitution—most of them with their parents' direct knowledge and consent. In situations where parents know they are accepting money to place their daughters in brothels, the girls are sometimes permitted to send a portion of their earnings home to their families and to visit on holidays. Indeed, "brokers and brothel owners . . . cultivate village families so they might buy more daughters as they come of age."[57] Nonetheless, the reality for these girls is not dissimilar to that faced by other girls trafficked into debt-bondage prostitution. One young Thai girl who was permitted to send money home to her parents, for instance, reported that she also had to have sex with 300 men per month to pay her rent at the brothel[58] and have sex with up to an additional 18 men per night—or 540 men per month—in order to make payments toward her bondage debt, food, and other necessities.[59]

CHILD SEX TOURISM

Child sex tourism (CST) is the practice of men or, less frequently, women, traveling away from their own regions or countries to perform sex acts with children. Many of the people who engage in CST are what the NGO End Child Prostitution, Child Pornography and Trafficking of Children for Sexual Purposes (ECPAT) and others refer to as situational abusers: people who would not engage in such sex acts near their own homes but who—with the promise or illusion of anonymity—do so in faraway destinations.[60] A majority of the sex tourists travel from western countries, most notably Australia, Germany, Great Britain, the Netherlands, and the United States,[61] with approximately 25 percent traveling from the United States.[62] The U.S. Department of State has found that these American child abusers come from wide-ranging backgrounds and, indeed, that "cases of child sex tourism involving U.S. citizens have included a pediatrician, a retired Army sergeant, a dentist, and a university professor."[63] Asian countries, most notably India, the Philippines, and Thailand, are the countries most often visited for child sex tourism.

Both girls and boys are trafficked into prostitution, and children as young as four have been reported among their numbers.[64] Whether forcibly abducted or placed into debt-bondage prostitution by their relatives, whether seemingly resistant or compliant, children under 18 fall into one category under the UN Protocol and other international treaties: persons whose consent or seeming consent is irrelevant. As the UN Protocol makes clear, harboring a child for prostitution is "trafficking in persons," even where no force, coercion, or deception is used while holding or sexually exploiting that child.[65]

Human Trafficking and Family Formation

Family formation is not immune from human trafficking. Forced marriage, in forms ranging from the most traditional to those assisted by the Internet, constitutes human trafficking, as does—according to some—baby selling.

BROKERED OR FORCED MARRIAGES

Since the mid-20th century, forced or brokered marriages have been prohibited by an international convention. That convention, the UN's 1956 Supplementary Convention on the Abolition of Slavery, the Slave Trade, and Institutions and Practices Similar to Slavery (1956 Supplementary Convention), classifies women in forced marriages as "person[s] of servile status." It also classifies forced marriage as an "institution[] and practice[] similar to slavery" and specifically prohibits

> *any institution or practice whereby . . . a woman, without the right to refuse, is promised or given in marriage on payment of a consideration in money or kind to her parents, guardian, family, or other person or group.*[66]

Despite this half-century-old agreement, however, forced marriage now exists in both old and new forms.

Traditional Forms of Forced Marriage
One of the oldest surviving forms of forced marriage is an arranged marriage with compensation to the bride's family and no meaningful consent or recognized right of refusal on the bride's part. In other situations, a bride's family may pay, rather than receive, monies in connection with the arranged marriage of their daughter. It should be noted, however, that arranged marriage remains common in many countries and that many of these marriages are arranged without the violation of human rights.

Girls may also be married to settle a family's debt,[67] to compensate for a family member's crime,[68] or to settle an argument between families.[69] Such marriages often take place when girls are quite young: "Africa's Young Brides," a video slide show accompanying a 2005 *New York Times* story's online version, for example, interviews young women whose families received monetary consideration upon their daughters' entries into arranged marriages. These girls were married at ages 10 (to a man believed to be between 55 and 65 years old at the time), 11 (to a man then in his 40s), and 14 (to a man who was then 58 years old).[70]

In Pakistan, a *jirga* (village court or council) has been traditionally empowered to award a girl in compensation for a family member's crime.[71] Such marriages, called *vani* marriage in some parts of Pakistan and *swara* or *sang-chati* marriage in others, were officially outlawed in January 2005.[72] These *jirga*-ordered marriages nonetheless continue to be performed and frequently involve very young girls.[73] Such compensatory marriages may also be arranged more informally, with young girls simply being sent by their families to marry in settlement of a dispute. Such a situation is described in the U.S. 2006 Trafficking in Persons Report (TIP Report):

> *In Afghanistan, a girl is promised to a man in a neighboring village to settle an age-old dispute between their families. Although young, she is taken out of school to marry a man she has never met. When she arrives, she is forced to cook, clean, and serve her husband's entire family for 18–20 hours per day. If she does something wrong, she is beaten and*

her new "family" threatens to kill her if she ever tries to leave. One day, her husband decides to marry someone new, so he sells his first wife to another man who also forces her to serve him and his family's needs.[74]

Early marriage generally puts an end to whatever educational opportunity a young girl might otherwise have had. It also increases the risk of obstetric fistula, a perforation of the wall between a mother's vagina and bladder and/or rectum, which results in a constant leaking of urine and/or feces. A consequence of obstructed labor with delayed or unavailable medical intervention, a fistula can occur in a woman of any age, but it is much more likely to occur when the delivering woman is very young. Regardless of the age of the mother, however, an obstructed labor that continues long enough to cause a fistula—a five days' labor is not uncommon if no medical help is available—will result in a stillborn baby. Fistula has been largely eliminated in Europe and North America, where most women have access to emergency Caesarian sections during labor, but it continues to occur in poor rural areas of Africa, Asia, and the Middle East. In many cases, a woman who develops a fistula will be shunned by her husband and community.[75]

In areas where very young marriage is traditional, families may feel that it is in the best interests of their daughters to marry young. As a recent United Nations Children's Fund (UNICEF) report makes clear, however, underage marriages are specifically included in the UN's foundation declaration against slavery and in the Pan-African Forum's definition of modern-day slavery:

> *Marriage before the age of 18 is a reality for many young women. In many parts of the world parents encourage the marriage of their daughters while they are still children in hopes that the marriage will benefit them both financially and socially, while also relieving financial burdens on the family. In actuality, child marriage is a violation of human rights, compromising the development of girls and often resulting in early pregnancy and social isolation, with little education and poor vocational training reinforcing the gendered nature of poverty.*
>
> *The right to "free and full" consent to marriage is recognized in the Universal Declaration of Human Rights—with the recognition that consent cannot be "free and full" when one of the parties involved is not sufficiently mature to make an informed decision about a life partner. The Convention on the Elimination of all Forms of Discrimination against Women mentions the right to protection from child marriage. . . . Child marriage was also identified by the Pan-African Forum against the Sexual Exploitation of Children as a type of commercial sexual exploitation of children.[76]*

In 2005, more than half of the women then aged 20 to 24 in Bangladesh, Burkina Faso, Cameroon, Central African Republic, Guinea, Mali, Mozambique, Nepal, Niger, Nigeria, and Uganda had been married before the age of 18.

Additional Forms of Forced Marriage
Other forced marriages are effected by brokers. These brokers may advertise on billboards or the Internet, take bride-seeking men on "organized tour[s] of the source country," or exhibit women at "trade shows." Many of the women trafficked in this manner are marketed to men in countries wealthier and more developed than their own. Women from Cambodia, Mongolia, Thailand, and Vietnam, for example, are marketed to men in Japan, Malaysia, and Taiwan. Similarly, women from Mongolia and Southeast Asia are marketed to men in South Korea.[77]

Such marketing of brides also occurs within countries. In India, for example, up to 90 percent of trafficking for sexual exploitation is internal, with girls and women being taken from one village to another for forced marriage and prostitution.[78] Women in China are also trafficked from one region to another—usually from a poorer inland province to a wealthier one—to be marketed and sold as brides.[79]

These patterns of transnational and internal bride trafficking are not mutually exclusive. In China men buy women who are trafficked within China, but they also buy women trafficked from North Korea, Burma, Russia, and Vietnam. (There are estimates that in some Chinese villages 30 to 90 percent of marriages may involve trafficked women.) In India, the majority of women sold into marriage have been trafficked from another region of the country, but women from Nepal and Bangladesh are sold as wives to Indian men as well.[80]

These women, who have been kidnapped or sold to brokers by their families, are frequently advertised as "commodities," and NGOs have observed that many of their purchasers are "exploitive men who feel they 'own' the foreign woman and can use her as a farm hand or domestic worker." Trafficked brides also face extramarital exploitation: According to governmental and NGO research, in a "significant percentage" of brokered marriages, the husband traffics his new wife into the commercial sex trades or forced labor.[81]

TRAFFICKING IN INFANTS
While the sale of babies is illegal, it is not uniformly considered a form of human trafficking when the baby is sold into adoption. The United States, for example, in its 2005 TIP Report, puts forth the view that human trafficking is not an issue so long as there is, ultimately, no exploitation of the child itself:

Baby selling, which is sometimes used as a means to circumvent legal adoption requirements, involves coerced or induced removal of a child, or situations where deception or undue compensation is used to induce the relinquishment of a child. Baby selling is not an acceptable route to adoption and can include many attributes in common with human trafficking. Though baby selling is illegal, it would not necessarily constitute human trafficking where it occurs for adoption. . . .

The purposes of baby selling and human trafficking are not necessarily the same. Some individuals assume that baby selling for adoption is a form of human trafficking because trafficking and baby selling both involve making a profit by selling another person. However, illegally selling a child for adoption would not constitute trafficking where the child itself is not to be exploited. Baby selling generally results in a situation that is nonexploitive with respect to the child. Trafficking, on the other hand, implies exploitation of the victims. If an adopted child is subjected to coerced labor or sexual exploitation, then it constitutes a case of human trafficking.[82]

Other conclusions can also be reached. The UNICEF database on child trafficking categorizes a number of baby-selling incidents as "baby trafficking," even when an adoptive home seems to have been the baby's ultimate destination.[83] Others who have closely examined the issue also classify baby selling as a form of human trafficking. Investigative journalism conducted by Nicola Smith Plovdiv of the *Sunday Times* (London) supports such a classification, regardless of the care subsequently lavished on purchased babies. Traveling to Bulgaria to investigate reports that "scores or perhaps hundreds of Bulgarian babies are being sold for adoption across Europe," she interviewed, among others, an impoverished woman from Bulgaria's Roma community. Promised a job in neighboring Greece while pregnant, the woman was driven across the border at night; she was then held captive with three other pregnant women, and it became clear that their babies would be taken at birth and sold. The women were rescued before their deliveries, and their traffickers—and arguably the traffickers of their babies—were arrested.[84] Spyridon Kloudas, a Greek lawyer specializing in that country's trafficking cases, is adamant in his view that, at the very least, the mothers in such cases should be considered victims of human trafficking.[85]

In China, the official view is less ambiguous, and the maximum penalty for trafficking three or more babies is death. Nonetheless, baby-trafficking gangs in China are reported to include doctors, midwives, and nurses.[86] Parental knowledge or consent is a factor in much of the baby selling: In some cases, driven by China's one-child policy and the traditional preference for boys, families clandestinely sell their newborn daughters in order to preserve their right to produce a male heir;[87] in other cases, driven by the same policy and traditional preference, parents sell their newborn sons for the premium price their baby boys can command.[88] In either case, the families receive far less for their children than do the middle persons. In May 2007, for example, police in eastern China's Jiangsu Province rescued 40 babies and arrested 47 suspected members of a baby-trafficking gang.[89] The traffickers of these Chinese infants stated that "they usually buy a baby girl for 1,500 yuan (US$219) but sell it for 8,000 yuan, while a baby boy usually cost them 8,000 yuan and can fetch 20,000 yuan (US$1,169) for them."[90]

Although the U.S. 2005 TIP Report expresses the view that children sold into nonexploitive adoptive homes are not trafficked, the U.S. Congressional-Executive Commission on China—a legislatively mandated commission of senators, members of the House of Representatives, and senior administration officials charged with monitoring human rights in China—acknowledged the issue of trafficking in the sale of babies in its own 2005 Annual Report:

> China's poorest families, who often cannot afford to pay the coercive "social compensation" fine that the government assesses when it discovers an extra child, often sell or give infants, particularly female infants, to traffickers. When police rescue them, many families do not come forward to claim their children because they are afraid of both the police and the local family and population planning officials. Authorities place some of these children in foster care, but many are eventually assigned to government-run orphanages. In 2004, police searching a bus found 28 newborn female infants who had been acquired by hospital staff in Guangxi province and then taken by middlemen to be sold in Henan and Anhui provinces.[91]

It must be noted that no definition of a trafficker in babies includes adoptive parents who have acted without knowledge of a child's abduction or sale.

Forced Labor

Again, the extent of human trafficking is so very difficult to measure that different governments and nongovernmental organizations frequently arrive at differing and even contradictory figures.[92] This is true not only with respect to the estimates of persons trafficked in total, but of estimates of persons trafficked into forced labor rather than sexual exploitation. While most reports conclude that the majority of modern-day slaves are trafficked into sexual exploitation, others conclude that forced labor is actually the larger category.[93] There is fairly wide acceptance, however, of figures cited in a 2005 ILO report: Approximately 98 percent of persons trafficked into sexual exploitation are female and 2 percent are male, while approximately 56 percent of persons trafficked into nonsexual economic exploitation are female and 44 percent are male.[94]

Introduction

Forced labor includes enslavement in private homes and enslavement in more public work spaces.

INVOLUNTARY DOMESTIC SERVITUDE

Involuntary domestic servitude is the official term for those enslaved to perform housekeeping chores in private homes. Women and girls comprise the majority of the victims in this category of forced labor. Most often, they are hired for what are represented as regular, paid positions, only to have their identity documents confiscated, their movements curtailed, and their paychecks cease:

> *Marlena traveled to the Persian Gulf to earn money for her family as a domestic servant in a wealthy household. Instead of a room of her own, Marlena slept on the kitchen floor and worked 20 hours every day of the week serving the family. The employer's wife confiscated her passport the day she arrived and forbade her from ever leaving the house. The family locked her inside whenever they left. The employer's wife beat her and called her names when she did not work hard enough. When Marlena tried to run away, the employer told her she would be arrested for leaving the house without permission. Though the recruitment agent promised her $200 per week, Marlena was never paid by her employers.*[95]

In other cases—especially those involving the children of North Africa and South Asia's rural villages—they may be sold by their families to employers in the more prosperous cities. Regardless of the method of recruitment or the final destination, victims are often subjected to beatings, sexual violence, and other forms of physical abuse, as well as psychological abuse.[96]

Such involuntary domestic service is found "throughout the world," including in the United States. This form of forced labor can be difficult to detect, given the private and easily hidden nature of domestic service. Moreover, if victims escape, they may be offered little protection since many countries do not consider involuntary domestic servitude a form of human trafficking. Rather than hold employers criminally liable when their escaped servants complain, such governments "generally encourage victims to return to the household or to seek civil penalties from abusive employers."[97]

FORCED LABOR IN THE WORKPLACE

Forced laborers are also held outside the home. According to the ILO, the highest ratio of forced laborers to country inhabitants is found in the Asian Pacific region, followed by the Caribbean and Latin America, then sub-Saharan Africa. These high ratios, the ILO concludes, "reflect the stubborn survival—and often the transmutation—of traditional forms of servitude."[98]

19

Forced Labor within Countries

While there is evidence that the descendants of slaves in Mauritania and perhaps other West African countries continue to be born into a form of slavery based on their family lineage,[99] most people born into slavery worldwide today are born into debt bondage—a form of slavery based on their family's debts or alleged debts. In Pakistan, for example, where entire families work in slavery to discharge paternal debt-bondage obligations, a father's unpaid debts and bonded servitude will be inherited by his sons and their descendants.[100]

People not born into debt bondage can become enslaved by it in various ways. Some men sell themselves and their families into bonded labor:

> "Salamat," a Christian Punjabi man in his forties, used to work as a daily wage-earner on a farm. When the owners of the farm no longer needed his labor he sought different types of work. He was unable to find a job and needed some money to meet his family's basic expenses. He had borrowed money from a number of people to meet such expenses. To repay his various debts he took out a loan of Rs.1,500 [$45] from a jamadar and sold himself, his wife and three children into bondage at a brick-kiln on the outskirts of Kasur [Pakistan].[101]

Others accept loans contingent on employment without realizing that their wages will not be sufficient to ever repay the original loan and the ever-accumulating loans toward daily living expenses. Still others—primarily children—are sold into debt bondage by their families.

Pakistan's poor have long worked within a system of employment based on wage advances (peshgi), and in cases where wages are sufficient and employers honest in their bookkeeping, these workers and their families may eventually earn their freedom. In many cases, however, these workers and their families find themselves perpetually enslaved. This designation is an accurate one: Debt-bondage employers exercise complete control over their bonded laborers. They routinely administer corporal punishment "ranging from mild beatings to outright torture,"[102] hold a man's wife and children hostage if he leaves the work site,[103] and even sell all or part of a family and its debts to other employers. In addition, while forced labor is not categorized as sexual exploitation, sexual exploitation often accompanies forced labor. Women are frequently "forced to have regular sexual relations with their employer or members of his family" and, if widowed, may find themselves sold into prostitution or forced marriages.[104]

Despite the passage of Pakistan's Bonded Labour System (Abolition) Act in 1992, debt-bondage enslavement in Pakistan continues to be "endemic and widespread,"[105] especially in the brick, carpet, and agricultural industries. Debt bondage is equally endemic and widespread within many other countries. In Brazil, for example, similarly enslaved laborers make charcoal, iron, and steel,[106] while in Peru, enslaved laborers make bricks, fell forests, and work in the mines.[107]

Transnational Forced Labor and Forced Labor on the Seas

Forced laborers are also trafficked globally. Bolivian and Peruvian forced laborers work in Argentina's fields and factories,[108] for example, while forced laborers from China perform various kinds of work in Costa Rica.[109] The seas are also a trafficking destination: In the Gulf of Thailand, on the Andaman Sea, the Sea of Japan, and the Black Sea, and on many other waters, men and boys are trafficked into the fishing industries. Cut off from any escape route or possible contact with family members, they work in "truly abhorrent" conditions:

Many are subjected to beatings; deprived of food, water, and sleep; exposed to highly unsanitary conditions and infectious diseases; and forced to perform life-threatening work in unsafe conditions without pay. Victims who do not die find themselves exploited by their traffickers anywhere from six months to four years.

The true extent of labor exploitation on the high seas is unknown, but cases that surface are truly abhorrent. In August 2006, more than 30 Burmese fishermen died from infectious diseases and lack of medical care on fishing vessels found off the coast of Thailand; the bodies of victims were tossed overboard, discarded like common refuse.[110]

Forced Child Labor

Children are especially vulnerable to forced labor exploitation. They may work alongside their parents in Pakistan's brick kilns and beside adults in some of the jobs described above, but they are also trafficked far from home and family. Roma girls from Bulgaria engage in forced thievery in Austria,[111] while boys from Togo perform agricultural work in Benin and Nigeria.[112] Children trafficked from Vietnam are forced to smuggle drugs in Great Britain, and children trafficked from Russia sell ice cream without pay in the United States.[113] Again, parents frequently consent to a child's departure when it is falsely presented as an opportunity for a better life. As a U.S. Department of State TIP Report summarizes one such case,

[t]he parents of 12-year-old Malik were convinced by a Koranic teacher— one of a revered group in Niger—that he would take the young boy to Mali, for further education. But once Malik and other Nigerian boys arrived in Niger, they were denied schooling and forced by the teacher to beg in the streets for long hours to earn money for him.[114]

21

In other cases, parents, too poor to care for their children themselves and seeing no opportunities for their children at home, knowingly place their children in forced labor situations.

Child Soldiers

It is estimated that there are more than 300,000 children currently involved in 30 or more armed conflicts. These child soldiers—some as young as seven years old—serve in rebel militias and in national armies. Many of these children have been abducted or otherwise forced to leave their families to become combatants.[115] Others have joined a conflict in return for food[116] or to exact vengeance for relatives who have been killed.[117] All are minor children and all are victims of modern-day slavery according to the UN Protocol, which makes clear that such recruitment of children under 18—with or without their consent—constitutes human trafficking.[118]

Child soldiers act as cooks, guards, messengers, porters, servants, and spies.[119] They are also placed into direct combat positions, ordered to walk into minefields ahead of older soldiers, and used in suicide missions.[120] These children are often brutally inducted into combat in a manner designed to desensitize them to violence; they may also be drugged as part of the desensitization process.[121] To ensure that all home ties are severed, child soldiers are also sometimes forced to maim and/or kill their own family and community members.[122] Regardless of the recruitment and induction process, a child soldier's experiences are frequently horrific:

> Michael was 15 when he was kidnapped by the Lord's Resistance Army (LRA) to serve as a combatant in the Ugandan insurgent force. During his forced service in the LRA, he was made to kill a boy who had tried to escape. He also watched another boy being hacked to death because he did not alert the guards when his friend successfully escaped.[123]

Girls are also used as armed combatants by rebel and paramilitary groups—indeed, HRW cites reports that more than a third of the child soldiers in Uganda, Nepal, and Sri Lanka are girls — and they face the added danger of sexual exploitation. In addition to their armed or camp-based roles in the conflict, female child soldiers are often made the forced sexual companions or wives of adult male soldiers. Furthermore, it is not uncommon for these young women to bear children in the midst of the conflict.[124] As Radhika Coomaraswamy, the United Nations Special Representative for Children and Armed Conflicts, describes it, "The girl child is often forced to play multiple roles in the conflict: She is often sex slave, mother and combatant at the same time."[125]

Child soldiers have been reported in Burundi, Burma, Sudan,[126] Sri Lanka,[127] Nepal,[128] Chad,[129] and Congo,[130] among other countries.

Trafficking for Involuntary Organ Harvests

Trafficking in persons for the removal of organs has also been documented, especially the trafficking in persons for removal of kidneys. Nancy Scheper-Hughes, founding director of Organs Watch, estimates that approximately 15,000 kidneys are taken from involuntary donors every year.[131] In what has become known as "transplant tourism," people from wealthier countries register for transplant surgeries with physicians in poorer countries; the procurement of kidneys for such operations has ranged from the "loss" of a poor Brazilian woman's kidney in a public hospital during gynecological surgery,[132] to the removal at gunpoint of day laborers' kidneys in India.[133] Coerced consent has also been documented, including cases between "employers and employees or wealthy people and their domestic workers in which the lower status individuals 'donated' their kidneys in return for secure employment, housing, or other basic needs."[134]

CAUSES OF HUMAN TRAFFICKING

The causes of transnational human trafficking must be examined in terms of what have been called "push and pull" factors: the factors that push people from countries of origin and the factors that "pull" people into destination countries. (The same factors are often applicable to the trafficking of persons from one region of a country to another.)

Countries of Origin

In its reports on transnational human trafficking, the United Nations designates countries as "countries of origin," "transit countries," and "destination countries." The origin countries with a "very high" reported incidence of human trafficking are Albania, Belarus, Bulgaria, China, Lithuania, Moldova, Nigeria, Romania, Russia, Thailand, and Ukraine. Each of these countries—and each of the 27 origin countries reported as having a "high," rather than "very high," incidence of trafficking[135]—has its own unique economic, historical, and cultural background. It is nonetheless possible to identify significant "push factors" common to many countries of origin.

POVERTY

Poverty is perhaps the greatest underlying cause of human trafficking from and within countries of origin. In West Africa, for example, almost two-thirds of the population subsist on less than $1 per day. When it is manifestly clear to families that they cannot feed their children, accepting a job offer

23

for one of the children—with or without promises of continued education, with or without the guise of a skill-fostering apprenticeship—is a "survival strategy." In regions with few opportunities for their children, parents also argue that, however menial or difficult the promised work is, their child is better served by leaving to learn a trade than by staying home to starve.[136] As for accepting money for the child, this, too, when viewed through the prism of very extreme poverty, can seem not only acceptable, but necessary if the remaining family is to survive. Extreme poverty is also a primary cause of adults' entry into debt bondage, either with full knowledge that they trade their freedom for at least minimal food and shelter or through the desperate grasping at what turns out to be false and imprisoning promises.[137]

Poverty is not only an individual matter, however, but a national one: An individual family's plight exists in the context of its country's resources and its extension of those resources to its people. The lack of educational access in the rural areas of many countries, for example, contributes to illiterate workers' reliance upon their employers' accounting of wages and accumulating debt.[138] The lack of employment opportunities, the lack of banking structures designed to aid low-wage workers, and the lack of social services also compound the effects of poverty upon these individuals.

> ... the problems of bonded labor are located in contemporary economic and political structures. In the Pakistani economy, where social services are often nonexistent, underemployment is high, and wages are low, access to credit is fundamental for survival, particularly when a failed harvest or a recessionary downturn can exhaust a worker's means of subsistence. If unable to obtain credit from alternative sources, workers fall prey to the advances of employers, landlords, and moneylenders who extend desperately needed cash in exchange for long-term control over their labor. In such an economic context, where alternatives for survival are limited, the male head of the family often enters into contracts which place himself, a member of his family, or his entire family into bondage.[139]

GENDER INEQUALITY

While poverty is a major cause of the trafficking of persons from and within origin countries, it does not fully explain the frequency of trafficking in women and girls. In these cases, gender inequality is also an issue.

Gender inequality is frequently multifaceted. It is an element of forced marriage, for example, but it is also the background against which Chinese infant girls are aborted or given up after birth, leading to an artificially low ratio of women to men and to an increase in bride selling when willing local women are unavailable.[140] Gender inequality is an element of the trafficking of Thailand's girls into brothels, but it is also a factor when many of Thailand's wives do not confront head-of-household husbands who regularly frequent and thus sustain their country's brothels.[141]

Gender inequality is also a factor in the use of fraud to enslave women. In many countries, girls still have fewer educational opportunities than boys and, as women, they may be denied employment, property, and inheritance rights. Women with so few resources are especially vulnerable to traffickers' false promises of employment and a more secure life.

Destination Countries

According to the United Nations, the countries reported "very high" as trafficking destinations are Belgium, Germany, Greece, Israel, Italy, Japan, the Netherlands, Thailand, Turkey, and the United States.[142] Again, each of these countries—and each of the 22 destination countries reported as having a "high" incidence of trafficking[143]—has its own unique economic, historical, and cultural background. Nonetheless, there are major "pull factors" common to many countries of origin.

ECONOMIC PROMISE

Traffickers often use the promise of a better economic future to deceive people into accepting fraudulent offers of employment abroad for themselves or their children. While the traffickers' promises are mere lies, their descriptions of economic opportunities in other countries reflect the firsthand knowledge of many origin country residents. According to Dilip Ratha of the World Bank, emigrant migrant workers send home private contributions that total $300 billion each year, an amount that is more than three times greater than the annual foreign aid donations of all countries combined.[144] These private contributions, known as remittances, help to fund housing, education, and other tangible needs of families in the receiving countries; neighbors who witness this evidence of successful emigration may misjudge the intentions of traffickers, but they are not basing their economic hopes on unsupported fantasy.

THE DEMAND FOR CONSUMER SEX

The demand for purchased sex (or, in the case of brokered brides, the demand for purchased sexual relationships and household labor) is what creates the supply of trafficked women for sale. The modern-day brokered bride industry is only possible because a number of men choose to buy their wives, just as women and girls can be trafficked into prostitution only because there is, ultimately, a clientele willing to pay for their use. Similarly, Asian children can profitably be trafficked for sex with adult males from wealthier neighboring and western countries only because a number of men travel to engage in pedophilia. This connection between consumer demand and global sex trafficking is stated quite bluntly in the U.S. 2005 TIP Report:

Market demand—especially from male sex buyers—creates a strong profit incentive for traffickers to entrap more victims, fueling the growth of trafficking in persons.[145]

According to NGOs, academics, and other researchers, the legalization of prostitution—viewed by some as providing more transparency in the industry and, therefore, more protection to women in the sex trades—only increases the demand for trafficked women by drawing additional consumers of purchased sex and by providing a legal facade for the enslavement of women. A study commissioned by the Swedish government concluded that a significant percentage of the profits from global prostitution, both legal and illegal, accrue to traffickers.[146]

This connection between the demand for commercial sex services and human trafficking has also been acknowledged by the UN Department of Peacekeeping Operations (DPKO). Following the discovery that women used as prostitutes in 2004 by UN peacekeeping troops in Congo were, in fact, trafficked persons, the DPKO issued a policy paper detailing the role of traffickers in meeting consumer demand and the effects of peacekeepers' perhaps unwitting reliance on human traffickers to satisfy their desire for purchased sex:

Any influx of peacekeeping troops and other personnel, contractors, local combatants and reconstruction money will create a source of demand and locally accessible revenue in otherwise poor economies. In such circumstances, UN peacekeepers should expect to find trafficking and exploitation emerging in its areas of operations, even as the first personnel arrive. Senior managers of missions should assume that traffickers will target UN personnel for revenue. . . .

The use of trafficking victims by peacekeepers for sexual and other services has been a source of major embarrassment and political damage to UN PKOs. Despite the fact that involvement is not usually widespread, the political and moral stigma attached to this behavior can taint entire missions. . . .[147]

The IOM has found similar evidence that traffickers respond to a demand for prostitution by enslaving women expressly to meet that consumer demand. Its 2002 report, "Women Trafficked for U.S. Military Bases," for example, found that more than 5,000 women had been trafficked from eastern Europe, the Philippines, and Russia to be prostituted to U.S. servicemen stationed in South Korea.[148]

PROFIT SEEKING, THE MINIMIZATION OF EXPENSES, AND OTHER MOTIVATIONS

Employers who arrange directly to use forced labor do so to maximize their profits. Other employers use forced labor when they subcontract to the lowest bidder and, knowingly or not, receive goods or services produced by enslaved laborers. In these cases, employers seek the lowest possible prices from suppliers and service providers without questioning the working conditions of those whose labor they subcontract.[149] Third-party traffickers hired to deliver labor at a fair market price may also use enslaved labor to inflate their own profit margins. In all these scenarios, the privileging of profit seeking over other values is a root cause of trafficking.

While employers use forced labor to maximize profits, consumers who purchase goods made with that forced labor are usually seeking to minimize the expense of acquiring desired items. While such items are often purchased without any suspicion that slave labor may be a factor, the consumers' insistence on a low price—and the consumers' failure to inquire as to how that low price may be secured—helps to drive the manufacturers' demands for cheap labor.

Individual decisions to enslave household workers or accept trafficked organs have simple, if unethical, motivations, according to those who have worked on many of these cases. Suzanne Tomatore, director of the Immigrant Women and Children Project of the New York City Bar Association, for example, has worked on many cases involving involuntary domestic servitude. Asked to comment on the motivation of those who enslave their household help, she replied:

> *Who would do this to another human being? . . . All kinds of people. Doctors, lawyers, professionals, business people, diplomats—the only thing the employers have in common as a group is they all have the resources to pay someone a fair wage, but they choose not to.[150]*

Medical anthropologist Nancy Scheper-Hughes of Organ Watch assigns similarly elemental motivations to those involved in trafficking persons for involuntary organ harvesting:

> *For most bio-ethicists, the "slippery slope" in transplant medicine begins with the emergence of a black market in organs and tissue sales. For the anthropologist, it emerges much earlier: the first time a frail and ailing human being looks at another living person and realizes that inside that other body is something that can prolong his or her [own] life.[151]*

At Every Stage

Official corruption and organized crime are also factors that contribute to human trafficking. Official corruption refers to governmental participation in circumventing local, national, and international anti-trafficking law. Such corruption ranges from police officers who take bribes to overlook women trafficked into the sex trades (indeed, there are reports of such bribes being added to women's debt-bondage accounts) to governments that make no effort to enforce national laws or international agreements.[152] As the U.S. 2004 TIPS Report describes it

> In many parts of the world … the involvement of police and immigration officials in trafficking seriously hobble[s] efforts to free victims of their misery and prosecute those responsible for modern-day slavery. Too many law enforcement operations [are] unsuccessful as brothel-keepers, sweatshop owners, or traffickers [are] tipped off by corrupt officials.[153]

Organized crime has also become a factor in human trafficking. According to UNODC, at least eight organized crime groups are now engaged in human trafficking. For six of the known groups, human trafficking is "one of a number of diversified criminal activities undertaken by the group." In the other two organized crime groups, human trafficking has become the primary—indeed, almost sole—illegal activity.[154] Again, research indicates that prostitution is frequently linked to organized crime and, increasingly, to human trafficking; moreover, research indicates that legalizing prostitution only increases sex trafficking and the already significant participation of organized crime.[155] Given these findings, it is perhaps not surprising that the primary victims of organized-crime traffickers are women and children.[156]

INTERNATIONAL EFFORTS TO END HUMAN TRAFFICKING

The United Nations and the International Labour Organization

During the last 80 years, the UN and the ILO have approved a number of documents intended to abolish slavery both in its traditional and modern-day forms. These multilateral agreements are legally binding on ratifying countries,[157] and all are relevant to the effort to end all aspects of slavery today. It must be noted, however, that the adoption of these documents has not ended slavery and there is, in the words of John R. Miller, the former U.S. ambassador-at-large on international slavery, "controversy surrounding the

United Nations and human trafficking." As he notes, in many cases, there has been no automatic correlation between a country's becoming party to the Protocol and renewed efforts to abolish slavery within its borders.[158]

The first group of documents was passed when codified chattel slavery was still practiced in a number of countries. The 1926 Slavery Convention, or the Convention to Suppress the Slave Trade and Slavery, was created under the auspices of the League of Nations and called on its signatory parties to "bring about, progressively and as quickly as possible, the complete abolition of slavery in all its forms."[159] The League of Nations was dissolved in 1946, but the UN, stating its interest in seeing the League's "duties and functions . . . continued," adopted the Slavery Convention with a few amendments in 1953.[160]

The UN Universal Declaration of Human Rights was adopted in 1948. Calling the signing of the Declaration a "historic act," the UN Assembly called for every member country to have the Declaration "disseminated, displayed, read and expounded principally in schools and other educational institutions, without distinction based on the political status of countries or territories."[161] Rather than repeat the 1926 Convention's call for slavery to end "progressively and as quickly as possible," the Universal Declaration of Human Rights proclaimed that "all human beings are born free and equal in dignity and rights" and "no one shall be held in slavery or servitude; slavery and the slave trade shall be abolished in all its forms."[162]

In addition, the trafficking of women and girls into prostitution was addressed as a separate issue during the first half of the 20th century. Between 1901 and 1933, the League of Nations had approved a number of instruments prohibiting the trafficking of women and children into prostitution. The UN, emphasizing that those documents remained in force, approved its own Convention for the Suppression of the Traffic in Persons and of the Exploitation of the Prostitution of Others in 1949. This Convention, while broad in its protection for women trafficked into prostitution, did not address the full spectrum of modern-day slavery.

The broader nature of slavery's midcentury survival began to be comprehensively addressed with the UN's 1956 Supplementary Convention. This document acknowledged that slavery and the slave trade continued to exist in some parts of the world, and it defined practices that create "servile status"—specifically, debt bondage, serfdom, unfree or forced marriage, and exploitive child labor—as practices similar to slavery.

The ILO, meanwhile, had adopted Convention 29, Concerning Forced Labour (1930), which had called for an end to that practice. Following the 1956 Supplementary Convention, the ILO addressed the issue of forced labor again in its Convention 105, Concerning the Abolition of Forced Labour (1957). This instrument, which specifically noted the 1926 Convention's concern that "compulsory or forced labour" not "develop into conditions analogous to slavery," and the 1956 Supplementary Convention's call "for the complete abolition of debt bondage and serfdom," pledged ILO members "to suppress and not make use of any form of forced or compulsory labour."[163]

The most recent group of relevant international instruments contains the UN Protocol (2000). This protocol sets forth what has become the most widely cited and accepted definition of human trafficking:

> the recruitment, transportation, transfer, harbouring or receipt of persons, by means of the threat or use of force or other forms of coercion, of abduction, of fraud, of deception, of the abuse of power or of a position of vulnerability or of the giving or receiving of payments or benefits to achieve the consent of a person having control over another person, for the purpose of exploitation.[164]

Addressing the many forms of modern-day slavery, the UN Protocol also defines exploitation as "the exploitation of the prostitution of others, or other forms of sexual exploitation, forced labour or services, slavery or practices similar to slavery, servitude or the removal of organs." It states that the victim's consent is "irrelevant" if the trafficker has used any of the coercive or fraudulent tactics described above, and it makes clear that, even if no fraudulent or coercive tactics are used, a child who "consents" to exploitation is nonetheless a trafficked child. ("Child" is defined as a person below the age of 18.)[165]

UNODC is the custodian of the UN Protocol, and UNODC's Global Programme against Trafficking in Human Beings (GPAT)—the only UN unit with a criminal justice mandate—helps member countries both to draft laws in compliance and furtherance of the UN Protocol and to devise and implement national strategies for fighting the crime of human trafficking. Where necessary, GPAT also contributes resources.[166]

A number of other important international conventions, adopted shortly before and after the UN Protocol, are related to one or another specific type of exploitation. Among the core international agreements on human trafficking, they include the Hague Convention on Protection of Children and Co-operation in Respect of Intercountry Adoption (1993), commonly referred to as the Hague Convention on Intercountry Adoption;[167] ILO Convention 182, Convention Concerning the Prohibition and Immediate Action for the Elimination of the Worst Forms of Child Labor (1999);[168] the UN Optional Protocol to the Convention on the Rights of the Child on the Sale of Children, Child Prostitution and Child Pornography (2000); and the UN Optional Protocol on the Rights of the Child in Armed Conflict (2000).[169]

In addition, the two major root causes of human trafficking in origin countries—gender inequality and poverty—are addressed by the 1979 UN

Convention on the Elimination of All Forms of Discrimination against Women (CEDAW) and the UN Millennium Development Goals of 2000. CEDAW, which is frequently referred to as "an international bill of rights for women," calls for the eradication of

> *... any distinction, exclusion, or restriction made on the basis of sex which has the effect or purpose of impairing or nullifying the recognition, enjoyment or exercise by women, irrespective of their marital status, on a basis of equality of men and women, of human rights and fundamental freedoms in the political, economic, social, cultural, civil or any other field.*[170]

Parties to CEDAW are required to submit reports to the Committee on the Convention on the Elimination of All Forms of Discrimination, which monitors the progress of the CEDAW's implementation.

Although the United Nations Millennium Declaration (2000) does not specifically mention modern-day slavery, it nonetheless addresses major root causes of human trafficking. In this declaration, member states pledged to eradicate extreme poverty and hunger, to achieve universal primary education, and to promote gender equality and empower women, among other goals, by 2015. These Millennium Development Goals (MDGs), as they are now known, are defined by specific benchmark criteria. The benchmarks for eradicating extreme hunger and poverty, for example, are to "reduce by half the proportion of people living on less than $1 a day" and to "reduce by half the proportion of people who suffer from hunger," while the goal of universal primary education is defined as "ensur[ing] that all boys and girls complete a full course of primary schooling." The specific task of promoting gender equality and empowering women is also tied to education: The MDGs specifically called upon member states to "eliminate gender disparity in primary and secondary education preferably by 2005, and at all levels by 2015." While the midpoint Millennium Development Goals Report (MDG Report) (2007) finds slow and mixed progress toward reaching these goals, it does find measurable achievement.[171]

The UN antislavery treaties and conventions require party nations to create certain standards within their own countries, and the UNODC is empowered to assist all UN member nations with the ensuing criminal justice issues. Nonetheless, there are limits to the United Nation's power to directly enforce the obligations of the countries that are party to the various antislavery measures. As Suzanne Miers describes the history of UN antislavery instruments in her book *Slavery in the Twentieth Century:*

> *... treaties had been negotiated. Standards had been set Some groups had been mobilized to claim their rights. Efforts had been made to*

alert the public to a whole range of abuses. Boycotts of goods produced by sweated and child labor had been organized. Many branches of the UN had discussed the issues. NGOs were active. But there remained no mechanism to enforce the conventions.[172]

UNODC concedes that enforcement remains a problem. Summarizing the worldwide impact of the most recent antislavery instrument, UNODC notes that "translating [the UN Protocol] into reality remains problematic. Very few criminals are convicted and most victims are probably never identified or assisted."[173]

The International Criminal Court (ICC), created by adoption of the Rome Statute of the International Criminal Court in 1998 and in effect as of 2002, also faces limitations. While it is authorized to try "persons accused of the most serious crimes of international concerns," specifically including slavery, the court must "rely on national governments to hand over the perpetrators; or on the international community to force them to do so." Moreover, the ICC has jurisdiction only over states that agree to be bound by its provisions, and a significant number of countries, including China, Russia, and the United States, have refused to agree.[174] As this is written, the Congolese warlord Thomas Lubanga is standing trial in the ICC on charges of using child soldiers in the 2002 to 2003 ethnic conflict in Congo's Ituri region. His case is the first to be heard before the ICC.

The few lawsuits brought against nations for failure to enforce their own or international antislavery cases have been brought in regional courts. In 2005, for example, the European Court of Human Rights found France guilty of violating the forced labor and servitude articles of the European Convention on Human Rights. In this case, a 15-year-old Togolese girl named Siwa-Akofa Siliadin was brought to France by a Mrs. D. with the promise of receiving an education and board in return for assistance with housework. Instead, her passport was confiscated and she became Mrs. D.'s unpaid servant. Mrs. D. then "lent" Siliadin to a Mr. and Mrs. B., in whose house she worked 15-hour days without pay and where, again, she was kept from education and her own identity papers. After four years, a neighbor reported the situation, and criminal proceedings were brought against Mr. and Mrs. B. The case ultimately reached the European Court of Human Rights, which ruled that Mr. and Mrs. B. were guilty of holding Siliadin in forced labor and servitude, and that France, in failing to prevent this, had violated its obligation under the European Convention on Human Rights.[175]

More recently, a regional court convicted Niger of failing to enforce its own antislavery laws and its obligations under international antislavery conventions and charters. Hadijatou Mani Koraou, the young woman who brought the lawsuit, was born a slave and sold to El Hadj Souleymane Naroua when she was 12 years old. While enslaved, she performed agricultural and household work; beginning at age 13, she was also subjected to sexual violence and became pregnant with three of Naroua's children. When an NGO worker informed Naroua that slavery was illegal in Niger, Naroua released Hadijatou from slavery but refused to grant her liberty, claiming that she was his wife under Niger's customary law. Hadijatou brought her case to the local Tribunal Civil et Coutumier, which ruled that Hadijatou and Naroua were not married and that Hadijatou was free. When Naroua appealed, the Tribunal de Grand Instance ruled in his favor, finding that "under Niger's customary law a slave girl is de facto married to her master once she is released."

In the course of subsequent appeals, Hadijatou married a man of her own choice. She was convicted of bigamy and sentenced to six months' imprisonment, along with her husband and her brother, who had consented to the marriage. Hadijatou, who served two months of her bigamy sentence, ultimately brought her case before the Economic Community of West African States (ECOWAS) Community Court of Justice in Niamey. Niger was charged with failure to enforce its own and international antislavery and gender discrimination law, including failure to uphold its obligations under the African Charter of Human and People's Rights; the Treaty of ECOWAS; the Convention for the Elimination of All Forms of Discrimination against Women; the Slavery Convention; the Supplementary Convention on the Abolition of Slavery, the Slave Trade, and Institutions and Practices Similar to Slavery; and the UN Protocol, among other instruments, all of which Niger had ratified.

In a decision that establishes precedent for all 15 ECOWAS member states, Niger was found guilty of gender discrimination (Niger's customary law was found to discriminate against women) and of failure to prevent slavery. While others have sued individuals involved in their enslavement—and while others have been the beneficiaries of criminal suits brought on their behalf—Hadijatou Mani Koraou is the first former slave to have herself sued a country for its action or inaction regarding slavery within its borders.[176]

Nongovernmental Organizations

NGOs play a significant role in the international effort to end human trafficking. For example, Anti-Slavery International (ASI), founded in 1839 and based in London, works to expose cases of modern-day slavery, educate the public about the issue, and pressure governments.[177] (It was also one of the NGOs to support Hadijatou Mani Koraou in her successful 2008 suit against Niger discussed above.) The Thailand-based Global Alliance Against Traffic in Women (GAATW), a network of more than 80 NGOs from all regions of the world, works to effect change in conditions and polices that encourage the trafficking of persons, paying special attention to the dangers faced by migrant workers.[178] The Coalition Against Trafficking in Women (CATW) works internationally against sexual exploitation and especially against the prostitution and trafficking of girls and women.[179] The NGO ECPAT, also based in Thailand, works worldwide to end the sexual exploitation of children.[180] The United States–based HRW as part of its mission to "protect the human rights of people all around the world" monitors countries and issues public reports regarding, among other human rights abuses, trafficking activities,[181] while the United States–based Organs Watch works to document and prevent trafficking for organ harvesting.[182] The Fair Trade Federation (FTF) based in the United States and the International Fair Trade Association (IFAT) based in the Netherlands both work internationally to certify that goods are fair trade; a "fair trade" designation means, among other things, that just conditions have prevailed during the production of a given good.

Other internationally active NGOs include direct rescue activities among their initiatives. FTS, a sister organization of ASI based in New York, works in the field to "knock down doors and help slaves escape" and funds education and other assistance to newly freed people all around the world.[183] Christian Solidarity International (CSI), controversially, raises money to purchase the freedom of individual modern-day slaves. UNICEF, among other organizations, has attacked this strategy as "absolutely intolerable," arguing that to purchase humans for any reason only increases the market for trafficked persons. Others defend and even applaud CSI's direct redemption program. Among them is Francis Bok, who himself was enslaved in Sudan for 10 years. Although his captivity ended without help from CSI, Bok, noting in 2003 that the organization had purchased the freedom of approximately 80,000 people, wrote "there is proof in the smiling faces of those liberated that redemptions have saved many lives and improved the lives of many more."[184]

---

[1] United Nations. "Universal Declaration of Human Rights" (1948). Available online. URL: http://www.un.org/Overview/rights.html. Accessed August 3, 2007.

[2] Kevin Bales. *Understanding Global Slavery: A Reader.* Berkeley: University of California Press, 2005, pp. 96–97, 112, 116; ———. *Disposable People: New Slavery in the Global Economy,* rev. 2nd ed. Berkeley: University of California Press, 2004, pp. 80–120; Jesse Sage and Loira Lasten, eds. *Enslaved: True Stories of Modern Day Slavery.* New York: Palgrave Macmillan, 2006, pp. 178–206.

[3] Bales. *Disposable People,* p. 202.

[4] HRW. "West Africa: Stop Trafficking in Child Labor" (2003). Available online. URL: http://hrw.org/english/docs/2003/04/01togo5489_txt.htm. Accessed October 1, 2007.

[5] UNESCO. "Trafficking Statistics Project." Available online. URL: http://www.unescobkk.org/index.php?id=1022. Accessed August 10, 2007.

[6] UNODC. "Trafficking in Persons: Global Patterns" (2006), p. 45. Available online. URL: http://www.unodc.org/pdf/traffickinginpersons_report_2006-04.pdf. Accessed June 6, 2006.

Introduction

[7] U.S. Department of State. "Trafficking in Persons Report" (2008), p. 7. Available online. URL: http://www.state.gov/g/tip/rls/tiprpt/2008. Accessed October 16, 2008.

[8] UN News Centre. "On bicentennial of slave trade's end, UN officials urge halt to modern-day exploitation" (3/26/07). Available online. URL: http://www.un.org/apps/news/story.asp?NewsID=220205&Cr=slave&Crl=#. Accessed July 30, 2007.

[9] U.S. Department of State. "Trafficking in Persons Report" (2007), p. 8.

[10] FTS. "What's the Story." Available online. URL: http://www.freetheslaves.net/NETCOMMUNITY/Page.aspx?pid=375&srcid=183. Accessed July 31, 2007.

[11] AASG. "Modern Slavery 101." Available online. URL: http://www.iabolish.org/modern_slavery101/. Accessed July 31, 2007.

[12] U.S. Department of State. "Trafficking in Persons Report," (2007), p. 8.

[13] UN News Centre. "On bicentennial of slave trade's end, UN officials urge halt to modern-day exploitation."

[14] HRW. "West Africa: Stop Trafficking in Child Labor."

[15] Thor Halvorssen (producer). *The Sugar Babies.* New Orleans: Siren Studios and the Hope, Courage and Justice Project, 2007.

[16] FTS. "Bal Vikas Ashram." Available online. URL: http://*freetheslaves*.net/NETCOMMUNITY/pAGE.ASPX?PID=288& SRCID=240. Accessed September 15, 2007.

[17] Dana Thomas. "Terror's Purse Strings." *New York Times* (8/7/07).

[18] U.S. Department of State. "Trafficking in Persons Report" (2007), p. 9.

[19] Michael Smith and David Voreacos. "Slaves in Amazon Forced to Make Material Used in Cars." Bloomberg.com (11/2/06). Available online. URL: http://www.bloomberg.com/apps/news?pid=2060109&sid=a4j1VKZq34TM<0x0026 >refer=home. Accessed October 1, 2007.

[20] John Bowe. *Nobodies: Modern American Slave Labor and the Dark Side of the New Global Economy.* New York: Random House, 2007, pp. 64–72.

[21] U.S. Department of State. "Trafficking in Persons Report" (2006), p. 19.

[22] HRW. "West Africa: Stop Trafficking in Child Labor."

[23] Smith and Voreacos. "Slaves in Amazon Forced to Make Material Used in Cars."

[24] UN News Centre. "UN and partners launch initiative to end 'modern slavery' of human trafficking." (3/26/07). Available online. URL: http://www.un.org/apps/news/story.asp?NewsID=22009&Cr=slave&Cr1. Accessed September 28, 2007.

[25] Bowe. *Nobodies: Modern American Slave Labor and the Dark Side of the New Global Economy,* p. xxii.

[26] Bales. *Disposable People,* p. 18.

[27] USINFO. "Human Trafficking a Global Problem, U.N. Report Says" (4/24/06). Available online. URL: http://usinfo.state.gov/xarchives/display.html?p=washfile-english&y=2006&m=April&x=20060424185515mbzemog0.2210504. Accessed October 4, 2007.

[28] U.S. Department of State. "Human Trafficking. Exploitation by U.N. Peacekeepers Condemned" (3/2/05). Available online. URL: http://www.america.gov/st/washfile-english/2005/March/20050302190435xlrenneF0.628216.html. Accessed April 28, 2008.

29 USINFO. "Human Trafficking a Global Problem, U.N. Report Says."

30 Bernard Lewis. *Race and Slavery in the Middle East: A Historical Inquiry.* New York: Oxford University Press, 1992, p. 3.

31 Sir Paul Harvey. *Oxford Companion to Classical Literature.* London: Oxford University Press, 1937, pp. 397–398.

32 Lewis. *Race and Slavery in the Middle East,* p. 4.

33 Stanley Engerman, Seymour Drescher, and Robert Paquette, eds. *Slavery.* Oxford: Oxford University Press, 2001, pp. 58, 149.

34 William Phillips. *Slavery from Roman Times to the Early Transatlantic Trade.* Minneapolis: University of Minnesota Press, 1985, p. 44.

35 John Wright. *The Trans-Saharan Slave Trade.* New York: Routledge, 2007.

36 Engerman. *Slavery,* p. 150.

37 Bales. *Disposable People,* p. 4.

38 ———. *Disposable People,* pp. 4, 18, 59.

39 International Organization for Migration. "Protection Schemes for Victims of Trafficking in Selected EU Member Countries, Candidate and Third Countries" (2003), p. 11. Available online. URL: http://www.old.iom.int/documents/publications/en/protection_scheme.pdf. Accessed June 7, 2007.

40 United Nations. "Protocol to Prevent, Suppress and Punish Trafficking in Persons Especially Women and Children, supplementing the United Nations Convention against Transnational Organized Crime" (2000), p. 2. Available online. URL: http://www.ohchr. org/english/law/protocoltraffic.html. Accessed June 7, 2007.

41 UNODC. "Protocol to Prevent, Suppress and Punish Trafficking in Persons, Especially Women and Children." Available online. URL: http://unodc.org/unodc/en/treaties/CTOC/ countrylist-traffickingprotocol.html. Accessed October 18, 2008.

42 U.S. Department of State. "Trafficking in Persons Report" (2007), p. 53.

43 ———. "Trafficking in Persons Report" (2007), pp. 8, 51, 53, 63.

44 ———. "Trafficking in Persons Report" (2007), pp. 8, 51, 53, 63.

45 USINFO. "Human Trafficking a Global Problem, U.N. Report Says" (4/24/06). Available online. URL: http://usinfo.state.gov/xarchives/display.html?p=washfile-english&y=2006&m =April&x=20060424185515mbzemog0.2210504. Accessed October 4, 2007.

46 McGill International Law Society. "Conference on Human Trafficking in Canada" (3/20/06). Available online. URL: http://mils.mcgill.ca/resources/Human_Trafficking.pdf. Accessed October 1, 2007.

47 U.S. Department of State. "Trafficking in Persons Report" (2007), p. 26.

48 McGill International Law Society. "Conference on Human Trafficking in Canada" (2006).

49 U.S. Department of State. "Trafficking in Persons Report" (2007), p. 26.

50 McGill International Law Society. "Conference on Human Trafficking in Canada" (2006).

[51] U.S. Department of State. "Trafficking in Persons Report" (2007), p. 26.

[52] McGill International Law Society. "Conference on Human Trafficking in Canada" (2006); U.S. Department of State. "Trafficking in Persons Report" (2007), p. 26.

[53] International Helsinki Federation for Human Rights. "A Form of Slavery: Trafficking in Women in OSCE Member States" (2000). Available online. URL: http://www.greekhelsinki. gr/English/reports/ihf-wit-july-2000-greece.html. Accessed August 29, 2007.

[54] International Helsinki Federation for Human Rights. "A Form of Slavery: Trafficking in Women in OSCE Member States."

[55] Socialsyrelsen. "Prostitution in Sweden" (2003). Available online: URL: http://www.social styrelsen.se.NR/rdonlyres/A688D624-4505-431F-A9CF-DCD7C12D0539/2719/200413128. pdf. Accessed June 19, 2007.

[56] U.S. Department of State. "Trafficking in Persons Report" (2007), p. 20.

[57] Bales. *Disposable People*, p. 42.

[58] ———. *Disposable People*, p. 41.

[59] ———. *Disposable People*, p. 36.

[60] "Child sex tourism raises its head in India." Indo-Asian News Service (10/14/07). Available online. URL: http://sify.com/news/fullstory.php?id=14542872. Accessed October 16, 2007.

[61] United Nations. "Press Conference on Human Trafficking and Sex Tourism" (10/21/04). Available online. URL: http://www.un.org/News/briefings/docs/2004/Martin_Press_Cfc_ 041020.doc.htm. Accessed October 16, 2008.

[62] ECPAT. End Child Prostitution, Child Pornography, and Trafficking of Children for Sexual Purposes. "Report on the Status of Action against Commercial Sexual Exploitation of Children: United States of America" (2006), pp. 12, 32. Available online. URL: http://www.ecpat. net/eng/AA-2005/PDF/Americas/Global_MonitoringReport-USA.PDF. Accessed September 3, 2007.

[63] U.S. Department of State. "Trafficking in Persons Report" (2007), p. 28.

[64] Emsie Ferreira. "South Africa Child Sex: Child Sex Trafficking Rising in South Africa as Poverty Spreads: Survey." Agence France-Presse (11/22/00). Available online. URL: http:// www.aegis.com/NEWSAFP/2000/AF001165.html. Accessed September 20, 2007.

[65] United Nations. "Protocol to Prevent, Suppress and Punish Trafficking in Persons Especially Women and Children, supplementing the United Nations Convention against Transnational Organized Crime" (2000), p. 2.

[66] ———. "Supplementary Convention on the Abolition of Slavery, the Slave Trade, and Institutions and Practices Similar to Slavery" (1956). Available online. URL: http://www.ohcr. orch.org/english/law/pdf.slavetrade.pdf. Accessed July 15, 2007.

[67] Sharon LaFraniere. "Forced to Marry Before Puberty, African Girls Pay Lasting Price." *New York Times* (11/27/05).

[68] Isambard Wilkinson. "Blood Debt Women Offered Up for Rape." Telegraph.Co.UK (9/11/05). Available online. URL: http://www.telegraph.co.ul/news.main.jhtml?xml=news/2 005/11/22/wdeb22.xml. Accessed October 1, 2007.

[69] U.S. Department of State. "Trafficking in Persons Report" (2006), p. 15.

[70] Sharon LaFraniere. "Forced to Marry Before Puberty, African Girls Pay Lasting Price."

[71] Isambard Wilkinson. "Blood Debt Women Offered Up for Rape."

[72] U.S. Department of State. "Country Reports on Human Rights Practices, 2006: Pakistan." Available online. URL: http://www.state.gov/g/drl/rls/hrrpt/2006/78874.htm. Accessed October 8, 2007.

[73] "Infants Saved from Wedlock to Landlord's Son." *Daily Times* (Pakistan) (7/19/06). Available online. URL: http://www.dailytimes.co.pk/default.asp?page=20060719story_19-7-2006_pg7_26. Accessed October 8, 2007, U.S. Department of State. "Country Reports on Human Rights Practices, 2006: Pakistan."

[74] U.S. Department of State. "Trafficking in Persons Report" (2006), p. 15.

[75] Sharon LaFraniere. "Nightmare for African Women: Birthing Injury and Little Help." *New York Times* (9/28/05); "Fistula Women." BBC World Service. Available online (audio and text). URL: http://www.bbc.co.uk/worldservice/sci_tech/highlights/010321_hospital.shtml; United Nations Population Fund's Campaign to End Fistula. Available online. URL: http://www.endfistula.org; Barbara Crossette. "U.N. Agency Sets Its Sights on Curbing Child Marriage." *New York Times* (3/8/01).

[76] UNICEF. "Early Marriage: A Harmful Traditional Practice" (2005), p. 1. Available online. URL: http://www.unicef.org/publications/index_26024.html. Accessed November 2, 2007.

[77] U.S. Department of State. "Trafficking in Persons Report" (2007), p. 17.

[78] ———. "Trafficking in Persons Report" (2007), p. 115.

[79] ———. "Trafficking in Persons Report" (2007), p. 80.

[80] ———. "Trafficking in Persons Report" (2006), p. 20.

[81] ———. "Trafficking in Persons Report" (2007), p. 17.

[82] ———. "Trafficking in Persons Report" (2005), p. 21.

[83] UNICEF Innocenti Research Center. Child Trafficking Research Hub. Available only online. URL: http://www.childtrafficking.org/eng/database.html. Search keywords: baby trafficking. Accessed October 4, 2007.

[84] Nicola Smith Plovdiv. "Revealed: Bulgaria's Baby Traders." *Sunday Times,* (10/01/06). Available online. URL: http://www.timesonline.co.uk/tol/news/world/article 656620.ece. Accessed October 2, 2007.

[85] Niki Kitsantonis and Matthew Brunwasser. "Baby Trafficking Is Thriving in Greece." *International Herald Tribune* (12/18/06). Available online. URL: http://www.iht.com/articles/2006/12/18/news/babies.php. Accessed October 20, 2007.

[86] UNICEF Innocenti Research Center. "Chinese Woman Sentenced to Death over Baby Trafficking" (5/14/04). Available online: URL: http://www.childtrafficking.org/cgi-bin/ct/main.sql?ID=702&file=view_document.sql<0x0026>TITLE=-1&AUTHOR=-1&THESAURO=-1&ORGANIZATION=-1&TYPE_DOC=-1&TOPIC=-1&GEOG=-1&YEAR=-1&LISTA=No&COUNTRY=-1&FULL_DETAIL=YES. Accessed September 20, 2007.

[87] ———. "Chinese Woman Sentenced to Death over Baby Trafficking" (5/14/04).

[88] "53 Babies Found, 110 Suspects Arrested for Baby Trafficking Case." *People's Daily* (Beijing) (10/08/04). Available online. URL: http://english.peopledaily.com.cn/200410/08/eng20041008_159275.html. Accessed October 4, 2007.

[89] "Gang Trafficking Over 60 Babies Cracked." China Economic Net (9/9/07). Available online. URL: http://en.ce.cn/National/Local/200709/08/t20070908_12834260.shtml. Accessed September 14, 2007.

[90] "Gang Trafficking Over 60 Babies Cracked."

[91] Congressional-Executive Commission on China. "2005 Annual Report," Section III(f), Status of Women. Available online. URL: http://www.cecc.gov/pgages/annualRPT/annualRpt05/2005_3F_women.php. Accessed October 5, 2007.

[92] UNESCO. "Trafficking Statistics Project." Available online. URL: http://www.unescobkk.org/index.php?id=1022. Accessed August 10, 2007.

[93] Debbie Nathan. "Oversexed." *The Nation*, (8/29/05). Available online. URL: http://www.thenation.com/doc/20050829/Nathan. Accessed December 1, 2007; International Labour Organization. "A Global Alliance against Forced Labour: Global Report under the Follow-up to the ILO Declaration on Fundamental Principles and Rights at Work, 2005." Available online. URL: http://www.ilo.org/dyn/declaris/DECLARATIONWEB.DOWNLOAD_BLOB?Var_Documen tID=5059. Accessed December 1, 2007.

[94] ILO. "A Global Alliance against Forced Labour: Global Report under the Follow-up to the ILO Declaration on Fundamental Principles and Rights at Work, 2005," p. 15. Available online. URL: http://www.ilo.org/dyn/declaris/DECLARATIONWEB.DOWNLOAD_BLOB?Var_Documen tID=5059. Accessed December 1, 2007.

[95] U.S. Department of State. "Trafficking in Persons Report" (2007), p. 13.

[96] ——. "Trafficking in Persons Report" (2007), p. 18.

[97] ——. "Trafficking in Persons Report" (2007), p. 13.

[98] ILO. "A Global Alliance against Forced Labour: Global Report under the Follow-up to the ILO Declaration on Fundamental Principles and Rights at Work, 2005," p. 12.

[99] ——. "A Global Alliance against Forced Labour: Global Report under the Follow-up to the ILO Declaration on Fundamental Principles and Rights at Work, 2005," pp. 42–43.

[100] Bales. *Disposable People.*

[101] HRW. "Contemporary Forms of Slavery in Pakistan" (1995), p. 44. Available online. URL: http://www.hrw.org/reports/pdfs/c/crd/pakistan957.pdf. Accessed November 19, 2007.

[102] ——. "Contemporary Forms of Slavery in Pakistan" (1995), p. 17.

[103] ——. "Contemporary Forms of Slavery in Pakistan" (1995), p. 56.

[104] ——. "Contemporary Forms of Slavery in Pakistan" (1995), p. 16.

[105] ——. "Contemporary Forms of Slavery in Pakistan" (1995), p. 2.

[106] Bales. *Disposable People*, p. 125.

[107] U.S. Department of State. "Trafficking in Persons Report" (2007), p. 167.

[108] ——. "Trafficking in Persons Report" (2007), p. 82.

[109] ———. "Trafficking in Persons Report" (2007), p. 54.

[110] ———. "Trafficking in Persons Report" (2007), p. 9.

[111] ———. "Trafficking in Persons Report" (2007), p. 58.

[112] Human Rights Watch. "Borderline Slavery: Child Trafficking in Togo" (2003), pp. 1–2. Available online. URL: http://www.hrw.org/reports/2004/togo003/. Accessed November 5, 2007.

[113] U.S. Department of State. "Trafficking in Persons Report" (2007), p. 7.

[114] ———. "Trafficking in Persons Report" (2007), p. 24.

[115] ———. "Trafficking in Persons Report" (2007), p. 24.

[116] HRW. "Facts about Child Soldiers." Available online. URL: http://www.hrw.org/campaigns/crp/fact_sheet.html. Accessed December 1, 2007; U.S. Department of State. "Trafficking in Persons Report" (2007), p. 24.

[117] ———. "Early to War: Child Soldiers in the Chad Conflict" (2007), p. 1. Available online. URL: http://hrw.org/reports/2007/chad0707webwcover.pdf. Accessed October 19, 2007.

[118] United Nations. "Protocol to Prevent, Suppress and Punish Trafficking in Persons, Especially Women and Children, supplementing the United Nations Convention against Transnational Organized Crime" (2000), p. 2.

[119] U.S. Department of State. "Trafficking in Persons Report" (2007), p. 24.

[120] HRW. "Facts about Child Soldiers."

[121] Ishmael Beah. "The Making, and Unmaking, of a Child Soldier: One Boy's Tortuous Entanglement in an African Civil War." New York Times Magazine (1/14/07), pp. 38–39.

[122] HRW. "Facts about Child Soldiers." "Trafficking in Persons Report" (2007), p. 24.

[123] U.S. Department of State. "Trafficking in Persons Report" (2006), p. 10.

[124] HRW. "Facts about Child Soldiers."

[125] U.S. Department of State. "Trafficking in Persons Report" (2007), p. 26.

[126] ———. "Trafficking in Persons Report" (2007), p. 21.

[127] HRW. "Complicit in Crime: State Collusion in Abductions and Child Recruitment by the Karuna Group" (2007). Available online. URL: http://www.hrw.org/reports/2007/srilanka0107/. Accessed November 5, 2007.

[128] ———. "Children in the Ranks: The Maoists' Use of Child Soldiers in Nepal" (2007). Available online. URL: http://www.hrw.org/reports/2007/nepal0207. Accessed November 5, 2007.

[129] ———. "Early to War: Child Soldiers in the Chad Conflict" (2007).

[130] Reuters. "Youths Again Forced to Fight in Congo, Aid Group Says." New York Times (12/25/07).

[131] "Top Transplant Surgeons Involved in Organ Trafficking, Expert Says." International Herald Tribune (2/14/08).

[132] Patricia McBroom. "An 'Organs Watch' to Track Global Traffick in Human Organs Opens Mon., Nov. 8, at UC Berkeley" (news release). University of California, Berkeley (11/03/99). Available online. URL: http://berkeley.edu/news/media/releases/99legacy/11-03-1999b.html. Accessed February 16, 2008.

[133] "Top Transplant Surgeons Involved in Organ Trafficking, Expert Says."

[134] Patricia McBroom. "An 'Organs Watch' to Track Global Traffick in Human Organs Opens Mon., Nov. 8, at UC Berkeley."

[135] UNODC. "Trafficking in Persons: Global Patterns" (2006), pp. 18–20. Available online. URL: http://www.unodc.org/pdf/traffickinginpersons_report_2006-04.pdf. Accessed June 6, 2007.

[136] Sharon LaFraniere. "Africa's World of Forced Labor, in a 6-Year-Old's Eyes." *New York Times* (10/29/06).

[137] U.S. Department of State. "Trafficking in Persons Report" (2007), p. 21.

[138] Bales. *Disposable People,* p. 167.

[139] HRW. "Contemporary Forms of Slavery in Pakistan" (1995), p. 17. Available online. URL: http://www.hrw.org/reports/pdfs/crd/pakistan957.pdf. Accessed November 19, 2007.

[140] U.S. Department of State. "Trafficking in Persons Report" (2006), p. 10.

[141] Bales. *Disposable People,* pp. 44–48.

[142] UNODC. "Trafficking in Persons: Global Patterns" (2006), pp. 18–20. Available online. URL: http://www.unodc.org/pdf/traffickinginpersons_report_2006-04.pdf. Accessed June 6, 2007.

[143] ———. "Trafficking in Persons: Global Patterns," pp. 18–20.

[144] Jason DeParle. "World Banker and His Cash Return Home." *New York Times* (3/17/08).

[145] U.S. Department of State. "Trafficking in Persons Report" (2005), p. 21.

[146] ———. "Trafficking in Persons Report" (2004), p. 15. Available online. URL: http://www.state.gov/documents/organization/34158.pdf. Accessed December 20, 2007.

[147] United Nations Department of Peacekeeping Operations. "Human Trafficking and United Nations Peacekeeping DPKO Policy Paper" (March 2004). Available online. URL: http://www.un.org/womenwatch/news/documents/DPKOHumanTraffickingPolicy03-2004.pdf. Accessed March 29, 2008.

[148] "Thousands of Women Forced into Sexual Slavery for US Servicemen in South Korea." *Feminist News Daily Wire* (9/09/02). Available online. URL: http://feminist.org/news/newsbyte/uswirestory.asp?id=6870. Accessed March 28, 2008.

[149] U.S. Department of State. "Trafficking in Persons Report" (2007), p. 35.

[150] Paul Vitello. "From Stand in Long Island Slavery Case, a Snapshot of a Hidden U.S. Problem." *New York Times* (12/30/07).

[151] Nancy Scheper-Hughes. "The Organ of Last Resort." Available online. URL: http://www.unesco.org/courier/2001_07/uk/doss34.htm. Accessed April 20, 2008.

[152] U.S. Department of State. "Trafficking in Persons Report" (2007), p. 35.

[153] ———. "Trafficking in Persons Report" (2004), p. 255.

[154] UNODC. "Trafficking in Persons: Global Patterns," pp. 68–70.

[155] Melissa Farley. *Prostitution and Trafficking in Nevada.* San Francisco: Prostitution Education and Research, 2007, pp. 117–130.

[156] UNODC. "Trafficking in Persons: Global Patterns," pp. 68–70.

41

[157] United Nations. "Basic Facts about the United Nations: International Law." Available online. URL: http://www.un.org/aboutun/basicfacts/intelaw.htm. Accessed December 31, 2007.

[158] John Miller. E-mail to Kathryn Cullen-DuPont, September 16, 2008.

[159] Office of the High Commissioner for Human Rights. "Slavery Convention" (1926). Available online. URL: http://www.unhchr.ch/html/menu3/b/f2sc.htm. Accessed October 7, 2007.

[160] ———. "Protocol amending the Slavery Convention signed at Geneva on 25 September 1926" (1953). Available online. URL: http://www.unhchr.ch/html/menu3/b/f2psc.htm. Accessed October 7, 2007.

[161] United Nations. "Universal Declaration of Human Rights" (1948). Available online. URL: http://www.un.org/Overview/rights.html. Accessed August 3, 2007.

[162] ———. "Protocol to Prevent, Suppress and Punish Trafficking in Persons, Especially Women and Children," p. 2.

[163] ———. "Convention (No. 105) Concerning the Abolition of Forced Labour" (1957). Available online. URL: http://www.unhchr.ch/html/menu3/b/32.htm. Downloaded December 31, 2007.

[164] United Nations. "Protocol to Prevent, Suppress and Punish Trafficking in Persons, Especially Women and Children, supplementing the United Nations Convention against Transnational Organized Crime" (2000), p. 2. Available online. URL: http://www.ohchr.org/english/law/protocoltraffic.html. Accessed June 7, 2007.

[165] ———. "Protocol to Prevent, Suppress and Punish Trafficking in Persons, Especially Women and Children, supplementing the United Nations Convention against Transnational Organized Crime" (2000), p. 2.

[166] UNODC. "UNODC and Human Trafficking." Available online. URL: http://www.undoc.org/undoc/en/human-trafficking/index.htm. Accessed December 31, 2007.

[167] Jane Gross. "U.S. Joins Overseas Adoption Overhaul Plan." *New York Times* (12/11/07).

[168] ILO. "ILO Convention 182, Convention Concerning the Prohibition and Immediate Action for the Elimination of the Worst Forms of Child Labour" (1999). Available online. URL: http://www.un.org/children/conflict/keydocuments/english/iloconvention1828.html. Accessed December 31, 2007.

[169] United Nations. "Optional Protocol to the Convention on the Rights of the Child on the Involvement of Children in Armed Conflicts" (2000). Available online. URL: http://www2.ohchr.org/english/law/pdf/crc-conflict.pdf. Accessed December 31, 2007.

[170] ———. "Convention on the Elimination of all Forms of Discrimination Against Women" (1979). Available online. URL: http://www.unhchr.ch/html/menu3/b/31cedaw.htm. Accessed December 31, 2007.

[171] ———. "The Millennium Development Goals Report" (2007). Available online. URL: http://www.un.org/millenniumgoals/pdf/mdg2007.pdf. Accessed December 1, 2007.

[172] Suzanne Miers. *Slavery in the Twentieth Century: The Evolution of a Global Problem.* Walnut Creek, Calif.: AltaMira Press, 2003, p. 454.

[173] UNOCD. "Human Trafficking." Available online. URL: http://www.unodc.org/unodc/en/human-trafficking/what-is-human-trafficking.html. Accessed March 12, 2009.

[174] Suzanne Miers. *Slavery in the Twentieth Century,* p. 454.

[175] European Court of Human Rights. "Press release issued by the Registrar, Chamber Judgment, *Siliadin v. France.*" Available online. URL: http://www.echr.coe.int/Eng/Press/2005/July/ChamberJudgmentSiliadinvFrance260705.htm. Accessed March 12, 2009.

[176] Lydia Polgreen. "Court Rules That Niger Failed by Allowing Girl's Slavery." *New York Times* (10/28/08); Jonathan Clayton. "Free at Last: Female Slave Who Dared to Take Niger to Court." *Times* (London; 10/28/08); Xan Rice. "Hope for West African Slaves after Landmark Ruling." *Guardian* (10/28/08); The International Centre for the Legal Protection of Human Rights. "*Hadijatou Mani v. Niger*"; Anti-Slavery International. "Briefing Papers: *Hadijatou Mani Koraou v. Niger.*"

[177] ASI. "About Anti-Slavery International." Available online. URL: http://www.antislavery.org/homepage/antislavery/about.com. Accessed December 2, 2007; United Nations. "Nongovernmental Organizations Database." Available online: URL: http://www.unodc.org/ngo/list.jsp. Accessed December 2, 2007.

[178] GAATW. "About Us." Available online. URL: http://www.gaatw.net/index.php?option=com_content&task=blogsection&id= 2&Itemid=59. Accessed December 2, 2007; United Nations. "Nongovernmental Organizations Database." Available online: URL: http://www.unodc.org/ngo/list.jsp. Accessed December 2, 2007.

[179] CATW. "An Introduction to CATW." Available online. URL: http://catwinternational.org/about/index.php. Accessed October 18, 2008.

[180] ECPAT. "About Us." Available online. URL: http://www.ecpat.net/EI/About_CSEC/About_CSEC/index.asp. Accessed February 29, 2008.

[181] HRW. "About HRW." Available online. URL: http://www.hrw.org/about. Accessed December 2, 2007; United Nations. "Nongovernmental Organizations Database." Available online. URL: http://www.unodc.org/ngo/list.jsp. Accessed December 2, 2007.

[182] Patricia McBroom. "An 'Organs Watch' to Track Global Traffic in Human Organs Opens Mon., Nov. 8, at UC Berkeley" (news release). University of California, Berkeley (11/8/99). Available online. URL: http://berkeley.edu/news/media/releases/99legacy/11-03-1999b.html. Accessed February 16, 2008.

[183] FTS. "What We Do." Available online. URL: http://www.freetheslaves.net/NETCOMMUNITY/Page.aspx?pid=240&srcid=341. Accessed December 2, 2007; United Nations. "Nongovernmental Organizations Database." Available online: URL: http://www.unodc.org/ngo/list.jsp. Accessed December 2, 2007.

[184] Francis Bok. *Escape from Slavery.* New York: St. Martin's Griffin, 2003.

2

Focus on the United States

THE UNITED STATES'S ROLE IN TRAFFICKING

The United States is a major destination country for traffickers and their victims. Indeed, the United States is one of only 10 destination countries—on a list of 139—that the United Nations Office on Drugs and Crime (UNODC) notes as having a "very high" reported incidence of human trafficking.[1] While UNODC's designation "very high" means that the United States received among the highest number of reported trafficking victims of any country in the years studied (1996–2000), the actual number of victims is very difficult to ascertain. The U.S. Department of State, for example, estimates that between 18,000 and 20,000 persons are trafficked across international borders and into the United States each year.[2] Other estimates, even when restricted to estimating women and children, are far greater. The U.S. Department of Justice has estimated that "approximately 50,000 women and children are trafficked into the United States annually,"[3] while the U.S. Central Intelligence Agency (CIA) cites estimates of 45,000 to 50,000 women and children.[4] Although estimates as high as 50,000 still appear in some documents, the U.S. government has, since 2004, used revised estimates of 14,500 to 18,000 victims trafficked into the United States each year.

The United States as a Destination Country

Despite the varying estimates of the total number of persons trafficked to the United States, there is general agreement as to the composite profile of the victims. UNODC analysis of North American trafficking victims suggests that, in keeping with overall global patterns, adult women are most frequently trafficked, followed by minors,[5] with about six girls trafficked to every boy.[6] Men— an estimated 5 percent of North American transnational victims according to UNODC—comprise the smallest group of the region's trafficked persons; however, the percentage is higher than in some other regions of the world. While noting that "[T]rafficking in men in [North America] is more frequently reported than in other regions of the world," UNODC also notes that many countries did not view men's forced labor as trafficking in the years studied.[7]

If it is difficult to estimate the number of persons trafficked to the United States, it is also difficult to estimate what percentage of victims are trafficked into which industries. A U.S. White House fact sheet on trafficking states that "[A]pproximately 80 percent of trafficking victims are female, and 70 percent of those female victims are trafficked for the commercial sex industry"—in other words approximately 56 percent of victims trafficked to the United States are forced into the sex trades.[8] The nongovernmental organization (NGO) Free the Slaves (FTS), in contrast, estimates that 46 percent of victims trafficked to the United States are forced into the sex trades. The remaining percentage are trafficked to a variety of industries, some of which may be legal, although poorly regulated.[9] FTS estimates that 27 percent of victims are found in domestic service, 10 percent in agriculture, 5 percent in sweat-shop manufacturing, and 4 percent in restaurant and hotel work.[10] Other sources may weigh these percentages differently, but most concur that these are the major destination industries in the United States.

The geographical dispersal of international trafficking victims within the United States is also broad. Forced labor situations, for instance, have been found in more than 90 American cities,[11] in the country's large agricultural tracts,[12] and—in anticipation of rebuilding in the wake of Hurricane Katrina—along the main highway corridor in Louisiana.[13] More widely, persons trafficked for forced labor and/or sexual exploitation have been documented in American Samoa, the Northern Mariana Islands, the District of Columbia, and in more than half of the U.S. states.[14] The largest concentrations of victims have been found in California, Florida, New York, and Texas, heavily populated states with considerable immigrant communities, all of which also serve as transit hubs for international travel.[15] Indeed, these four states account for 48 percent of all human trafficking cases opened by U.S. attorneys between 2001 and 2005.[16]

The United States as a Transit and Origin Country

While the United States is absent from UNODC's list of transit countries (that is, from the list of countries through which victims pass from their country of origin to the countries in which they are ultimately enslaved), it is not absent from the list of origin countries. Although UNODC lists the United States as having a low reported incidence of origin-country trafficking,[17] the number still indicates that U.S. citizens or residents are trafficked transnationally into modern-day slavery.

FTS, examining modern slavery within U.S. borders, reports that "Some victims are born and raised in the United States and find themselves pressed into servitude by fraudulent or deceptive means."[18] The California Alliance to Combat Trafficking, reaching a similar conclusion, states that "[A]lthough the majority of human trafficking victims in the United States are foreign nationals, there are many U.S. citizen victims who are trapped in forced labor and involuntary servitude."[19] While there is no official estimate of enslaved American citizens, it is undeniable that some number of Americans have been trafficked within and from the United States.

In a 2003 study of verified forced-labor cases in the United States, FTS found that the United States was the second most common origin country for rescued victims, per trafficking case detected. Since each of 149 cases involved a different number of trafficking victims, the same study also tallied origin-country representation by the absolute number of victims; by this method, the United States was the eighth most common country of origin in American forced-labor trafficking cases.[20] Studies restricted to sex trafficking also document the United States's role as a country of origin. The Coalition Against Trafficking in Women (CATW), in an analysis of 38 prosecuted cases of trafficking for sexual exploitation, found American women and/or girls to be the exclusive victims of three of the cases and among the victims in one of the cases.[21] Examining the particular plight of children trafficked within the United States, End Child Prostitution, Child Pornography and Trafficking of Children for Sexual Purposes (ECPAT) notes that American children who are forced into prostitution are not generally viewed as trafficking victims, despite the clear statement in the United Nations Protocol to Prevent, Suppress and Punish Trafficking in Persons, Especially Women and Children (UN Protocol) and in the United States's own Trafficking Victims Protection Act of 2000 that minors are unable to give meaningful consent and that the harboring of a minor for sexual exploitation should be deemed trafficking, regardless of the circumstances. Charity and aid workers who work with runaway and abandon youth report that "thousands" of American runaway and castaway teenaged girls are recruited and harbored in a manner that meets the UN Protocol and other definitions of human trafficking.[22]

ORIGINS OF PERSONS TRAFFICKED TO THE UNITED STATES

Transnational Victims

Women, children, and men are trafficked to the United States from every known region, but most frequently from Asia, Latin America, the Commonwealth of Independent States, and eastern Europe.[23] While definitive information as to the extent of this illegal and often hidden activity is not available, an analysis of the available credible information provides irrefutable evidence that people from more than 40 countries are trafficked into the United States.[24]

This list of origin countries includes both developing and developed nations from all across the world, with specific country representation varying from year to year. As of April 2008, the Department of Health and Human Services (HHS) identified 77 origin countries from which among those persons in the United States who were verified as victims of human trafficking had come. The regions included Africa, the Americas, Asia, Europe, and the Pacific Islands, with the largest number of victims from Latin America. Of the Latin American trafficking victims, 20 percent came from Mexico and 28 percent from El Salvador.[25]

Victims are also exploited in their own countries through sex tourism. This exploitive situation reverses travel patterns since persons from wealthier, more developed countries travel to less wealthy, less developed countries as sex tourists. American men make up 25 percent of sex tourists.[26]

American Victims

When discussing the origins of domestic trafficking victims, it is useful to examine the sociological factors that contribute to their existence. Studies indicate that the persons most at risk for trafficking within the United States are disaffected, runaway, or castaway children. Children of the Night, an organization dedicated to the rescue of child prostitutes, finds that these children are deliberately targeted:

Child prostitution is national in scope. Pimps have become more sophisticated in their recruitment and maintenance of the children they force into prostitution, moving their victims from state to state, often forcing them to work as prostitutes outside the larger cities and in small towns, where police are unfamiliar with the operations of child prostitution rings. Children are recruited by pimps in arcades, malls, entertainment centres, at tourist attractions and concerts. The pimp seduces a new recruit with the lure of wealth and the luxury of designer clothes, fancy cars, and exclusive nightclubs. Pimps move from city to city looking for children who are easy prey: alone, desperate, and alienated. Once he moves a child from her hometown to a strange city, the pimp can easily force her to work as a prostitute. Thousands of children are victimized by this horrible con game every year.[27]

American children who have been lured into prostitution are more often charged with prostitution than treated as victims in the United States,[28] even though the harboring of a minor child for exploitation is specified as human trafficking under the UN Protocol, regardless of the child's consent or seeming consent. In September 2008, however, New York State passed the country's first law recognizing prostituted minors as victims. Under the Safe Harbor for Exploited Youth Act, apprehended boys and girls under age 18 will be sent to counseling and rehabilitation programs, rather than charged with prostitution.[29]

While disaffected, runaway, or castaway children are the group most at risk for trafficking within the United States—and while prostitution is the most frequent destination—children and adults are sometimes trafficked into other industries.

EXPLOITATION OF TRAFFICKED PERSONS IN THE UNITED STATES

Whatever their precise numbers or countries of origin, those enslaved in the United States, like those enslaved anywhere else in the world, "find a hell of servitude."[30] As FTS and the University of California at Berkeley's Human Rights Center report, trafficking victims in the United States have been

> . . . tortured, raped, assaulted, and murdered. They have been held in absolute control by their captors and stripped of their dignity. Some have been subjected to forced abortion, dangerous working conditions, poor nutrition, and humiliation. Some have died during their enslavement. Others have been physically or psychologically scarred for life. Once freed, many will suffer from a host of health-related problems. . . .[31]

Such victims have been found in America's brothels and strip clubs, in its private homes, in its fields and factories, and on its street corners.

Sexual Exploitation

Most persons trafficked into the United States are trafficked for sexual exploitation, including stripping, pornography, and prostitution. Most of these victims are female, and many are minor children. Prostitution is illegal in every state but Nevada and, unless it is solicited outdoors or from cars, Rhode Island; stripping and pornography are, in many circumstances, legal trades.

These victims are enslaved in operations that range from one person's home to a network's nationwide prostitution ring. In *U.S. v. Reddy* (2000), a California businessman Lakireddy Bali Reddy pleaded guilty to federal charges resulting from his trafficking of women and minor girls into the United States. The women were forced to work in his home and in his places of business, but they were also forced to serve "as a quasi-harem for his sexual gratification."[32] A 1999 case in Georgia, *U.S. v. Yong Hui McCready, et al.*, in contrast, exposed a national network of traffickers. In this case, FBI agents found eight minor girls held captive in a brothel in Atlanta, Georgia. Further investigation uncovered a network of brothels in 14 states, through which 500 to 1,000 trafficked women (many of them under the age of 18) were rotated. The women spent approximately two weeks at a time in each location, primarily to meet male customers' demands to have paid sex with a series of different women.[33]

It should be noted that even when women are trafficked into legal sex-related work, sexual violence is often a factor. *U.S. v. Maksimenko*, for example, involved two men's trafficking of at least nine women from Russia and Ukraine to be held in servitude as exotic dancers in their Michigan strip clubs. These women were held captive through the use of force, including rape.[34]

Involuntary Domestic Servitude

Involuntary domestic servitude is widely estimated to be the second largest category of modern-day slavery in the United States. Enslavers of domestic servants are assisted by several factors. First is the fact that live-in domestic servants are employed and housed in private homes, which generally eliminates casual public observation of their working conditions. The completely privatized nature of domestic service is further compounded by the fact that domestic workers are not classified as "employees" under the U.S. National Labor Relations Act (NLRA) and are specifically excluded from the legal protections offered to many other workers who wish to organize for better working conditions and wages.[35] The fact that many enslaved workers do not speak English furthers their isolation.

The range of individuals guilty of enslaving domestic workers is broad and inclusive. Within it are "doctors, lawyers, business people, [and] diplomats," all of whom go to great lengths to ensure the public is not aware of their actions. Claudia Flores, an attorney with the American Civil Liberties Union (ACLU) who has represented victims of involuntary domestic servitude in the United States, explains the measures such employers use to control their domestic workers:

Many times, they are forbidden to talk to people who come into the house ... If there are two of them, they are often forbidden to talk to each other. Their phone calls are monitored. They are not allowed to go anywhere unaccompanied.[36]

The recent case of *U.S. v. Sabhnani* (2007) has drawn national attention to this form of modern-day slavery in the United States. In this case, Varsha and Mehender Sabhnani, who ran a multimillion dollar perfume business from their home in the wealthy Long Island hamlet of Muttontown, New York, were convicted on federal charges related to keeping two Indonesian women in involuntary domestic servitude. According to testimony provided to the grand jury and at the trial, the women were forced to sleep on the floors of closets, given inadequate food, and allowed to leave the house only to take out the garbage. Ordered to call their employers Master and Missus, the women were beaten with rolling pins and brooms, deliberately burned with scalding water, purposely cut with a knife on at least one occasion, and forced to eat their own vomit, among other abuses. As further measures of control, the Sabhnanis also kept the women's Indonesian passports locked away from them and made threats against their family members in Indonesia. The women's enslavement was discovered only when one of the women escaped, wearing nothing more than pants and a towel; employees at the local Dunkin' Donuts, seeing her disheveled state and a number of bruises, called 911 on her behalf.[37]

While the dramatic nature of one victim's escape called wide attention to the Sabhnanis' crime, other recently exposed cases of involuntary domestic servitude have been equally egregious. These include the case of a 24-year-old African woman enslaved and kept from school since the age of six by African diplomats in New York[38]; an 11-year-old Cameroonian girl trafficked to Maryland to care for her employer's home and two children without pay, a situation in which she was beaten with cable cords and a broken metal broomstick; an Indian woman trafficked to Florida and forced to care for her employer's home and invalid son without pay and without one day off in more than five years[39]; and a Ghanaian woman trafficked to Maryland and forced to clean her traffickers' home and the homes of others without compensation.[40]

Agriculture

Like domestic workers, agricultural workers are excluded from NLRA protections for workers wishing to organize for better working and wage conditions. While the Migrant and Seasonal Agricultural Worker Protection Act (MSPA) and the Fair Labor Standards Act (FLSA) require that agricultural workers be paid at least the federal minimum wage, and MSPA does require the contractors who act as labor brokers to growers be registered with the Department of Labor, the actual federal oversight of workers in the field is often minimal.

Much of America's farm labor is arranged through labor contractors who hire seasonal workers and, in turn, make the workers' labor available to growers without the growers' assumption of the liabilities of employment. This has enabled some of the largest agricultural concerns to disassociate themselves from the working and wage conditions in their own fields. Ramiro, Jose, and Juan Ramos, farm labor contractors who supplied agricultural workers to some of the largest citrus farms in Florida, for example, were convicted in 2002 on 15 federal charges related to forced labor.[41] While charges were levied only against the Ramos family, trial testimony elicited from the director of human resources of Lakes Brothers, one of Florida's larger citrus growers, illustrates both corporate involvement and legal disassociation:

A: *We don't employ those people.*

Q: *Technically you don't, but they are in your groves all day picking fruit?*

A: *Yes.*

Q: *They are on your property picking fruit from your tree?*

A: *That's correct.*

Q: *They are loading oranges into containers that are shipped to companies that process fruit based on your contractor?*

A: *That's correct.*

Q: *So it is your fruit, it is your worker, too, isn't he?*

A: *No, he is not my worker.*

Q: *Because there's a piece of paper that says he is provided by a contractor? That's it, right?*

A: *Our relationship is with the contractor to provide workers.*

The Ramoses were found guilty on 15 of the 16 charges. Presiding district court judge K. Michael Moore, ordering the Ramoses to forfeit $3 million in personal and business property and sentencing two of the Ramoses to 12 years and the third to 10 years, clearly held the labor contractors responsible for their actions. Nonetheless, he also suggested that the prosecutors focus on "others at a higher level of the fruit-picking industry [who] seem complicit in one way or another with how these activities occur."[42] (In 2004, "for reasons unrelated to his trafficking charges," Juan Ramos's sentence was reduced.)[43]

Other cases of agricultural forced labor include men trafficked from Jamaica to work in a New Hampshire tree-cutting business; men trafficked from Tongo to Hawaii to work in a landscape business and pig farm;[44] and men and boys trafficked from Mexico to upstate New York by farm contractors who supplied them to squash farmers and other agricultural concerns.[45]

Efforts are underway, with some evidence of success, to have end-user corporations exercise greater oversight over the production and harvesting of their ingredients. The Coalition of Immokalee Workers, an NGO responsible for bringing many of the facts of the Ramos case to light, for instance, has led boycotts against Taco Bell, McDonald's, and Burger King; within the past few years, these corporations have agreed to require verifiable improvements in their suppliers' labor practices.[46]

Sweatshop Manufacturing

Sweatshop manufacturing refers to the work done in factories where labor laws are routinely and deliberately violated.[47] Conditions in such factories can include overtime and minimum wage abuses, the use of child labor, and/ or the violations of health and safety laws.[48] Approximately 170,000 people are estimated to work in sweatshops located in the United States[49] and some number of these people are trafficked.[50] Both the resurgence of sweatshops and the use of modern-day slaves to staff them have occurred against the background of ever-increasing global competition. Fees charged for manufacturing in developing countries reflect wages that are far lower than the minimum wages set by U.S. labor law, making it difficult for American manufacturers to compete. As FTS reports

> competition is pressing manufacturers who chose to remain in the United States to reduce their labor costs to a minimum. In some cases, that can mean forced labor.[51]

One of the most highly publicized cases of modern-day slavery in an American factory was *U.S. v. Kil Soo Lee* (2003). In this case, five men trafficked more than 250 people from Vietnam and China to their garment factory in American Samoa (a territory of the United States, located in the South Pacific Ocean). The victims, most of whom were young women, were forced to go without food, physically restrained at work stations, held in guarded barracks when not working, and beaten. So abusive was their treatment that one of the young woman "had an eye gouged out by a defendant who struck her with a jagged pike in order to punish her. . . ."[52] Other cases of modern-day slavery in American factories include 72 Thai workers enslaved behind barbed wire in a sweatshop in El Monte, California,[53] and Indian men trafficked to Oklahoma to manufacture pressure valves.[54]

Other Forced Laborers

Modern-day slavery has been found in many other occupations, both legal and illegal. Victims have been forced to produce marijuana in Oregon[55]; to tend bar in New Jersey[56]; to labor in a marble and granite business in Georgia; and to beg in New York City. This last case involved the trafficking of 60 persons from Mexico—all of whom were deaf and unable to speak, 12 of whom were children, and three of whom were pregnant at the time of their rescue—for the forced selling of trinkets in the New York City subways in the 1990s.[57] These victims were forced to leave key chains beside subway riders along with cards stating "I am deaf"; if they did not earn at least $100 per day for their captors, they were beaten.[58] Further measures of control included the confiscation of the victims' documents, the use of stun guns, and the hunting down and recapture of those who tried to escape. During their four-and-one-half years of enslavement, it is estimated that these victims turned over to their captors approximately $8 million.[59]

CONSIDERATIONS PARTICULAR TO TRAFFICKING IN THE UNITED STATES

The primary destination country "pull factors" in the United States are the same as those found, to one or another degree, in other destination countries: the commodification of sex and sexual relationships and the elevation of monetary concerns—specifically profit seeking and the desire to acquire consumer goods at ever lower prices—above all else. Traffickers of persons to the United States are also increasingly connected to organized crime, as are traffickers worldwide.

There are, however, additional considerations relevant to human trafficking in the United States. It is not uncommon, for instance, to discover that traffickers are recently naturalized citizens of the United States who have maintained close ties to their countries of origin, ties that they use to deceive former neighbors into enslavement.[60] Generally, such traffickers return to their origin country displaying trappings of supposed success, then offer to "help" others secure their own chance to live "an American dream." In one such case, a naturalized American family, originally from Mexico, trafficked at least two dozen women and girls from their common hometown in Veracruz. The victims, who had expected to work as waitresses, housekeepers, and childcare workers, were forced into prostitution near camps of migrant workers in Florida and the Carolinas. In addition to forced prostitution, these women were also subjected to beatings, rape, and forced abortions.[61]

Another trafficking pattern particular to the United States is the abuse of temporary work visas for the live-in migrant domestic workers of certain international visitors. The United States has special classes of visas for the "personal employees, attendants, domestic workers or servants" of foreign diplomats and government officials, international organization officials, and others. These visas grant domestic workers legal status in the United States only so long as they remain in the employ of the person with whom they have traveled to the United States.[62] While these international employers must agree to pay their employees at least the U.S. federal minimum wage and abide by other requirements designed to protect the employee—and while most of these arrangements remain free of any taint of human trafficking—Human Rights Watch (HRW) has identified a pattern of abuse in connection with these special visas. As the organization's report on the issue describes it, domestic workers who become enslaved in this fashion "become some of the world's most disadvantaged workers held captive by some of the world's most powerful employers, who exploit, abuse, degrade, mock and humiliate them."[63]

U.S. EFFORTS TO END HUMAN TRAFFICKING

The United States is a party to many of the international instruments that prohibit various forms of modern slavery. It has signed and ratified the UN Protocol, the Optional Protocol to the Convention on the Rights of the Child on the Sale of Children, Child Prostitution and Child Pornography, and the Optional Protocol to the Convention on the Rights of the Child in Armed Conflict. It has also ratified ILO Convention 182, Concerning the Prohibition and Immediate Action for the Elimination of the Worst Forms of Child Labor, ILO Convention 105, Abolition of Forced Labor, and the Hague Convention on Intercountry Adoption. It has not ratified ILO Convention 29, Concerning Forced Labor, however.

Two other UN instruments address poverty and discrimination against women, two of the root causes of human trafficking. The UN Millennium Declaration (2000) was unanimously adopted by the leaders of 189 member nations, including the United States. The United States has signed but not ratified the UN Convention on the Elimination of All Forms of Discrimination against Women (meaning that it is obligated to act in good faith to uphold the aims of the convention, but that it is not legally bound to abide by it).

Efforts to End Domestic Human Trafficking
A CONSTITUTIONAL AMENDMENT AND LEGISLATION (NINETEENTH AND TWENTIETH CENTURIES)

With ratification of the Thirteenth Amendment to the Constitution in 1865, the United States abolished slavery within its borders and in any place subject to its jurisdiction. Subsequent domestic legislation related to slavery and slavelike conditions included the so-called Padrone statute, passed in 1874 to prohibit "padrones in Italy [from] inveigl[ing] from their parents young boys whom the padrones then used without pay as beggars, bootblacks, or street musicians" in American cities,[64] and the 1910 Mann Act (also known as the White Slave Traffic Act), designed to combat sex trafficking in women.[65] Section 1584, the so-called Anti-Peonage Act, was passed in 1948 to consolidate and expand these two predecessor statutes, but even this broader law remained focused on the "involuntary labor performed by particularly vulnerable persons."[66] Despite language that might have been interpreted to the contrary, Statute 1584 was generally interpreted by the courts, even as late as 1988, to apply only in cases where victims were held by or as a result of physical force or the credible threat of force, rather than through psychological intimidation, fraud, or similar means.[67]

THE U.S. TRAFFICKING VICTIMS PROTECTION ACT OF 2000

The U.S. Trafficking Victims Protection Act of 2000 (TVPA),[68] the first comprehensive federal law to address modern-day slavery, specifically encompasses all manner of modern-day slavery tactics, including fraud, coercion, the confiscation of documents, and debt bondage. It also specifically states that in the case of a minor child (a person under 18 years of age) the harboring or possession of that child for exploitation is evidence enough of human trafficking, without any requirement to prove force, fraud, or other means of acquisition. (However, the minor child provision is not regularly applied to prostituted children who resided in the United States prior to sex-trade activity.)[69] Such children are generally charged with prostitution; a notable exception, discussed below, is New York State.[70]

The TVPA

Criminalizes procuring and subjecting another human being to peonage, involuntary sex trafficking, slavery, involuntary servitude, or forced labor;

Provides social services and legal benefits to survivors of these crimes, including authorization to remain in the country;

Provides funding to support protection programs for survivors in the United States as well as abroad; and

Includes provisions to monitor and eliminate trafficking in countries outside of the United States.[71]

It also requires convicted traffickers to make restitution to their victims and permits survivors to file suit for additional civil damages.[72]

While the TVPA has been widely praised by human rights workers and labor activists, it has also earned some criticism. FTS, for example, criticizes the TVPA's requirement that victims cooperate with U.S. law enforcement and prosecutors in order to be eligible for the special "T-visas" issued to such victims,[73] and the resulting reality that not all trafficking victims are permitted to remained in the United States following their rescue.

THE PROTECT ACT OF 2003

The Prosecutorial Remedies and Other Tools to end the Exploitation of Children Today (PROTECT Act of 2003)[74] significantly expanded "law enforcement's ability to prevent, investigate, prosecute and punish violent crimes committed against children." The PROTECT Act of 2003 set a goal for the establishment of a national AMBER Alert Program (named for nine-year-old Amber Hagerman, who was kidnapped and murdered in 1996), which is a partnership between law enforcement agencies, broadcasters, and others to immediately publicize the abduction of a child. It also expands the permissible use of wiretaps in cases of suspected child sexual abuse and child sex trafficking, eliminates all statutes of limitations for crimes involving child sexual abuse or child abduction, and makes it more difficult for persons charged with such crimes to obtain bail. Under the PROTECT Act of 2003, sentences for crimes involving the sexual abuse of children are significantly increased: Sentences for the first conviction of using a child to produce pornography are 15 to 30 years, and life imprisonment is required in the case of a second serious sexual offense against a child.[75]

THE MODEL STATE STATUTE

The Department of Justice has developed a "Model State Anti-Trafficking Criminal Statute" that it makes available for adoption by states or as a starting point for a state's development of anti-trafficking legislation. As of the end of 2008, 33 states have adopted such comprehensive legislation,[76] and comprehensive legislation on modern-day slavery is currently pending in a number of other states.[77]

New York's 2007 anti-trafficking law, one of the most recent to be passed, is one of the toughest and most comprehensive laws in the nation. It categorizes labor trafficking and sex trafficking as state felony offenses with sentences upon conviction of three to seven years and three to 25 years, respectively. In addition, it makes it a state felony offense to sell "travel-related services to facilitate prostitution" regardless of whether prostitution is legal in the destination country or U.S. state.[78] The new law also mandates that emergency health care, housing, and other state services be provided to trafficking survivors.[79]

In 2008, the New York State legislature also passed a related measure, the Safe Harbor for Exploited Youth Act. This legislation, which ends the criminalization of child prostitutes in New York, was passed only after four years of debate. Opponents of the act, including New York City mayor Michael Bloomberg, key members of his administration, and a number of law enforcement officials, argued that children were persuaded to testify about their sexual exploitation only under threat of extended jail time, since reduced sentences for prison or juvenile detention were frequently offered in exchange for testimony. Law enforcement officials who supported the continued criminalization of child prostitutes also expressed the view that "jail, or its equivalent, is one way to keep them from running right back to the predators."[80]

There is a long history in the United States of viewing children—especially girls—as not entitled to full "age of consent" protection if they have had any association with prostitution. A Wisconsin law passed in 1889, for example, set the age of consent for girls at 12, but provided a lighter sentence for men found to have had intercourse with girls under age 12 "if the child shall be a common prostitute."[81]

Others see issues of race, class, and social disadvantage rather than the historical bias against protecting the already prostituted child. A study commissioned by the New York State legislature estimated that 75 percent of the children involved in New York City's sex trades had been in the foster care system, for example, while 85 percent of the state's sexually exploited children came from families that had come into contact with the child welfare system.[82] Many of these children are also from minority backgrounds. Rachel Lloyd, director of Girls Educational & Mentoring Services, a New York City organization that works with teenaged prostitutes, feels strongly that "it's . . . race and class" that make the criminalization of underage prostitutes acceptable. "If we served 250 white girls from . . . middle class homes," she said prior to one of the act's early defeats, "we'd be changing the law."[83] As this book is written, New York State is the only state acting to treat underage prostitutes as victims rather than criminals.

THE TRAFFICKING INFORMATION AND REFERRAL HOTLINE

HHS, through a contract with the Polaris Project, sponsors and funds a Trafficking Information and Referral Hotline (Trafficking Hotline) at 1-888-373-7888. The Trafficking Hotline is available seven days per week and 24 hours per day to take phone calls from victims of trafficking or people who believe they may have come in contact with a trafficked person. Hotline operators are trained to help the caller assess the immediate safety of the victim and coordinate the appropriate governmental and nongovernmental response. The hotline receives between 400 and 450 calls per month.

ENFORCEMENT

Enforcement of both state and federal anti-trafficking legislation has not yet met expectations. Although 33 states now have anti-trafficking laws, almost no convictions have been won under them. As Chris Johnson, the attorney general's policy director in Washington State explains it, police officers do not yet recognize the signs of trafficking. One difficulty in identifying victims is the fact that many fear retaliation against their family members or themselves if they bring the true nature of their situation to the attention of law enforcement officials. Finally, as former U.S. ambassador-at-large on modern slavery John Miller has noted, the laws' requirement that "force, fraud or coercion" be proved has been a difficult standard for local prosecutors to meet.[84]

While some of the same factors are present in the enforcement of federal law, the federal agencies charged with this responsibility—the Department of Justice's Civil Rights Division, Criminal Division, and U.S. Attorney's Offices, along with the Federal Bureau of Investigation (FBI) and Immigration and Customs Enforcement—have had more success in identifying victims and obtaining convictions in trafficking cases. In the fiscal year 2007, for example, the Department of Justice's Civil Rights Division and U.S. Attorney's Office conducted 182 investigations; charged 89 individuals; and won 189 convictions (including cases initiated in prior years), while the FBI and the Justice Department's Criminal Division made 308 arrests and won 106 convictions.[85]

Efforts to End International Human Trafficking

In addition to participation in a number of international instruments that address human trafficking, the United States has taken unilateral action to address global human trafficking.

TRAFFICKING IN PERSONS REPORTS

Starting in 2001, the U.S. State Department has issued an annual Trafficking in Persons Report (TIP Report), the "primary diplomatic tool through which the U.S. Government encourages partnership and increased determination in the fight against ... modern-day slavery."[86] Specifically, the TIP Report analyzes the type and extent of modern-day slavery in the world's countries, as well as each country's efforts to combat it. The United States does not assign itself to a tier; beginning with the 2007 TIP Report, however, it has included an assessment of its own role in trafficking and its efforts to abolish slavery within its borders. It also provides a country ranking that markedly differs from that found in the UN Global Patterns report: Where the UN Global Patterns report ranks countries by the numbers of persons trafficked from, through, or to the listed countries, the United States ranks countries by their efforts to eradicate modern-day slavery, particularly as measured against the minimum standards set in TVPA. Those minimum standards are quite specific:

> ... [T]he minimum standards for the elimination of trafficking appli-cable to the government of a country of origin, transit, or destination for a significant number of victims of severe forms of trafficking [defined in the 2007 report as 100 or more persons] are as follows:
>
> > (1) The government of the country should prohibit severe forms of trafficking in persons and punish acts of such trafficking.
> >
> > (2) For the knowing commission of any act of sex trafficking involv-ing force, fraud, coercion, or in which the victim of sex trafficking is a child incapable of giving meaningful consent, or of trafficking which includes rape or kidnapping or which causes a death, the government of the country should prescribe punishment commensurate with that for grave crimes, such as forcible sexual assault.
> >
> > (3) For the knowing commission of any act of a severe form of traf-ficking in persons, the government of the country should prescribe pun-ishment that is sufficiently stringent to deter and that adequately reflects the heinous nature of the offense.
> >
> > (4) The government of the country should make serious and sus-tained efforts to eliminate severe forms of trafficking in persons.[87]

The United States considers the TIP "Tier 1" countries to be in compli-ance with the minimum standards set in the TVPA, "Tier 2" to be out of compliance but making significant efforts, and "Tier 3" countries to be out of compliance and not making significant efforts. The report also includes a "Tier 2 Watch List" for countries that have moved from Tier 2 to Tier 1, moved from Tier 3 to Tier 2, or remain at Tier 2 with (a) evidence of an increasing trafficking problem, (b) promised improvement in the following year, or (c) evidence that efforts against trafficking have not increased.[88]

According to TVPA, the United States may withhold "non-humanitar-ian, non-trade related foreign assistance" from Tier 3 countries. It may also oppose International Monetary Fund and World Bank assistance to those countries.[89] Any such sanctions take effect on October 1 following the June issuance of the report, with the provision that the president may waive the sanctions if the country in question takes significant action prior to that date. (The president may also waive such sanctions to prevent harm to vulnerable populations or if it is deemed that waiving the sanctions will aid in the imple-menting of TVPA standards.)[90]

While such sanctions have proved to be a powerful means of securing "increased determination in the fight against . . . modern-day slavery,"[91] they are not the only U.S. response to poor placement on the TIP list: From the TIP release date in July through the following February, the Office to Monitor and Combat Trafficking in Persons (TIP office, a unit of the State Department currently led by Ambassador Mark P. Lagon) works to help willing countries effect change.[92]

While the TIP Reports have been widely praised by national and international NGOs, they have also prompted controversy. Women's organizations, for example, have objected to the Tier 1 status of European countries that have legalized prostitution, and some Belizean officials have argued that the reports are politicized in that their Tier 3 status in 2006 was due, at least in part, to their county's good relationship with Venezuela (U.S. relations with Venezuela have been strained since the election of Venezuelan president Hugo Chávez). The TIPS rankings have also caused occasional controversy within U.S. administrations: It was widely reported, for instance, that Secretary of State Condoleezza Rice and Deputy Secretary of State John Negroponte disagreed about India's tier placement. Negroponte reportedly argued that India should be listed as a Tier 3 country, while Rice—whose position that it was not in the United States's best interest to alienate the Indian government ultimately prevailed—argued that India should remain a Tier 2 Watchlist country.[93]

Among the antislavery actions for which the United States claims the TIP deserves at least partial credit are:

Cambodia shut down a red-light district where 10-year-olds openly were sold and prostituted and "cheap girls" were advertised on the Internet; Japan slashed the number of entertainment visas issued to certified Filipina dancers, singers or other entertainers because traffickers were forcing many of these women into prostitution; the United Arab Emirates eliminated the exploitation of South Asian boys as camel-racing jockeys and paid for the repatriation of more than 1,000 boys to their home countries; Jamaica pledged to step up prosecutions [in 2008]; Saudi Arabia said it intended to adopt the 2000 U.N. Trafficking in Persons Protocol; and Taiwan vowed to strengthen its antitrafficking laws.[94]

EFFORTS AGAINST CHILD SEX TOURISM

The PROTECT Act of 2003, together with the Trafficking Victims Protection Reauthorization Act of 2003 (TVPA Reauthorization of 2003), established maximum penalties of 30 years in prison for Americans convicted of child sex tourism.[95] The identification and prosecution of sex tourists is also aided by "Operation Predator," a domestic and international initiative launched by the Department of Homeland Security in 2003 that "identif[ies], investigate[s], and arrest[s] child predators," including American sex tourists. The penalties are substantial. Michael Lewis Clark was arrested in Cambodia and charged with two counts of engaging in sex with a minor. The first U.S. citizen to be convicted under the child sex tourism provision of the PROTECT Act, he was sentenced to 97 months in jail.[96] There is no similar effort to apprehend U.S. citizens engaged in commercial sexual relations with adults while abroad.

ANTI-TRAFFICKING FUNDS

The TIP Office funds international anti–human trafficking programs, among other things. In fiscal year 2007, the TIP Office supported 73 international projects with funds totaling $16.5 million. Each of the 73 projects originated with a source-country proposal, and each was chosen through a competitive grant application process. The TIP Office funded a wide variety of organizations and efforts, including a grant of $16,650 to assist the Islamic Association in Population Development in working with Guinea's Islamic Associations "to develop training modules and manuals, . . . and work with Muslim Councils to spread [anti-trafficking] messages"; a grant of $99,700 to assist Save the Children UK with work "in four townships of Mandalay State [Burma] to develop community-based child protection systems . . . includ[ing] . . . conducting awareness campaigns on trafficking, children's rights, and child protection, and developing protection and reintegration procedures for trafficked children"; and a grant of $244,000 to assist the U.S. Agency for International Development (AID) in helping Jamaica to "provide better sheltering and protection for [trafficking] victims, as well as increase the efficacy of government-run hotlines for reporting [trafficking] cases." [97]

NONGOVERNMENTAL ORGANIZATIONS

There are many NGOs based in the United States that are working to end modern-day slavery and to address the root causes of human trafficking in the United States and worldwide. These include the American Anti-Slavery Group (AST), the Break the Chain Campaign, Children of the Night, the Coalition of Immokalee Workers (CIW), Equality Now, FTS, the International Justice Mission (IJM), HRW, Physicians for Human Rights (PHR), the Polaris Project, and the SAGE Project.

These NGOs work on their own to combat trafficking and aid victims, but they also work in concert with the U.S. government. Many anti-trafficking projects, for instance, are funded by the TIP Office but conducted under the auspices of NGOs. NGOs also assist the U.S. Immigration and Customs Enforcement (ICE) staff in disseminating information about special visa and other immigration protections available to trafficking victims. These efforts are broadly based: More than 120 NGOs have working relationships with domestic ICE field offices, while more than 50 NGOs have working relationships with ICE offices abroad. NGOs are also involved in the preparation of the annual TIP Reports. In 2006, for instance, the TIP Office evaluated information from the NGOs as part of its preparation of the TIP Report, then held "a post–TIP Report briefing" for the NGOs.[98]

The NGOS have tremendous records of accomplishment. Equality Now, for example, was instrumental in the passage of New York State's anti-trafficking legislation in 2007 and in the passage of the state's Safe Harbor for Exploited Youth Act in 2008. Not every NGO based in the United States has been without criticism, however. IJM, for example, has been responsible "for as many rescued victims as any international organization," but it has also been criticized for infiltrating brothels to obtain the documentation necessary to build court cases against traffickers.[99]

CONCLUSION

The United States is one of the leading destination countries for transnational human trafficking, and it also has a significant problem with the exploitation of underage U.S. nationals in the commercial sex industry. It has taken significant legislative efforts to address transnational trafficking within its borders, and it is beginning to recognize prostituted minors as victims rather than as criminals. With its annual TIP Report rankings—and the potential U.S. sanctions that accompany a poor ranking—the United States has also taken unilateral action to address worldwide human trafficking. As the next chapter's discussion of Belize will show, this unilateral move has been an effective one.

[1] UNODC. "Trafficking in Persons: Global Patterns" (2006), p. 20. Available online: URL: http://www.unodc.org/pdf/traffickinginpersons_report_2006-04.pdf. Accessed June 6, 2006.

[2] U.S. Department of State. "Fighting Human Trafficking Inside the United States." Available online. URL: http://uninfo.sate.gov/gi/Archive/2004/May /23-381449.html. Accessed January 27, 2008.

[3] U.S. Department of Justice, Civil Rights Division. "Trafficking in Persons: A Guide for Non-Governmental Organizations." Available online. URL: http://www.usdoj.gov/crt/crim/wetf/trafficbrochure.html. Accessed January 3, 2008.

[4] Amy O'Neill Richard. "International Trafficking in Women to the United States: A Contemporary Manifestation of Slavery and Organized Crime" (1999). Available online. URL: http://www.cia.gov/library/center-for-the-study-of-intelligence/csi-publications/book-and-mon ographs/trafficking/pdf. Accessed September 29, 2008

[5] UNODC. "Trafficking in Persons: Global Patterns" (2006), p. 98.

[6] ———. "Trafficking in Persons: Global Patterns" (2006), p. 78.

[7] ———. "Trafficking in Persons: Global Patterns" (2006), p. 98.

Focus on the United States

[8] The White House. "Human Trafficking: A New Form of Slavery." Available online. URL: http://www.whitehouse.gov/infocus/traffic/. Accessed January 3, 2008.

[9] Free the Slaves and Human Rights Center. "Hidden Slaves: Forced Labor in the United States" (2004), p. 9. Available online. URL: http://www.digitalcommons.ilr.cornell.edu/cgi/viewcontent.cgi?article=1007&content=forcedlabor. Accessed October 24, 2008.

[10] ———. "Hidden Slaves: Forced Labor in the United States" (2004), p. 1.

[11] ———. "Hidden Slaves: Forced Labor in the United States" (2004), p. 1.

[12] John Bowe. *Nobodies: Modern American Slave Labor and the Dark Side of the New Global Economy.* New York: Random House, 2007, pp. 35–77.

[13] Jane Morse. "U.S. Intensifying Efforts to Combat Human Trafficking; Additional Funding to Cement Law Enforcement and Victims' Services Partnerships." State Department Documents and Publications (10/03/06).

[14] CATW. "Sex Trafficking of Women in the United States: International and Domestic Trends" (2001), p. 18. Available online. URL: http://www.ojp.usdoj.gov/nij/international/programs/sex_traff_s.pdf. Accessed December 8, 2007 (Analysis of Attorney General's Reports 2003–2006).

[15] Free the Slaves and Human Rights Center. "Hidden Slaves: Forced Labor in the United States" (2004), p. 1.

[16] U.S. Department of Justice. "Bureau of Justice Statistics: Federal Prosecution of Human Trafficking, 2001–2005." Available online. URL: http://ojp.usdoj.gov/bjs/abstract/fpht05.htm. Accessed August 20, 2008.

[17] UNODC. "Trafficking in Persons: Global Patterns" (2006), p. 20.

[18] Free the Slaves and Human Rights Center. "Hidden Slaves: Forced Labor in the United States" (2004), p. 1.

[19] California Alliance to Combat Trafficking and Slavery Task Force. "Human Trafficking in California" (2007). Available online. URL: http://safestate.org/documents/HT_Final_Report_ADA.pdf. Accessed November 15, 2007.

[20] Free the Slaves and Human Rights Center. "Hidden Slaves: Forced Labor in the United States" (2004), p. 13.

[21] CATW. "Sex Trafficking of Women in the United States." (2001), pp. 100–105.

[22] ECPAT. "Global Monitoring Report on the Status of Action against the Sexual Exploitation of Children" (2007). Available online. URL: http://www.ecpat.net/eng/A4A_2005/PDF/Americas/Global_Monitoring_Report-USA.pdf. Accessed November 16, 2007.

[23] HHS. "Fact Sheet: Human Trafficking." Available online. URL: http://www.acf.hhs.gov/trafficking/about/fact_human.html. Accessed November 16, 2007; Amy O'Neill Richard. "International Trafficking in Women to the United States" (1999).

[24] U.S. Department of Justice. "Attorney General's Annual Report to Congress on U.S. Government Activities to Combat Trafficking in Persons, Fiscal Year 2006," p. 4. Available online. URL: http://www.usdoj.gov/ag/annualreports/tr2006/agreporthumantrafficking2006.pdf. Accessed November 26, 2007.

[25] Mark Lagon. Speech at Georgetown University, Washington, D.C. (4/9/08). Available online. URL: http://fora.tv/2008/04/09/Mark_Lagon_T-Visas_for_Victims_of_Human_Trafficking. Accessed October 20, 2008.

[26] ECPAT. "Global Monitoring Report on the Status of Action against the Sexual Exploitation of Children: USA," pp. 11, 32. Available online. URL: http://ecpat.net/AYA/2005/americas. html. Accessed October 19, 2008.

[27] ———. "Global Monitoring Report," p. 11.

[28] Bob Herbert. "The Wrong Target." *New York Times* (2/19/08).

[29] Nicholas Confessore. "New Law Shields Children from Prostitution Charges." *New York Times* (9/22/08); Thomas Adock. "Legal, Social Services Communities Prepare for Enactment of Safe Harbor Act." *New York Law Journal* (10/03/08).

[30] U.S. Department of State. "Trafficking in Persons Report" (2007), p. 235. Available online. URL: http://www.state.gov.documents.organization/82902.pdf. Accessed July 31, 2008.

[31] Free the Slaves and Human Rights Center. "Hidden Slaves: Forced Labor in the United States" (2004), p. 5.

[32] U.S. Department of Justice. "Report on Activities to Combat Human Trafficking, Fiscal Years 2001–2005." Available online. URL: http://www.usdoj.gov/olp/human_trafficking.htm. Accessed October 24, 2008.

[33] CATW. "Sex Trafficking of Women in the United States," pp. 100–105.

[34] U.S. Department of Justice. "Attorney General's Annual Report to Congress on U.S. Government Activities to Combat Trafficking in Persons, Fiscal Year 2006," p. 19.

[35] National Labor Relations Board. "Employees/Employers NOT covered by NLRA." Available online. URL: http://www.nlrb.gov/workplace_rights/employees_or_employers_not_covered_by_nlra.aspx. Accessed January 10, 2007; ———. "Basic Guide to the National Labor Relations Act" (1977). Available online. URL: http://www.nlrb.gov.nlrb/shared_files/brochures/basicguide.pdf. Accessed January 10, 2007.

[36] Paul Vitello. "From Stand in Long Island Slavery Case, a Snapshot of a Hidden U.S. Problem." *New York Times* (12/03/07).

[37] *U.S. v. Sabhnani.* Superseding Indictment. Cr. No. 07 CR 429 (S-1) (TCP) (E.D.N.Y., 2007); Paul Vitello. "Couple Held Two Servants Captive for Years, U.S. Says." *New York Times* (5/16/07); ———. "From Stand in Long Island Slavery Case, a Snapshot of a Hidden U.S. Problem"; Corey Kilgannon. "N.Y. Couple Convicted in Slave Case." *New York Times* (12/17/07).

[38] Vitello. "From Stand in Long Island Slavery Case, a Snapshot of a Hidden U.S. Problem."

[39] U.S. Department of Justice. "Report to Congress from Attorney General Alberto R. Gonzales on U.S. Efforts to Combat Trafficking in Persons in Fiscal Year 2004," p. 24.

[40] U.S. Department of Justice. "Report to Congress from Attorney General John Ashcroft on U.S. Efforts to Combat Trafficking in Persons in Fiscal Year 2003," p. 23. Available online. URL: http://www.usdoj.gov/olp/human_trafficking.htm. Acessed October 24, 2008.

[41] Bowe. *Nobodies: Modern American Slave Labor and the Dark Side of the New Global Economy,* pp. 64–72.

[42] Bowe. *Nobodies: Modern American Slave Labor and the Dark Side of the New Global Economy,* p. 70.

[43] *U.S. v. Ramiro Ramos* (No. 04-11152-EE), on appeal from the U.S. District Court for the Southern District of Florida. Brief for the United States as Appellee, pp. 3–4; Department of Justice. "Report to Congress from Attorney General John Ashcroft on U.S. Efforts to Combat Trafficking in Persons in Fiscal Year 2003," p. 25.

[44] U.S. Department of Justice. "Report to Congress from Attorney General John Ashcroft on U.S. Efforts to Combat Trafficking in Persons in Fiscal Year 2003," pp. 22–23.

[45] U.S. Department of Justice press release. "Six Indicted in Conspiracy for Trafficking and Holding Migrant Workers in Conditions of Forced Labor in Western New York" (6/19/02). Available online. URL: http://www.usdoj.gov/opa/pr/2002/June/02_crt_360.htm. Accessed January 20, 2007; Stephen Greenhouse. "Migrant-Camp Operators Face Forced Labor Charges." *New York Times* (6/21/02).

[46] Bowe. *Nobodies: Modern American Slave Labor and the Dark Side of the New Global Economy,* pp. 72–75.

[47] Free the Slaves and Human Rights Center. "Hidden Slaves: Forced Labor in the United States" (2004), p. 1.

[48] Robert J. S. Ross. *Slaves to Fashion: Poverty and Abuse in the New Sweatshops."* Ann Arbor: University of Michigan Press, 2004.

[49] Pamela H. Sacks. "The Resurgence of Sweatshops: Exploring Abuses in America's Garment Industry." *Worcester Telegram and Gazette* (1/11/05).

[50] Free the Slaves and Human Rights Center. "Hidden Slaves: Forced Labor in the United States" (2004), p. 18.

[51] California Alliance to Combat Trafficking and Slavery Task Force. "Human Trafficking in California: Final Report" (2007).

[52] U.S. Department of Justice. "Report to Congress from Attorney General John Ashcroft on U.S. Efforts to Combat Trafficking in Persons in Fiscal Year 2003," p. 24.

[53] Free the Slaves and Human Rights Center. "Hidden Slaves: Forced Labor in the United States" (2004), p. 18.

[54] ———. "Hidden Slaves: Forced Labor in the United States" (2004), p. 8.

[55] Department of Justice. "Attorney General's Annual Report to Congress on U.S. Government Activities to Combat Trafficking in Persons, Fiscal Year 2006," p. 44.

[56] ———. "Attorney General's Annual Report to Congress on U.S. Government Activities to Combat Trafficking in Persons, Fiscal Year 2006," p. 47.

[57] ———. "Attorney General's Annual Report to Congress on U.S. Government Activities to Combat Trafficking in Persons, Fiscal Year 2006," p. 48.

[58] Deborah Sontag. "7 Arrested in Abuse of Deaf Immigrants." *New York Times* (7/01/97).

[59] Amy O'Neill Richard. "International Trafficking in Women to the United States: A Contemporary Manifestation of Slavery and Organized Crime" (1999), p. 20.

[60] Free the Slaves and Human Rights Center. "Hidden Slaves: Forced Labor in the United States" (2004), pp. 13–14.

[61] ———. "Hidden Slaves: Forced Labor in the United States" (2004), p. 1; Amy O'Neill Richard. "International Trafficking in Women to the United States: A Contemporary Manifestation of Slavery and Organized Crime" (1999), p. 47.

[62] U.S. Department of State, Bureau of Consular Affairs. "Visas: Diplomats and Foreign Government Officials." Available online. URL: http://travel.state.gove/visa/temp/types/types_2637.html#how. Accessed January 2, 2008.

[63] HRW. "Hidden in the Home: Abuse of Domestic Workers with Special Visas in the United States" (2001), pp. 1–2. Available online. URL: http://www.hrw.org/reports/2001/usa dom0501.pdf. Accessed December 1, 2007.

[64] *United States v. Kozminski,* 487 U.S. 931 (1988). Available online. URL: http://caselaw. lp.findlaw.com/scripts/getcase.pl?navby=search&court=US&cas e=/us487/931.html. Accessed January 22, 2008.

[65] Kathryn Cullen-DuPont. *The Encyclopedia of Women's History in America,* 2nd ed. New York: Facts On File, 2000, p. 152.

[66] *United States of America, Petitioner v. Ike Kozminsi, et al.* "Brief for the United States." Available online. URL: http://www.usdoj.gov/osg/briefs/1987/sg870333.txt. Accessed January 22, 2008.

[67] *United States v. Kozminski,* 487 U.S. 931 (1988).

[68] U.S. Public Law 106-386 (10/28/00). "Victims of Trafficking and Violence Protection Act of 2000." Available online. URL: http://www.state.gov/documents/organization/10492.pdf. Accessed October 20, 2008.

[69] Bob Herbert. "The Wrong Target." *New York Times* (2/19/08).

[70] Nicholas Confessore. "New Law Shields Children from Prostitution Charges." *New York Times* (9/22/08); Thomas Adock. "Legal, Social Services Communities Prepare for Enactment of Safe Harbor Act." *New York Law Journal* (10/03/08).

[71] Free the Slaves and Human Rights Center. "Hidden Slaves: Forced Labor in the United States" (2004), p. 21.

[72] U.S. Public Law 106-386 (10/28/00). "Victims of Trafficking and Violence Protection Act of 2000."

[73] Free the Slaves and Human Rights Center. "Hidden Slaves: Forced Labor in the United States" (2004), p. 21.

[74] U.S. Public Law 108-21 (4/30/03). "The Prosecutorial Remedies and Other Tools to end the Exploitation of Children Today (Protect) Act of 2003." Available online. URL: http://www.amberillinois.org/PDF/protectact2003.pdf. Accessed October 20, 2008.

[75] U.S. Department of Justice. "Fact Sheet: PROTECT Act." Available online. URL: http://www.usdog.gov/opa/pr/2003/April/03_ag_266.htm. Accessed December 22, 2007.

[76] Michael B. Mukasey. "Remarks Prepared for Delivery by Attorney General Michael B. Mukasey at the American Legislative Exchange Council Annual Meeting." Available online. URL: http://www.usdoj.gov/ag/speeches/2008/ag_speech_080801.html. Accessed October 22, 2008.

[77] U.S. Department of Justice. "Attorney General's Annual Report to Congress on U.S. Government Activities to Combat Trafficking in Persons, Fiscal Year 2006," p. 23.

[78] Danny Hakim and Nicolas Confessore. "Albany Agrees on Law against Sexual and Labor Trafficking." *New York Times* (5/17/07).

[79] Editorial board. "Slaves of New York." *New York Times* (5/20/07).

[80] Clyde Haberman. "The Sexually Exploited Ask for Change: Help, Not Jail." *New York Times* (6/12/07).

[81] Kathryn Cullen-DuPont. *The Encyclopedia of Women's History in America*, 2nd edition. New York: Facts On File, 2000, p. 7.

[82] Editorial board. *New York Times* (9/15/07).

[83] Nicholas Kristof. "The Pimps' Slaves." *New York Times* (3/16/08).

[84] Ruth Tiechroeb. "State's Human Trafficking Law Fails to Snag a Conviction." *Seattle Post-Intelligencer* (7/22/08).

[85] U.S. Department of State. "TIP Report, 2008," p. 51.

[86] ———. "Office to Monitor and Combat Trafficking in Persons." Available online. URL: http://www.state.gov.g/tip/. Accessed January 21, 2008.

[87] U.S. Public Law 106-386. (10/28/00). "Victims of Trafficking and Violence Protection Act of 2000."

[88] U.S. Department of State. "TIP Report, 2007," p. 12.

[89] ———. "TIP Report, 2007," p. 12.

[90] ———. "TIP Report, 2007," p. 15.

[91] ———. "Office to Monitor and Combat Trafficking in Persons."

[92] Solmaz Sharifi. "Modem Abolitionists at the U.S. State Department: How the U.S. Government Fights Human Trafficking." *State* magazine (January 2008). Available online. URL: http://www.america.gov/st/hr-english/2008/January/2008117162306ajesroM0.7160913.html. Accessed January 21, 2008.

[93] "India Escapes U.S. List of Worst Human Traffickers." CNN.com (6/13/07). Available online. URL: http://www.cnn.com/2007/US/06/12/human.trafficking/index.html. Accessed April 27, 2008.

[94] Sharifi. "Modern Abolitionists at the U.S. State Department: How the U.S. Government Fights Human Trafficking."

[95] U.S. Department of State. "The Facts about Child Sex Tourism." Available online. URL: http://www.state.gov/g/tip/rls/fs/2005/51351.htm. Accessed January 21, 2008

[96] The White House. "Fact Sheet: Operation Predator." Available online. URL: http://www.whitehouse.gov/news/releases/2004/07/print/20040707-10.htm. Accessed January 21, 2008; Michael B. Farrell. "Global Campaign to Police Child Sex Tourism." *Christian Science Monitor* (4/22/04).

[97] U.S. Department of State. "Office to Monitor and Combat Trafficking in Persons."

[98] U.S. Department of Justice. "Attorney General's Annual Report to Congress on U.S. Government Activities to Combat Trafficking in Persons, Fiscal Year 2006," pp. 33–34.

[99] John Miller. E-mail to author (9/16/08); Quentin Hardy. "Hitting Slavery Where It Hurts." Available online. URL: http://www.forbes.com/global/2004/0112/055_print.html. Accessed October 26, 2008.

3

Global Perspectives

Different countries have felt the impact of modern-day slavery in different ways. These differences reflect each country's role as an origin, transit, or destination country for human trafficking and each country's response—or lack of response—to the activity within its borders. Also, on a less obvious level, there are many historical, cultural, economic, and legal factors that have influenced national experiences with modern-day slavery. A close examination of the Netherlands, Nigeria, India, and Belize illustrates some of these differences, while also helping to make clear what is common to human trafficking in any setting.

NETHERLANDS
Netherlands's Role in Human Trafficking

Like the United States, the Netherlands is listed by the United Nations (UN) as among the world's top 10 destination countries for modern-day slaves.[1] Where the United States is listed as "low" on the list of origin countries, however, the Netherlands is listed as "very low,"[2] and where the United States is absent from the list of transit countries, the Netherlands is listed as a "medium"-level transit country.[3] The UN rankings are based on the number of persons reported trafficked from, through, or within a given country.

The United States—which considers evidence of 100 or more trafficked persons as evidence of significant trafficking and which classifies countries according to their efforts to eradicate trafficking rather than number of persons trafficked—classifies the Netherlands as a Tier 1 country.[4] This ranking identifies the Netherlands as having a trafficking problem, but it also places it among only 28 of 152 countries that the United States considers in full compliance "with the minimum standards for the elimination of trafficking."[5]

While these rankings provide two valuable evaluations of the Netherlands's role in trafficking, they do not offer an estimate of the country's actual numbers of trafficked persons. A 2001 Commission of European Communities report, attempting to estimate that number, concluded that approximately 3,500 persons were trafficked into the Netherlands each year from 1997 to 2000.[6] The Foundation against Trafficking in Women reached a similar conclusion as late as 2003, estimating that 3,000 women and girls were trafficked into the Netherlands each year.[7] During those years, however—and indeed, until 2005—only trafficking for sexual exploitation was classified as human trafficking under Dutch law.[8] Since the U.S. Trafficking in Persons Reports (TIP Reports) and reports released by reputable nongovernment organizations (NGOs)[9] have consistently found forced nonsexual labor as well as sexual exploitation when examining human trafficking in the Netherlands, the estimates of 3,000 to 3,500 persons per year are undoubtedly too low.

The Netherlands also plays a role as a medium-level transit country,[10] meaning that traffickers pass through the Netherlands with their victims en route to a final destination. In addition, trafficking victims may be enslaved first in the Netherlands and then later in another country. Most domestically recruited victims who are enslaved in this manner are ultimately brought to Belgium or Germany. Internationally trafficked victims who are not kept in the Netherlands are ultimately brought to a broad range of destination countries, most frequently to Italy.[11]

Origin of Persons Trafficked to and through the Netherlands
INTERNATIONAL TRAFFICKING

Persons are trafficked to the Netherlands from more than 30 countries.[12] The majority of these modern-day slavery victims are females trafficked into the sex trades, most notably from Bulgaria, China, Nigeria, Poland, and Romania.[13] Young adult women are the most frequently trafficked, with two-thirds of the victims estimated to be between 18 and 24 years of age. Fewer than 1 percent of sex trafficking victims who have come to the attention of NGOs or charitable organizations have been male[14], but, as forced labor was not part of the Netherlands's definition of human trafficking until fairly recently, trafficked males have been the least noted of the country's victims. Men from Bangladesh, China, India, and Turkey are known to be trafficked into forced labor in the Netherlands's factories, ports, private homes, and restaurants.[15]

The Netherlands also has a serious problem with child trafficking, with one of every six enslaved persons estimated to be a minor child.[16] One known method of child recruitment involves the all-too-frequent disappearance of unaccompanied girls entering the Netherlands to seek asylum or otherwise entering the country as unaccompanied minors (UM). These underage women—most of whom come from West Africa and China—are targeted by traffickers; as ECPAT describes it, they "disappear" from UM centers and asylums shortly after arrival and are then forced into prostitution.[17]

DOMESTIC TRAFFICKING

While the UN ranks the Netherlands as a low-level country of origin, that ranking reflects only those Dutch nationals and residents reported as victims of international, or transnational, trafficking. A significant percentage of the Netherlands's trafficking victims—and especially its child trafficking victims—are Dutch nationals or residents trafficked *within* the country. Approximately 30 percent of children prostituted in the Netherlands are estimated to be of Dutch birth. Another 30 percent of the Netherlands's prostituted children are estimated to be of Antillean, Moroccan, Surinamese, or Turkish ethnicity, and approximately 60 percent of these children are also Dutch nationals.[18] Reporting figures for all verified victims per annum, regardless of age, the Bureau National Rapporteur Mensenhandel (BNRM), or National Reporter on Human Trafficking, finds that Dutch nationals were 32 percent of victims in 2000, 25 percent in 2001, 24 percent in 2002, and 26 percent in 2003.[19] It is noteworthy that the percentage of Dutch national victims declined and the percentage of transnational victims increased immediately following the Netherlands's legalization of brothels in 2000: by 2007 Amsterdam's mayor, among others, would conclude that legalization had attracted increased trafficking by organize crime.

Exploitation of Trafficking Victims in the Netherlands

There is a wide range of methods used to recruit persons for trafficking in or to the Netherlands. Outright kidnapping is one such method, as is the outright purchase of victims from family members or other mistakenly trusted contact persons. As happens in many other countries, victims are frequently lured with false promises of employment in domestic service or the restaurant, catering, hotel, or entertainment industries. Victims may also be deceived into believing that they are traveling for studies abroad or to engage with a marriage agency. A widespread method of recruitment, especially in cases of domestic trafficking of young women, is the so-called lover boy system, whereby a man earns a woman's trust through a seeming romance, only to force her into prostitution once she has been separated from her family. Finally, since prostitution is legal in the Netherlands, victims are also recruited into what they know will be prostitution, but do not expect to be enslavement. Regardless of the method of recruitment, most modern-day slaves in the Netherlands are females trafficked into the sex trades.

EXPERIENCES OF ADULT VICTIMS

In approximately 60 percent of transnational sex trafficking cases, a woman is removed from her country of origin and forced to work in the sex trades through a number of transit countries en route to the Netherlands. In order to force a woman into compliance, traffickers may use or threaten rape and other forms of violence against her; threaten violence against her family; seize her travel documents; force the use of drugs and alcohol upon her; and tattoo signs of ownership upon her body, among other measures.[20] The threats against family members frequently include evidence that the traffickers are, indeed, able to inflict violence on those the woman herself can no longer contact. As one Baltic woman rescued in the Netherlands testified:

> *When we arrived in the Netherlands we were brought to a hotel. We were told that we would be working as prostitutes the next night. I screamed and said I would never do that. But they showed me a photo of my son and told me to quiet down, because something nasty might happen to him otherwise.[21]*

The red light districts in Amsterdam, the Netherlands's capital, are known for the open display of sex for sale. In what is called window prostitution, women in various states of undress advertise their availability to passing men from storefront-style windows. Even women who have agreed to come to the Netherlands to engage in legalized prostitution may not have anticipated these circumstances. One rescued Czech woman testified about the gap between her expectations—in terms of both her working conditions and her state of freedom—and the reality she found:

> *I was shocked when I saw the women, practically naked behind the windows; I had never seen this before. I did not want to expose myself like that. Then when I started work, I had no say in the hours I worked. I was not allowed to leave the house and I was not allowed to refuse clients.[22]*

Multiple forced abortions are also reported by women rescued from brothels.[23]

EXPERIENCES OF CHILD VICTIMS

The Dutch police regularly inspect licensed brothels for evidence of underage prostitution, and licensed brothel owners are careful not to have minor girls in evidence.[24] Nonetheless, children are prostituted in the Netherlands. Research based on a "careful extrapolation of the data from police, asylum centres, youth, and prostitution-relief institutions" suggests that one in five of the Netherlands's prostituted women were first prostituted as minor children, and that outright force was used in 45 percent of these cases.[25] Almost half of prostituted girls are recruited by lover boys, and more than half of these child lover-boy victims are Dutch nationals.[26] It is important to note that the United Nations Protocol to Prevent, Suppress and Punish Trafficking in Persons,

Especially Women and Children (UN Protocol) and other international instruments clearly state that the harboring of any child for exploitation is human trafficking, regardless of any seeming consent.

End Child Prostitution, Child Pornography and Trafficking of Children for Sexual Purposes (ECPAT) notes that while the ban on underage girls in sex shop windows is widely observed, there have been instances of seemingly experienced girls being placed in such windows on their 18th birthdays, something that speaks of underage "preparation":

> ... care organizations and the police come across cases of girls being put on display in the windows of sex shops when they turn 18. Before this, many of the girls might have already been "prepared" for prostitution, via gang rapes, forced sex, and having sex with the friends of the pimp. The existence of this "preparatory" treatment that minor girls are subjected to is extremely difficult to prove, not least because money does not always change hands.

Prior to age 18, girls are known to be prostituted in venues outside of the Netherlands's legally sanctioned system "within illegal escort services, in hotels, in parked cars, in private houses, and in illegal private clubs (mostly in towns but also in the countryside)." Such activity is reportedly abetted by use of cell phones and the Internet.[27]

While the majority of victims trafficked into the sex trades are female, prostituted boys are also found in the Netherlands. While many of these minor boys fall between the ages of 15 and 18, care organizations report that boys seem to be first prostituted in the Netherlands "at a slightly younger age than girls, i.e., between 9 and 15 years old."[28] There is also a ploy specific to the recruitment of boys: the fraudulent offering of a football contract. In such cases, the families of African boys pay sizeable fees to traffickers posing as football (American soccer) agents able to secure sports contracts in the Netherlands. Upon arrival in the Netherlands, the boys may be pressed directly into enslaved work by the so-called football agent. Boys enslaved in this scam are also abandoned at the airport by agents who pocket all the maintenance and other monies provided by the boys' families, leaving the boys to be preyed upon by traffickers of unaccompanied minors.[29] (Prior to 2001, there were numerous reports of professional Dutch football clubs actually hiring such underage African players without legitimate wages, contracts, or housing permits.)[30]

Most of the country's trafficked children, like most of its trafficked adults, are concentrated in the sex trades. Trafficked children have also been found working in involuntary domestic servitude, as forced laborers in the catering industry, and as captive participants in the illegal sectors of the Netherlands's drug trade.[31]

Considerations Particular to Trafficking in the Netherlands

Prostitution has always been legal in the Netherlands, absent any evidence of force or coercion, but the operation of brothels was banned in 1911. That ban was overturned in October 2000, when brothels and pimping were both made legal.[32] Proponents of these changes in the law—and, later, the Netherlands's Ministry of Foreign Affairs itself—argued, among other things, that the licensing and routine inspection of brothels would help to end abuse of women in the sex trades, including trafficking:

> *An important spin-off of the policy is that it prevents human trafficking, which is characterised by exploitation, coercion and violence. The lifting of the ban on brothels makes prostitution a legitimate occupation and gives prostitutes the same rights and protections as other professionals. The labour laws offer the most effective protection against exploitation, violence and coercion. The policy is based on the conviction that strengthening the position of women is the best way to combat sexual violence. Moreover, abuses are easier to detect when prostitutes operate publicly and legally rather than in a clandestine subculture.*
>
> *The introduction of a municipal licensing system enables the police and other law enforcement agencies to conduct inspections of brothels, subject to the mayor's consent. Through regular inspections to ensure that brothels conform to the licensing conditions, the police are in a position to pick up signs of human trafficking. They obtain invaluable information that can be used immediately to trace and prosecute offenders in both the regulated and unregulated sectors.[33]*

Opponents of legal prostitution and brothels in the Netherlands argued that legalization has only increased human trafficking. As Dr. Janice G. Raymond, co-executive director of the Coalition Against Trafficking in Women (CATW), wrote to the U.S. Department of State in protest of the Netherlands's favorable ranking as a Tier 1 country:

> *Evidence is mounting that legalized/decriminalized pimping and brothels contribute to the sex trafficking of women and children. For example, countries such as Holland and Germany, both of which have recognized prostitution as work and as a legal economic sector, are precisely the countries that experience higher rates of women illegally trafficked into the country for trafficking. . . .*
>
> *Essentially, legalization is a gift to pimps and traffickers, transforming them overnight into third party business agents and international entrepreneurs. Legalized systems of prostitution allow the sex industry to flourish with impunity, transforming prostitution into "sex work" and sex trafficking into "migration for sex work."[34]*

While there are voices on both sides of the issue, it appears to an increasing number of observers that legalized prostitution—by providing a legal veneer behind which illegal activity can flourish and by providing what Bob Herbert of the *New York Times* has called "a friendlier climate for demand"[35]—has not reduced the abuse or trafficking of women.[36]

In addition, some of the Netherlands's youth workers have come to believe that legalization has caused young girls to view prostitution as increasingly acceptable.[37] As one such worker expressed it:

> *The morals on prostitution have changed. Girls are aware of the fact that they can make money by selling sex, and they have less hesitation in doing so. Earning money and buying things with the proceeds of prostitution is not seen as such a bad thing any more.*

While there is no consensus on the influence of legalization on children's views on prostitution, there *is* consensus on risk factors that make children vulnerable to sex trafficking in the Netherlands. These include extreme dependence on other people and a lack of self-esteem; having been a victim of rape or other sexual abuse; a strict religious upbringing that unduly restricted personal freedom; a difficult family situation involving divorce, blended families, or single parenthood; parental neglect or abuse; adventure-seeking behavior; becoming a runaway; having survived war or another national or natural disaster; poverty; loneliness and the actual or perceived lack of a social-support network; and "parents who are unable to cope with Dutch society or their own child."[38]

The Netherlands's Efforts to End Trafficking
DOMESTIC EFFORTS TO END TRAFFICKING

As noted above, the Netherlands legalized brothels and pimping in 2000 to, among other things, attempt to introduce a transparency that might help end the trafficking of women into prostitution. Indeed, the United States noted in its 2005 TIP Report that the Netherlands had begun to interview prostituted women to verify that they worked voluntarily, in accord with the stated goals of the legalization act.[39] Nevertheless, as 2007 neared an end, Amsterdam mayor Job Cohen announced that legalization had failed to curb the trafficking of women into prostitution or reduce the abuse of prostituted women.[40] In fact, brothel legalization has increased, as opponents argued it would, the amount of human trafficking and even the presence of organized crime.[41] As a result, the city now plans to close at least 25 percent of the window brothels and increase the age of legal prostitution from 18 to 21, among other reforms designed to limit, but not outlaw, prostitution, pimping, and brothels.[42]

At the national level, the BNRM was established in 2000 to report to parliament about trafficking in the Netherlands. The United States credits the Netherlands with aggressive investigation and prosecution of traffickers, including investigations that led to the shutting down of several major international sex-trafficking rings including one based in Turkey, one based in Romania, and another that trafficked in Nigerian children.[43]

Rescued victims of trafficking are registered by Stichting Tegen Vrouwenhandel, the Foundation against Trafficking in Women, Netherlands (STV), an organization subsidized by the government and charged with offering assistance to victims. Victims who either cooperate in the prosecutions of their traffickers or face violence upon return to their countries of origin are permitted to remain in the Netherlands. Other victims may be deported to their countries of origin.

The Dutch government has also instituted a national campaign in high schools to warn young women about lover boy scams.[44] A broader national campaign targeting, among others, the clients of prostituted women is designed to raise the country's general awareness of modern-day slavery and of a trafficking hotline run by the government.[45]

A number of NGOs are also working to combat trafficking in the Netherlands. These include Project 13, an NGO that assists girls and young women aged 13 to 23 who have been abused either by boyfriends or in prostitution; Beauty and the Beast, a prostitution prevention group targeting girls aged 13 to 16; Pretty Woman, a mobile project to assist girls aged 12 to 18 who are vulnerable to prostitution and girls and young women aged 18 to 23 who have been forced into prostitution; Veilige Haven (Safe Harbour), which offers a protected meeting place for Moroccan girls vulnerable to prostitution; and Bonded Labour in the Netherlands Project, which offers language, computer, and other courses to rescued victims, as well as job-placement assistance.[46]

Prior to 2005, all Dutch anti-trafficking efforts were directed at sex trafficking, since other forms of forced labor were not recognized as human trafficking under Dutch law. With the implementation of Criminal Code Article 273a, forced labor was included in the Dutch definition for the first time, and efforts against nonsexual forms of trafficking have begun.[47] In 2006, the most recent year for which statistics are available, 216 sex trafficking cases were prosecuted, and 90 convictions obtained. In the same year, four forced labor cases were prosecuted; all defendants were acquitted, but the Dutch government is appealing in two of the cases.[48]

THE NETHERLANDS'S PARTICIPATION IN INTERNATIONAL EFFORTS TO END TRAFFICKING

The Netherlands is a party to many of the international instruments that prohibit various forms of modern slavery. It has signed and accepted the UN

Protocol, and it has signed and ratified the Optional Protocol to the Convention on the Rights of the Child on the Sale of Children, Child Prostitution and Child Pornography and the Hague Convention on Intercountry Adoption. It has signed, but not ratified, the Optional Protocol to the Convention on the Rights of the Child in Armed Conflict (meaning that it is not legally bound to abide by that convention.) It also has ratified the three major International Labour Organization (ILO) instruments relating to modern-day slavery: ILO Convention 182, Concerning the Prohibition and Immediate Action for the Elimination of the Worst Forms of Child Labor; ILO Convention 29, Concerning Forced Labor; and ILO Convention 105, Abolition of Forced Labor.[49]

In addition, the Netherlands is a party to UN instruments that address poverty and discrimination against women, two of the root causes of human trafficking. The UN Millennium Declaration (2000) was unanimously adopted by the leaders of 189 member nations, including the Netherlands.[50] The Netherlands has also signed and ratified, subject to reservation, the UN Convention on the Elimination of All Forms of Discrimination against Women. (The reservation concerns Dutch objections to statements made in the convention's preamble concerning apartheid, colonialism, neocolonialism, nuclear disarmament and other issues it deemed "not directly related to the achievement of total equality between men and women.")[51]

Conclusion

One of the leading destination countries for transnational human trafficking, the Netherlands also has an identifiable problem with the internal trafficking of young girls into its sex industry. It has taken legislative steps to address human trafficking, including the addition of forced labor to its anti-trafficking statute; public awareness measures, such as campaigns intended to alert teenaged girls to the dangers posed by "lover boy" traffickers; and reforms to its legalized brothel system, including a reduction in the size of its red-light district and an increase in the legal age for prostitution from 18 to 21.

NIGERIA
Nigeria's Role in Human Trafficking

Nigeria is listed by the United Nations as among the world's top 11 origin countries for modern-day slaves.[52] It is also listed as a "medium"-level destination country[53] and a "low"-level transit country.[54]

While the UN ranks countries according to the number of persons reported trafficked between and through countries, the United States ranks countries according to their efforts to eliminate all trafficking. On this basis, the

United States ranks Nigeria as a Tier 2 country, classifying Nigeria as a country that "does not fully comply with the minimum standards for the elimination of trafficking [but] is making significant efforts to do so."[55] This ranking, which Nigeria has held since 2005, is an improvement over Nigeria's earlier placement: As recently as 2004, the United States listed Nigeria as a Tier 2 Watch List country due to the "significant complicity of Nigerian security personnel in human trafficking and the lack of evidence of increasing efforts to address this complicity," and the finding that Nigeria, ". . . commits inadequate funding and personnel to fight against Nigeria's serious trafficking problem."[56]

There is no question that Nigeria's trafficking problem is as serious as the United States claims. Africans Unite Against Child Abuse (AFRUCA), an organization dedicated to protecting African children in the United Kingdom, confirms that ". . . Nigeria unfortunately has a reputation for being one of the leading African countries with cross border and internal trafficking."[57] The same view is expressed within Nigeria itself: The Women's Consortium of Nigeria (WOCON), a Nigerian-based women and girls' rights organization, notes that Nigeria "has often been referred to as 'the most donating African country in the global sex industry.' Nigerian women comprise a large percentage of the African victims of trafficking in Europe."[58]

Despite the certainty about Nigeria's role as a major source country for modern-day slaves, there is no certainty regarding the specific number of persons trafficked every year. It is estimated that 200,000 children are trafficked every year from West African countries and that "Nigeria is the centre of this regional child-trafficking market."[59] There are also estimates that, each year, 45,000 Nigerians—mostly women and girls—are trafficked to Europe alone.[60] Tabulations made in the field seem to verify that many of Europe's modern-day slaves are, indeed, Nigerian. In Italy, more than 60 percent of prostitutes are found to be Nigerian, and many of these women and girls are believed to be trafficking victims; in Great Britain, more than 80 percent of the African trafficking victims assisted by AFRUCA are found to have come from Nigeria.[61]

Nigeria's role as an origin country is also evidenced by the deportations of victims from various destination countries back to Nigeria. These numbers reflect only the victims who are discovered and, at the end of official proceedings, deported home rather than assisted in their countries of exploitation. While these numbers, then, represent only some portion of the trafficked population, they speak to a constant stream of Nigerians discovered in slavery. Figures compiled by Women Trafficking and Child Labour Eradication Foundation (WOTCLEF) and the Nigerian police force, for example, indicate that from March 1999 to April 2000, 1,126 trafficked Nigerian women were returned home through deportation.[62]

Victims are also enslaved within Nigeria. The United Nations Children's Fund (UNICEF) Innocenti Research Centre correctly notes that there is more information available about African transnational trafficking than there is about trafficking within individual African countries,[63] but it is nevertheless possible to suggest the size of this problem. According to the ILO, for example, there are approximately 12 million child laborers aged 10 to 14 in Nigeria.[64] Without specifying an age range, the Network Against Human Trafficking In West Africa (NAHTIWA) estimates the number of child laborers in Nigeria to be 15 million.[65] While it is not known what percentage of Nigeria's total child-labor workforce is trafficked, a study conducted by ILO/International Programme on the Elimination of Child Labour (IPEC) concluded that 19 percent of children interviewed in Nigerian schools and 40 percent of "street children and hawkers (those who sell goods on the street)" interviewed in seven Nigerian towns were trafficking victims.[66]

Origins and Destinations of Persons Trafficked from, within, and to Nigeria

Nigerians, mostly women and girls, are trafficked internationally to Austria, Belgium, the Central African Republic, France, Gabon, Germany, Italy, Mali, the Netherlands, Norway, Saudi Arabia, Spain, the United States, and countries in North Africa, among other destinations.[67] Women and girls from other countries are also trafficked into Nigeria, most notably from Benin, Cameroon, the Central African Republic, Chad, Ghana, Niger, and Togo. There is substantial internal trafficking in Nigeria as well, with most domestic victims being trafficked from rural communities to urban ones.[68]

Many of Nigeria's internationally trafficked victims are from Edo State, a state in central southern Nigeria that includes both rural areas and Benin City. Indeed, if Nigeria is a leading source country, "Edo state has been labeled as the most endemic state known for human trafficking."[69] According to Nogi Imoukhuede, project co-coordinator of Women's Rights Watch Nigeria, girls and women from Edo State's poorest villages and urban areas are specifically targeted by traffickers for exploitation in Europe.[70] It is estimated that 92 percent of Nigerian women and girls enslaved in European prostitution have been trafficked from Edo State,[71] an estimate that is supported by the fact that approximately 80 percent of Nigerian trafficking victims deported from Europe have been found to come from Edo State.[72] A significant percentage of these women and girls may not have originally resided in Edo State, however. Benin City is often a destination for those seeking employment, and it also has a "national reputation as the headquarters for illegal immigration fixers." Thus, trafficking victims counted as coming "from Edo State" may also include those who first traveled to Benin City in search of employment there or a route to what they thought would be illegal immigration, but not slavery.[73]

As noted above, rural areas are also a primary source for internally trafficked victims and especially for children trafficked within Nigeria. These children are most often trafficked from rural areas in Akwa Ibom, Benue, Cross River, Kwara, and Oyo States to various Nigerian cities within and without their home states, including Abeokuta, Calabar, Ibadan, Kano, Lagos, and Port Harcourt.[74] While women and girls are most often trafficked in, from, and to Nigeria, boys and, far less often, men are also trafficked.[75] Indeed, Nigerian men are so rarely trafficked that there is no discussion of them as victims in the 2008, 2007, or 2006 TIP Reports.

Exploitation of Nigerian Trafficking Victims

Nigerian victims are enslaved in the commercial sex trades and in various forms of forced labor. Nigerian girls and women, whether trafficked within Nigeria or to another country, generally find themselves enslaved in sexual or domestic servitude. Nigerian boys, both those trafficked domestically and internationally, generally find themselves enslaved as domestic laborers, as forced agricultural, mining, and stone quarry laborers, and as forced beggars and street hawkers.[76] Along with other boys from West Africa, Nigerian boys are also lured into fraudulent football "academies," only to be turned over or abandoned to traffickers in Europe.[77]

While some trafficking victims are flown directly to destination countries using fraudulent documents obtained from corrupt Nigerian officials, most victims take a combination of land, sea, rail, and air routes.[78] The overland route through the Sahara to North Africa, where victims board boats bound for Europe, is particularly dangerous. Some victims make the journey in severely overcrowded container and refrigerator trucks.[79] Many others make a month long walk, during which victims have been known to drink their own urine in order to survive.[80] A number of trafficked persons die every year during this Sahara crossing.[81]

SEXUAL EXPLOITATION

Prostitution

The vast majority of Nigeria's modern-day slavery victims are girls and women trafficked into prostitution. One method of recruiting these women is well established, with Nigerian-based madams or pimps (also called mamans) having established ties with mamans in destination countries[82] and messengers willing to transport the trafficked women.[83] These traffickers approach postpubescent girls and young women in public places such as markets.[84] They make false promises involving nonsexual employment or, in some cases, work described as prostitution, but not described as including slavery.[85] The victims who accept these deceptive offers are generally warned not to inform their families that they will be leaving Nigeria.[86] In the case of children, parents may be approached by traffickers posing as friends or even by actual relatives acting as or cooperating with traffickers.[87] As the *Logos Daily Sun* reported one such case:

> *Clara, 12, was picked up by her aunty having agreed with her parents that she would work as a house-help somewhere in Lagos on a salary of N7,000 [about U.S. $60 in 2008] and this money was to be sent to her parents in the village.*
>
> *Unknown to Clara and her relatives, the aunt, who is involved in human trafficking, was to hand her over to [a] syndicate. By the arrangement of her aunt, whose plans were not disclosed to her relatives, Clara would continue her voyage to an undisclosed destination as soon as she arrived.*
>
> *As agreed, Clara was handed over in exchange for the money, part of which was sent to her parents as salary for two years. Soon after the deal was sealed, Clara began her journey to Italy where she was forced into prostitution.[88]*

Italy and Spain are major destinations for Nigerian girls and women trafficked into prostitution. Indeed, Titi Abubakar, the founder of WOTCLEF and wife of former Nigerian vice president Atiku Abubakar, says that despite all efforts to end trafficking, "Nigerian girls still litter the streets of Spain and Italy."[89] The Netherlands has also long been a major destination country for Nigerian women trafficked into prostitution.[90]

Nigerian girls and women trafficked into prostitution in Europe and elsewhere are subjected to the seizure of identity documents, threats of brutality against family members, and the infliction of violence, including beatings and rape.[91] In addition, they are subjected to a means of enforcement specific to their culture: the use of Voodoo ritual (Voodoo is a religion that blends elements of traditional West African religion and French Catholicism). When trafficking victims or their parents agree to "employment" contracts, albeit often based on false information, Voodoo priests are frequently enlisted to perform ceremonies binding victims to oaths of obedience and silence. Belief in these religious rituals is strong, and trafficking victims trust that whatever punishment the priest has indicated—madness, illness, death—will befall them or members of their families if escape is attempted:[92]

> *When traffickers draw up a contract, they often call on a traditional priest to give approval. This is usually done at a traditional 'shrine'. The*

priest takes something deeply personal from the girl. It might be hair from her head, some pubic hair, a nail clipping, or some underwear. This trophy is wrapped up with a flourish, and the priest leaves no doubt that it will be used to control the victim from a distance. This use of voodoo is a way of keeping the girl in bondage . . .[93]

When Nigerian women trafficked for sexual purposes are rescued or deported, they are often found to be terminally ill and destitute. They are exposed to HIV/AIDS with such frequency that, according to Nigeria's National Agency for the Prohibition of Trafficking in Persons and Other Related Matters (NAPTIP), 60 percent of returned Nigerian trafficking victims are HIV positive.[94] Many returning victims also arrive in Nigeria in a state of absolute destitution. According to NAPTIP spokesperson Arinze Orakwue, if a prostituted woman earns freedom from debt bondage her trafficker will alert authorities. When the formerly trafficked woman is deported, the trafficker claims her accumulated possessions. As Orakwue describes it: "These victims are being used from the beginning to the end. . . ."[95]

Internally trafficked girls and women are also sold into sexual exploitation, as are girls and women trafficked into Nigeria from Benin, Ghana, Togo, and other nearby countries.[96]

Child Marriage
In northern Nigeria, early marriage for girls is the norm, especially in the rural areas. In the rural northwest of Nigeria, for example, approximately 66 percent of girls are married before age 15 and more than 80 percent before age 18.[97] (Across Nigeria as a whole, girls' median age at marriage is 16.)[98] Child marriages are generally arranged by the girls' fathers, with varying degrees of support from the girls' mothers.[99] The girls themselves are not generally asked to provide consent (and, indeed, the UN Protocol and other international instruments reject the idea that minor children are capable of giving informed consent to marriage), nor are they generally well informed about reproductive matters. As the Population Council summarizes the experiences of adolescent wives in Nigeria:

Their experience of marriage was often unwanted and traumatic, with their not knowing what was happening to them and not giving their consent to marriage.[100]

These adolescent girls are generally younger than the men they marry. The average age difference between an adolescent wife and her husband in a monogamous marriage (about 66.6 percent of such marriages) is 12 years; the average difference between an adolescent girl and her husband in a polygamous marriage (about 33.3 percent of such marriages) is 18 years.[101] Interviews with married Nigerian girls indicate that "Once married, girls' participation in household decision-making is limited."[102] In most cases, child marriage also means an end to educational opportunity; only 2 percent of married girls in Nigeria attend school.[103]

In addition, girls married at adolescence are at extreme risk for complications of pregnancy, given their state of physical development and the circumstances in which they generally deliver their children. More than half the girls in northwest Nigeria and almost half the girls in northeast Nigeria receive no medical care whatsoever during their first pregnancy. Most of these girls (approximately 86 percent in the northwest and 78 percent in the northeast) deliver their first babies at home. During these home births, the girls may be completely unattended (approximately 21 percent in the northwest and 11 percent in the northeast) or attended only by a friend or relative without any medical training (approximately 42 percent in the northwest and 52 percent in the northeast). The consequences are often fatal: A Nigerian woman has a 1 in 18 lifetime chance of dying in childbirth,[104] and approximately 1 in 9 children delivered in northern Nigeria die at or shortly after birth.[105] Poor nutrition, early pregnancy, and lack of medical care during pregnancy and childbirth are also risk factors for obstetric fistula,[106] a tear in the wall between the vagina and/or bladder or rectum. Nigeria is believed to have one of the highest rates of fistula in the world, with approximately 20,000 girls and women suffering this injury every year and approximately 400,000 to 800,000 Nigerian girls and women currently living with the injury. Woman with fistulas cannot control their bladder and/or bowel functions; they are often abandoned by their husbands.[107]

FORCED LABOR

Trafficked prepubescent Nigerian girls are usually sold into forced labor,[108] although they are sometimes trafficked twice: first, to one country for domestic servitude, then, at adolescence, to a second country for sexual exploitation.[109] Nigerian boys and women are also trafficked into forced labor.

Women and older girls may be approached directly by those intending to traffic them into forced labor, in the same manner as they are approached by sex traffickers. While young children are also approached directly—and, indeed, there are documented cases of children being lured into slavery with the promise of a radio or a bicycle[110]—it is their parents who are most often contacted by traffickers. Parents are generally approached by friends, by people posing as friends of friends, by relatives, or by other seemingly trustworthy intermediaries. In these cases of forced labor recruitment, it is generally made clear that the child will be leaving home to work, but it is not always made clear under what circumstances the child will toil.

Global Perspectives

Involuntary Domestic Servitude

Most Nigerian girls and women trafficked into forced labor are sold into involuntary domestic servitude[111]; trafficked house boys have been found as well.[112] While Nigerians are trafficked into servitude abroad, many are also enslaved in Nigeria's cities, where the increasing number of two-income households has increased demand for household help. Estimates are that 80 percent of household servants in these cities are children, "most of whom are trafficked victims." Harsh debt-bondage arrangements are common. As WOCON describes it:

> As domestic workers, the children are subjected to 12–18 hours of clean-ing, baby care, cooking and other forms of household chores. They are the first to get up in the morning and the last to go to bed at night.... The wages paid to the children average about N1000 or an equivalent of less than $10 US per month. However, a large percentage of these wages are deducted by the traffickers as repayment for the upkeep of the children before employment and the facilitation of employment.[113]

Persons from Benin, Ghana, Togo, and other nearby countries are also trafficked into domestic servitude in Nigeria.[114] Adult Nigerian women are often trafficked into domestic servitude abroad, including to Great Britain and the United States, where they work as childcare providers.[115]

Other Forms of Forced Labor

Nigerian girls and women trafficked internally into forced labor are some-times also found working on plantations,[116] while internally trafficked boys are most often found working as beggars (most often under the direction of religious teachers), street hawkers, stone quarry and mine workers, agri-cultural laborers,[117] and "washers of feet."[118] Persons trafficked into Nigeria from other African countries and to those countries from Nigeria are also found in these forced labor positions. [119] Many of Nigeria's forced labor vic-tims, whether trafficked to, from, or within the country, are children younger than 14; indeed, trafficked Beninese children as young as five have been found in Nigerian rock quarries.[120] These children—like those of all ages trafficked into Nigerian rock quarries—faced working conditions that were, unquestionably, "exploitative and slave-like." As WOCON describes it:

> ... the children who were recently rescued from slave camps in Ogun State were found to be between the ages of 4–16 years. They were made to work in open camps where they dig the soil with their bare hands, to get stones, which they break by hitting one stone against another to get granite at illegal mining sites. Each child collects almost a tipper load of

83

stone per day. They are poorly fed merely for survival and made to sleep on a bare floor in open air. Their working hours are between 16–18 hours per day. They rarely have their baths and are denied proper clothing.[121]

OTHER FORMS OF EXPLOITATION

Trafficked Nigerians suffer other forms of exploitation as well. One additional form of exploitation, the trafficking of children for *diya* or "blood money," has been documented in Saudi Arabia. In Islamic law the person who kills or injures another—whether accidental or premeditated—has to pay *diya* to the victim (if alive) or his family or clan. In these trafficking cases, an agent secures a Nigerian child from parents with promises of paid work and then takes the child to Saudi Arabia to be killed. The trafficker pushes the child before an expensive, oncoming car. If the child is killed, the Saudi Arabian person has two legal options: paying compensation to the victim's family (an option the victim's family can refuse) or being sentenced to death. The trafficker, posing as the victim's family, accepts the compensation and receives the equivalent of approximately $27,000. In Nigeria, the parents are told of their child's death—but not of the circumstances—and given approximately $775 to represent what would have been the child's wages during his or her short stay in Saudi Arabia.[122]

There is also concern about the rise in what United Nations Educational, Scientific and Cultural Organization (UNESCO) terms "baby harvesting"[123] in Nigeria. In these cases, orphanages and medical personnel provide care for pregnant girls and women who have decided not to keep their babies. The mothers are paid off after taking oaths of silence or signing papers to relinquish their babies to be sold. It is often unclear as to where these children go. As UNESCO reports, "There is no trace of many of the babies that are sold, and one cannot be sure exactly how they are used."[124]

The trafficking of persons for the involuntary harvesting of organs has also been reported.[125]

Considerations Particular to Trafficking in Nigeria

There are many intertwined push factors that influence trafficking in Nigeria. These include extreme poverty, a low rate of universal education, a tradition of child labor and fostering, the unequal status of women, a high number of orphans, and official corruption.

POVERTY

Despite its oil reserves and other resources, Nigeria is a country with endemic poverty. According to the World Bank's latest available figures, fully 70.8 percent of Nigerians live on less than one dollar per day.[126] Much of Nigeria's worst poverty is in its rural areas, where many subsistence or near-subsistence farmers depend on small plots of land farmed without supplemental irrigation. (The International Fund for Agricultural Development [IFAD], a UN agency, reports that approximately 90 percent of the country's food is grown in this manner.) These small farmers and their families may "manage to eke out a subsistence living but often go short of food, particularly during the pre-harvest period." Countrywide indicators of poverty include the facts that only 26 percent of children are immunized against diphtheria, pertussis, and tetanus and 38 percent of the population is without access to clean drinking water. (Among the rural poor, almost 50 percent are without access to clean drinking water.)[127]

The consequences of such poverty are dire. The infant mortality rate in Nigeria is 98 deaths per 1,000 live births. The under-five mortality rate, that is, the rate at which Nigerian children die before turning five, is 198 children per 1,000.[128] Among children who survive, malnutrition is common. Against this background of extreme poverty, opportunities to travel for work and/or schooling seem, to many, a chance at survival.

EDUCATION AND ACCESS TO MASS MEDIA

The deceptive promises of traffickers—which often involve exaggerated claims about life outside of Nigeria—are difficult for intended victims to properly assess when their educational opportunities and access to mass media have been limited.

According to Nigeria's most recent Demographic and Health Survey (DHS), conducted in 2003, "Although the majority of the household population age 6 and older has some education, 46 percent of females and 31 percent of males have never attended school." Among the general population, approximately 33 percent of men and 25 percent of women have received some secondary education, but "the median number of years of schooling is 0.2 for females and 3.6 for males."[129] Despite governmental efforts to realize the UN Millennium Development Goal (MDG) of universal primary education by 2015, the attendance ratio of Nigeria's school-aged children has not significantly improved: The DHS found that only 60 percent of primary school age children were, in fact, receiving a primary school education in 2003.[130] (A ratio that includes over-age students was, however, higher.)[131] Among the reasons the Nigerian government cites for boys and girls' failure to attend or complete primary school are the family's need for the child to earn money; the lack of family funds to pay for school books, uniforms, and other school-related expenses; illnesses arising from unsafe drinking water and other sanitation-related deficits; and the distance of many children's homes from their schools.[132]

If one's own lack of education makes it difficult to accurately assess a trafficker's promises, the lack of educational opportunities for one's children can make those very same deceptive offers—and particularly those that refer to educational opportunities abroad—seem especially compelling.

Access to mass media is also limited. According to the 2003 DHS, only 58.5 percent of Nigerians listened to the radio, only 36.5 percent watched television, and only 11.5 percent read a newspaper; 35.5 percent of Nigerians had no access whatsoever to mass media.[133] This limited-information environment also favors would-be traffickers and not their intended victims.

TRADITIONS OF CHILD LABOR AND FOSTERING

Two Nigerian cultural traditions—the early introduction of children to work and the fostering of poor children—have been widely exploited by traffickers and, at times, abused by parents and other family members of victims.

The African continent has the world's highest child labor rate: 41 percent of its children aged five to 14 are engaged in labor,[134] including labor that meets ILO convention standards for child labor, such as assisting on family farms or helping with the rearing of younger siblings. If Africa has the highest child-labor rate of any continent, Nigeria has one of the highest child-labor rates in Africa. In 2005, for example, fully 68.6 percent of its primary school children were engaged in labor[135] and the rate was even higher among children not attending primary school.

Nigeria also has a long tradition of fostering, whereby well-off family and friends assume responsibility for rearing their poorer connections' children, and the children, in turn, help with family chores and other child-appropriate tasks. Within Nigeria, this practice is considered a way to spread the pain of an extended family's worst poverty among all its members, ameliorating poverty's most devastating effects upon children and reducing the burden upon their parents. Fostering has also included parents sending their children abroad, especially to relatives and friends in Great Britain. (Many Nigerians had relocated to that country to accept various educational and scholarship opportunities offered to Nigerians following Nigeria's independence from Great Britain in 1960.)[136]

These combined cultural practices—an acceptance of child labor and a tradition of fostering that sometimes includes a child leaving Nigeria—create a climate in which a so-called friend of a friend may find it easier than in other countries to gain a parent or a victim's trust. However, many observers find that desperately poor parents may accept child labor and relocation knowing that the engagement includes forced labor and prostitution.[137]

STATUS OF WOMEN

As the Nigerian government itself acknowledged in its most recent Millennium Development Goal Report (MDG Report) to the UN, "all forms of discrimination against women in all spheres of life do exist [in Nigeria]."[138] One of the areas in which this is most readily apparent is in girls and women's limited access to education. While educational attainment levels remain low in Nigeria in general, they are substantially lower for females than for males. Many more girls than boys never attend school at all, due to what the MDG describes as "the traditional attitude of parents to … invest in the education of boys thereby denying girls the opportunity to participate."[139] The MDG Report also lists several reasons that Nigerian girls may begin, but not complete their primary school education: The requirement that pubescent girls begin to observe purdah (a system of sex segregation and the seclusion of women practiced in some Muslim and Hindu communities); female child marriage; and early motherhood.[140] Lack of education can be a contributing factor to origin-country trafficking. In the case of Nigerian girls, lack of attendance at school can also be—and often is—an indication that absent students already live in the slavery-like conditions of child marriage.[141]

Other gender-discriminatory factors that add to Nigerian women's vulnerability are laws that prevent women from inheriting property and a culture in which "the will of men is to be respected."[142] These factors diminish a woman's decision-making role not only at critical junctures in her own life, but when decisions are made for her daughters.

ORPHANHOOD

In 2004, a UNICEF-supported study concluded that there were 7 million orphans in Nigeria and that 1.8 million of those children had been orphaned due to HIV/AIDS. The report also projected that by 2010 the spread of HIV/AIDS would increase the number of Nigerian orphans to 8.2 million.[143]

Married girls in Nigeria may be at particular risk for HIV/AIDS-related deaths:

> Child marriage may put girls at increased risk of HIV infection compared to unmarried sexually active girls. Married girls have sex more often, have more unprotected sex, and have partners who are more likely to be HIV-positive because of their older age.

Indeed, studies in individual African countries indicate that more married adolescent girls test positive for HIV than unmarried sexually active adolescent girls and that across sub-Saharan Africa 17 to 22 percent of girls ages 15 to 19 are infected with HIV, while 3 to 7 percent of same-aged boys are infected.

Many of the factors under discussion tend to be interrelated. The fact that married girls have more unprotected sex, for example, is related to the practice of young girls being married to much older men, many of whom have a sexual history, and the limited decision-making role girls frequently have within these marriages. As a Population Council briefing summarizes the consequences of these combined factors, "Married girls have limited ability to negotiate condom use."[144]

While married girls may be at particular risk for HIV/AIDS, they are not the only Nigerians at risk. Moreover, HIV/AIDS is not the only cause of Nigerian orphanhood. Poverty, malnutrition, lack of access to potable water, insufficient medical care, and other circumstances all contribute to Nigeria's low life expectancy, which was only 44 years for males and females born in 2005.[145]

Regardless of the cause of parental death, the consequences of orphanhood in a country where, "[w]ith the burden of poverty, families and communities cannot cope with an increased number of orphans," is catastrophic. As UNICEF's country representative in Nigeria, Mr. Ayalew Abai, describes it, "The negative impact . . . of orphanhood of so many children is evident through the growing number of children living in the streets, exposed to the worst forms of child labour and child trafficking."[146]

EXPLOITATION OF RELIGIOUS BELIEFS

The exploitation of religious beliefs is also a factor in human trafficking in Nigeria. Muslim teenage boys in northern Nigeria often study with Islamic teachers (also called *malams*) in what is known as *almajirci* scholarship. This sometimes involves boys traveling with the scholar, and circumstances can, intentionally or not, devolve into trafficking:

> *The pupils learn from the scholar as they move from one town to another. They are often inadequately prepared for such a journey. The Malam is frequently too poor to sustain his family or the pupils entrusted to him. Consequently, both the Malam and his pupils often rely on the benevolence of the community in which they happen to be guests. In most instances, the Malam lives on the support of his pupils who beg or perform menial tasks for food sellers and shopkeepers in public places and motor parks all over northern Nigeria.[147]*

While a 2006 UNESCO report points out that "both the benefactors and the pupils are often unaware that this constitutes an aberration from international norms,"[148] the U.S. State Department classifies such "forced begging" of boys for religious leaders as human trafficking.[149]

Women's religious beliefs, both Voodoo and Muslim, are exploited as well. As was discussed above, Voodoo priests oversee ritual ceremonies to help ensure victims' obedience and silence; indeed, female adherents of Voodoo may be preyed upon precisely because their participation in ritual ceremonies can eliminate the need to beat them into submission when they are ultimately delivered into the sex trades.[150] The religious practices of Muslim women in Nigeria are likewise exploited. Many devout Nigerian Muslim women, particularly from the northern part of the country, wish to make the hajj (pilgrimage to Mecca), one of the five fundamental duties of Islam. They are sometimes preyed on in transit or by traffickers who offer to assist them with travel, but instead sell them into slavery.[151]

OFFICIAL CORRUPTION

Official corruption, cited as one of the primary reasons Nigeria was listed as a Tier 2 Watch List country in the 2004 TIP Report, remains a problem. Reports of Nigerian officials facilitating the production of forged or false documents and assisting traffickers with border crossings and other clandestine travel continue to surface, as do reports of law enforcement personnel who fail to intervene.[152] Despite improvements that led to Nigeria's elevation to a Tier 2 country in 2005—and its continued Tier 2 listing in 2006 and 2007—Babacar Ndiaye, head of United Nations Office on Drugs and Crime (UNODC) regional office for West and Central Africa, described corruption in Nigeria as a widespread problem as recently as May 2007. Human traffickers in Nigeria, he claimed, "work quietly and in the open," without worrying about interference from law enforcement personnel.[153]

PULL FACTORS

Against a background of poverty and other hardships in Nigeria, the thought that life might be better elsewhere serves as an exploitable "pull factor." Quite often, the seeming promise of an entry-level job in another country is sufficient to lure victims into a trafficker's control. In other cases, however, such as when promises of professional football contracts abroad are used to secure custody of young boys, traffickers are also able to exploit exaggerated and inflated impressions of life in other countries.

Legalized prostitution in some European Union (EU) countries is also cited—and condemned—by Nigerian officials as being a significant pull factor. While many Nigerian women and girls are trafficked into the sex trades after accepting offers of what they believe to be nonsexual forms of work, other Nigerian women and girls accept work they understand to involve legalized prostitution, but do not expect to involve enslavement. The head of media and communication for Nigeria's National Agency for the Prohibition of Traffic in Persons, Arinze Orakwue, blames the legalization of prostitution outside of Nigeria for the fact that prostitution has become, in some cases, an acceptable job offer with which to camouflage the intent to traffic. As he expressed his frustration in November 2007:

> *It is disgusting to think that those who indulge in commercial sex in these countries [with legalized prostitution] pay tax to the government. It has been made a normal business and . . . these girls who sleep with*

an average of 10 men in a day, mostly do not use the money for their
personal use, rather they give it to their traffickers until they are able
to buy their freedom.[154]

Push and pull factors in Nigeria combine to create an environment favorable to the traffickers. As a result, almost all Nigerian transnational trafficking victims consent—or have their family consent—to their leaving the country, albeit usually based on deceptive information.[155]

Nigeria's Efforts to End Trafficking
DOMESTIC EFFORTS TO END TRAFFICKING

Although significant problems with official corruption remain, the U.S. State Department reports that "the Nigerian government continues to show a clear commitment to anti-trafficking reforms."[156] Specifically targeting corruption in September 2006, for instance, Nigeria dismissed documentation staff involved in issuing false travel documents and, as of June 2007, was bringing the suspects to trial.[157]

Nigeria has also passed significant anti-trafficking legislation. In 2003, Nigeria passed the Trafficking in Persons Law Enforcement and Administration Act (NAPTIP Act) and, as the act mandated, established NAPTIP to oversee the country's anti-trafficking activities and to prosecute traffickers. The 2003 NAPTIP emphasized a prohibition against sex trafficking, but it did not adequately address forced labor trafficking;[158] a 2005 amendment more explicitly included nonsexual forced labor in the NAPTIP Act's definition of human trafficking. Nigeria's Child Rights Act (CRA), passed in 2003, prohibiting children from being "separated from . . . parents against their will, except where it is in the best interests of the child,"[159] is also viewed as instrumental in Nigeria's legal fight against human trafficking.

Traffickers have been prosecuted in Nigeria, but convictions have been difficult to attain. While trafficking convictions have not been easy to obtain in any country, efforts in Nigeria are particularly "hampered by a lack of funding for thorough investigations and a lack of awareness of trafficking among judges, many of whom conflate trafficking with smuggling."[160] In the year preceding the 2007 TIP Report, for example, 81 investigations resulted in 23 prosecutions for trafficking and only three convictions. Moreover, the sentences were not severe (indeed, the U.S. State Department termed them "inadequate"): two years in prison for those convicted in two sex trafficking cases, and one year in a child forced begging case.[161]

A number of Nigerian NGOs are also working to end human trafficking in the country. These include WOTCLEF, which, among other things, initiated the bill that ultimately became the NAPTIP Act;[162] WOCON, which, also among other things, organized a 2007 panel discussion on "Cultural Challenges to the Elimination of Girl Child Trafficking and Commercial Sexual Exploitation in West Africa" during the 51st session of the UN Commission on the Status of Women (CSW);[163] and Girls' Power Initiative (GPI), which seeks to broaden the "exposure of girls to information and skills that enhance personal development . . . [to] equip them to resist negative cultural and modern practices such as FGM [female genital mutilation] and trafficking," and to help them become "catalysts of change in their own environment."[164]

NIGERIA'S PARTICIPATION IN
INTERNATIONAL EFFORTS TO END TRAFFICKING

Nigeria is a party to a number of the international instruments that prohibit various forms of modern slavery. It has signed and ratified the UN Protocol. It has signed but not ratified the Optional Protocol to the Convention on the Rights of the Child on the Sale of Children, Child Prostitution and Child Pornography and the Optional Protocol to the Convention on the Rights of the Child in Armed Conflict (meaning that it is not legally bound to abide by these conventions). It has also ratified the three major ILO instruments relating to modern-day slavery: ILO Convention 182, Concerning the Prohibition and Immediate Action for the Elimination of the Worst Forms of Child Labor; ILO Convention 29, Concerning Forced Labor; and ILO Convention 105, Abolition of Forced Labor.[165] It has neither signed nor ratified the Hague Convention on Intercountry Adoption.

Nigeria is also a party to UN instruments that address poverty and discrimination against women, two of the root causes of human trafficking. The UN Millennium Declaration (2000) was unanimously adopted by the leaders of 189 member nations, including Nigeria.[166] Nigeria has also signed and ratified the UN Convention on the Elimination of All Forms of Discrimination against Women.[167]

In addition, Nigeria has joined other Economic Community of West African States (ECOWAS) in a declaration and action plan to combat human trafficking in the region. The Declaration on the Fight against Trafficking in Persons (2001) committed the ECOWAS member states—Benin, Burkina Faso, Cap Verde, Côte d'Ivoire, Gambia, Ghana, Guinea, Guinea-Bissau, Liberia, Mali, Niger, Nigeria, Senegal, Sierra Leone, and Togo—to the elimination of trafficking and set forth various initiatives, including preparation of an action plan. The action plan itself, the ECOWAS Initial Plan of Action against Trafficking in Persons (2002–03), calls for, among other things, new law enforcement units dedicated specifically to trafficking and special training for officials from police officers to judges.[168]

Conclusion

Nigeria is a leading origin country for human trafficking. While anti-trafficking legislation has been passed, legal prohibition does not address the long list of factors that facilitate human trafficking in Nigeria. These include poverty, limited educational opportunity, limited access to mass media, traditions of child labor and fostering, discrimination against women, and high rates of orphanhood due to HIV/AIDS. Progress against human trafficking in Nigeria will be achieved only in concert with progress on these root-cause issues.

INDIA
India's Role in Human Trafficking

India is listed by the UN as a high-level origin and a high-level destination country for today's enslaved persons, a designation that places it among the world's top 38 origin countries and top 23 destination countries. It is also listed as a medium-level transit country.[169]

While the UN ranks countries according to the number of persons reported trafficked between and through countries, the United States ranks countries according to their efforts to eliminate all trafficking. On this basis, the United States ranks India as a Tier 2 Watch List country, classifying it as a county that "should receive special scrutiny" with regard to its trafficking record.[170] India has been a so-called Watch List country since 2004, when it lost its more favorable Tier 2 listing.[171] The U.S. State Department acknowledges that India does, in fact, meet the Tier 2 definition of a country "not fully comply[ing] with the minimum standards for the elimination of trafficking . . . but mak[ing] significant efforts to do so." Nevertheless, India remains on the Tier 2 Watch List "for its failure to show increasing efforts to tackle India's large and multidimensional problem."[172]

The human trafficking problem in India is indeed severe. While the exact number of victims is not known, it is estimated that 25,000 to 40,000 women and children are trafficked into India for sexual exploitation from Nepal and Bangladesh every year.[173] India's Ministry of Home Affairs (MHA) estimates, however—and outside observers agree—that 90 percent of its country's sex trafficking is internal, meaning that the 25,000 to 40,000 Nepalese and Bangladeshi victims may constitute less than 10 percent of India's sex trafficking victims.

In addition to persons trafficked for sexual exploitation, India also has an estimated 20 million to 65 million bonded laborers, most of whom are Indian nationals and many of whom live in conditions that meet the definition of modern-day slavery. As a medium-level transit country, India is also a temporary location for at least some number of trafficked persons who are passed through its borders. As the 2007 TIP Report summarizes, "India's trafficking in persons problem is estimated to be in the millions."[174]

Origins and Destinations of Persons Trafficked from, within, and to India

The Congressional Reporting Service (CRS) estimates that 150,000 persons are trafficked regionally in South Asia every year and that India is a primary destination country for many of them.[175] India itself is also a high-level source country. Internationally trafficked Indians are most often enslaved in the Gulf States, primarily for involuntary domestic servitude. India also serves as a medium-level transit country, especially for Nepalese and Bangladeshi traffickers and their victims. Nepalese and Bangladeshi women and girls are trafficked through India to Pakistan, generally for sexual exploitation, while Nepalese and Bangladeshi men, women, and children are trafficked through India to the Middle East, primarily for involuntary domestic servitude.[176]

An estimated 250,000 to 500,000 women and girls are trafficked internally every year for prostitution and other commercial sex work. The NGO Shakti Vahini reports that "The problem of trafficking and prostitution is acute in [the states of] Andhra Pradesh, Karnataka, Maharastra, Tamil Nadu, Rajasthan, Uttar Pradesh and West Bengal."[177] Internal trafficking for forced marriage "by coercion or trade"[178] likewise occurs frequently in India. Examining examples from just two states, Shakti Vahini estimates that there are 5,000 to 10,000 such forced marriages in Haryana State's Rewari and Faridabad districts and 4,000 to 5,000 such marriages in Punjab State's Mansa district.[179]

Much forced labor in India is internal as well. In terms of geographic origin, most domestic workers in India's cities—many of whom meet the definition of trafficked persons—are from the country's rural areas.[180] Gender, age, caste, and Scheduled Tribe membership are also origin factors pertinent to domestic servitude recruitment. Of India's domestic workers, for instance, 92 percent are women and children, with 25 percent being between the ages of 15 and 20, and 20 percent being under the age of 14.[181] (Indeed, 90 percent of Indian households surveyed acknowledged that girls 12 to 15 years old would be their "preferred choice" of servant.)[182] Caste and tribal membership are also significant origin factors. Most domestic workers in India are Dalits (members of Hinduism's lowest hereditary social class, formerly known as the untouchables); many others are members of the Scheduled Tribes[183] (tribal peoples also known as *adivasis* or original inhabitants,[184] their approximately 573 communities are "among the poorest in India").[185]

India also has many forced laborers who are not in domestic service, and many of these workers are also held in conditions that meet the definition of modern-day slavery. Here caste and Scheduled Tribe membership are the central origin factors. Although Indian law prohibits caste-based discrimination and the government has "embarked on consultations to protect the rights of Dalits, other marginalized castes, and vulnerable communities," such discrimination, in fact, continues to exist.[186] One consequence is that members of the lower castes (officially referred to as the Scheduled Castes) and Scheduled Tribe communities are the Indians most often enslaved in bonded labor in India.[187]

Exploitation of Trafficking Victims in India
SEXUAL EXPLOITATION

Prostitution

Prostitution is legal in India as long as "no third party is involved, it is not done in or near a public place, it is not forced, there is no solicitation, or when the prostitute resides alone." Nonetheless, the commercial sex trade in India is conducted by third parties in, among other places, massage parlors, nightclubs, hotels, private houses, and, especially, brothels. Trafficking is often involved, and many of those trafficked are under age: UNICEF estimates that of 1 million children engaged in sex work worldwide, half are in India.[188] Moreover, since 1980, the age of these trafficked girls has fallen. As Gary Lewis, chief of UNODC, described it prior to a 2007 regional conference of the UN Global Initiative to Fight Human Trafficking (UN.GIFT):

> The . . . devastating fact is that now Nepali girls below 10 years are being forced into the trade. In the 1980s (trafficked) girls were mostly in the age group of 14–16 and in 1994 the age further reduced to 10–14. But last year girls below the age of 10 were found trapped into the human trafficking business [in India].[189]

As in other countries, victims may be deceived into their enslavement with offers of nonsexual work or with offers of work they understand to involve prostitution, but do not understand to involve enslavement. They may also be abducted and sold into prostitution by strangers[190] or sold into prostitution by their own family members.[191] Regardless of the method by which girls and women are trafficked into sexual enslavement, their experiences are often horrific. Nicholas D. Kristof of the *New York Times* has written that "The brothels of India are the slave plantations of the 21st century," a claim that is borne out by the details of one trafficked woman's story. As Kristof relates, Meena Khatun was abducted from her north Indian village.

While still a child and well before her first menses, she was beaten "with a belt, sticks and an iron rod," forcibly made drunk enough to pass out, and then, while she was still unconscious, prostituted for the first time. Her subsequent life in the brothel included the servicing of 10 to 25 customers each night. It also included being "bred." As Kristof explains, breeding prostitutes "is common in Indian brothels." Sons born to prostituted mothers are used for labor; daughters are used, first, as hostages to influence their mothers' behavior and, later, as prostitutes themselves.[192]

Meena and her children are now free, but most women and girls enslaved in India's sex trades are not as lucky. According to the Global Alliance Against Traffic in Women (GAATW), laws intended to punish traffickers are instead being used to arrest and charge prostituted women, many of whom are actually trafficking victims.[193] This frequently results in trafficking victims becoming "even more deeply enslaved":

> A particularly troubling consequence of the conviction of the large number of women who have been trafficked for purposes of prostitution is that the criminal justice system becomes a means through which trafficked women become even more deeply enslaved. A "spiral of exploitation" was identified in the NHRC [National Human Rights Commission of India] report, whereby trafficked women are arrested and charged for soliciting for prostitution. They are then bailed out by brothel-owners who add the amount paid to secure their release to the debt the women were previously working to pay off, and the women are then forced to work more than before to pay off their higher financial burden.[194]

Reports also indicate that rescued girls are sometimes re-trafficked following rejection by their families and communities of origin.[195]

The consequences of sex trafficking for prostitution in India extend beyond the lives of the victims and, indeed, beyond India's borders. A recent study of Nepalese sex trafficking victims rescued in India, for example, suggests that the transnational spread of HIV/AIDS is due, in part, to human trafficking.[196]

As early as 2002, Holly Burkhalter, director of U.S. Policy for Physicians for Human Rights, testified before the House International Relations Committee about such a possibility:

> Sex trafficking is an almost inevitable death sentence for the victims for several reasons. First, because they are virtually or literally enslaved, trafficking victims have no ability to insist upon condom use and are vulnerable to dangerous sexual practices most associated

with transmission. Second, trafficking victims are forced to endure intercourse with multiple partners. And third, violence is common in commercial sex and particularly prevalent when women or children are forcibly subjected to sex against their will. Injuries and abrasions heighten physical vulnerability to AIDS transmission. And young girls' physically immature bodies are highly vulnerable to injuries, significantly heightening their risk of infection. Moreover, having other sexually transmitted diseases (STDs) heightens the risk of contracting HIV by up to a factor of 10. STDs are more common among women than men, and women often contract STDs at a younger age than men.

. . . Though the percentage of HIV transmissions that can be attributed to trafficking has not, to my knowledge, been determined, it seems highly likely that coercion or forcing millions of cases of girls and women into violent, unprotected sex acts with multiple partners is a significant factor in the spread of the AIDS pandemic. [internal citations omitted][197]

The study of India's Nepalese sex trafficking victims confirms the fears expressed by Dr. Burkhalter. The 2007 study, conducted by Dr. Jay G. Silverman of Harvard's School of Public Health and published in the *Journal of the American Medical Association,* found that, overall, 38 percent of the Nepalese sex trafficking victims tested positive for HIV, and 61 percent of those who had been trafficked before age 15 (one in seven victims) tested HIV positive. Whether accepted upon repatriation, rejected, and/or re-trafficked, these rescued victims leave India to become, as the report describes it, "AIDS risk factor[s] in their home countries."[198] (It should be noted that these HIV infection rates are similar to those found in sex trafficking victims repatriated to Nigeria and discussed above.)

Boys are also trafficked for prostitution in India, a fact that, due to social mores, has only recently begun to be acknowledged.[199]

Forced and Child Marriage
Every year, a large number of women and girls are sold, coerced, or placed by parental decision into forced and/or child marriage in India. Some of these marriages involve adult women, but many involve minors. While the legal age for marriage in India is 18 for girls and 21 for boys, more than half of Indian females marry before 18,[200] and half marry by age 15. Child marriage is not restricted to any one Indian community. Many thousands of Hindu Indian girls in Chhattisgarh, Madhya Pradesh, and Rajasthan are married every year during the festival of Askhay Tritiya, for example, while girls from Scheduled Tribes and Scheduled Castes in Tamil Nadu's Krishnagiri district are routinely married between eight and 12 years of age.[201] There have been reports of marriages involving girls as young as five years old.[202]

The early childbirths associated with early marriage increase the risk of obstructed labor and other complications of childbirth. According to the Office of the Registrar of India, "240 girls die every day due to pregnancy-related complications in early child marriages."[203]

Adult women are also forcibly married in India. Women trafficked internally from the states of Assam and West Bengal, for instance, are sold into marriage in more affluent Haryana and Punjab, two states where a changing male/female sex ratio (due primarily to the selective aborting of female fetuses) has resulted in a "shortage of brides." Girls and women are also trafficked transnationally from neighboring countries, especially Bangladesh, for forced marriages to Indian men.

The experience of being sold into these forced marriages can be every bit as devastating as the experience of being sold into the commercial sex trades. As Kamal Kumar Pandey, secretary of Shakti Vahini, describes it:

> . . . [T]he plight of the victims [is] similar to those in the brothel based sexual exploitation.
> . . . in the trafficking that is going on in Haryana and Punja, these victims of trafficking into coerced marriage never become the part of society (they remain "Paro" or the "Bought" or "Kept" and their children "Children of Paro"), and are sold several times in the life. Living for a period of time as a wife and bearing children does not guarantee them any security. There are cases of women with three children being sold along with children. She at times is separated from her children when sold, at times the buyer may not be willing to take the children along. . . . [T]he victims of coerced marriages are kept in bondage for whole life with only movement when she is resold to another person. These victims of coerced marriages are being forced to live life very akin to medieval sex slavery and are doubled as labour for domestic and agricultural works.
> The victims in brothels are money spinning machines for their Madams, thus have some value but here the victims are merely cheap labour and sex slave, even her medicinal expenses cost more than her real cost and thus have to die early inflicted by various kinds of diseases and infections for want of any medication.[204]

Arranging marriages for young women is a traditional practice in India, as it is in many parts of the world. Child marriages may also be arranged by parents who believe that early marriage benefits their daughters despite evidence that interrupted educations, increased risk for obstetrical problems, and other negative impacts are generally among the consequences, even where the emotional dynamic of a couple is far different from that described above by Secretary Pandey. Moreover, regardless of the intent of those who arrange, coerce, or force a marriage, such unions are in violation of the Universal Declaration of Human Rights's recognition of the right to give "free and full" consent to one's marriage—a consent that a minor is deemed too young to meaningfully give,[205] and a consent that is, all to often, not requested of adult women.[206]

FORCED LABOR

Indian men, women, and children are trafficked into forced labor abroad, including the trafficking of women and children into involuntary domestic servitude in Asian, Middle Eastern, and Western countries, and the trafficking of Indian men into the construction trades in the Arabian Gulf.[207] Persons from other countries are also trafficked into forced labor in India, most often women and girls from Nepal and Bangladesh who are trafficked into involuntary domestic service. Most forced labor in India, is, however, internal.[208]

Involuntary Domestic Servitude

There are approximately 20 million domestic workers in India,[209] most of whom are female,[210] and many of whom are from the Scheduled Castes or Scheduled Tribes. While many of the adult female domestic workers are hired and paid in an aboveboard manner, others—of an indeterminate number—are trafficking victims, ensconced in involuntary domestic servitude.[211]

A greater portion of young domestic workers can be clearly identified as living in involuntary domestic servitude. Almost half of India's domestic workers are younger than 20 years old, with children younger than 14 constituting 20 percent of the domestic workforce and children and young adults between the ages of 15 and 20 constituting 25 percent. The NGO Social Alert reported in 2000:

> Live-in child domestic workers can be boys or girls. Very young boys are employed to fetch water and milk, scrub floors and do some shopping. Young girls live "invisibly" and hidden in the households that adopt them, from the age of 4 on, as orphans or from broken families. Middlemen, agencies, or domestic workers who return to their villages recruit them. Many however go on their own to the big cities to earn money to support their families in the villages. At the age of 12 a girl will be expected to perform all the tasks of a middle-class household. She starts at 5 in the morning by fetching water. Then she prepares the breakfast, cleans the house, prepares lunch, washes and irons clothes, prepares dinner, washes the dishes and goes to bed around midnight. These girls generally sleep on the floor of the kitchen.[212]

A study conducted by Save the Children in 2005 found similar conditions; it also noted a pattern of debt-bondage agreements whereby rural parents send their children to become domestic workers in urban areas, and their child's wages are sent home.[213] Referring to these children as well as to those who were abducted or deceived by strangers, the report concludes, "The treatment and servitude that child domestic workers suffer is akin to slavery."[214]

Other Forms of Forced Labor
Indian men, women, and children are trafficked into forced labor in a variety of settings, and their labor is used in the production of brassware, bricks, carpets, cigarettes, embroidered cloth and other textiles, fireworks, jewelry, milled rice, pottery, semiprecious and gemstones, sugar, tea and all manner of agricultural products, timber, and other goods.[215] Despite the wide range of settings, however, there is an element common to most forced labor in India: debt bondage.

There are an estimated 20 to 65 million persons in India, most of them Indian nationals, currently held in debt bondage.[216] Many are held in the modern-day form of debt bondage that has evolved since the end of legal chattel slavery and become common in many countries, but many others are held in an earlier form of debt-bondage enslavement. This form of debt bondage, what Kevin Bales of Free the Slaves (FTS) calls perhaps "the most ancient and long-lasting of all the world's enslavements," is agricultural debt bondage.[217]

In this system, landlords give full-time laborers a daily portion of rice or unground wheat, plus the farming rights to a small plot of land. There is no other payment. The only income such a bonded laborer can earn is from the sale of any excess food grown on the portion of land set aside for his use and sustenance. When, inevitably, the cost of medicines, fertilizers, and other necessities exceeds a laborer's income, money is borrowed—often, at a high interest rate—from the landlord. Such a cycle can recur year after year, so that debt mounts without hope of repayment. If a man dies with unpaid debt, his debt and bondage status are inherited by his sons. This has occurred in generation after generation in India—Bales posits that it is not impossible for a currently bonded agricultural laborer to represent the 300th generation of his family to be enslaved in agricultural debt bondage—and, despite recent laws to the contrary, it continues still.[218]

OTHER FORMS OF EXPLOITATION

Child Soldiers
Child soldiers have been found in various of India's armed conflicts, including conflicts in Jammu, Kashmir, and Chhattisgarh.[219]

Since the late 1960s, for example, Naxalite insurgents, a communist group originating in West Bengal, have been waging war against the Indian government. The Maoist-inspired Naxalites have a presence in at least 106 of the administrative districts in India and exert control over approximately 20 percent of the country's forests. Naxalite forces use boys and girls as soldiers, most often from the tribal communities whose interests they claim to represent. (Indeed, they are estimated to have the support, "through choice or coercion," of about half the people living in the tribal areas.)[220] In addition to serving as soldiers, girls in the Naxalite forces "are reportedly used for the sexual gratification of older cadres" and also to help disguise Naxalite camps as "ordinary villages."[221]

The Salwa Judum, an anti-Naxalite group based in Chhattisgarh state, also recruits children. There are conflicting reports as to whether the Salwa Judum was created during a spontaneous people's uprising against the Naxalites, or whether its creation was instigated by the Chhattisgarh state government, but there is no dispute that its activities are now assisted by the state. There is also no dispute that it engages in extreme violence. As the Asian Centre for Human Rights reports:

> *The Salwa Judum is far from a peaceful campaign with hundreds of the cadres, 3,200 in Dantewada alone, being given full military training as Special Police Officers (SPOs). The security forces and Salwa Judum activists have been responsible for gross violations of human rights including torture, killings and rape especially during joint operations to bring scattered villages under the Salwa Judum.[222]*

Naxalite and Salwa Judum child soldiers are generally recruited at about age 14. On both sides of the conflict, they act as spies and messengers, walk ahead of adult soldiers to check for antipersonnel mines and other dangers, and fight in combat. When these children die in combat, their leaders often claim that they fought for the other side or that they were bystanders. There have also been reports of child soldiers' bodies being deliberately mutilated after death to eliminate traces of individual identity and obscure the indications of age.[223]

Organ Harvesting

Trafficking for organ harvesting has also become a visible problem in India in recent years, particularly the trafficking in persons for the forced removal of kidneys.[224] In January 2008, police uncovered a kidney-trafficking ring of a size they called "unprecedented." Headed by Dr. Amit Kumar, the trafficking ring included 20 paramedics, five nurses, four doctors, five diagnostic centers, and 10 pathology clinics. Indian newspapers have demanded further investigation into the possibility that police officers were also complicit.[225]

In this trafficking ring, "kidney scouts" traveled to day-laborer sites in India's poorer states, looking for donor matches for prospective transplant patients who had contacted Dr. Kumar. The kidney scouts' cars were outfitted with medical equipment that enabled them to test for donor matches on site. Day laborers in India may make little more than a dollar per day, if hired,[226] and many of them seem to have been induced to take a fraudulently represented test for a small payment. When found to be a donor match to a specific patient, some day laborers apparently agreed to sell one of their kidneys. Others were kidnapped and drugged, however, and some "were held at gunpoint before their organs were harvested."[227] Afterward, the victims were told they would be killed if they ever spoke of what had been done to them.

Between 400 and 500 "transplant tourists" are believed to have received the involuntarily harvested kidneys. When the ring was broken, written inquiries from 48 new foreigners in search of kidneys were found in Dr. Kumar's office.[228]

Considerations Particular to Trafficking in India

POVERTY

India has the world's second most rapidly growing economy, second only to China's. Its gross domestic product (GDP) grew 9.2 percent in 2005, 9.2 percent in 2006, and 8.7 percent growth in 2007. While final figures are not available as this is written, it is believed to be on target for 7 percent growth in 2008. Many millions of people in India have not, however, been reached by this economic boom.

While the percentage of people living in poverty in India has fallen steadily from 39.1 percent in 1987–88, to 29 percent in 2006, about 285 million people still lived in poverty in 2007. Other figures help to illustrate the impact of such poverty on the people affected: In 2005, 24 percent of the population was found to be undernourished,[229] 35 percent of children aged 12 to 23 months had not been vaccinated against measles, 25 percent lacked access to an "improved," or cleaned, water source, and 62 percent lacked access to improved sanitation facilities.[230]

STATUS OF WOMEN

In India, a bias against females is observable even before birth. Although performing ultrasound for the purpose of determining a fetus's sex without a compelling medical reason has been illegal since the passage in 1994 of the Pre-natal Diagnostic Techniques Act (PNDT), such sex-determining ultrasounds have become common in India, as has the aborting of fetuses found to be female. *The Lancet*, a British medical journal, estimates that perhaps 10 million female fetuses have been aborted in this manner during the past two decades, a figure some have criticized as too high. Other figures are not in dispute: In 2006, the national rate of girl to boy births was 927 to 1,000, with a rate of 776 girls to 1,000 boys in one state. (In the United States, the ratio was 952 girls to 1,000 boys, and worldwide it was 935 girls to 1,000 boys.) Moreover, "The problem was also acute among some of the wealthiest and best-educated communities." Female infanticide has also been reported.[231]

Since 1961, dowries have also been prohibited in India. Nonetheless, the dowry tradition has continued in many parts of India, and it contributes to both the demand and supply sides of trafficking in women. The burden of having to provide dowries for one's daughters is "one factor that makes daughters less desirable." Believed to be a contributing factor in female foeticide and infanticide and, thus, in the resulting low rate of female to male births,[232] the need to provide dowries contributes to a shortage of marriageable women and the ensuing demand for trafficked brides. Dowries contribute more directly to the supply side of trafficking in women: Poor parents who know they will not be able to provide an adequate dowry for their daughters are more often—and more easily—induced to sell them.[233]

The prevalence of child marriage is also a reflection and a consequence of the status of women in India.

DISCRIMINATION AGAINST THE SCHEDULED CASTES AND THE SCHEDULED TRIBES

Members of both the Scheduled Castes and the Scheduled Tribes face discrimination in India. Among the Scheduled Castes, Dalits face the most severe discrimination. As Prime Minister Manmohan Singh described it in December 2007:

Dalits have faced a unique discrimination in our society that is fundamentally different from the problems of minority groups in general. The only parallel to the practice of "untouchability" was Apartheid in South Africa. Untouchability is not just social discrimination. It is a blot on humanity.[234]

While Dalits are sometimes able to rise above the barriers and obstacles created by discrimination—indeed, Kocheril Raman Narayanan became India's first Dalit president in 1997—they more often experience a lack of social and occupational mobility. In 2006, for example, many rural Dalits continued to work in agricultural bondage.[235] The fact that caste-bound social structures such as inherited agricultural bondage endure, despite legal repeal, is both an example and a cause of human trafficking.

Discrimination against members of the Scheduled Tribes also results in circumstances favorable to trafficking recruiters. The India Centre for Indigenous and Tribal People reports that the marginalization and poverty so often experienced by tribal women increase their vulnerability to sex traf-ficking and trafficking into forced labor. A study by Sunlaap, an NGO based in West Bengal, further reports that some tribal communities in the states of Uttar Pradesh and Madhya Pradesh now rely on prostitution for suste-nance, including the prostitution of their own children and of children they purchase and raise as their own for the purpose of prostitution. These tribal children are often prostituted in metro stations.[236]

EDUCATION

With more than 300 universities and 15,000 colleges, India has the third larg-est system of higher education in the world.[237] It also has very little gender disparity among children currently attending primary school and a youth (persons aged 12 to 24) literacy rate that has climbed from 64 percent in 1990 to 74 percent in 2005.[238] Nonetheless, the poorest of India's children are frequently ill served by the country's educational system.

In cases where families can afford to send their children to private schools, many choose to do so. More poor families now send their children to school than at any time in India's history, but the government schools they attend "have sunk to spectacularly low levels." The results of a 2007 survey of primary government schools in 16,000 Indian villages found that four out of 10 fifth graders were unable to read at a second-grade level, while seven out of 10 could not perform subtraction. School administrators interviewed following the release of the survey acknowledged underfunded, understaffed, and under-equipped schools, but they also pointed to studies indicating that the children of illiterate parents, as many of these students are, perform worse in school than the children of literate parents. Others questioned whether "poor children from lower castes" were receiving the necessary attention from their teachers. Regardless of the reasons for the test results among these poorest students, the likelihood of a significant percentage progressing to secondary school is small: among the poorest 20 percent of Indian men, only 2 percent have gradu-ated from college.[239] Again, these factors are interrelated and self-reinforcing: Poverty can be both a cause and a consequence of interrupted education, and poverty and lack of education can both be risk factors for trafficking.

GOVERNMENT INACTION AND OFFICIAL CORRUPTION

India has passed anti-trafficking legislation, but that legislation primarily addresses sex trafficking, to the ensuing neglect of bonded laborers. As the U.S. State Department summarizes it, "India's anti-trafficking laws, policies and programs . . . did not recognize the country's huge population of bonded laborers, which NGOs estimate to range from 20 to 65 million laborers, as a significant problem."[240] The 2007 TIP Report, examining the situation in 2006, found that "no substantial efforts" were made to investigate or try those who used bonded labor.[241]

In addition to anti-trafficking legislation, India has passed legislation designed to address such contributory factors as gender, caste, and ethnic minority discrimination. Enforcement of many of these laws is, however, lax.[242] It is also not uncommon for law enforcement officials to be complicit in trafficking activities.[243] Corruption also reduces the effects of government aid: Monies intended to assist bonded agricultural workers or fund schools, for instance, are often diverted away from the proper recipients.[244]

NATURAL DISASTERS

Natural disasters—and the loss of family members, destruction of property, and homelessness that they often cause—are also contributing factors to human trafficking in India. Floods and cyclones, for example, are cited "among the main causes" for the transnational sex trafficking of Bangladeshi girls from Satkhira and Jessore into India for forced marriages in Uttar Pradesh or brothel prostitution in Kolkata (Calcutta) and Mumbai (Bombay), India.[245]

Similarly, natural disasters are a factor in internal trafficking. As Shakti Vahini reports:

> *The perennial problem of floods in Assam, Bihar and droughts and cyclone in Orrisa and Andhra . . . has left a large section of the population in these states at the mercy of nature, suffering untold miseries for long duration[s] . . . and thus compelling them to migrate and hence vulnerable to trafficking and has provided an opportunity to the traffickers to develop well established networks due to regular and continuous availability of the victims.[246]*

India's Efforts to End Trafficking

DOMESTIC EFFORTS TO END TRAFFICKING

As the U.S. State Department asserts, India's anti-trafficking law (the 1956 Prevention of Immoral Traffic Act) does focus its attention on sexual exploitation to the exclusion of debt bondage.[247] That said, India has enacted a number of other measures that address issues related to human trafficking, including debt bondage.

The 1976 Bonded Labour System (Abolition) Act, for example, while not defining bondage as trafficking, nonetheless releases all bonded laborers, cancels their bondage debts, forbids new bondage agreements, and requires the state to provide economic assistance to the individuals who are freed. The Child Labour (Prohibition and Regulation) Act, as passed in 1986, defined child labor as work performed by a child under the age of 14. It neither forbade all child labor nor required that a child worker be of a certain age, but it did regulate hours and safety conditions. It also prohibited the use of child labor in 25 hazardous occupations, including three occupations commonly held by bonded laborers.[248] This act was amended in 2006 to also prohibit the employment of children younger than 14 as domestic servants and in other newly specified occupations.[249]

India has also passed legislation to address child marriage, dowry, female foeticide, and discrimination against lower caste and tribal peoples. The Child Marriage Restraint Act, passed in 1929, set the age of consent at 14 for girls and 18 for males; amended in 1949 and 1978, it now sets the age of consent at 18 for girls and 21 for boys. The Dowry Prohibition Act, passed in 1961 and amended in 1984 and 1986, forbids the paying of dowries and provides for prosecution and criminal penalties for grooms and families who request dowries. The Prohibition of Sex Selection Act (also known as the Pre-natal Diagnostic Techniques Act) was passed in 1994; intended to combat female foeticide, this act forbids the use of ultrasound to determine the sex of a fetus, unless there is a compelling medical reason. The Scheduled Caste and the Scheduled Tribes (Preventions of Atrocities) Act, intended to combat two forms of discrimination that are root causes of trafficking in India, was passed in 1989.

However, there are serious deficits in the enforcement of all of these legislative measures. In some areas, the government has taken few or no enforcement measures. As reported in the 2008 TIP Report, "[g]overnment authorities made no progress in addressing one of India's largest human trafficking problems—bonded labor. . . . government authorities do not proactively identify and rescue bonded laborers. . . ." Likewise, although legislation was passed to prohibit children from working in hotels or as domestic servants, "the government did not demonstrate efforts to enforce the law." Official corruption also remains a problem, with corrupt officers, among other things, "protect[ing] brothels that exploit women and protect[ing] traffickers and brothel keepers from arrest and other threats of enforcement." While sex traffickers are arrested, convictions are rare: In 2006, for example, 1,289 people were arrested for trafficking, but only four of these people were convicted and sentenced to jail.[250]

There are also a number of NGOs working to end human trafficking in India. These include the South Asian Coalition on Child Servitude (SACCS), which assists individual child laborers (its head, Kailash Satyarthi, is credited with "liberat[ing] more than 75,000 bonded and child laborers since 1980);[251] Shakti Vahini, which, among other things, publishes a TIP Report that examines human trafficking in each of India's states; and Apne Aap, an organization devoted to assisting prostituted women and eliminating sex trafficking. The National Campaign on Dalit Human Rights works to eliminate caste discrimination, and Bharathi Trust works among the tribal communities in Tamil Nadu to, among other things, secure the freedom of bonded laborers.

INDIA'S PARTICIPATION IN INTERNATIONAL EFFORTS TO END TRAFFICKING

India is a party to a number of the international instruments that prohibit various forms of modern slavery. It has signed but not ratified the UN Protocol (meaning that it is not legally bound to abide by this convention). It has signed and ratified the Optional Protocol to the Convention on the Rights of the Child on the Sale of Children, Child Prostitution and Child Pornography, the Optional Protocol to the Convention on the Rights of the Child in Armed Conflict, and the Hague Convention on Intercountry Adoption. While it ratified two of the three ILO conventions relating to modern-day slavery—ILO Convention 29, Concerning Forced Labor, and ILO Convention 105, Abolition of Forced Labor—it has not ratified the third major convention, ILO Convention 182, Concerning the Prohibition and Immediate Action for the Elimination of the Worst Forms of Child Labor.

India is also a party to UN instruments that address poverty and discrimination against women and ethnic minorities, three of the root causes of human trafficking in the country. The UN Millennium Declaration (2000) was unanimously adopted by the leaders of 189 member nations, including India. India has also signed and ratified the UN Convention on the Elimination of All Forms of Discrimination against Women, subject to declaration and reservation. (Of particular importance among the declarations and reservations is India's declaration that it will work to modify "cultural patterns of conduct of men and women" to eliminate prejudices only insofar as it can do so while conforming to its country's "policy of non-interference in the personal affairs of any Community without its initiative and consent," and a reservation stating that India will not be bound by an article requiring that men and women have [t]he same right to enter into marriage.")[252] India is also a party to the UN Convention on the Elimination of all Forms of Racial Discrimination (1965), without reservation.

In addition, India is a party with other members of the South Asian Association for Regional Cooperation (SAARC)—a political and economic association that also includes Afghanistan, Bangladesh, Bhutan, Maldives, Nepal, Pakistan, and Sri Lanka—to the 2002 SAARC Convention on Trafficking and 2002 SAARC Convention on Child Welfare.

Conclusion

Of all the countries discussed in this chapter, India has, by far, the largest number of enslaved people. It is not only a high-level origin and a high-level destination country for internationally trafficked persons, but a country that has up to 65 million of its own nationals enslaved—many of them from birth—within its borders. These internally enslaved people are held in a debt bondage that is now illegal in India, but tacitly permitted. Other illegal but nonetheless practiced forms of human trafficking in India include trafficking into the sex trades, forced and child marriage, involuntary domestic servitude, the use of child soldiers, and organ harvesting. The list of root causes is also long: poverty, discrimination against women and members of the scheduled castes and scheduled tribes, limited educational opportunities, government inaction and official corruption, and even natural disasters; all these are among the factors facilitating human trafficking in India.

BELIZE

Belize's Role in Human Trafficking

Belize is listed by the United Nations as a low-level origin[253] and a very low-level destination country.[254] In addition, it is absent from the UN's list of transit countries.[255] In terms of the number of persons trafficked, then, Belize has a considerably smaller problem than many other countries.

The United States's rankings are based, however, not on the reported number of trafficked persons, but on a country's efforts to eliminate all trafficking activity within its borders. Based on this criteria, Belize was one of only 12 countries to receive a Tier 3 ranking in the 2006 TIP Report. Moreover, this was not the first time Belize received this so-called worst offender ranking: It was also listed as a Tier 3 country in 2003. (Belize is the only one of the four countries considered herein ever to have received this lowest-possible ranking.)

The U.S. State Department described its 2006 decision as being based on an assessment of Belize's traffic prevention strategies, its enforcement and victim-assistance efforts, and its legislative initiatives:

> *The Government of Belize does not fully comply with the minimum standards for the elimination of trafficking and is not making significant efforts to do so. . . . Laws against trafficking remain weak and largely unenforced, adult victims received no attention or assistance, and the government made no significant effort to raise public awareness and work with vulnerable populations.*[256]

A Tier 3 ranking is accompanied by the possible loss of U.S. financial aid and other sanctions meant to be punitive and meant to prompt change in a country's response to human trafficking within its borders.

There is no dispute that far fewer persons are trafficked to and from Belize than are trafficked to many other countries. Indeed, so few incidents of trafficking were reported in 2001 and 2002 that Belize was not even considered for a tier ranking in those years.[257] That said, human trafficking does take place in Belize. Women and children (primarily female children) are trafficked to and from Belize for sexual exploitation and forced labor. Internal trafficking is also reported, particularly the trafficking of girls into the sex trades or underage marriages.[258]

After its debut as a Tier 3 country in 2003, the Belize government commissioned a study of human trafficking within its borders[259] and passed anti-trafficking legislation. Following these measures, Belize received an improved Tier 2 Watch List ranking in both 2004 and 2005. (Countries are placed on this list if a tier-placement improvement is based on promised future action, if efforts against trafficking stall or decrease, or if the number of trafficking victims increases rather than decreases. Generally speaking, countries moving from either Tier 1 or 3 are often initially placed on the Tier 2 Watch List, where they will receive "special scrutiny.")

After two years as a Watch List country—two years in which the U.S. State Department found, among other things, that enforcement of the new anti-trafficking legislation was lax—Belize was returned to the Tier 3 list in 2006 where it once again faced U.S. financial sanctions. Belize then "made substantial improvement in combating human trafficking" and was listed as a Tier 2 country in the 2007 TIPS Report.[260]

Origins and Destinations of Persons Trafficked from, within, and to Belize

Most women and girls trafficked into the commercial sex trades in Belize are from other Central American countries, including Guatemala and El Salvador. Women and girls from Central America have also been trafficked into forced labor in Belize, as have Chinese and Indian nationals. Belizean girls are trafficked internally into the sex trades. Belizean women have also reportedly been trafficked from Belize for sexual exploitation in other countries.

Exploitation of Belize's Trafficking Victims
SEXUAL EXPLOITATION

Women and girls trafficked into Belize for sexual exploitation are prostituted or forced to engage in stripping and exotic dancing.[261] These internationally trafficked victims are most often deceived by trafficking agents who themselves deliver them into enslavement, but there have also been reports of complicit Belizean taxi drivers "deliver[ing] women to brothels." The brothel or bar owners generally confiscate the passports and other identity documents of internationally trafficked victims. These women and girls are then housed in substandard conditions, including in the bars where many of them are forced to work.

Belizean girls are also trafficked internally into Belize's sex trades, sometimes with the knowledge and consent of their parents or other family members. In many of these cases, a family's daughter is not the first in the family to be so prostituted:

> *The government's National Committee for Families and Children reported instances of minors engaged in prostitution with older male clientele, in some cases of their own volition, in others arranged by their family. The girls were typically of high-school age, but some as young as 12 were reported, and came from economically disadvantaged families in which their mothers were also victims of the same abuse.*[262]

The U.S. State Department found in 2005 that many girls had been sold to older men (usually family friends) as brides. In 2006, there were also reports that some girls had been sold to older men for sexual exploitation,[263] while other girls have engaged in sexual relations with older men in return for clothing, school fees and books, or jewelry.[264]

FORCED LABOR

Forced labor in Belize has included the use of children to sell newspapers and shine shoes and the use of Chinese nationals to staff sweatshops. In addition, there have been reports of victims being trafficked from India to Belize as bonded laborers. In the case of Chinese and Indian victims, the traffickers are generally Chinese and Indian immigrants who settle in Belize and then exploit their former countrymen and women.[265]

Considerations Particular to Trafficking in Belize

Belize has a low incidence of persons trafficked. The following considerations shed light on the trafficking that currently occurs but, equally important, they also point to where Belize is vulnerable to increased trafficking.

HISTORY AND GEOGRAPHY

Having achieved independence from Britain on September 21, 1981, Belize is a young nation and one still at work on its institutional and public policy framework. Its geography—Belize is located south of Mexico and east of Guatemala, with its entire eastern boundary open to the Caribbean Sea—combines with this still-developing political framework to invite both entry and human trafficking. As Juan Miguel Petit, the UN rapporteur on the sale of children, child prostitution, and child pornography, describes it in the TIP in Belize Preliminary Report:

> *Belize has a long and open border particularly difficult to control without a large amount of human, technological and economic resources. . . .*
> *As a young country, Belize is still building its institutional area. . . . the model of a cohesive public policy system able to react with flexibility when facing new challenges, is still under construction. Hence, migratory flow towards Belize is, on occasions, a serious problem that doesn't find an effective answer. . . . It is well known that . . . the multiplication of human trafficking . . . flourishes in a society where . . . the policies are too weak to tackle the intense migratory flow.*[266]

SHIFTING DEMOGRAPHICS

A former British colony, Belize's population was for many years primarily composed of native Mayans and English-speakers of African descent. The country is now a multiethnic one, with a large Spanish-speaking population and immigrants from China, Europe, India, and the Middle East. Of concern to those working against human trafficking is evidence that the Chinese and Indian communities are isolated within Belize; social service groups and other organizations report that these groups' limited contact with other Belizeans makes it difficult to identify cases of human trafficking. Other studies point to the incomplete "socio-economic integration of Central American immigrants into Belize" and suggest that their lower standard of living may reflect an "anti Central American" bias in a country that, as a British colony, may have identified more with its Caribbean neighbors than its Central American neighbors.[267] While there is little or inconclusive evidence of forced labor among Central American immigrant workers on Belizean plantations, there is evidence that they are frequently deceived as to the working conditions they will find.

While some immigrant groups may be more at risk than others by virtue of isolation or discrimination, the level of immigration into Belize has itself become sufficient to cause political and social strains that contribute to human trafficking:

> *Some of the conclusions . . . point out the big impact that immigration is producing in the society of Belize, particularly in the coverage of social matters. These effects are very important . . . because they show an increase of social risk situations. This means lack of resources for family needs, difficulties in school coverage and no responses for the starting up of social deterioration in which family violence, prostitution at young ages and lack of socialization possibilities, become the first step to trafficking cases.*[268]

POVERTY

According to Belize's 2002 Poverty Assessment Report, 33 percent of its people are poor and 13.4 percent were extremely poor (defined as being unable to meet basic food needs).[269] Rural Belizeans are more often poor than their urban counterparts (44.2 percent v. 23.7 percent). Native Maya are the poorest Belizeans, with 77 percent of the Mayan population assessed as poor and 54.8 percent meeting the definition of very poor.

EDUCATION

Belize's educational system is better run and better utilized than others in the region. Almost 100 percent of children matriculate in the early years of primary school, and the country has a primary school student-teacher ratio of 25-1. Moreover, the country has a 93 percent literacy rate. That said, only 55 percent of the children who begin primary school actually complete that stage of their education, and only 50 percent of children who take the entrance exam to secondary school pass it. An investigation by the Human Rights Commission of Belize in 2003 into the country's high rates of primary school absenteeism and incompletion found that "families aren't really motivated" and that many of the children hold wage-paying jobs. There is also low attendance among those admitted to secondary school and, here, financial strains are an additional factor. While no tuition is charged, there are ancillary fees that many families cannot afford, including fees for uniforms, school books, and the like.[270] (Indeed, payment of school fees is specifically cited in many cases of sexual exploitation involving girls.)[271]

PROSTITUTION

In Belize, there has long been a demand for prostitutes from foreign countries. Most observers agree that this demand is related to Belizean men wishing to remain anonymous and/or unrecognized when using a prostitute.[272] While there have been fewer trafficking victims in Belize than elsewhere, there have been reports of foreign-born women being trafficked into brothels.[273]

SEX TOURISM

Belize has become an adventure and ecotourism destination, one that its official tourism board has successfully sought to position as a site for destination weddings, family adventure holidays, honeymoons, and couple getaways. There have also been reports of sex tourism, however, including the exploitation of children.[274]

OFFICIAL INACTION AND CORRUPTION

It is widely acknowledged that Belize does not have many reported instances of human trafficking and that its debut as a Tier 3 country in the 2003 TIP Report "was a surprise for many people and officials in Belize."[275] That said, there were at least some cases of human trafficking prior to 2003, no Belizean law prohibiting it until 2003, and limited enforcement of that law in 2004 and 2005. Official inaction between 2004 and 2005 included limited investigation of trafficking cases; an application of the lightest possible sentences in the few trafficking convictions sought and obtained (one-year sentences were the norm, when up to five were permitted under the 2003 law); inadequate social, health, and witness-protection assistance for victims; and no notable efforts to raise public awareness about human trafficking.[276] Beginning in 2006, the government of Belize has significantly increased its efforts to end human trafficking within its borders.

Belize's Efforts to End Human Trafficking
DOMESTIC EFFORTS TO END TRAFFICKING

Following its listing as a Tier 3 country in 2003, Belize passed its Trafficking in Persons Prohibition Act of 2003. In that same year, it also commissioned Juan Miguel Petit, the UN's Special Rapporteur on the sale of children, child prostitution, and child pornography, to prepare a report on human trafficking in Belize. In response to these measures, the U.S. State Department moved Belize to the Tier 2 Watch List (a category for nations moved up from Tier 3 and, in the State Department's view, requiring special scrutiny). In August 2005, Belize also raised the age at which girls were permitted to marry with parental consent from 14 to 16, a move intended to prevent men from evading prosecution for rape by marrying their child victims. Enforcement of these new laws and implementation of Petit's report were deemed minimal, however, and Belize was returned to the Tier 3 list in 2006.

In 2006, Belize increased its investigation of trafficking, including conducting unannounced raids on brothels that resulted in the rescue of seven trafficked women during a two-month period. It also "revitalize[d]" its Anti-trafficking Committee, which held a number of anti-trafficking training programs for Belize's immigration officials, police officers, and social workers.[277] Taking further action, the government arrested three police officers (two for trafficking and one for exploiting victims of trafficking).

The Belizean government also worked to heighten public awareness of human trafficking. During the summer of 2006, for example, it held meetings to discuss involuntary domestic servitude and human trafficking with members of the Indian community, and it began a nationwide, multimedia trafficking awareness campaign.

The Belizean government also acted against child sex tourism in 2006, prosecuting four foreigners for sexual offenses against children and returning a fifth, untried, to his country.[278] The country's tourist industry organized to combat child sex tourism as well. In August 2006, the Belize Tourism Industry Association (BTIA)—the representative organization of more than 500 tourism businesses in Belize—signed ECPAT's Code of Conduct for the Protection of Children from Commercial Sexual Exploitation in Travel and Tourism, which commits tourism personnel to abide by six criteria intended to prevent the trafficking of children for sexual exploitation. ECPAT-USA and BTIA also launched the Protect Children in Tourism Project to provide compliance training for Belize's tourism industry personnel and to publicize the code of conduct.

Citing Belize's "substantial improvement in combating human trafficking since the release of the 2006 Report," the U.S. State Department listed Belize as a Tier 2 country in 2007, bypassing the Tier 2 Watch List placement that is generally given to countries moving up from the Tier 3 "black list."

BELIZE'S PARTICIPATION IN INTERNATIONAL EFFORTS TO END TRAFFICKING

Belize is a party to a number of the international instruments that prohibit various forms of modern slavery. It has not signed the UN Protocol or the Hague Convention on Intercountry Adoption, but it has assented to both instruments (an action equivalent to ratification). It has signed and ratified the Optional Protocol to the Convention on the Rights of the Child on the Sale of Children, Child Prostitution and Child Pornography and the Optional Protocol to the Convention on the Rights of the Child in Armed Conflict. It has also ratified all three of the ILO conventions directly relating to modern-day slavery—ILO Convention 29, Concerning Forced Labor; ILO Convention 105, Abolition of Forced Labor; and ILO Convention 182, Concerning the Prohibition and Immediate Action for the Elimination of the Worst Forms of Child Labor.

Belize is also a party to UN instruments that address poverty and discrimination against women, two root causes of human trafficking. The UN Millennium Declaration (2000) was unanimously adopted by the leaders of 189 member nations, including Belize. Belize has also signed and ratified the UN Convention on the Elimination of All Forms of Discrimination against Women. Finally, Belize is a member of the Latin American Network for Missing Persons.

Conclusion

Compared to other countries discussed in this chapter, Belize has a small number of trafficking victims. In the United States's view, Belize nonetheless merited a Tier 3 ranking in 2003 and 2006 due to insufficient action to prevent modern slavery within its borders. While the United States has sometimes been criticized for appearing to take political alliances and other issues into account when assigning a TIP ranking, an examination of Belize's response to its 2003 and 2006 Tier 3 rankings—and the U.S. sanctions Tier 3 countries face—provide evidence that the U.S. TIP Reports and rankings are having an effect in the fight against modern-day slavery.

---

[1] UNODC. "Trafficking in Persons: Global Patterns" (2006), p. 20. Available online. URL: http://www.unodc.org/pdf/traffickinginpersons_report_2006-04.pdf. Accessed June 6, 2006.

[2] ———. "Trafficking in Persons: Global Patterns" (2006), p. 18.

[3] ———. "Trafficking in Persons: Global Patterns" (2006), p. 19.

[4] U.S. Department of State. "Trafficking in Persons Report: (2007)," p. 42. Available online. URL: http://www.state.gov.documents/organization/82902.pdf. Accessed July 31, 2007.

[5] ———. "Trafficking in Persons Report: (2007)," p. 156.

[6] Commission of the European Communities, DG Justice & Home Affairs. "Research Based on Case Studies of Victims of Trafficking in Human Beings in 3 EU Member States, i.e., Belgium, Italy, and the Netherlands" (2003), p. 274. Available online. URL: http://www.ontheroadonlus.it/rootdown/RapIppocra.pdf. Accessed January 12, 2008.

[7] United Nations Economic and Social Council. "Integration of the Human Rights of Women and the Gender Perspective: Violence Against Women" (2003), p. 314. Available online. URL: http://www.unhchr.ch/Huridocda/Huridoca.nsf/0/a9c6321593428acfc1256cef0038513e?Open document. Accessed January 2, 2008.

[8] Freedom House. "Freedom in the World—Netherlands (2006)." Available online. URL: http://www.freedomhouse.org/inc/content/pubs/fiw/inc_country_detail.cfm?year=2006<0x0026>country=7026&pf. Accessed January 15, 2008.

[9] U.S. Department of State. "Trafficking in Persons Report: (2007)," p. 156; Freedom House. "Freedom in the World—Netherlands (2006)."

[10] UNODC. "Trafficking in Persons: Global Patterns" (2006), p. 19.

[11] Bureau Nationaal Rapporteur Mensenhandel. "Trafficking in Human Beings, Supplementary Figures: Fourth Report of the Dutch National Rapporteur" (2005), pp. 17–18, 39. Available online. URL: http://rechten.uvt.nl/victimology/national/NL-NRMEngels4.pdf. Accessed December 26, 2007.

[12] ECPAT. "Global Monitoring: Report on the Status of Action against Commercial Sexual Exploitation of Children, the Netherlands" (2006), p. 11. Available online. URL: http://www.ecpat.nl/ariadne/loader.php/en/ecpat/documenten/Global_Monitoring_Report<0x2014>NETHERLANDS.pdf/. Accessed January 2, 2008.

[13] U.S. Department of State. "Trafficking in Persons Report: (2007)," p. 156.

[14] Commission of the European Communities, DG Justice & Home Affairs. "Research Based on Case Studies," p. 275.

[15] U.S. Department of State. "Trafficking in Persons Report: (2007)," p. 156.

[16] Commission of the European Communities, DG Justice & Home Affairs. "Research Based on Case Studies," p. 275.

[17] ECPAT. "Global Monitoring: Report on the Status of Action against Commercial Sexual Exploitation of Children, the Netherlands" (2006), p. 11.

18 ———. "Global Monitoring: Report on the Status of Action against Commercial Sexual Exploitation of Children, the Netherlands" (2006), p. 11.

19 Bureau Nationaal Rapporteur Mensenhandel. "Trafficking in Human Beings, Supplementary Figures: Fourth Report of the Dutch National Rapporteur" (2005), p. 21. Available online. URL: http://rechten.uvt.nl/victimology/national/NL-NRMEngels4.pdf. Accessed December 26, 2007.

20 Commission of the European Communities, DG Justice & Home Affairs. "Research Based on Case Studies," pp. 286–287.

21 ———. "Research Based on Case Studies," p. 311.

22 ———. "Research Based on Case Studies," p. 306.

23 ———. "Research Based on Case Studies," p. 298.

24 ECPAT. "Global Monitoring: Report on the Status of Action against Commercial Sexual Exploitation of Children, the Netherlands" (2006).

25 Commission of the European Communities, DG Justice & Home Affairs. "Research Based on Case Studies," p. 275.

26 Stichting Defense for Children International the Netherlands. "Investigating Exploitation: Research into Trafficking in Children in the Netherlands" (2005), p. 27. Available online. URL: http://polis.osce.org/library/f/2716/549/NGO-NLD-RPT-2716-EN-Investigating%20 Exploitatio n.pdf. Accessed December 21, 2007.

27 ECPAT. "Global Monitoring: Report on the Status of Action against Commercial Sexual Exploitation of Children, the Netherlands" (2006).

28 ———. "Global Monitoring: Report on the Status of Action against Commercial Sexual Exploitation of Children, the Netherlands" (2006).

29 Stichting Defense for Children International the Netherlands. "Investigating Exploitation: Research into Trafficking in Children in the Netherlands" (2005), p. 45.

30 ———. "Investigating Exploitation: Research into Trafficking in Children in the Netherlands" (2005), p. 49.

31 ———. "Investigating Exploitation: Research into Trafficking in Children in The Netherlands" (2005), p. 5.

32 The Netherlands Ministry of Foreign Affairs. "Dutch Policy on Prostitution: Questions and Answers, 2005," p. 1. Available online. URL: http://www.prostitutionprocon.org/pdf/ netherlnds/pdf. Accessed December 26, 2007.

33 ———. "Dutch Policy on Prostitution: Questions and Answers, 2005," p. 6.

34 Dr. Janice G. Raymond. "Letter to the Office to Monitor and Combat Trafficking in Persons, Department of State, March 6, 2002." Available online. URL: http://action.web. ca/home/catw/readingroom.shtml?x=12782. Accessed December 26, 2007.

35 Bob Herbert. "Fantasies, Well Meant." *New York Times* (9/11/07).

36 "Amsterdam to Clean Up 'Red Light' District." Reuters (12/17/07); "Amsterdam Turns off the Red Lights as Mayor Seeks a Smarter Image." *Times* (London, 9/29/07).

37 ECPAT. "Global Monitoring: Report on the Status of Action against Commercial Sexual Exploitation of Children, the Netherlands" (2006); Stichting Defense for Children Interna-

tional the Netherlands. "Investigating Exploitation: Research into Trafficking in Children in the Netherlands" (2005), p. 33.

[38] ———. "Investigating Exploitation: Research into Trafficking in Children in the Netherlands" (2005), p. 58.

[39] U.S. Department of State. "Trafficking in Persons Report" (2006), p. 188. Available online. URL: http://www.state.gov/documents/organization66086.pdf. Accessed June 5, 2007.

[40] "Amsterdam to Clean Up 'Red Light' District." Reuters (12/17/07); "Amsterdam Turns off the Red Lights as Mayor Seeks a Smarter Image." *Times* (London, 9/29/07).

[41] Marlise Simons. "Amsterdam Tries Upscale Fix for Red Light District Crime." *New York Times* (2/24/08).

[42] "Amsterdam to Clean Up 'Red Light' District." Reuters (12/17/07).

[43] U.S. Department of State. "Trafficking in Persons Report: (2007)," p. 156; ———. "Trafficking in Persons Report: (2008)", p. 191.

[44] ———. "Trafficking in Persons Report: (2007)," p. 156.

[45] ———. "Trafficking in Persons Report: (2007)," p. 156; United Nations Information Service. "UNODC Head Welcomes Dutch Campaign against Sexual Exploitation" (1/12/06). Available online. URL: http://www.unis.unvienna.org/unis/pressrls/2006/uniscp259.html. Accessed March 20, 2008.

[46] Commission of the European Communities, DG Justice & Home Affairs. "Research Based on Case Studies," pp. 266–268.

[47] Bureau Nationaal Rapporteur Mensenhandel. "Trafficking in Human Beings, Supplementary Figures: Fourth Report of the Dutch National Rapporteur" (2005), pp. 17–18, 39. Available online. URL: http://rechten.uvt.nl/victimology/national/NL-NRMEngels4.pdf. Accessed December 26, 2007.

[48] U.S. Department of State. "Trafficking in Persons Report: (2008), p. 191.

[49] ———. "Trafficking in Persons Report: (2007)," p. 226.

[50] United Nations. "United Nations Millennium Declaration, State Parties." Available online. URL: http://www.un.org/millennium/declaration/ares552e.htm. Accessed December 31, 2007.

[51] ———. "Convention on the Elimination of All Forms of Discrimination against Women." Available online. URL: http://www.un.org/womenwatch/daw/cedaw/states.htm. Accessed January 2, 2008.

[52] UNODC. "Trafficking in Persons: Global Patterns" (2006), p. 19.

[53] ———. "Trafficking in Persons: Global Patterns" (2006), p. 20.

[54] ———. "Trafficking in Persons: Global Patterns" (2006), p. 19.

[55] U.S. Department of State. "Trafficking in Persons Report: (2007)," p. 12.

[56] ———. "Trafficking in Persons Report: (2004)," p. 71. Available online. URL: http://www.state.sou/g/tip/rls/tiprpt/2004. Accessed October 25, 2008.

[57] AFRUCA. "Nigerians in London: Working Together to Safeguard Trafficked Children." Available online. URL: http://www.afruca.org/documents/nigerian_trafficking_event_advert.pdf. Accessed January 4, 2008.

[58] WOCON. "Special Focus on Human Trafficking." Available online. URL: http://www.wocononline.org/about_us.html. Accessed February 1, 2008.

[59] Jonathan Clayton. "The Lost Children of Nigeria's Sex Trade." *Times* (London, 4/5/04).

[60] Toye Olori. "Nigeria Imposes Life Sentence for Human Traffickers." Inter Press Service (7/28/03). Available online. URL: http://us.oneworld.net/article/view/64448/1/. Accessed February 1, 2008.

[61] AFRUCA. "Nigerians in London: Working Together to Safeguard Trafficked Children." Available online. URL: http://www.afruca.org/documents/nigerian_trafficking_event_advert.pdf. Accessed January 4, 2008.

[62] Hamila Oyagbola. "Human Trafficking: The Nigerian Woman as an Endangered Species." Available online. URL: http://www.globaljusticecenter.org/papers2005/oyagbola_eng.htm. Accessed October 2, 2008.

[63] UNICEF Innocenti Research Centre. "Trafficking in Human Beings, Especially Women and Children, in Africa," p. 21. Available online. URL: http://www.unicef.org/protection/files/insight8e.pdf. Accessed January 15, 2008.

[64] Adeze Ojukwu. "Nigeria/West Africa: Human Trafficking." *Daily Champion* (Lagos, 9/21/06). Available online. URL: http://www.stopdemand.com/afawcs0112878ID=180/newsdetails.html. Accessed February 1, 2008.

[65] NAHTIWA. "Country Reports: Nigeria." Available online. URL: http://nahtiwa.virtualactivism.net/countryreports.htm. Accessed February 1, 2008.

[66] ILO/International Programme on the Elimination of Child Labour. "Combating Trafficking in Children for Labour Exploitation in West and Central Africa," pp. 12–13. Available online. URL: http://portal.unesco.org/shs/en/files/3602/10718321711ilochildtrafficking.pdf/ilochildtrafficking .pdf. Accessed January 20, 2008.

[67] U.S. Department of State. "Trafficking in Persons Report: (2007)," p. 160; "Trafficking in Persons Report" (2006), p. 193.

[68] ———. "Trafficking in Persons Report" (2006), p. 193.

[69] Atika Balal. "Nigeria: Human Trafficking—A View from Edo State." Available online. URL: http://www.ungift.org/index.php?option=com_content&task=view&id=365<0x0026>Itemid=676. Accessed February 2, 2008.

[70] NAHTIWA. "Country Reports: Nigeria." Available online. URL: http://nahtiwa.virtualactivism.net/countryreports.htm. Accessed February 1, 2008.

[71] UNESCO. "Policy Paper No. 14.2(E), Human Trafficking in Nigeria: Root Causes and Recommendations" (2006), p. 14. Available online. URL: http://unesdoc.unesco.org/images/0014/001478/147844E.pdf. Accessed December 17, 2007.

[72] NAHTIWA. "Country Reports: Nigeria."

[73] Deborah Thomas, Kamari Clarke, et al. *Globalization and Race: Transformations in the Cultural Production of Blackness*. Durham, N.C.: Duke University Press, 2006, pp. 217–218.

[74] WOCON. "Special Focus on Human Trafficking."

[75] Oyagbola. "Human Trafficking: The Nigerian Woman as an Endangered Species."

[76] U.S. Department of State. "Trafficking in Persons Report: (2007)," p. 160.

[77] Dan McDougall. "The Scandal of Africa's Trafficked Players." *Observer* (London, 1/6/08).

[78] UNODC. "Measures to Combat Trafficking in Human Beings in Benin, Nigeria and Togo" (2006), p. 32. Available online. URL: www.unodc.org/documentsw/humantrafficking/ht_researchreports_nigeria.pdf. Accessed December 17, 2007.

[79] Joe Bavier. "Children's Rescue Highlights Nigeria's Battle with Trafficking." Voice of America (3/8/05). Available online. URL: http://www.voanews.com/english/archive/2005-03/2005-03-08-voa28.cfm?CFID=201675665< 0x0026>CFTOKEN=29018006. Accessed February 2, 2008.

[80] UN Office for the Coordination of Human Affairs, Integrated Regional Information Networks. "Nigeria: Dream of Freedom Turns to Prostitution Nightmare." Available online. URL: http://www.irinnews.org/report.aspx?reportid=57008. Accessed: February 2, 2007.

[81] "Nigeria: Stepping Up Anti-Human Trafficking Crusade." *Daily Champion* (Lagos, 8/31/04); Ian Pannell. "Trafficking Nightmare for Nigerian Children." BBC News (1/20/01). Available online. URL: http://news.bbc.co.uk/1/hi/world/africa/841928.stm. Accessed February 19, 2008.

[82] UNESCO. "Policy Paper No. 14.2(E), Human Trafficking in Nigeria: Root Causes and Recommendations" (2006), p. 28.

[83] Donna M. Hughs, Laura Joy Sporcic, Nadine Z. Mendelsohn, Vanessa Chirgwin. CATW. "The Factbook on Global Sexual Exploitation—Italy" (1999). Available online. URL: http://www.uri.edu/artsci/wms/hughes/factbook.htm. Accessed February 19, 2008.

[84] UNESCO. "Policy Paper No. 14.2(E), Human Trafficking in Nigeria: Root Causes and Recommendations" (2006), p. 28.

[85] ———. "Policy Paper No. 14.2(E), Human Trafficking in Nigeria: Root Causes and Recommendations" (2006), p. 37.

[86] ———. "Policy Paper No. 14.2(E), Human Trafficking in Nigeria: Root Causes and Recommendations" (2006), p. 28.

[87] UNODC. "Measures to Combat Trafficking in Human Beings in Benin, Nigeria and Togo" (2006), p. 65; Ekemini Yemi-Ladejobi. "Nigeria—Evils of Human Trafficking." *Daily Champion* (Lagos, 8/18/07).

[88] Yemi-Ladejobi. "Nigeria—Evils of Human Trafficking."

[89] Francis Awowole-Browne. "Shameful—In Spite of Efforts at Curbing Prostitution, Nigerian Girls Still Litter Streets of European Countries." *Daily Sun* (Nigeria, 7/3/06).

[90] Bureau Nationaal Rapporteur Mensenhandel. "Trafficking in Human Beings, Supplementary Figures: Fourth Report of the Dutch National Rapporteur" (2005), p. 21. Available online. URL: http://rechten.uvt.nl/victimology/national/NL-NRMEngels4.pdf. Accessed December 26, 2007.

[91] Atika Balal. "Nigeria: Human Trafficking—A View from Edo State."

[92] Jonathan Clayton. "The Lost Children of Nigeria's Sex Trade." *Times* (London, 4/5/04); CNN. "Inside Africa: A Look at Human Trafficking in Nigeria" (9/16/06). Transcript available online. URL: http://transcripts/cnn/.com/TRANSCRIPTS/0609/16/i_if.0.1.html. Accessed January 20, 2008; Yemi-Ladejobi. "Nigeria—Evils of Human Trafficking"; UNODC. "Measures to Combat Trafficking in Human Beings in Benin, Nigeria and Togo" (2006), p. 65.

[93] UNODC. "Measures to Combat Trafficking in Human Beings in Benin, Nigeria and Togo" (2006), p. 52.

[94] "Victims of Trafficking Contract Aids." *Daily Champion* (Lagos, 8/16/07).

[95] Atika Balal. "Nigeria: Human Trafficking—A View from Edo State."

[96] ILO. "Review of Legislation and Policies in Nigeria on Human Trafficking and Forced Labour" (2006), p. 1. Available online. URL: http://www.ilo.org/wcmsp5/groups/publication/wcms_083149.pdf. Accessed December 20, 2007.

[97] Population Council. "The Experience of Married Adolescent Girls in Northern Nigeria" (2007), pp. vii, 16. Available online. URL: http://www.popcouncil.org/pdfs/Nigeria_MarriedAdol.pdf. Accessed January 2, 2008.

[98] ———. "Nigeria: Addressing Child Marriage in Northern Nigeria." Available online. URL: http://www.pspcouncil.org/Projects/TA_NigeriaChildMarriage.html. Accessed October 25, 2008.

[99] ———. "The Experience of Married Adolescent Girls in Northern Nigeria" (2007), pp. 6–7.

[100] ———. "The Experience of Married Adolescent Girls in Northern Nigeria" (2007), p. 16.

[101] ———. "The Experience of Married Adolescent Girls in Northern Nigeria" (2007), p. vii; "Nigeria: Addressing Child Marriage in Northern Nigeria." Available online. URL: http://www.pspcouncil.org/Projects/TA_NigeriaChildMarriage.html. Accessed October 25, 2008.

[102] ———. "The Experience of Married Adolescent Girls in Northern Nigeria" (2007), p. 7.

[103] ———. "Child Marriage Briefing: Nigeria." Available online. URL: http://www.popcouncil.org.pdfs/briefingsheet/NIGERIA.pdf. Accessed December 18, 2007.

[104] UNICEF. "Nigeria: At a Glance." Available online. URL: http://www.unicef.org/infoby country/nigeria_statistics.html#29. Accessed January 20, 2008.

[105] Population Council. "The Experience of Married Adolescent Girls in Northern Nigeria" (2007), p. 10.

[106] United Nations. "Press Briefing: Press Conference on UNFPA Project to Treat Obstetric Fistula in Nigeria." Available online. URL: http://www.un.org/News/briefings/docs/2005/UNFPA_Briefing_050222.doc.htm. Accessed February 1, 2008.

[107] Population Council. "The Experience of Married Adolescent Girls in Northern Nigeria" (2007), pp. 10–11.

[108] UNODC. "Measures to Combat Trafficking in Human Beings in Benin, Nigeria and Togo" (2006), p. 32.

[109] UNICEF Innocenti Research Centre. "Trafficking in Human Beings, Especially Women and Children, in Africa," p. 21.

[110] UNODC. "Measures to Combat Trafficking in Human Beings in Benin, Nigeria and Togo" (2006), p. 65.

[111] U.S. Department of State. "Trafficking in Persons Report: (2007)," p. 160.

[112] Allen Little. "Nigeria's 'Respectable' Slave Trade." BBC News, (4/17/04). Available online. URL:http://news.bbc.co.uk/1/hi/programmes/from_our_own_correspondent/3632203.stm. Accessed February 2, 2008.

[113] WOCON. "Forms and Routes." Available online. URL: http://www.wocononline.org/children.html. Accessed February 1, 2008.

[114] ILO. "Review of Legislation and Policies in Nigeria on Human Trafficking and Forced Labour" (2006), p. 1.

[115] ———. "Review of Legislation and Policies in Nigeria on Human Trafficking and Forced Labour" (2006), p. 3.

[116] ———. "Review of Legislation and Policies in Nigeria on Human Trafficking and Forced Labour" (2006), p. 1.

[117] U.S. Department of State. "Trafficking in Persons Report: (2007)," p. 160.

[118] Little. "Nigeria's 'Respectable' Slave Trade."

[119] U.S. Department of State. "Trafficking in Persons Report: (2007)," p. 160.

[120] UNODC. "Measures to Combat Trafficking in Human Beings in Benin, Nigeria and Togo" (2006), p. 48.

[121] WOCON. "Forms and Routes."

[122] UNESCO. "Policy Paper No. 14.2(E), Human Trafficking in Nigeria: Root Causes and Recommendations" (2006), p. 30.

[123] ———. "Policy Paper No. 14.2(E), Human Trafficking in Nigeria: Root Causes and Recommendations" (2006), p. 30.

[124] ———. "Policy Paper No. 14.2(E), Human Trafficking in Nigeria: Root Causes and Recommendations" (2006), p. 31.

[125] Balal. "Nigeria: Human Trafficking—A View from Edo State."

[126] The World Bank. "Africa: Countries" (interactive map). Available online. URL: http://web.worldbank.org/WBSITE/EXTERNAL/COUNTRIES/AFRICAEXT/0,,contentMD K:20226042~menuPK:258664~pagePK:146736~piPK:226340<0x 007E>theSitePK:258644,00.html. Accessed December 21, 2007.

[127] IFAD. "Enabling the Rural Poor to Overcome Poverty in Nigeria." Available online. URL: http://www.ifad.org/operations/projects/regions/PA/factsheets/ng.pdf. Accessed February 1, 2008.

[128] ———. "Rural Poverty Portal: Nigeria Statistics." Available online. URL: http://www.ruralpovertyportal.org/english/regions/africa/nga/statistics.htm. Accessed February 2, 2008.

[129] Federal Republic of Nigeria, National Population Commission. "Nigeria Demographic and Health Survey, 2003," p. 13. Available online. URL: http://www.measuredhs.com/pubs/pdf/FR148/00FrontMatter.pdf. Accessed January 10, 2008.

[130] ———. "Nigeria Demographic and Health Survey, 2003," p. 15.

[131] ———. "Nigeria Demographic and Health Survey, 2003," p. 15.

[132] Federal Republic of Nigeria. "Millennium Development Goals Report, 2004," p. 28. Available online. URL: http://www.undoc.org/index.cfm?P=87&f=N. Accessed February 4, 2008.

[133] Federal Republic of Nigeria, National Population Commission. "2003 Nigeria Demographic Health Survey Fact Sheet." Available online. URL: http://www.measuredhs.com/pubs/pdf/GF5/Nigeria2003generalfactsheet.pdf. Accessed January 10, 2008.

[134] UNODC. "Measures to Combat Trafficking in Human Beings in Benin, Nigeria and Togo" (2006), p. 24.

[135] Bonale M. Fetuga, Fidelis O Njokama, and Abediyi O Olowu. "Prevalence, Types and Demographic Features of Child Labour among School Children in Nigeria." Available online. URL: http://www.pubmedcentral.nig.gov/articlerender.fcgi?artic=554995. Accessed February 10, 2008.

[136] Vicky Nwogu. "Trafficking of Persons to Europe: The Perspective of Nigeria as a Sending Country." Available online. URL: http://www.unicef.orginfobycountry/nigeria_statistics.html#29 www.nuoveschiavitu.it/ns/doc_leggi/relazione_nigeria.doc. Accessed January 11, 2008.

[137] Sarah Crowe. "West and Central African Nations Join Forces to End Child Trafficking." UNICEF Newsline (7/7/06). Available online. URL: http://www.unicef.org/infobycountry/nigeria_34868.html. Accessed February 19, 2008; UN Office for the Coordination of Human Affairs. "Nigeria: Dream of Freedom Turns into Prostitution Nightmare" (11/4/05). Available online. URL: http://irinnews.org/report.aspx?reportid=57008. Accessed February 24, 2008; Stephen Faris. "Italy's Sex Trade Pulls Teens Pushed by Poverty." Women's e-News, (8/15/02). Available online. URL: http://www.womensenews.org/article.cfm/dyn/aid/1005. Accessed February 24, 2008; Little. "Nigeria's 'Respectable' Slave Trade."

[138] Federal Republic of Nigeria. "Millennium Development Goals Report, 2004."

[139] ———. "Millennium Development Goals Report, 2004," p. 22.

[140] ———. "Millennium Development Goals Report, 2004," p. 28.

[141] United Nations. "Supplementary Convention on the Abolition of Slavery, the Slave Trade, and Institutions and Practices Similar to Slavery" (1956). Available online. URL: http://www.ohcr.orch.org/english/law/pdf.slavetrade.pdf. Accessed July 15, 2007; Federal Republic of Nigeria. "Millennium Development Goals Report, 2004," p. 28.

[142] UNESCO. "Policy Paper No. 14.2(E), Human Trafficking in Nigeria: Root Causes and Recommendations" (2006), p. 37.

[143] UNICEF Press Centre. "Millions of Orphans in Nigeria Need Care and Access to Basic Sevices." Available online. URL: http://www.unicef.org/media/media_27420.html. Accessed February 10, 2008.

[144] Population Council. "Child Marriage Briefing: Nigeria."

[145] UNICEF. "Nigeria: At a Glance."

[146] UNICEF Press Centre. "Millions of Orphans in Nigeria Need Care and Access to Basic Sevices."

[147] UNESCO. "Policy Paper No. 14.2(E), Human Trafficking in Nigeria: Root Causes and Recommendations" (2006), p. 35.

[148] ———. "Policy Paper No. 14.2(E), Human Trafficking in Nigeria: Root Causes and Recommendations" (2006), p. 36.

[149] U.S. Department of State. "Trafficking in Persons Report: (2007)," p. 160.

[150] Jonathan Clayton. "The Lost Children of Nigeria's Sex Trade." Times (London, 4/5/04).

[151] UNESCO. "Policy Paper No. 14.2(E), Human Trafficking in Nigeria: Root Causes and Recommendations" (2006), p. 36; Balal. "Nigeria: Human Trafficking—A View from Edo State."

[152] UNESCO. "Policy Paper No. 14.2(E), Human Trafficking in Nigeria: Root Causes and Recommendations" (2006), p. 40.

[153] François Tillinac. "Trafficking of African Women Is Thriving." Independent Newspapers Online (South Africa, 5/10/07). Available online. URL: http://www.int.iol.co.za/index.php?set_id=1&click_id=3016&art_id=nw20070 510150022241C437730. Accessed February 25, 2008.

[154] Balal. "Nigeria: Human Trafficking—A View from Edo State."

[155] UNESCO. "Policy Paper No. 14.2(E), Human Trafficking in Nigeria: Root Causes and Recommendations" (2006), p. 36.

[156] U.S. Department of State. "Trafficking in Persons Report: (2007)," p. 226.

[157] ———. "Trafficking in Persons Report: (2007)," p. 161.

[158] ILO. "Review of Legislation and Policies in Nigeria on Human Trafficking and Forced Labour" (2006), p. 24.

[159] ———. "Review of Legislation and Policies in Nigeria on Human Trafficking and Forced Labour" (2006), p. 29.

[160] U.S. Department of State. "Trafficking in Persons Report: (2008)," p. 198.

[161] ———. "Trafficking in Persons Report: (2007)," p. 161.

[162] ILO. "Review of Legislation and Policies in Nigeria on Human Trafficking and Forced Labour" (2006), p. 23.

[163] WOCON. "Women's Consortium of Nigeria." Available online. URL: http://www.wocononline.org. Accessed February 29, 2008.

[164] Girls' Power Initiative. "Comprehensive Sexuality Education as a Tool for Reducing Trafficking in Girls: The Girls' Power Initiative (GPI) Nigeria Experience." Available online. URL: http://gpinigeria.org/comprehensive.html. Accessed February 29, 2008.

[165] U.S. Department of State. "Trafficking in Persons Report: (2007)," p. 226.

[166] United Nations. "United Nations Millennium Declaration, State Parties." Available online. URL: http://www.un.org/millennium/declaration/ares552e.htm. Accessed December 31, 2007.

[167] ———. "Convention on the Elimination of All Forms of Discrimination against Women." Available online. URL: http://www.un.org/womenwatch/daw/cedaw/states.htm. Accessed January 2, 2008.

[168] United Nations Information Service. "Significant Progress in the Fight against Trafficking in Human Beings in West African States." Available online. URL: http://www.unis.unvienna.org/unis/pressrls/2001/cp400.html. Accessed February 20, 2008.

[169] UNODC. "Trafficking in Persons: Global Patterns" (2006), p. 19.

[170] U.S. Department of State. "Trafficking in Persons Report: (2007)," p. 12.

[171] ———. "Trafficking in Persons Report" (2004), p. 116. Available online. URL:http://www.state.gov/g/tip/rls/tiprpt/2004. Accessed October 25, 2008.

[172] ———. "Trafficking in Persons Report: (2007)," p. 115.

[173] "India among Top Human Trafficking Destinations: UN." MSN News (10/3/07). Available online. URL: http://content.msn.co.in/News/National/NationalIndA_031007_1833.htm. Accessed February 20, 2008.

[174] U.S. Department of State. "Trafficking in Persons Report: (2007)," p. 115.

[175] Congressional Research Service. "Trafficking in Women and Children: The U.S. and International Response" (updated 2002). Available online. URL: http://fpc.state.gov/documents/organization/9107.pdf. Accessed February 20, 2008.

[176] U.S. Department of State. "Trafficking in Persons Report: (2007)," p. 115.

[177] Shakti Vahini. "Trafficking in India Report—2004." Available online. URL: http://www.crin.org/docs/traffickingreport.pdf. Accessed January 17, 2008.

[178] ———. "Female Foeticide, Coerced Marriage & Bonded Labour in Haryana and Punjab; a Situational Report" (2003). Available online. URL: http://www.ungift.org/pdf/situational_report.pdf. Accessed January 17, 2008.

[179] ———. "Female Foeticide, Coerced Marriage & Bonded Labour in Haryana and Punjab; a Situational Report" (2003), p. 7.

[180] Social Alert. "Invisible Servitude: An In-Depth Study on Domestic Workers in the World" (2000), p. 20. Available online. URL: http://www.socialalert.org/k/index.php?option=com_content&task=view&lang =fr&id=94. Accessed February 29, 2008.

[181] ———. "Invisible Servitude: An In-Depth Study on Domestic Workers in the World" (2000), p. 19.

[182] Shakti Vahini. "Trafficking in India Report—2004."

[183] Social Alert. "Invisible Servitude: An In-Depth Study on Domestic Workers in the World" (2000), p. 20.

[184] Minorities at Risk Project. "Assessment for Scheduled Tribes in India." Available online. URL: http://www.cidcm.umd.edu/mar/assessment.asp?groupId=75011. Accessed February 1, 2008.

[185] Federal Research Division, Library of Congress. "Country Reports, India: Tribes." Available online. URL: http://countrystudies.us.inia/70.htm. Accessed February 1, 2008.

[186] HRW. "Human Rights Overview: India." Available online. URL: http://www.hrw.org/english/docs/2006/01/18/india12272.htm. Accessed December 30, 2007.

[187] Human Rights Watch and Center for Human Rights and Global Justice, NYU School of Law. "Hidden Apartheid: Caste Discrimination against India's 'Untouchables' (Shadow Report to the UN Committee on the Elimination of Racial Discrimination)," p. 86. Available online. URL: http://www.hrw.org/reports/2007/india0207/india0207webwcover.pdf. Accessed February 6, 2008.

[188] U.S. Department of State. "Country Reports on Human Rights Practices, 2005: India." Released March 2006. Available online. URL: http://www.state.gov/g/drl/rls/hrrpt/2005/61707.htm. Accessed January 16, 2008.

[189] "India among Top Human Trafficking Destinations: UN." MSN (10/3/07). Available online.URL: http://www.giftasia.in/index.php?option=com_content&task=view&id=234<0x0026>Itemid=353. Accessed February 9, 2008.

[190] Nicholas D. Kristof. "The 21st-Century Slave Trade." *New York Times* (4/22/07).

[191] U.S. Department of State. "Country Reports on Human Rights Practices, 2005: India." Released March 2006. Available online. URL: http://www.state.gov/g/drl/rls/hrrpt/2005/61707.htm. Accessed January 16, 2008.

[192] Nicholas D. Kristof. "The 21st-Century Slave Trade." *New York Times* (4/22/07).

[193] Global Alliance against Traffic in Women. "Collateral Damage: The Impact of Anti-Trafficking Measures on Human Rights around the World" (2007). pp. 121–122. Available online. URL: http://www.gaatw.net/Collateral%20Damage_Final/singlefile_CollateralDamagefinal.pdf. Accessed February 8, 2008.

[194] ———. "Collateral Damage: The Impact of Anti-Trafficking Measures on Human Rights around the World" (2007), p. 121. Available online. URL: http://www.gaatw.net/Collateral%20Damage_Final/singlefile_CollateralDamagefinal.pdf. Accessed February 8, 2008.

[195] ECPAT. "Global Monitoring: Report on the Status of Action against Commercial Sexual Exploitation of Children, India" (2006), p. 12.

[196] Donald G. McNeil, Jr. "Sex Slaves Returning Home Raise AIDS Risks, Study Finds." *New York Times* (8/1/07).

[197] PHR. "Sex Trafficking and the HIV/AIDS Pandemic: Testimony of Holly Burkhalter, Physicians for Human Rights Before the House International Relations Committee." Available online. URL: http://physiciansforhumanrights.org/library/2003-06-25.html. Accessed February 29, 2008.

[198] Donald G. McNeil, Jr. "Sex Slaves Returning Home Raise AIDS Risks, Study Finds." *New York Times* (8/1/07).

[199] ECPAT. "Global Monitoring: Report on the Status of Action against Commercial Sexual Exploitation of Children, India" (2006), p. 14.

[200] International Institute for Population Sciences and Macro International. "National Family Health Survey (NFHS-3), 2005–06: India." Available online. URL: http://www.measuredhs.com/pubs/pdf/FRIND3/00FrontMatter00.pdf. Accessed January 3, 2008.

[201] U.S. Department of State. "Country Reports on Human Rights Practices, 2005: India." Released March 2006. Available online. URL: http://www.state.gov/g/drl/rls/hrrpt/2005/61707.htm. Accessed January 16, 2008.

[202] Shakti Vahini. "Trafficking in India Report—2004."

[203] U.S. Department of State. "Country Reports on Human Rights Practices, 2006: India." Released March 2007. Available online. URL: http://www.state.gov/g/drl/rls/hrrpt/2006/78871.htm. Accessed January 16, 2008.

[204] Shakti Vahini. "Female Foeticide, Coerced Marriage & Bonded Labour in Haryana and Punjab; a Situational Report" (2003), pp. 3–4.

[205] UNICEF. "Early Marriage: A Harmful Traditional Practice" (2005), p. 1. Available online. URL: http://www.unicef.org/publications/index_26024.html. Accessed November 2, 2007.

[206] Shakti Vahini. "Female Foeticide, Coerced Marriage & Bonded Labour in Haryana and Punjab; a Situational Report" (2003), pp. 3–4.

[207] U.S. Department of State. "Country Reports on Human Rights Practices, 2006: India."

[208] ———. "Country Reports on Human Rights Practices, 2006: India."

[209] Save the Children. "Child Domestic Work: A Violation of Human Rights: Report on the Legal Position of Child Domestic Workers in India" (2005). Available online. URL: http://www.unicef.orginfobycountry/nigeria_statistics.html#29 www.savethechildren.in/india/key_sectors/LegalprovisionsinIndiaforCDW.pdf. Accessed January 7, 2008.

[210] Social Alert. "Invisible Servitude: An In-Depth Study on Domestic Workers in the World" (2000), p. 20.

[211] U.S. Department of State. "Trafficking in Persons Report: (2007)," p. 115.

[212] Social Alert. "Invisible Servitude: An In-Depth Study on Domestic Workers in the World" (2000), p. 19.

[213] Save the Children. "Child Domestic Work: A Violation of Human Rights: Report on the Legal Position of Child Workers in India" (2005), p. 12.

[214] ———. "Child Domestic Work: A Violation of Human Rights: Report on the Legal Position of Child Workers in India" (2005), p. 13.

[215] Bales. *Disposable People,* revised edition. Berkeley: University of California Press, 2000, pp. 198, 201; U.S. Department of State. "Trafficking in Persons Report: (2007)," p. 115.

[216] U.S. Department of State. "Trafficking in Persons Report: (2007)," p. 116.

[217] Bales. *Disposable People,* p. 197.

[218] ———. *Disposable People,* pp. 203–213.

[219] Coalition to Stop the Use of Child Soldiers. "Global Report: India." Available online. URL: http://www.child-soldiers.org/regions/country?id=99. Accessed October 26, 2008.

[220] Randeep Ramesh. "Inside India's Hidden War: Mineral Rights Are behind Clashes between Leftwing Guerrillas and State-Backed Militias." *Guardian* (5/9/06).

[221] Asian Legal Resource Centre. "India: Child Soldiers Being Used as Expendable Pawns in Armed Conflicts (A Written Statement Submitted by the Asian Legal Resource Center to the 6th Session of the UN Human Rights Council)." Available online. URL: http://www.alrc.net/doc/mainfile.php/alrc_statements/442. Accessed February 14, 2008.

[222] Asian Centre for Human Rights. "Chhattisgarh Government and Naxalites Urged to Talk: Naxalites Killing More Civilians, State Government Recruiting Child Soldiers." Available online. URL: http://www. achrweb.org/press/2006/IND0606.htm. Accessed October 25, 2008.

[223] Asian Legal Resource Centre. "India: Child Soldiers Being Used as Expendable Pawns in Armed Conflicts."

[224] Amelia Gentlemen. "Kidney Theft Ring Preys on India's Poorest Laborers." *New York Times* (1/30/08).

[225] Asian Legal Resource Centre. "India: Child Soldiers Being Used as Expendable Pawns in Armed Conflicts."

[226] Somini Sengupta. "Push for Education Yields Little for India's Poor." *New York Times* (1/17/08).

[227] "India: Kidney Ring Suspect Arrested." *New York Times* (2/8/08).

[228] Asian Legal Resource Centre. "India: Child Soldiers Being Used as Expendable Pawns in Armed Conflicts."

[229] Government of India. Ministry of Statistics and Programme Implementation. "Millennium Development Goals: India Country Report, 2005." Available online. URL: http://www.unicef.orginfobycountry/nigeria_statistics.html#29wbplan.gov.in/docs.MDG_India_country_Report.pdf. Accessed October 25, 2008.

[230] World Bank. "India: Data and Statistics." Available online. URL: http://www.worldbank.org.in/WBSITE/EXTERNAL/COUNTRIES/SOUTHASIAEXT/INDI AEXTN/0,,menuPK:295609~pagePK:141132~piPK:141109~theS itePK:295584,00.html. Accessed February 14, 2008.

[231] U.S. Department of State. "Country Reports on Human Rights Practices, 2006: India." Released March 2007. Available online. URL: http://www.state.gov/g/drl/rls/hrrpt/2006/78871.htm. Accessed January 16, 2008.

[232] ———. "Country Reports on Human Rights Practices, 2006: India."

[233] Shakti Vahini. "Female Foeticide, Coerced Marriage & Bonded Labour in Haryana and Punjab; a Situational Report" (2003), pp. 3–4.

[234] Human Rights Watch and Center for Human Rights and Global Justice, NYU School of Law. "Hidden Apartheid: Caste Discrimination against India's 'Untouchables' (Shadow Report to the UN Committee on the Elimination of Racial Discrimination)," p. 3. Available online. URL: http://www.hrw.org/reports/2007/india0207/india0207webwcover.pdf. Accessed February 6, 2008.

[235] U.S. Department of State. "Country Reports on Human Rights Practices, 2006: India."

[236] ECPAT. "Global Monitoring: Report on the Status of Action against Commercial Sexual Exploitation of Children, India" (2006), p. 15.

[237] Kaushik Basu. "India's Faltering Education System." BBC News (8/18/06). Available online. URL: http://news.bbc.co.uk/go/pr/fr/-/2/hi/south_asia/4793311.stm. Accessed February 20, 2008.

[238] World Bank. "India: Data and Statistics."

[239] Sengupta. "Push for Education Yields Little for India's Poor."

[240] U.S. Department of State. "Trafficking in Persons Report: (2007)," pp. 115–116.

[241] ———. "Trafficking in Persons Report: (2007)," p. 12.

[242] ———. "Country Reports on Human Rights Practices, 2006: India."

[243] U.S. Department of State. "Trafficking in Persons Report: (2007)," pp. 115–116.

[244] Bales. *Free the Slaves*, pp. 214–215.

[245] ECPAT. "Global Monitoring: Report on the Status of Action against Commercial Sexual Exploitation of Children, India" (2006), p. 11.

[246] Shakti Vahini. "Female Foeticide, Coerced Marriage & Bonded Labour in Haryana and Punjab; a Situational Report" (2003), p. 50.

[247] Republic of India. "The Immoral Traffic (Prevention) Act, 1956. Available online. URL: http://www.prsindia.org/docs/bills/1167469313/bill51_2007010251_Immoral_Traffic_Preventi on_Act1956.pdf. Accessed March 3, 2008.

[248] Human Rights Watch, Children's Rights Project. "The Small Hands of Slavery: Bonded Child Labor in India." Available online. URL: http://www.hrw.org.reports/1996/India3.htm. Accessed March 3, 2008.

[249] Republic of India. "The Child Labour (Abolition and Rehabilitation) Bill, 2006. Available online. URL: http://rajyasabha.nic.in/bills-ls-rs/2006/CVII_2006.pdf. Accessed March 14, 2008.

[250] U.S. Department of State. "Trafficking in Persons Report: (2008)," pp. 139–140.

[251] ———. "Trafficking in Persons Report: (2007)," p. 40.

[252] United Nations. "Convention on the Elimination of All Forms of Discrimination against Women." Available online. URL: http://www.un.org/womenwatch/daw/cedaw/states.htm. Accessed January 2, 2008.

[253] UNODC. "Trafficking in Persons: Global Patterns" (2006), p. 18.

[254] ———. "Trafficking in Persons: Global Patterns" (2006), p. 20.

[255] ———. "Trafficking in Persons: Global Patterns" (2006), p. 19.

[256] U.S. Department of State. "Trafficking in Persons Report" (2006), p. 72.

[257] ———. "Trafficking in Persons Report: (2007)," p. 83.

[258] ———. "Trafficking in Persons Report: (2007)," p. 83; U.S. Department of State. "Country Reports on Human Rights, 2005: Belize." Released 2006. Available online. URL: http://www.state.goav/g/rls/hrrpt/2005/61716.htm. Accessed March 4, 2008.

[259] Government of Belize, Press Office. "Study of Trafficking in Persons Commissioned" (2004). Available online. URL: http://www.governmentofbelize.gov.bz/press_release_details.php?pr_id=2697. Accessed February 19, 2008.

[260] U.S. Department of State. "Trafficking in Persons Report: (2007)," p. 83.

[261] ———. "Country Reports on Human Rights Practices, 2006: Belize."

[262] ———. "Country Reports on Human Rights Practices, 2006: Belize."

[263] U.S. Department of Labor, Bureau of International Labor Affairs. "Belize." Available online. URL: http://dol.gov/ilab/media/reports/iclp/tda2004/belize.htm. Accessed March 4, 2008.

[264] U.S. Department of State. "Country Reports on Human Rights Practices, 2006: Belize."

[265] ———. "Country Reports on Human Rights Practices, 2006: Belize."

[266] Juan Miguel Petit. "Trafficking in Persons in Belize. Preliminary Report: November 2004." Available online. URL: http://www.oas.org.atip/Belize/BELIZE-%20Petit.pdf. Accessed February 19, 2008.

[267] ———. "Trafficking in Persons in Belize. Preliminary Report: November 2004," p. 21.

[268] ———. "Trafficking in Persons in Belize. Preliminary Report: November 2004," p. 25.

[269] Government of Belize, Ministry of National Development. "First Millennium Development Goals Report" (2004). Available online. URL: http://www.undg.org/index.cfm?P=87&f-B. Accessed January 10, 2008.

[270] Petit. "Trafficking in Persons in Belize. Preliminary Report: November 2004," pp. 16–17.

[271] U.S. Department of State. "Country Reports on Human Rights Practices, 2006: Belize."

[272] Petit. "Trafficking in Persons in Belize. Preliminary Report: November 2004," p. 59.

[273] U.S. Department of State. "Country Reports on Human Rights Practices, 2005: Belize." Released 2006. Available online. URL: http://www.dol.gov/ilab/media/reports/tda/tda2006/belize.pdf. Accessed October 25, 2007.

[274] ———. "Country Reports on Human Rights Practices: 2002." Released 2003. Available online. URL: http://www.asylumlaw.org/docs/belize/usdocs02_belize_w.pdf. Acccessed October 25, 2008.

[275] Petit. "Trafficking in Persons in Belize. Preliminary Report: November 2004," p. 28.

[276] U.S. Department of State. "Trafficking in Persons Report" (2006), p. 72.

[277] ———. "Country Reports on Human Rights Practices, 2006: Belize."

[278] ———. "Trafficking in Persons Report: (2007)," p. 83.

PART II

Primary Sources

4

United States Documents

This chapter contains excerpts of primary source documents concerning chattel slavery and human trafficking in the United States, as well as the efforts of the United States to end human trafficking in other parts of the world. It is divided into the following sections:

Legislation and executive orders, chronologically arranged

Media, briefs, and press releases

Forced labor and domestic servitude

Sex trafficking

Child sexual exploitation

U.S. efforts to end human trafficking

LEGISLATION AND EXECUTIVE ORDERS

The Slave Trade Act of 1808 (excerpt)

This act, whose full title is "An act to prohibit the importation of slaves into any port or place within the jurisdiction of the United States, from and after the first day of January, in the year of our Lord one thousand eight hundred and eight," ended the legal importation of enslaved persons into the United States. It changed neither the status of those already enslaved in the United States nor the status of their children.

Be it enacted by the Senate and House of Representatives of the United States of America in Congress assembled, That from and after the first day of January, one thousand eight hundred and eight, it shall not be lawful to import or bring into the United States or the territories thereof from any foreign kingdom, place, or country, any negro, mulatto, or person of colour, with intent to hold, sell, or dispose of such negro, mulatto, or person of colour, as a slave, or to be held to service or labour.

Source: U.S. Congress. "An act to prohibit the importation of slaves into any port or place within the jurisdiction of the United States, from and after the first day of January, in the year of our Lord one thousand eight hundred and eight." Available online. URL: http://amistad.mysticseaport.org/library/govt.papers/legis/1807.act.barsslavetrade. html. Accessed March 28, 2008.

Emancipation Proclamation (1863, excerpts)

The Emancipation Proclamation ended legal chattel slavery in states "in rebellion against the United States" (the Confederate states) during the Civil War.

By the President of the United States of America:

A Proclamation.

Whereas, on the twenty-second day of September, in the year of our Lord one thousand eight hundred and sixty-two, a proclamation was issued by the President of the United States, containing, among other things, the following, to wit:

"That on the first day of January, in the year of our Lord one thousand eight hundred and sixty-three, all persons held as slaves within any State or designated part of a State, the people whereof shall then be in rebellion against the United States, shall be then, thenceforward, and forever free; and the Executive Government of the United States, including the military and naval authority thereof, will recognize and maintain the freedom of such persons, and will do no act or acts to repress such persons, or any of them, in any efforts they may make for their actual freedom.

... And upon this act, sincerely believed to be an act of justice, warranted by the Constitution, upon military necessity, I invoke the considerate judgment of mankind, and the gracious favor of Almighty God.

In witness whereof, 1 have hereunto set my hand and caused the seal of the United States to be affixed.

Done at the City of Washington, this first day of January, in the year of our Lord one thousand eight hundred and sixty three, and of the Independence of the United States of America the eighty-seventh.

By the President: ABRAHAM LINCOLN
WILLIAM H. SEWARD, Secretary of State.

Source: Abraham Lincoln. "Emancipation Proclamation." Available online. URL: http://www.ourdocuments. gov/doc.php?doc=34&page=transcript. Accessed March 28, 2008.

The Thirteenth Amendment to the U.S. Constitution (1865)

This amendment to the U.S. Constitution abolished legal slavery in the United States.

Amendment 13—Slavery Abolished

1. Neither slavery nor involuntary servitude, except as a punishment for crime whereof the party shall have been duly convicted, shall exist within the United States, or any place subject to their jurisdiction.

2. Congress shall have power to enforce this article by appropriate legislation.

Source: U.S. Constitution. Available online. URL: http://www.usconstitution.net/xconst_Am13.html. Accessed March 28, 2008.

Mann Act (1910, excerpts)

This act, also known as the White Slave Traffic Act, forbids the transportation of women and girls across state or national borders for purposes of prostitution or "other immoral purposes."

. . . SEC. 2. That any person who shall knowingly transport or cause to be transported, or aid or assist in obtaining transportation for, or in transporting, in interstate or foreign commerce, or in any Territory or in the District of Columbia, any woman or girl for the purpose of prostitution or debauchery, or for any other immoral purpose, or with the intent and purpose to induce, entice, or compel such woman or girl to become a prostitute or to give herself up to debauchery, or to engage in any other immoral practice; . . . shall be deemed guilty of a felony . . .

SEC. 3. That any person who shall knowingly persuade, induce, entice, or coerce, or cause to be persuaded, induced, enticed, or coerced, or aid or assist in persuading, inducing, enticing or coercing any woman or girl to go from one place to another in interstate or foreign commerce, or in any Territory or the District of Columbia, for the purpose of prostitution or debauchery, or for any other immoral purpose, or with the intent and purpose on the part of such person that such woman or girl shall engage in the practice of prostitution or debauchery, or any other immoral practice, whether with or without her consent, . . . shall be deemed guilty of a felony . . .

133

SEC. 4. That any person who shall knowingly persuade, induce, entice or coerce any woman or girl under the age of eighteen years from any State or Territory or the District of Columbia to any other State or Territory or the District of Columbia, with the purpose and intent to induce or coerce her, or that she shall be induced or coerced to engage in prostitution or debauchery, or any other immoral practice, and shall in furtherance of such purpose knowingly induce or cause her to go and to be carried or transported as a passenger in interstate commerce upon the line or route of any common carrier or carriers, shall be deemed guilty of a felony,

. . . SEC. 8. That this Act shall be known and referred to as the "White-slave traffic Act."

Source: "Unforgivable Blackness, a film by Ken Burns: About the Film/Full Text of the Mann Act." PBS. Available online. URL: http://www.pbs.org/unforgivableblackness/knockout/mannact_text.html. Accessed March 28, 2008.

Trafficking Victims Protection Act of 2000 (excerpts)

The United States's first comprehensive federal law to address modern-day slavery, the Trafficking Victims Protection Act prohibits trafficking in persons within the United States. It also sets criteria for the U.S. to evaluate other countries' efforts to eliminate trafficking, rank those countries, and, in some cases, sanction countries for failure to act against human trafficking.

. . . SEC. 102. PURPOSES AND FINDINGS.

(a) PURPOSES.—The purposes of this division are to combat trafficking in persons, a contemporary manifestation of slavery whose victims are predominantly women and children, to ensure just and effective punishment of traffickers, and to protect their victims. . . .

. . . SEC. 103. DEFINITIONS.

In this division: . . .

(2) COERCION.—The term "coercion" means—

(A) threats of serious harm to or physical restraint against any person;

(B) any scheme, plan, or pattern intended to cause a person to believe that failure to perform an act would result in serious harm to or physical restraint against any person; or

(C) the abuse or threatened abuse of the legal process.

(3) COMMERCIAL SEX ACT.—The term "commercial sex act" means any sex act on account of which anything of value is given to or received by any person.

(4) DEBT BONDAGE.—The term "debt bondage" means the status or condition of a debtor arising from a pledge by the debtor of his or her personal services or of those of a person under his or her control as a security for debt, if the value of those services as reasonably assessed is not applied toward the liquidation of the debt or the length and nature of those services are not respectively limited and defined.

(5) INVOLUNTARY SERVITUDE.—The term "involuntary servitude" includes a condition of servitude induced by means of—

(A) any scheme, plan, or pattern intended to cause a person to believe that, if the person did not enter into or continue in such condition, that person or another person would suffer serious harm or physical restraint; or

(B) the abuse or threatened abused of legal process. . . .

. . . (8) SEVERE FORMS OF TRAFFICKING IN PERSONS.—The term "severe forms of trafficking in persons" means—

(A) sex trafficking in which a commercial sex act is induced by force, fraud, or coercion, or in which the person induced to perform such act has not attained 18 years of age; or

(B) the recruitment, harboring, transportation, provision, or obtaining of a person for labor or services, through the use of force, fraud, or coercion for the purpose of subjection to involuntary servitude, peonage, debt bondage, or slavery.

(9) SEX TRAFFICKING.—The term "sex trafficking" means the recruitment, harboring, transportation, provision, or obtaining of a person for the purpose of a commercial sex act. . . .

. . . SEC. 105. INTERAGENCY TASK FORCE TO MONITOR AND COMBAT TRAFFICKING.

(a) ESTABLISHMENT.—The President shall establish an Inter-agency Task Force to Monitor and Combat Trafficking.

(b) APPOINTMENT.—The President shall appoint the members of the Task Force, which shall include the Secretary of State, the Administrator of the United States Agency for International Development, the Attorney General, the Secretary of Labor, the Secretary of Health and Human Services, the Director of Central Intelligence, and such other officials as may be designated by the President.

(c) CHAIRMAN.—The Task Force shall be chaired by the Secretary of State.

(d) ACTIVITIES OF THE TASK FORCE.—The Task Force shall out the following activities:

(1) Coordinate the implementation of this division,

(2) Measure and evaluate progress of the United States and other countries in the areas of trafficking prevention, protection, and assistance to victims of trafficking, and prosecution and enforcement against traffickers, including the role of public corruption in facilitating trafficking. The Task Force shall have primary responsibility for assisting the Secretary of State in the preparation of the reports described in section 110.

(3) Expand interagency procedures to collect and organize data, including significant research and resource information on domestic and international trafficking. Any data collection procedures established under this subsection shall respect the confidentiality of victims of trafficking.

(4) Engage in efforts to facilitate cooperation among countries of origin, transit, and destination. Such efforts shall aim to strengthen local and regional capacities to prevent trafficking, prosecute traffickers and assist trafficking victims, and shall include initiatives to enhance cooperative efforts between destination countries and countries of origin and assist in the appropriate reintegration of stateless victims of trafficking.

(5) Examine the role of the international "sex tourism" industry in the trafficking of persons and in the sexual exploitation of women and children around the world.

(6) Engage in consultation and advocacy with governmental and nongovernmental organizations among other entities, to advance the purposes of this division. . . .

. . . SEC. 108. MINIMUM STANDARDS FOR THE ELIMINATION OF TRAFFICKING.

(a) MINIMUM STANDARDS.—For purposes of this division, the minimum standards for the elimination of trafficking applicable to the government of a country of origin, transit, or destination for a significant number of victims of severe forms of trafficking are the following:

(1) The government of the country should prohibit severe forms of trafficking in persons and punish acts of such trafficking.

(2) For the knowing commission of any act of sex trafficking involving force, fraud, coercion, or in which the victim of sex trafficking is a child incapable of giving meaningful consent, or of trafficking which includes rape or kidnapping or which causes a death, the government of the country should prescribe punishment commensurate with that for grave crimes, such as forcible sexual assault.

(3) For the knowing commission of any act of a severe form of trafficking in persons, the government of the country should prescribe punishment that is sufficiently stringent to deter and that adequately reflects the heinous nature of the offense.

(4) The government of the country should make serious and sustained efforts to eliminate severe forms of trafficking in persons.

(b) CRITERIA.—In determinations under subsection (a)(4), the following factors should be considered as indicia of serious and sustained efforts to eliminate severe forms of trafficking in persons:

(1) Whether the government of the country vigorously investigates and prosecutes acts of severe forms of trafficking in persons that take place wholly or partly within the territory of the country.

(2) Whether the government of the country protects victims of severe forms of trafficking in persons and encourages their assistance in the investigation and prosecution of such trafficking, including provisions for legal alternatives to their removal to countries in which they would face retribution or hardship, and ensures that victims are not inappropriately incarcerated, fined, or otherwise penalized solely for unlawful acts as a direct result of being trafficked.

(3) Whether the government of the country has adopted measures to prevent severe forms of trafficking in persons, such as measures to inform and educate the public, including potential victims, about the causes and consequences of severe forms of trafficking in persons.

(4) Whether the government of the country cooperates with other governments in the investigation and prosecution of severe forms of trafficking in persons.

(5) Whether the government of the country extradites persons charged with acts of severe forms of trafficking in persons on substantially the same terms and to substantially the same extent as persons charged with other serious crimes (or, to the extent such extradition would be inconsistent with the laws of such country or with international agreements to which the country is a party, whether the government is taking all appropriate measures to modify or replace such laws and treaties so as to permit such extradition).

(6) Whether the government of the country monitors immigration and emigration patterns for evidence of severe forms of trafficking in persons and whether law enforcement agencies of the country respond to any such evidence in a manner that is consistent with the vigorous investigation and prosecution of acts of such trafficking, as well as with the protection of human rights of victims and the internationally recognized human right to leave any country, including one's own, and to return to one's own country.

(7) Whether the government of the country vigorously investigates and prosecutes public officials who participate in or facilitate severe forms of trafficking in persons, and takes all appropriate measures against officials who condone such trafficking.

SEC. 110. ACTIONS AGAINST GOVERNMENTS FAILING TO MEET MINIMUM STANDARDS.

(a) STATEMENT OF POLICY.—It is the policy of the United States not to provide nonhumanitarian, nontrade-related foreign assistance to any government that—

(1) does not comply with minimum standards for the elimination of trafficking; and

(2) is not making significant efforts to bring itself into compliance with such standards. . . .

Source: U.S. Public Law 106-386—October 28, 2000. "Victims of Trafficking and Violence Protection Act of 2000." Available online. URL: http://www.state.gov/documents/organization/10492.pdf. Accessed October 20, 2008.

The Prosecutorial Remedies and Other Tools to End the Exploitation of Children Today (PROTECT) Act of 2003 (excerpt)

This act expanded the permissible use of wiretaps and other investigatory measures in cases of suspected child abuse and child sex trafficking, eliminated all statutes of limitations for crimes involving child abuse or child abduction, and called for the establishment of a national AMBER Alert program to immediately publicize the abduction of a child. As evidenced in the excerpts below, it also criminalized sex tourism by American citizens and significantly increased the sentences for persons convicted of the sexual exploitation of children.

... SEC. 104. STRONGER PENALTIES AGAINST KIDNAPPING.

(a) SENTENCING GUIDELINES.—Notwithstanding any other provision of law regarding the amendment of Sentencing Guidelines, the United States Sentencing Commission is directed to amend the Sentencing Guidelines, to take effect on the date that is 30 days after the date of the enactment of this Act—

(1) so that the base offense level for kidnapping in section 2A4.1(a) is increased from level 24 to level 32;

(2) so as to delete section 2A4.1(b)(4)(C); and

(3) so that the increase provided by section 2A4.1(b)(5) is 6 levels instead of 3.

(b) MINIMUM MANDATORY SENTENCE.—Section 1201(g) of title 18, United States Code, is amended by striking "shall be subject to paragraph (2)" in paragraph (1) and all that follows through paragraph (2) and inserting "shall include imprisonment for not less than 20 years."

SEC. 105. PENALTIES AGAINST SEX TOURISM.

(a) IN GENERAL.—Section 2423 of title 18, United States Code, is amended by striking subsection (b) and inserting the following:

"(b) TRAVEL WITH INTENT TO ENGAGE IN ILLICIT SEXUAL CONDUCT.—A person who travels in interstate commerce or travels into the United States, or a United States citizen or an alien admitted for permanent residence in the United States who travels in foreign commerce, for the purpose of engaging in any illicit sexual conduct with another person shall be fined under this title or imprisoned not more than 30 years, or both.

"(c) Engaging in Illicit Sexual Conduct in Foreign Places.— Any United States citizen or alien admitted for permanent residence who travels in foreign commerce, and engages in any illicit sexual conduct with another person shall be fined under this title or imprisoned not more than 30 years, or both.

"(d) Ancillary Offenses.—Whoever, for the purpose of commercial advantage or private financial gain, arranges, induces, procures, or facilitates the travel of a person knowing that such a person is traveling in interstate commerce or foreign commerce for the purpose of engaging in illicit sexual conduct shall be fined under this title, imprisoned not more than 30 years, or both. . . .

SEC. 106. TWO STRIKES YOU'RE OUT.

(a) In General.—Section 3559 of title 18, United States Code, is amended by adding at the end the following new subsection:

"(e) Mandatory Life Imprisonment for Repeated Sex Offenses Against Children.—

"(1) In general.—A person who is convicted of a Federal sex offense in which a minor is the victim shall be sentenced to life imprisonment if the person has a prior sex conviction in which a minor was the victim, unless the sentence of death is imposed. . . .

Source: U.S. Public Law 108-21—April 30, 2003. "The Prosecutorial Remedies and Other Tools to end the Exploitation of Children Today (Protect) Act of 2003." Available online. URL: http://www.amberillinois.org/PDF/protectact2003.pdf. Accessed October 20, 2008.

Model State Anti-Trafficking Criminal Statute (2003, excerpts)

Developed by the U.S. Department of Justice, this "model state anti-trafficking criminal statue" is available for adoption by states or as a starting point for a state's development of its own anti-trafficking legislation.

AN ACT relating to criminal consequences of conduct that involves certain trafficking of persons and involuntary servitude.

BE IT ENACTED BY THE LEGISLATURE OF THE STATE OF ___:

(A) Title ___, Penal Code, is amended by adding Article XXX to read as follows:

ARTICLE XXX: TRAFFICKING OF PERSONS AND INVOLUNTARY
SERVITUDE

SEC. XXX.02. CRIMINAL PROVISIONS.

(1) INVOLUNTARY SERVITUDE. Whoever knowingly subjects, or attempts to subject, another person to forced labor or services shall be punished by imprisonment as follows, subject to Section (4), *infra:*

(A) by causing or threatening to cause physical harm to any person, not more than 20 years;

(B) by physically restraining or threatening to physically restrain another person, not more than 15 years;

(C) by abusing or threatening to abuse the law or legal process, not more than 10 years;

(D) by knowingly destroying, concealing, removing, confiscating or possessing any actual or purported passport or other immigration document, or any other actual or purported government identification document, of another person, not more than 5 years,

(E) by using blackmail, or using or threatening to cause financial harm to [using financial control over] any person, not more than 3 years.

(2) SEXUAL SERVITUDE OF A MINOR. Whoever knowingly recruits, entices, harbors, transports, provides, or obtains by any means, or attempts to recruit, entice, harbor, provide, or obtain by any means, another person under 18 years of age, knowing that the minor will engage in commercial sexual activity, sexually-explicit performance, or the production of pornography (see [relevant state statute] (defining pornography)), or causes or attempts to cause a minor to engage in commercial sexual activity, sexually-explicit performance, or the production of pornography, shall be punished by imprisonment as follows, subject to the provisions of Section (4), *infra:*

(A) in cases involving a minor between the ages of [age of consent] and 18 years, not involving overt force or threat, for not more than 15 years;

(B) in cases in which the minor had not attained the age of [age of consent] years, not involving overt force or threat, for not more than 20 years;

141

(C) in cases in which the violation involved overt force or threat, for not more than 25 years.

(3) TRAFFICKING OF PERSONS FOR FORCED LABOR OR SERVICES. Whoever knowingly (a) recruits, entices, harbors, transports, provides, or obtains by any means, or attempts to recruit, entice, harbor, transport, provide, or obtain by any means, another person, intending or knowing that the person will be subjected to forced labor or services; or (b) benefits, financially or by receiving anything of value, from participation in a venture which has engaged in an act described in violation of Sections XXX.02(1) or (2) of this Title, shall, subject to the provisions of Section (4) *infra*, be imprisoned for not more than 15 years.

Source: U.S. Department of Justice. "Model State Anti-Trafficking Criminal Statute." Available online. URL: http://www.usdoj.gov/crt/crim/model_state_law.pdf. Accessed October 20, 2008.

MEDIA, BRIEFS, AND PRESS RELEASES

Modern Slaves; Paul Wellstone Seeks to Free Them (October 2000)

Senator Paul Wellstone (D-Minnesota) and Senator Sam Brownback (R-Kansas) cosponsored the Trafficking Victims Protection Act of 2000 in the Senate. The Senate passed it on July 27, 2000.

(The House of Representatives had passed its own version earlier.)

. . . The modern slaves who concern Senator Paul Wellstone are mostly women and children imported illegally into the United States and then forced into the sex trade, into industrial sweatshops or into abused service as domestic workers. Some pay to come because they think they are going to be placed in a well-paying job. Others are abducted or sold by their families.

This week both Senate and House passed Wellstone's Trafficking Victims Protection Act of 2000, sending it on for President Clinton's signature. So convincing was Wellstone's case on this bill that it passed unanimously in the Senate and just one vote shy of unanimous in the House. . . .

Source: "Modern Slaves; Paul Wellstone Seeks to Free Them." *Star Tribune* (Minneapolis, 10/12/00).

Passage in Senate Sends Bill on Forced Labor to President (October 2000)

The Trafficking Victims Protection Act created the Office to Monitor and Control Trafficking, established as framework for victim assistance, and set forth the laws and sentencing guidelines that would apply to traffickers.

... The measure enacted today establishes specific laws against trafficking, punishing the worst violators with prison terms of 20 years to life and forcing them to compensate their victims.

It also provides special visas for some victims, so they could stay in the United States while their exploiters are prosecuted and perhaps even permanently. ...

... The bill also provides for an office within the State Department that would direct and coordinate federal efforts to deal with trafficking in human beings.

Source: David Stout. "Passage in Senate Sends Bill on Forced Labor to President." *New York Times* (10/12/00).

U.S. Criticizes Major Allies for Inaction in Slave Trade (July 2001)

The first U.S. Trafficking in Persons Report was released in July 2001. Countries identified as taking insufficient efforts to the trafficking faced U.S. sanctions beginning in 2003.

The State Department today criticized several of the United States' closest allies, inching Saudi Arabia, Israel, Greece and South Korea, saying they had not made sufficient efforts to stop the trafficking of slaves within their borders.

The assessments came in the department's first annual Trafficking in Persons Report, mandated under a law enacted last fall. It is similar to the reports on human rights and drug trafficking. Like those, it offers the option to apply sanctions, in this case to countries that are not, in the government's view, making adequate efforts to fight the slave trade.

. . . because the law is new, the sanctions provision does not take effect until 2003.

Source: Joel Brinkley. "U.S. Criticizes Major Allies for Inaction in Slave Trade." July 13, 2001. Available online. URL: http://www.usdoj.gov/opa/pr/2001/February/076crt.htm. Accessed March 28, 2008.

Secretary of State Colin L. Powell's Special Briefing on Release of Trafficking in Persons Report (June 2002)

The second U.S. Trafficking in Persons Report was issued in July 2002.

Good morning, ladies and gentlemen, I am here today to present the Department of State's Second Annual Trafficking in Persons Report. The Trafficking Victims Protection Act that mandates the report condemns trafficking as a modern form of slavery. This report represents the resolve of the entire US Government to stop this appalling assault on the dignity of men, women and children. . . .

Trafficking leaves no land untouched, including our own. Approximately 50,000 people are trafficked into the United States every year. Here and abroad, the victims of trafficking toil under inhuman conditions—in brothels, sweatshops, fields and even in private homes.

The Annual Trafficking in Persons Report shines a much-needed light on this global problem. We use the information that we collect to bolster the will of the international community to combat this unconscionable crime. . . .

Countries that make a serious effort to address the problem will find a partner in the United States, ready to help them design and implement effective programs. Countries that do not make such an effort, however, will be subject to sanctions under the Trafficking Victims Protection Act beginning next year.

For our own part, President Bush has directed all relevant United States agencies to combine forces to eradicate trafficking and help rehabilitate its victims.

Source: U.S. Department of State. "Special Briefing on Release of Trafficking in Persons Report, June [5], 2002." Available online. URL: http://www.state.gov/secretary/former/powell/remarks/2002/10748.htm. Accessed March 28, 2008.

John R. Miller, Director of the Office to Monitor and Combat Trafficking in Persons, Testimony Before the House International Relations Committee Subcommittee on Terrorism, Nonproliferation and Human Rights (June 2003)

In June 2003, John R. Miller, director of the Office to Monitor and Combat Trafficking, presented the third U.S. Trafficking in Persons (TIP) Report to the House International Relations Committee Subcommittee on Terrorism, Non-proliferation and Home Rights and outlined among other thing, the impact of U.S. sanctions against countries failing to act against trafficking, set to begin with the release of the 2003 TIP Report.

Mr. Chairman and other Members of the Committee,

I want to thank you for the opportunity to personally present to the Congress the third annual Trafficking Persons Report prepared by the Department of State.

This third annual report carries special significance because for the first time, governments that are not making significant efforts to bring themselves into compliance with the Act's minimum standards could face consequences that include the loss of non-humanitarian-, non-trade-related assistance. I would like to assure the Committee that the Department views the imposition of penalties on other countries as a very serious matter and that my staff conducted extensive research into the anti-trafficking activities of other governments. Our embassies submitted serious and detailed reports, and international and non-governmental organizations continued to share with us their experiences and understanding of trafficking developments around the world. . . .

My staff is working actively with several of our embassies to outline the steps that we believe a country can and should be taking. . . .

Finally, I would like to emphasize that the Administration's State Department efforts to fight trafficking in persons is not confined to this annual report. In February, we convened 400 people from the United States and abroad who were active participants in the fight against sex trafficking. Congressmen Frank Wolf and Chris Smith addressed the delegates who came from all strata of society and represented an enormous range of anti-trafficking experiences. The conference brought together many groups and individuals who had no knowledge of each other but who now seek to work together. At another level, I am convening next week the latest quarterly meeting of a multi-agency meeting group to coordinate the anti-trafficking strategies and programs of the federal agencies involved in this fight against traffickers. Our ambassadors throughout the world are keeping this issue on our bilateral agenda, raising awareness, and calling for action. Through our outreach efforts here and abroad, we are raising awareness about this issue so that everyone who learns of the problem can be part of the solution. My staff has traveled to scores of countries to meet with foreign government officials, non-governmental representatives and others who are joining the fight. . . .

Source: John R. Miller. "Testimony Before the House International Relations Committee Subcommittee on Terrorism, Nonproliferation and Human Rights," June 25, 2003. Available online. URL: http://www.state.ov//tip/rls/rm/22241.htm. Accessed March 29, 2008.

President George W. Bush's Address to the General Assembly of the United Nations (September 23, 2003)

In September 2003, President George W. Bush addressed the General Assembly of the United Nations about human trafficking and the United States's efforts to combat it.

. . . There's another humanitarian crisis spreading, yet hidden from view. Each year, an estimated 800,000 to 900,000 human beings are bought, sold or forced across the world's borders. Among them are hundreds of thousands of teenage girls, and others as young as five, who fall victim to the sex trade. This commerce in human life generates billions of dollars each year—much of which is used to finance organized crime. . . .

This problem has appeared in my own country, and we are working to stop it. The PROTECT Act, which I signed into law this year, makes it a crime for any person to enter the United States, or for any citizen to travel abroad, for the purpose of sex tourism involving children. The Department of Justice is actively investigating sex tour operators and patrons, who can face up to 30 years in prison. Under the Trafficking Victims Protection Act, the United States is using sanctions against governments to discourage human trafficking. . . .

Source: U.S. Department of State. "President Addresses UN General Assembly," September 23, 2003. Available online. URL: http://www.state.gov/g/tip/rls/rm/24336.htm. Accessed March 29, 2008.

Examples of Trafficking Convictions Secured in the U.S. in 2003

These are examples of convictions won in 2003 under the Trafficking Victims Protection Act of 2000.

United States v. Blackwell (**Maryland**)

After a three-week trial, a husband and wife (natives of Ghana) were convicted in June 2003 of conspiring to smuggle a woman from Ghana into the United States to work as an unpaid domestic servant and nanny. The defendants hid the victim's passport and required her to perform household chores, including cleaning other people's homes, with little or no compensation. . . .

The local U.S. Attorney's Office and the Civil Rights Division prosecuted the case; this is the first conviction after trial under 18 U.S.C. § 1589 (the forced labor provision of the Trafficking Victims Protection Act). The wife was sentenced to 63 months in prison, while the husband received six months of home detention and three years probation.

United States v. Quinton Williams (**Nevada**)

The defendant was convicted on April 2, 2003 of sex trafficking of children, transporting both a minor and an adult for prostitution, money laundering, and interstate travel in aid of racketeering. Williams was sentenced on June 20, 2003 to 125 months in prison and ordered to pay a $2,500 fine.

United States v. Lozoya (**Texas**)

Two defendants pled guilty to charges arising from their illegal transportation of a young Mexican woman into the United States to perform domestic work. The Mexican woman, along with her baby daughter, was held in a trailer where the family mistreated them; the family's failure to obtain medical assistance resulted in the death of the baby. . . .

United States v. Guzman, et al. (**Georgia**)

Four defendants were charged in a superseding indictment on January 30, 2003 with conspiring to transport and harbor three female aliens for prostitution, including two juveniles, from Mexico into the United States and forcing them to engage in prostitution in the Atlanta metropolitan area. . . .

Source: U.S. Department of Justice, U.S. Department of Health and Human Services, U.S. Department of State, et al. "Assessment of U.S. Government Activities to Combat Trafficking in Persons," June 2004. Available online. URL: http://www.justice.gov/crt/crim/wetf/us_assessment_2004.pdf. Accessed March 29, 2008.

U.S. Adds Gulf Allies to Trafficking Blacklist (June 2007)

It was widely noted in the media that the 2007 Trafficking Persons Report added four Arab allies to the list of Tier 3 countries.

The United States added four Arab allies—Bahrain, Kuwait, Oman, and Qatar—to its list of countries with the worst records of preventing people from being sold into the sex trade and servitude. In its annual report on human trafficking, the State Department also added Algeria, Equatorial Guinea, and Malaysia to the list of countries with the lowest ranking. . . .

Source: "U.S. Adds Gulf Allies to Trafficking Blacklist." *New York Times* (6/13/07).

U.S. Assessed in the Trafficking in Persons Report (June 2007)

Beginning in 2007, an assessment of the United States's role in the trafficking and its efforts to combat it was included in the annual Trafficking in Persons Report.

The United States is a source and destination country for thousands of men, women, and children trafficked for the purposes of sexual and labor exploitation. Women and girls, largely from East Asia, Eastern Europe, Mexico and Central America are trafficked to the United States into prostitution. Some men and women, responding to fraudulent offers of employment in the United States, migrate willingly—legally and illegally—but are subsequently subjected to conditions of involuntary servitude at work sites or in the commercial sex trade. An unknown number of American citizens and legal residents are trafficked within the country primarily for sexual servitude and, to a lesser extent, forced labor. . . .

Source: U.S. Department of State. "Trafficking in Persons Report (2007)," p. 49. Available online. URL: http://www.state.gov.documents/organization/82902.pdf. Accessed July 31, 2007.

FORCED LABOR AND DOMESTIC SERVITUDE

Imported Servants Allege Abuse by Foreign Host Families in U.S. (January 1999)

In 1999, the Washington Post *reported on the involuntary servitude of domestic workers among the households of special visa holders in the United States.*

Thousands of domestic servants are being brought into the United States from impoverished countries and then severely exploited by foreign employers, many of whom work for embassies and international organizations in the Washington area, according to human rights groups, immigration attorneys and former domestics. . . .

The domestic servants, most of them women from poor backgrounds in Africa, Asia and Latin America, are typically imported under a provision of immigration law that allows foreign diplomats, embassy employees and officials of organizations such as the World Bank, International Monetary Fund and United Nations to bring in personal household workers with the understanding that the employers will abide by U.S. labor laws. There is, however, virtually no oversight into whether they comply. . . .

So far this decade, more than 30,000 domestics have been brought to the United States under special work visas. Many are treated equitably. But among the others are some of the most exploited workers in the United States today, ...

One FBI-led team is investigating a well-off Brazilian businessman and his wife who allegedly held an illiterate servant from their homeland in slave-like conditions for 19 years while she worked in their suburban Maryland home.

The servant, who is about 60, came to authorities' attention recently when she had to be hospitalized for treatment of a long-neglected stomach tumor. She told local social workers that she sometimes had to beg neighbors for food and clothing and was regularly beaten by the wife. She said the couple told her that if she fled their home, she would be arrested immediately because she is black. . . .

Source: William Branigin. "Imported Servants Allege Abuse by Foreign Host Families in U.S." *Washington Post* (1/5/99).

Six Indicted by Conspiracy for Trafficking and Holding Migrant Workers in Conditions of Forced Labor in Western New York (June 2002)

In 2002, forced laborers were rescued in Buffalo, New York, and trafficking charges levied against their captors.

Assistant Attorney General Ralph F. Boyd, Jr., and Michael A. Battle, United States Attorney for the Western District of New York, announced an eighteen-count indictment against six defendants who participated in a scheme to recruit, transport and harbor undocumented Mexican migrant workers, and then held them in conditions of forced labor at migrant labor camps near Buffalo, New York. . . .

The indictment further alleges that the Garcia operation used guards to monitor workers' movements, engaged in verbal abuse and threats of physical harm, deportation and arrest. As part of the plan to control and exploit the workers, Garcia and members of her operation took large deductions from the workers' earnings, leaving them with virtually no pay. The indictment further charges that the defendants refused to let workers leave until deductions from their earnings paid off charges for transportation, food, housing, and other items that were not disclosed at the time of recruitment.

Source: Department of Justice, Press Release. "Six Indicted by Conspiracy for Trafficking and Holding Migrant Workers in Conditions of Forced Labor in Western New York" (6/19/02). Available online. URL: http://www.usjoj. gov/opa/pr/June/02_crt_360.htm. Accessed March 28, 2008.

Suffolk County Couple Plead Guilty to Forced Labor, Alien Smuggling Charges (November 2004)

In 2004, a Suffolk County couple pleaded guilty to charges involving the forced labor of 69 people.

Martin D. Ficke, Special Agent-in-Charge of the Department of Homeland Security's Immigration and Customs Enforcement (ICE), Roslynn R. Mauskopf, United States Attorney for the Eastern District of New York, and R. Alexander Acosta, Assistant Attorney General, United States Department of Justice today announced that Marlluz Zavala and Jorge Ibanez pleaded guilty to conspiring to commit forced labor; conspiring to recruit, harbor, transport and house undocumented workers; engaging in extortionate credit transactions; and transferring false alien registration cards.

The guilty plea proceedings were conducted before United States District Judge Sandra J. Feuerstein at the U.S. Courthouse in Central Islip, New York.

At the time of the defendants' arrests on June 21, federal agents executed search warrants at three Suffolk County, New York, residences owned by the defendants located at 5 Felway Drive in Coram, 4 Fourth Avenue in Brentwood, and 3524 Great Neck Road in Amityville, and took into custody 69 Peruvian illegal aliens, including 13 children, who had been living in cramped and squalid conditions . . .

The defendants confiscated the aliens' passports and threatened to turn the aliens over to law enforcement authorities if they refused to work. The aliens were forced to turn over almost all of their earnings to the defendants, who used the money to purchase houses, real property, and vehicles, and to pay for their own living expenses. In most cases, the aliens were left with only $50 or less per week to support themselves and their families. . . .

When sentenced, Zavala and Ibanez each face a maximum punishment of 50 years imprisonment and a fine of up to $1 million.

Source: U.S. Department of Homeland Security, Immigration and Customs Enforcement (Press Release). "Suffolk Country Couple Plead Guilty to Forced Labor, Alien Smuggling Charges" (11/5/04). Available online. URL: http://usinfo.state.ov/i/Archive/2004/Nov/09-464819.html. Accessed March 29, 2008.

Woman Pleads Guilty to Holding a Domestic Worker in Involuntary Servitude (March 2004)

In 2004, a Los Angeles woman pleaded guilty to holding a domestic worker in involuntary servitude.

The Justice Department announced today that an Indonesian national pleaded guilty in United States District Court in Los Angeles to holding a young Indonesian woman in involuntary servitude.

In 1997, the defendant, Mariska Trisanti, arranged for the victim to travel from Indonesia to Los Angeles on a tourist visa, with the expectation that the victim would work for her for two years as a nanny and housekeeper. When the victim arrived in the United States however, Trisanti confiscated her passport to prevent her from running away and put her to work for 17 hours or more per day, seven days a week. The victim received virtually no compensation for her labor. Although Trisanti initially made some payments to the victim's relatives, even those payments stopped entirely after the first year of service. . . .

Source: U.S. Department of Justice, Press Release. "Woman Pleads Guilty to Holding a Domestic Worker in Involuntary Servitude" (3/25/04). Available online. URL: http://www.usdoj.gov/opa/pre/2004/March/04_crt_1888.htm. Accessed March 28, 2008.

Taco Bell Agrees to Meet All Immokalee Worker Demands (March 2005)

In 2005, Taco Bell agreed, among other things, to prohibit human rights violations in its supply chain.

After an almost four-year boycott, a hunger strike, and several bus tours promoting their cause, a farmworkers organization based in southern

Florida declared a victory yesterday in its battle to improve working conditions for Taco Bell's tomato pickers. In an unusual conclusion to the pro-
longed campaign. Taco Bell and its parent company, Yum! Brands, agreed
to all of the Coalition of Immokalee Workers' demands.

The workers will receive a penny-per-pound raise for the tomatoes they
pick—nearly double their current pay. Taco Bell says it will terminate contracts with subcontractors who fail to implement the raise.

The fast food chain also agreed to institute a code of conduct with its growers, explicitly prohibiting human rights violations.

Source: Andrew Stelzer. "Taco Bell Agrees to Meet All Immokalee Worker Demands." *The NewStandard* (3/9/05).
Available online. URL: http://newstandardnews.net/content/index.cfm/items/1523. Accessed March 30, 2008.

10 Charged in International Human Smuggling Ring That Lured Young Honduran Women to U.S. for Forced Labor (July 2005)

*In 2005, 10 were charged with smuggling young Honduran women for forced
labor is New Jersey's bars.*

Ten people were indicted today, all alleged members of a ring operating
in the United States and Honduras that smuggled young, undocumented
Honduran women into the U.S. and forced them to work off their smuggling debt in bars in Hudson County, U.S. Attorney Christopher J. Christie
announced.

The women, mostly from rural, poor villages in Honduras—some as young
as 14—were recruited under the false promise of getting legitimate jobs as
waitresses in restaurants in New Jersey. Once brought to Hudson County
by way of a safehouse in Houston, Texas, however, they were put to work at
several bars owned by the ringleader and subject to physical and emotional
abuse, according to the Indictment.

The 31-count Indictment returned today describes, among other abuses,
young victims being raped while smuggled to the United States; victims
sometimes far younger than 21 forced to continually drink alcohol and
dance with male customers at the bars to raise money to pay human
smuggling fees of between $10,000 and $20,000; victims being beaten if

they were not compliant; victims forced to work in the bars up to seven days a week from 6 p.m. to 2 a.m.; threats of deportation or harm to them and their families in Honduras if they did not comply with the ring's demands.

Young women who became pregnant were forced to terminate pregnancies to maintain them as income-producers for the ring, according to the Indictment. . . .

Source: U.S. Immigration and Customs Enforcement. "10 Charged in International Human Smuggling Ring That Lured Young Honduran Women to U.S. for Forced Labor" (7/21/05). Available online. URL: http://www.ice.gov/pi/newsreleases/articles/050721neward.htm. Accessed March 30, 2005.

Frosty Treat Managers and Others Charged with Forced Labor (September 2006)

In 2006, eight students from Russia were rescued from forced labor as ice cream salespersons in Kansas City, Missouri.

According to an affidavit filed in support of the criminal complaint, eight Russian students from Voronozh, Russia, were recruited to work in the United States under a student work program. The students registered with a company named InterAir in Russia, which advertised a program offering a cultural, educational, and financially rewarding summer in the United States. The students signed an employment contract in order to gain a visa that would allow them to legally travel and be employed within the United States. Each of the students borrowed $2,500 to pays fees to travel to the United States, arriving on different dates in June 2006. None of the students had previously traveled to the United States and some did not speak any English.

[David L.] Carslake and [David H.] Mackintosh, managers of Frosty Treats, 620 E. Linwood Blvd., Kansas City, allegedly used threats and psychological and financial pressure to force the Russian students to work driving ice cream trucks for the company. Filiminov, an employee who worked at Frosty Treats' Kansas City office and traveled to Russia, and Aleksandvovich-Tokarev, who worked in Russia, were involved in recruiting the students.

. . . The students worked 13 hours a day, seven days a week, for less than minimum wage, which was paid in cash. In one example cited by the affidavit, a Russian student told investigators that he worked 13 hours a day for 62 days for $700—averaging 87 cents per hour.

Frosty Treats provided the students with an old van, which they were told could only be used to travel between their apartment and Frosty Treats. Fili-monov allegedly told the students that there was a global positioning tracker on the van, so that Carslake and Mackintosh would know if they deviated from their path. They were not permitted to use the van to buy groceries and would secretly try to buy food during their working hours.

The students were not permitted to have a mailbox key or a telephone in their apartment, and were ordered to stop using a telephone at the apart-ment complex lobby. . . .

Source: Office of the U.S. Attorney, Western District of Missouri. "Human Trafficking Initiative: Three KC Men, Two Russian Nationals Charged with Forced Labor of Eight Russian Students" (9/19/06). Available online: URL: http://www.usdoj.ov.usao/now/news20006/carslake.com.htm. Accessed March 30, 2008.

Immokalee Workers, McDonald's Reach Agreement (April 2007)

In 2007, McDonald's agreed to improve conditions for the tomato pickers in its supply chain.

The Coalition of Immokalee Workers (CIW) and fast-food giant McDonald's announced an agreement yesterday that will double the wages and improve working conditions for tomato pickers in Florida who supply McDonald's with tomatoes. . . .

After reaching a 2005 agreement with YUM! Brands—the parent com-pany of Taco Bell—the CIW turned its attention to McDonald's. . . .

According to a joint statement issued by Lucas Benitez of the CIW and William Whitman of McDonald's, the hamburger giant will pay a penny per pound more for tomatoes picked by Florida farmworkers and will insure that the extra wages are paid by its suppliers directly to the tomato pickers.

The CIW and McDonald's produce suppliers also agreed to work together to develop a new code of conduct for Florida tomato growers . . .

Source: Jerry Van Marter. "Immokalee Workers, McDonald's Reach Agreement." Presbyterian News Service, Office of Communication (4/10/07). Available online. URL: http://www.pcusa.org/pcnews/2007/07210.htm. Accessed March 31, 2008.

U.S. v. Sabhnani, Superseding Indictment (September 2007)

In 2007, a New York couple was charged with holding two domestic workers in involuntary servitude. The following is an excerpt from the superseding indictments.

UNITED STATES OF AMERICA
- against -
VARSHA MAHENDER SABHNANI,
also known as "Madame,"
"Shirley" and "Shelly," and
MAHENDER MURLIDHAR SABHNANI,
Defendants.

THE GRAND JURY CHARGES:

COUNT ONE
(Conspiracy to Commit Forced Labor)

1. On or about and between February 5, 2002 and May 13, 2007, both dates being approximate and inclusive, within the Eastern District of New York and elsewhere, the defendants VARSHA MAHENDER SABHNANI, also known as "Madame," "Shirley" and "Shelly," and MAHENDER MURLIDHAR SABHNANI, together with others, did knowingly and intentionally conspire to obtain the labor and services of Jane Doe #1 and Jane Doe #2 . . . in violation of Title 18, United States Code, Section 1589.

2. In furtherance of the conspiracy and to effect its objectives . . . the defendants, together with others, committed and caused to be committed, among others, the following:

OVERT ACTS

a. On or about February 5, 2002, unindicted coconspirator #1, a relative of the defendants who resided in Indonesia and whose identity is known to the Grand Jury ("UC #1"), and Jane Doe #1 traveled from Indonesia to John F. Kennedy International Airport located in Queens, New York ("Kennedy Airport").

b. On or about February 5, 2002, VARSHA MAHENDER SABHNANI and MAHENDER MURLIDHAR SABHNANI met Jane Doe #1 and UC #1 at Kennedy Airport.

c. On or about February 5, 2002, MAHENDER MURLIDHAR SABH-NANI drove VARSHA MAHENDER SABHNANI, UC #1 and Jane Doe

#1 from Kennedy Airport to 205 Coachman Place East, Muttontown, New York (the "residence").

d. On or about February 5, 2002, in the residence, VARSHA MAHENDER SABHNANI took Jane Doe #1's Indonesian passport. . . .

g. In or about and between 2002 and May 13, 2007, in the residence, VARSHA MAHENDER SABHNANI struck Jane Doe #1's arm, causing bruising. . . .

j. On or about January 2, 2005, MAHENDER MURLIDHAR SABH-NANI drove to Kennedy Airport where he met Jane Doe #2, who had arrived from Indonesia.

k. On or about January 2, 2005, in the residence, VARSHA MAHENDER SABHNANI took Jane Doe #2's Indonesian passport.

l. In or about and between September 2005 and May 13, 2007, in the residence, VARSHA MAHENDER SABHNANI struck Jane Doe #2's face.

m. In or about and between 2005 and May 13, 2007, in the residence, VARSHA MAHENDER SABHNANI struck Jane Doe #1 on the back.

n. In or about and between 2005 and May 13, 2007, in the residence, VARSHA MAHENDER SABHNANI threatened to have Jane Doe #2's husband arrested in Indonesia.

o. In or about and between 2005 and May 13, 2007, in the residence, VARSHA MAHENDER SABHNANI threatened to falsely report to the police in Nassau County, New York, that Jane Doe #1 and Jane Doe #2 had stolen jewelry and money.

p. In or about and between 2005 and May 13, 2007, in the residence, VARSHA MAHENDER SABHNAHI forced Jane Doe #1 to eat several hot chili peppers.

q. In or about and between 2005 and May 13, 2007, in the residence, VARSHA MAHENDER SABHNAN1 forced Jane Doe #1 to eat her own vomit.

r. In or about and between 2005 and May 13, 2007, in the residence, VARSHA MAHENDER SABHNANI forced Jane Doe #1 and Jane Doe #2 to take cold showers.

s. In or about and between 2005 and May 13, 2007, in the residence, VARSHA MAHENDER SABHNANI forced Jane Doe #1 and Jane Doe #2 to repeatedly run up flights of stairs.

t. In or about and between 2005 and May 13, 2007, in the residence, VARSHA MAHENDER SABHNANI cut Jane Doe #1's face with a knife.

u. In or about and between 2005 and May 13, 2007, in the residence, VARSHA MAHENDER SABHNANI pulled on Jane Doe #1's ears and dug her fingernails into the back of Jane Doe #1's ears, causing open lacerations behind Jane Doe #1's ears.

v. In or about and between 2005 and May 13, 2007, in the residence, VARSHA MAHENDER SABHNANI pinched Jane Doe #1's arm, causing open lacerations.

w. In or about June 2006, in Muttontown, New York, VARSHA MAHENDER SABHNANI drove Jane Doe #1 and Jane Doe #2 to 135 Coachman place East, Muttontown, New York, and ordered them to perform domestic services at that location. . . .

y. In or about and between 2006 and May 13, 2007, in the residence, VARSHA MAHENDER SABHNANI cut Jane Doe #1's chest with a knife.

z. In about 2007, in the residence, VARSHA MAHENDER SABHNANI poured hot water on Jane Doe #1, causing burns to Jane Doe #1's thigh area. . . .

Source: U.S. v. Sabhnani, Cr. No. 07 CR 429(S-I) (TCP) (U.S. District Court E.D.N.Y), Robert E. Kessler. "Couple Found Guilty in Slave Case." *Newsday* (Melville, NY, 12/18/07).

SEX TRAFFICKING

Four Indicted in Alaska for Luring Russian Girls and Women to U.S. and Enslaving Them in a Strip Club (February 2001)

In 2001, six Russian women and girls were rescued for enslavement in Alaska strip club and their captors charged with human trafficking.

Four people were charged today in Alaska with conspiring to enslave Russian women and girls in a strip club in Anchorage, the Justice Department announced. This is the first case prosecuted under the Victims of Trafficking and Violence Protection Act of 2000, enacted by Congress in October 2000 to stop the practice of trafficking in humans.

Victor Virchenko, Pavel Agafonov, Tony Kennard and Rachel Kennard were charged under a 23-count indictment with conspiring to lure six Russian women and girls to Alaska to enslave them. . . .

Today's . . . indictment charges that the defendants recruited the females under false pretenses—to perform Russian folk dances in a cultural festival—only to force them into servitude once they arrived in the United States. The charges against the defendants include six counts of forced labor . . . for coercing the victims to perform in a strip club by employing a scheme that relied on threats, isolation, and confiscation of the victims' passports, visas, and plane tickets.

Source: U.S. Department of Justice, Press Release. "Four Indicted in Alaska for Luring Russian Girls and Women to U.S. and Enslaving Them in a Strip Club" (2/22/01). Available online. URL: http://www.usdoj.gov/opa/pr/2001/February/076crt.htm.

Thousands of Women Forced into Sexual Slavery for US Servicemen in South Korea (September 2002)

In 2002, the International Organization for Migration reported that more than 5,000 women had been trafficked from various international locations to service American soldiers in South Korea, beginning in the mid-1990s.

Since the mid 1990s, more than 5,000 women have been trafficked into South Korea for sexual services for United States servicemen, according to a report from the International Organization for Migration. These trafficked women have typically come from the Philippines, Russia and Eastern Europe and were lured to work as prostitutes in bars frequented by US servicemen stationed in South Korea.

Many of these women live a life similar to that of a slave as they are kept from a regular income, live in horrible conditions, are forced to sell sex, and often face violence. . . .

In June, the US military stated that it would investigate whether the military's prohibition on trafficking and prostitution in South Korea is actually being followed.

Source: "Thousands of Women Forced into Sexual Slavery for US Servicemen in South Korea." *Feminist News Daily Wire* (9/9/02). Available online. URL: http://feminist.org/news/newsbyte/uswirestory.asp?id=6870. Accessed March 28, 2008.

Sex Trafficking: San Francisco Is a Major Center for International Crime Networks That Smuggle and Enslave (October 2006)

In this article, a prosecutor, law enforcement officer, and an aid worker discuss trafficked women's fears of testifying against their enslavers.

Many of San Francisco's Asian massage parlors—long an established part of the city's sexually permissive culture—have degenerated into something much more sinister: international sex slave shops.

Once limited to infamous locales such as Bombay and Bangkok, sex trafficking is now an $8 billion international business, with San Francisco among its largest commercial centers. . . .

It thrives because it's so hard to prosecute—the same women who are needed on the stand to help win cases are the ones who are being threatened into silence by their captors, said Heidi Rummel, a former federal prosecutor with the sex trafficking unit in Los Angeles.

"We have to explain the woman's mind-set—that she's often unsophisticated, comes from a country with a corrupt government and would believe her captors' lies that if she flees she could get arrested by police," she said. "Juries have a hard time. They wonder: If the door was open why didn't she just run?"

Sex traffickers who get caught are rarely convicted of sex trafficking—and they know it. It's a frustrating cat-and-mouse game for federal investigators and prosecutors, who spend a year or more keeping a sex slavery network under surveillance, and then none of the women held in captivity is willing to testify.

Local police face the same problems.

"Our undercover officers arrest women for prostitution weekly in the massage parlors," said Hettrich of the San Francisco vice unit. "We let her know if she cooperates with us, she won't go to jail. But she is more afraid of her traffickers than us."

Women are scared for good reason. Those who have become witnesses have been burned with acid, have disappeared, or have had their homes ransacked and their families harmed or threatened in their home countries, said Dong Shim Kim, head counselor at Du Re Bang (My Sister's Place), a shelter for sex trafficking victims in South Korea. . . .

Source: Meredith May. "Sex Trafficking: San Francisco Is a Major Center for International Crime Networks That Smuggle and Enslave (part one of a four-part special report)." *San Francisco Chronicle* (10/6/06).

Free, You Mi Begins to Put Her Life Back Together (October 10, 2006)

In this article, a sex trafficking survivor speaks of her experience.

Ivy Lee, an attorney specializing in human trafficking at Asian Pacific Islander Legal Outreach in San Francisco, helped You Mi apply for the T-1 visa. After a five-month investigation, the government concluded that You Mi was a sex-trafficking victim and granted her the visa on July 25.

HUMAN TRAFFICKING

You Mi is ready for her new life in California. . . .

But she never truly can escape her past.

She keeps her head down when serving food at the restaurant, in case someone at the table is a former customer who would recognize her.

It's been hard for her to start over, to make new friends. She doesn't like to say much because even the most innocent questions about where she came from force her to change the subject.

Sex work has left her with lingering health problems. A gynecologist told her that she is at high risk for cervical cancer.

And she knows the Korean criminal syndicate could easily find her.

You Mi got a terrible scare earlier this year, when a moneylender in South Korea sent her a threatening e-mail, claiming that she still owed him $7,000 and that she'd better wire immediately to a certain account. Whoever sent the note discovered her American e-mail address through her home page on Cyworld, the Korean equivalent of myspace.com.

You Mi wrote back, telling the sender that she would keep his threatening e-mail with her attorney. She hasn't heard from him since. . . .

For You Mi, her time as a sex slave has left a permanent bruise on her soul, A year of her life was taken away. Her innocence is gone. Her trust obliterated. Tension is woven into her personality.

You Mi misses her family. She misses her life before it went so wrong. The T-1 visa has given her a sense of justice, but she wants men to know what really goes on inside a massage parlor.

"Most customers come into a massage parlor thinking nothing is wrong; that it's a job we choose," she said. "It doesn't occur to them that we are slaves."

Source: Meredith May. "Diary of a Sex Slave" (fourth in a four-part special report). *San Francisco Chronicle* (10/9/06).

Leader of New York–Connecticut Sex-Trafficking Ring Pleads Guilty (March 2008)

This article describes the operation of a sex trafficking ring in New York, New Jersey, and Connecticut.

Corey Davis, also known as "Magnificent," pleaded guilty today in federal court in Bridgeport, Conn., to a federal civil rights charge for organizing and leading a sex-trafficking ring. A co-conspirator previously pleaded guilty to a related charge of conspiring to violate the Mann Act, which prohibits the interstate transport of individuals for prostitution. Davis is scheduled to be sentenced on June 2, 2008. Under the terms of his plea agreement, Davis faces up to 296 months imprisonment.

During his guilty plea hearing, Davis admitted that he recruited a girl under the age of 18 years to engage in prostitution, that he was the organizer of a sex-trafficking venture, and that he used force, fraud and coercion to compel the victim to commit commercial sex acts from which he obtained the proceeds. . . .

According to the indictment, Davis lured victims to his operation with promises of modeling contracts and a glamorous lifestyle. Davis then forced the girls to work a grueling schedule each day that entailed dancing and performing sex acts at strip clubs in Connecticut, New York and New Jersey. The victims earned up to $5,000 a night in these activities, which Davis confiscated and kept for himself.

The indictment also alleged that Davis beat many of the victims to force them to work for him and for violations of stringent rules he imposed to isolate and control them. In one attack, Davis slashed the head, shoulder, and hand of a girl with a box cutter to punish her for keeping some of the money she had earned. On another occasion, Davis stuck a pistol into the mouth of a victim and threatened to kill her.

Source: "Leader of New York–Connecticut Sex-Trafficking Ring Pleads Guilty." PR Newswire (4/1/08).

CHILD SEXUAL EXPLOITATION

Notice for Prospective Camp Volunteers (November 2006)

The Prosecutorial Remedies and Other Tools to End the Exploitation of Children Today Act of 2003 (PROTECT Act of 2003) requires, among other things, background checks on people who volunteer to work with children. Below is a notification of such a requirement.

To the potential volunteer regarding fingerprinting and the PROTECT Act:

The PROTECT Act (Public Law 108-21) was signed into law by the US Congress in 2003. A portion of the law authorized a pilot program that would allow selected youth-serving organizations access to the Federal Bureau of Investigations (FBI) criminal history database through fingerprinting of prospective volunteers. The pilot contained a provision for the development of criteria that would be used to determine a volunteer's fitness to serve in a volunteer role in a youth-serving organization. The American Camp Association (ACA) was accepted into this pilot in July 2006. For the American Camp Association (ACA), this pilot is named "PROTECTScreen."

Pursuant to the PROTECT Act, the ACA-Accredited Camp to which you have applied to serve as a volunteer may request an FBI fingerprint background check, and determination of your fitness to serve as a volunteer. This check will access criminal history record information held by the FBI and a determination of your fitness to serve will be rendered by the National Center for Missing and Exploited Children (NCMEC). . . .

Source: American Camp Association. "Notice for Prospective Camp Volunteers Pursuant to the PROTECT Act— PROTECTScreen Pilot, November 2006. Available online. URL: http://www.acacamps.org/publicpolicy/documents/ CampVolunteerNotice_000.pdf. Accessed March 29, 2008.

Report Finds That 2,000 of State's Children Are Sexually Exploited, Many in New York City (April 2007)

In 2007, a report by the New York State Office of Children and Family Services estimated that there were more than 2,000 sexually exploited minors in New York City.

At first it seemed like an innocent flirtation. Shaneiqua was 12 years old and walking around Brownsville, Brooklyn, when a man pulled up alongside her in a car and called to her from his window.

"He was just, like, 'You're cute. I really see myself being with you.' Stuff like that," she said.

Shaneiqua had just run away from home and had nowhere to go, so she got into his car. It was a decision that changed her life.

Eventually, she would learn that the man, known as Handsome, was a pimp. In exchange for room and board, she said, he asked her to dance at a strip club and give him her earnings. When that wasn't enough money, she said, he told her to start taking men into the "VIP room," trading sex for cash.

Shaneiqua reluctantly agreed. In her mind, she said, it was just part of being in a relationship. "The only thing that really mattered to me was whether he was still going to love me after I slept with other men," she said. "As long as he said yes, I didn't really have any problem with it."

A report released Friday by the New York State Office of Children and Family Services estimates that New York City is home to more than 2,000 sexually exploited children under 18. . . .

Source: Cassi Feldman. "Report Finds 2,000 of State's Children are Sexually Exploited, Many in New York City." New York Times (4/24/07).

U.S. EFFORTS TO END HUMAN TRAFFICKING

"Modern-Day Slavery" Prompts Rescue Efforts: Group Targets Abuse of Foreign Maids, Nannies (May 2004)

This article describes the rescue of a domestic worker held in involuntary domestic servitude.

Alexandra Santacruz pressed up to the kitchen window on a recent spring night and peered anxiously down the street. She had done everything she could to get ready, tying her belongings neatly into four plastic bags and hiding them in the trash bin outside the Falls Church townhouse.

Just past 8 P.M., two hours after Santacruz began her vigil, a maroon van eased to a stop in front. Its passengers stepped out to begin their work: They were there to rescue her, The 24-year-old was desperate to leave her job as a live-in nanny, but her employers had threatened to call police if she did.

Two lawyers from CASA of Maryland, a workers' rights group, knocked on the door and confronted her stunned employer. They had become practiced at this exchange, now a common part of their jobs, and they were prepared for the accusations and denials that followed.

In minutes, Santacruz bounded out of the house, an enormous stuffed dog in her arms. *"Estoy feliz!"* she shouted, "I'm so happy."

For nearly two years, she had worked 80-hour weeks cooking, cleaning and baby-sitting for an Ecuadoran official of the Organization of American States, For that, her attorneys said, she was paid little more than $2 an hour. She had worked for the same family in Ecuador, but since arriving, she said, her employer had taken her passport, she had no money and she was afraid that if she left, she would lose her visa and police would come for her.

Stories like hers are increasing among the thousands of women who are recruited every year from impoverished countries as live-in domestic help, according to law enforcement officials and advocacy groups. Now, a growing number of organizations are reaching out to mistreated domestic workers, helping them leave their employers and providing emergency housing and legal advice. . . .

Source: Lena H. Sun. "Modern-Day Slavery" Prompts Rescue Efforts." *Washington Post* (5/3/04).

Our Trafficking Signal: Stop! (June 2004)

In June 2004, Secretary of State Colin L. Powell presented the fourth U.S. Trafficking in Persons Report to President George W. Bush and the members of Congress.

Today I presented the 2004 State Department Report on Trafficking in Persons to the President and the Congress, as mandated by the Trafficking Victims Protection Act. . . .

Trafficking in persons is high on President Bush's priority list, as he emphasized during his UN General Assembly speech this past September. "There's a special evil in the abuse and exploitation of the most innocent and vulnerable," the President said, and all the agencies represented on the Interagency TIP Task Force that I chair agree.

We are genuinely "seized of the matter," to use the standard diplomatic parlance, and the reason is obvious; The more you learn about how the most innocent and vulnerable among us are savaged by these crimes, the more impossible it becomes to look the other way. Women and girls as young as 6 years old being trafficked into commercial sexual exploitation; men are being trafficked into forced labor; children are being trafficked into war as child soldiers.

And the victims are not few. We estimate 600,000–800,000 cases each year of trafficking victims taken across international frontiers. And that does not include those who are victimized within their own countries. The vast majority of victims, international and otherwise, are women and children.

Numbers so large can freeze our imaginations. But every case is different, and every case is monstrous. Consider just one example. Southeast Asian traffickers took Khan, an 11-year-old girl living in the hills of Laos, to an embroidery factory in a large city. She and other children were made to work 14 hours a day for food and clothing, but no wages. When Khan protested this, she was beaten. When she protested again, she was stuffed into a closet where the factory owner's son fired a gun pellet into her cheek and poured industrial chemicals over her.

Such horrors, multiplied hundreds of thousands-fold, must not stand unchallenged. Under the President's direction, we have drawn unprecedented attention to the trafficking problem. The 2004 *Report*, like its predecessors, puts pressure on countries whose performances are deficient. Our TIP monitoring system has three tiers, and if a country's practices land it in Tier 3, it faces significant sanctions. Several countries have cleaned up their acts to avoid Tier 3 status, and real people have been helped, real lives have been saved, as a result. . . .

But we are not satisfied with our progress. Up to 18,000 cases a year afflict our own country. . . .

I urge everyone to read this

Report—it's posted at http://www.state.gov/—and to do what you can, in your own communities, to help us confront this challenge.

Source: Colin L. Powell. "Our Trafficking Signal: Stop!" (op-ed). *International Herald Tribune* (6/14/04).

U.S. Faults 4 Allies Over Forced Labor (June 2005)

The fifth U.S. Trafficking in Persons Report named 14 countries—including four Middle East allies—as Tier 3 countries subject to U.S. sanctions for failure to adequate address human trafficking.

The United States criticized four of its closest allies in the Middle East on Friday, saying Kuwait, Qatar, Saudi Arabia and the United Arab Emirates are doing little if anything to stop forced labor and other forms of "modern slavery" within their borders.

The four countries are among 14 "Tier III" nations that the State Department said had a serious problem with trafficking in persons and made little or no effort to control it, despite prodding from the United States. Citation as a Tier III country can trigger economic penalties. . . .

Source: Joel Brinkley. "U.S. Faults 4 Allies Over Forced Labor." June 4, 2005.

HUMAN TRAFFICKING

The Real Deal: As the Hound of Human Traffickers, John Miller Believes Playing Politics Is Not an Option (August 2005)

In this interview, John R. Miller, the U.S. ambassador-at-large on modern slavery, explained what the United States hoped would be the effect of the annual Trafficking in Persons Report.

. . . THERE's A nine-hour difference between Kuwait and Washington, D.C., and an even greater difference of opinion. A video conference has been arranged for Ambassador John Miller of the federal Trafficking Persons Office and his team to explain to Kuwait why it has landed on the bottom tier of this year's Trafficking In Persons report, an annual review of all nations' efforts to curtail traffickers. The three-tier TIP rankings rankle some countries. As the screen opens, a huddle of irritated journalists is staring back from Kuwait City. The trafficking crisis in Kuwait is so bad that Bangladeshi servants and construction workers recently rioted in front of their embassy, seeking help to escape employers or get paid.

But the Kuwaiti journalists jump on Miller. They want to know: *Who is the U.S. to tell us what we should do inside our country?*

The aim, Miller finally tells them, is to "create discussion."

That's all?

No, Miller explains later. "We hope they will respond to the "name and shame" factor. . . .

Source: Alan Berner. "The Real Deal: As the Hound of Human Traffickers, John Miller Believes Playing Politics Is Not an Option." *Seattle Times* (8/05).

Specialized Anti-Trafficking Unit Launched in Justice Department (Winter 2006)

In 2006, the U.S. Justice Department created the Human Trafficking Prosecution Unit to focus solely on the prosecution of human trafficking crimes.

Attorney General Alberto R. Gonzales and Assistant Attorney General for the Civil Rights Division Wan J. Kim have announced the formation of the Human Trafficking Prosecution Unit (HTP Unit) within the Criminal Section of the Civil Rights Division. The HTP Unit will be the Department's

166

specialized enforcement unit focused exclusively on combating the crime of human trafficking. The New Unit will enhance the Department's ability to investigate and prosecute significant human trafficking and slavery cases, including those that cross jurisdictional boundaries and involve complex financial crimes. The Unit will also serve as a resource for training, outreach, and policy development on human trafficking and slavery issues.

Source: U.S. Department of Justice, Civil Rights Division. "Specialized Anti-Trafficking Unit Launched in Justice Department." *Anti-Trafficking News Bulletin* (Winter 2006–2007). Available online. URL: http://www.justice.gov/crt/crim/trafficking_newsletter/antitraffnews_dec06.pdf. Accessed March 31, 2008.

Albany Agrees on Law against Sexual and Labor Trafficking (May 2007)

In 2007, New York State passed one of the strongest state anti-trafficking laws in the country.

State lawmakers and Gov. Eliot Spitzer said Wednesday that they had agreed to make labor- and sex-trafficking felonies, breaking a deadlock on an issue many thought should have been resolved long ago.

Although there are federal laws against human trafficking—essentially a modern form of slavery—some state lawmakers and advocacy groups say they are insufficient. Federal law enforcement has focused mostly on the largest criminal trafficking rings, rather than smaller operations like sweatshops and brothels, advocacy groups say.

Moreover, although local law enforcement officials are most likely to stumble across victims of trafficking, the advocacy groups say, the absence of a state trafficking law has provided little incentive for local prosecutors to tackle such cases.

"New York is finally joining the ranks of other states in ensuring that those who exploit innocent people and children and cause extreme suffering are subject to strict punishment under state law," Governor Spitzer said in a statement.

At least 29 states already have laws specifically addressing human trafficking. The State Department has estimated that 14,500 to 17,500 people a year are brought into the United States and then used for forced labor or sex, although experts say such statistics are inexact estimates. . . .

"This bill will be the model for any state law on trafficking in the country," said Taina Bien-Aimé, the executive director Of Equality Now, which has pushed for a trafficking law.

Source: Danny Hakim and Nicholas Confessore. "Albany Agrees on Law against Sexual and Labor Trafficking," May 17, 2007.

A Closing Note from the Drafters of the U.S. Trafficking in Persons Report (June 2007)

The terms vary: trafficking, forced labor, involuntary servitude, slavery . . . but the basic elements are the same. Someone seeks a better life and takes a risk by accepting an offer of employment often outside his or her country—and finds a hell of servitude instead. We have shed light on the most vulnerable—women and children—but in the modern age of exploitation through debt and deception, there are many men who fall prey to traffickers. This Report shows the servitude suffered by so many men who have taken risks for themselves and their families, but end up enslaved by labor recruiters and employers.

At the age of 22, Ko Maung left his home in Mon State, Burma with his new bride to find work in a neighboring country. The newlyweds dreamed of earning enough money to return to Burma and build a home for their children. Ko Maung's wife went to work in a fish-processing factory; he took jobs aboard fishing vessels that took him to sea for two to three months. In 2003, he accepted what, he thought, was a safe offer of work on a fishing boat for two years. "You stay here, he told his wife as he left. "I will come back with money and we can go back to Burma." Later, his wife was told he had died during the final months of the fishing boat's three-year voyage.

From accounts of survivors who made it back, Ko Maung and 30 other Burmese recruited to work on a fleet of six fishing boats died at sea from forced labor, starvation, and vitamin deficiencies. They had been forced to remain at sea for years, denied pay, and fed only fish and rice. Workers made repeated requests to leave the boats, but were denied. They requested medical attention but were ignored. As one after another grossly exploited man died at the end of the fishing voyage, their bodies were unceremoniously dumped overboard. They were used in forced labor until they could breathe no more. Those who survived were not paid for their work—which amounted to three years of enslavement.

This Report Is dedicated to Ko Maung, who paid the ultimate price of slavery, and to his family whose dreams were crushed. Through the courage of his compatriots, and advocates who assist male victims of slavery, we have heard his voice of agony. We pledge to project his voice, breaking down the walls of indifference and corruption that protect businesses that rely on this despicable trade in disposable humans.

Thank you for your support. Thank you for joining us.

Rebecca Billings	Jennie Miller
Kathleen Bresnahan	Sally Neumann
Jennifer Schrock	Amy O'Neill Richard
Donnelly	Gayatri Patel
Dana Dyson	Catherine Pierce
Shereen Faraj	Solmaz Sharifi
Barbara Fleck	Jane Nady Sigmon
Mark Forstrom	Andrea Smail
Eleanor Kennelly Gaetan	Felecia A. Stevens
Paula R. Goode	Mark B. Taylor
Megan L. Hall	Caroline S. Tetschner
Mark P. Lagon	Jennifer Topping
Amy	Rachel Yousey
LeMar-Meredith	Raba
Carla Menares Bury	Veronica Zeitlin

Source: U.S. Department of State. "Trafficking in Persons Report (2007)," p. 235. Available online. URL: http://www.state.gov/documents/organization/82902.pdf. Accessed July 31, 2007.

Senators Durbin and Coburn Introduce Human Trafficking Bill (June 2007)

In 2007, Senators Dick Durbin (D-Illinois) and John Coburn (R-Oklahoma) introduced legislation to permit prosecution of Americans who commit trafficking crimes outside the United States.

U.S. Senator Dick Durbin (D-IL), Chairman of the Senate Subcommittee on Human Rights and the Law, and Senator Tom Coburn, M.D. (R-OK), who serves as Ranking Member of the subcommittee, today introduced legislation that will close a legal loophole that currently prevents the U.S. Justice Department from prosecuting people in the United States who have committed the crime of human trafficking in other countries.

"We cannot allow our country to continue providing a safe haven for those trafficking in human misery," said Durbin. "For the third year in a row, the number of countries who are not doing enough to combat human trafficking has increased. If these countries won't prosecute those who engage in human trafficking, the United States should be empowered to bring justice to those traffickers who are in the United States."

Under current law, federal prosecutors can only pursue human trafficking crimes if they are committed within the United States or by a U.S. citizen abroad. In contrast, other violations of fundamental human rights—such as torture, terrorism, and hostage taking—may be prosecuted even when committed outside the United States by non-U.S. citizens, The Trafficking in Persons Accountability Act would close the current loophole by amending the Peonage, Slavery, and Trafficking in Persons chapter of the federal criminal code to allow prosecution of non-U.S. citizens for human trafficking committed outside the United States.

"This bill gives our country the option to prosecute those who engage in human trafficking when they are found on our soil. It is contrary to our system of justice to allow perpetrators of these reprehensible crimes to go free without fear of prosecution," Dr. Coburn said. . . .

Source: "Senators Durbin and Coburn Introduce Human Trafficking Bill." States News Service (6/27/07).

5

International Documents

This chapter contains excerpts of primary source documents concerning international human trafficking. It is divided into the following sections:

International treaties amd declarations

International accounts of human trafficking

Netherlands

Nigeria

India

Belize

INTERNATIONAL TREATIES AND DECLARATIONS

The League of Nations 1926 Slavery Convention (excerpt)

While earlier regional conventions had called for abolition, this was the first truly international convention to address slavery. Rather than calling on its signatory parties to abolish slavery immediately, it called on them to "bring about, progressively and as quickly as possible, the complete abolition of slavery in all its forms." It acknowledges forced labor but, unlike later international conventions, does not categorize it as slavery. The League of Nations was dissolved in 1946, but the United Nations adopted this convention in 1953.

Article 1

For the purpose of the present Convention, the following definitions are agreed upon:

(1) Slavery is the status or condition of a person over whom any or all of the powers attaching to the right of ownership are exercised.

(2) The slave trade includes all acts involved in the capture, acquisition or disposal of a person with intent to reduce him to slavery; all acts involved

in the acquisition of a slave with a view to selling or exchanging him; all acts of disposal by sale or exchange of a slave acquired with a view to being sold or exchanged, and, in general, every act of trade or transport in slaves.

Article 2

The High Contracting Parties undertake, each in respect of the territories placed under its sovereignty, jurisdiction, protection, suzerainty or tutelage, so far as they have not already taken the necessary steps:

(a) To prevent and suppress the slave trade;

(b) To bring about, progressively and as soon as possible, the complete abolition of slavery in all its forms.

Source: Office of the High Commissioner for Human Rights. "Slavery Convention" (1926). Available online. URL: http://www.unhchr.ch/html/menu3/b/f2sc.htm. Accessed October 7, 2007.

International Labour Organization, Convention (No. 29) Concerning Forced Labour (1930) (excerpt)

This convention calls for an end to all forms of forced labor "within the shortest period possible" and provides guidelines for a transition period, including a provision for the continued use of forced labor for public works.

Article 1

1. Each Member of the International Labour Organisation which ratifies this Convention undertakes to suppress the use of forced or compulsory labour in all its forms within the shortest possible period.

2. With a view to this complete suppression, recourse to forced or compulsory labour may be had, during the transitional period, for public purposes only and as an exceptional measure, subject to the conditions and guarantees hereinafter provided.

3. At the expiration of a period of five years after the coming into force of this Convention, and when the Governing Body of the International Labour Office prepares the report provided for in article 31 below, the said Governing Body shall consider the possibility of the suppression of forced or compulsory labour in all its forms without a further transitional period and the desirability of placing this question on the agenda of the Conference.

Source: International Labour Organization. "Convention (No. 29) Concerning Forced Labour" (1930). Available online. URL: http://www.unhchr.ch/html/medu3/b/31.htm. Accessed December 31, 2007.

United Nations Universal Declaration of Human Rights (1948)

One of five documents said to constitute an international bill of rights, the Universal Declaration of Human Rights recognizes the "equal and inalienable rights of all members of the human family" and specifically prohibits slavery. This document is reproduced here in its entirety.

Article 1

All human beings are born free and equal in dignity and rights. They are endowed with reason and conscience and should act towards one another in a spirit of brotherhood.

Article 2

Everyone is entitled to all the rights and freedoms set forth in this Declaration, without distinction of any kind, such as race, colour, sex, language, religion, political or other opinion, national or social origin, property, birth or other status. Furthermore, no distinction shall be made on the basis of the political, jurisdictional or international status of the country or territory to which a person belongs, whether it be independent, trust, non-self-governing or under any other limitation of sovereignty.

Article 3

Everyone has the right to life, liberty and security of person.

Article 4

No one shall be held in slavery or servitude; slavery and the slave trade shall be prohibited in all their forms. . . .

Article 16

1. Men and women of full age, without any limitation due to race, nationality or religion, have the right to marry and to found a family. They are entitled to equal rights as to marriage, during marriage and at its dissolution.

2. Marriage shall be entered into only with the free and full consent of the intending spouses.

3. The family is the natural and fundamental group unit of society and is entitled to protection by society and the State. . . .

Source: United Nations. "Universal Declaration of Human Rights" (1948). Available online. URL: http://www.un.org/Overview/rights.html. Accessed August 3, 2007.

United Nations Convention for the Suppression of the Traffic in Persons and of the Exploitation of the Prostitution of Others (1949) (excerpt)

This convention addressed the trafficking in persons, specifically women and children, for sexual exploitation. It did not address other forms of trafficking in persons.

Article 1

The Parties to the present Convention agree to punish any person who, to gratify the passions of another:

(1) Procures, entices or leads away, for purposes of prostitution, another person, even with the consent of that person;

(2) Exploits the prostitution of another person, even with the consent of that person.

Article 2

The Parties to the present Convention further agree to punish any person who:

(1) Keeps or manages, or knowingly finances or takes part in the financing of a brothel;

(2) Knowingly lets or rents a building or other place or any part thereof for the purpose of the prostitution of others. . . .

Source: United Nations. "Convention for the Suppression of the Traffic in Persons and of the Exploitation of the Prostitution of Others." Available online. URL: http://www.unhchr.ch/html/menu3/b/33.htm. Accessed March 25, 2008.

United Nations Supplementary Convention on the Abolition of Slavery, the Slave Trade, and Institutions and Practices Similar to Slavery (1956) (excerpt)

This convention acknowledged that chattel slavery still existed in some parts of the world, and it classified practices that create "servile status"—specifically debt bondage, serfdom, unfree or forced marriage, and exploitive child labor— as practices similar to slavery. Parties to the convention agreed to abolish all such practices "as soon as possible."

Section I.—Institutions and practices similar to slavery
Article 1

Each of the States Parties to this Convention shall take all practicable and necessary legislative and other measures to bring about progressively and as soon as possible the complete abolition or abandonment of the following institutions and practices, where they still exist and whether or not they are covered by the definition of slavery contained in article 1 of the Slavery Convention signed at Geneva on 25 September 1926:

(a) Debt bondage, that is to say, the status or condition arising from a pledge by a debtor of his personal services or of those of a person under his control as security for a debt, if the value of those services as reasonably assessed is not applied towards the liquidation of the debt or the length and nature of those services are not respectively limited and defined;

(b) Serfdom, that is to say, the condition or status of a tenant who is by law, custom or agreement bound to live and labour on land belonging to another person and to render some determinate service to such other person, whether for reward or not, and is not free to change his status;

(c) Any institution or practice whereby:

(i) A woman, without the right to refuse, is promised or given in marriage on payment of a consideration in money or in kind to her parents, guardian, family or any other person or group; or

(ii) The husband of a woman, his family, or his clan, has the right to transfer her to another person for value received or otherwise; or

(iii) A woman on the death of her husband is liable to be inherited by another person;

(d) Any institution or practice whereby a child or young person under the age of 18 years, is delivered by either or both of his natural parents or by his guardian to another person, whether for reward or not, with a view to the exploitation of the child or young person or of his labour.

Article 2

With a view to bringing to an end the institutions and practices mentioned in article 1 (c) of this Convention, the States Parties undertake to prescribe, where appropriate, suitable minimum ages of marriage, to encourage the use of facilities whereby the consent of both parties to a marriage may be freely expressed in the presence of a competent civil or religious authority, and to encourage the registration of marriages.

Section II.—The slave trade
Article 3

1. The act of conveying or attempting to convey slaves from one country to another by whatever means of transport, or of being accessory thereto, shall be a criminal offence under the laws of the States Parties to this Convention and persons convicted thereof shall be liable to very severe penalties. . . .

Source: United Nations. "Supplementary Convention on the Abolition of Slavery, the Slave Trade, an Institutions and Practices Similar to Slavery." Available online. URL: http://www/ohcr.org/english/law/pdf/slavetrade.pdf. Accessed July 15, 2007.

International Labour Organization, Convention (No. 105) Concerning the Abolition of Forced Labour (1957) (excerpt)

This convention, which referenced both the 1926 Slavery Convention and the 1956 Supplementary Convention on the Abolition of Slavery, the Slave Trade, and Institutions and Practices Similar to Slavery in its introductory section, committed ILO member signatories "to suppress and not make use of any form of forced or compulsory labour."

Article 1

Each Member of the International Labour Organisation which ratifies this Convention undertakes to suppress and not to make use of any form of forced or compulsory labour:

(a) As a means of political coercion or education or as a punishment for holding or expressing political views or views ideologically opposed to the established political, social or economic system;

(b) As a method of mobilising and using labour for purposes of economic development;

(c) As a means of labour discipline;

(d) As a punishment for having participated in strikes;

(e) As a means of racial, social, national or religious discrimination.

Article 2

Each Member of the International Labour Organisation which ratifies this Convention undertakes to take effective measures to secure the immediate and complete abolition of forced or compulsory labour as specified in article 1 of this Convention. . . .

Source: International Labour Organization. "Convention (No. 105) Concerning the Abolition of Forced Labour" (1957). Available online. URL: http://www.unhchr.ch/html/menu3/b/32.htm. Accessed December 31, 2007.

United Nations Convention on the Elimination of All Forms of Discrimination against Women (1979) (excerpt)

This convention, which is sometimes referred to as an international bill of rights for women, calls for the elimination of all forms of discrimination against women and defines what that would entail in civil, cultural, economic, social, political, and other areas of life. In addressing discrimination against women, it addresses one of the root causes of human trafficking.

Noting that the Charter of the United Nations reaffirms faith in fundamental human rights, in the dignity and worth of the human person and in the equal rights of men and women,

Noting that the Universal Declaration of Human Rights affirms the principle of the inadmissibility of discrimination and proclaims that all human beings are born free and equal in dignity and rights and that everyone is entitled to all the rights and freedoms set forth therein, without distinction of any kind, including distinction based on sex,

Noting that the States Parties to the International Covenants on Human Right have the obligation to ensure the equal rights of men and women to enjoy all economic, social, cultural, civil and political rights,

Considering the international conventions concluded under the auspices of the United Nations and the specialized agencies promoting equality of rights of men and women,

Noting also the resolutions, declarations and recommendations adopted by the United Nations and the specialized agencies promoting equality of rights of men and women,

Concerned, however, that despite these various instruments extensive discrimination against women continues to exist,

Recalling that discrimination against women violates the principles of equality of rights and respect for human dignity, is an obstacle to the participation of women, on equal terms with men, in the political, social, economic and cultural life of their countries, hampers the growth of the prosperity of society and the family and makes more difficult the full development of the potentialities of women in the service of their countries and of humanity,

Concerned that in situations of poverty women have the least access to food, health, education, training and opportunities for employment and other needs,

Convinced that the establishment of the new international economic order based on equity and justice will contribute significantly towards the promotion of equality between men and women,

Emphasizing that the eradication of apartheid, all forms of racism, racial discrimination, colonialism, neo-colonialism, aggression, foreign occupation and domination and interference in the internal affairs of States is essential to the full enjoyment of the rights of men and women,

Affirming that the strengthening of international peace and security, the relaxation of international tension, mutual co-operation among all States irrespective of their social and economic systems, general and complete disarmament, in particular nuclear disarmament under strict and effective international control, the affirmation of the principles of justice, equality and mutual benefit in relations among countries and the realization of the right of peoples under alien and colonial domination and foreign occupation to self-determination and independence, as well as respect for national sovereignty and territorial integrity, will promote social progress and development and as a consequence will contribute to the attainment of full equality between men and women,

Convinced that the full and complete development of a country, the welfare of the world and the cause of peace require the maximum participation of women on equal terms with men in all fields,

Bearing in mind the great contribution of women to the welfare of the family and to the development of society, so far not fully recognized, the social significance of maternity and the role of both parents in the family and in the upbringing of children, and aware that the role of women in procreation should not be a basis for discrimination but that the upbringing of children requires a sharing of responsibility between men and women and society as a whole,

Aware that a change in the traditional role of men as well as the role of women in society and in the family is needed to achieve full equality between men and women,

Determined to implement the principles set forth in the Declaration on the Elimination of Discrimination against Women and, for that purpose, to adopt the measures required for the elimination of such discrimination in all its forms and manifestations. . . .

Source: United Nations. "Convention on the Elimination of all Forms of Discrimination against Women" (1979). Available online. URL: http://www.unhchr.ch/html/menu3/b/31cedaw.htm. Accessed December 31, 2007.

Hague Convention on Protection of Children and Co-Operation in Respect of Intercountry Adoptions (1993)

Following a preamble that stressed the importance to children of growing up in a loving family and the role intercountry adoption can play in the life of a child who has not found an adoptive home in his or her native country, the Hague Convention on Intercountry Adoption set forth the following origin country requirements for intercountry adoption, in part "to prevent the abduction, the sale of, or traffic in children."

CHAPTER 11—REQUIREMENTS FOR INTERCOUNTRY ADOPTIONS

Article 4

An adoption within the scope of the Convention shall take place only if the competent authorities of the State of origin—

a) have established that the child is adoptable;

b) have determined, after possibilities for placement of the child within the state of origin have been given due consideration, that an intercountry adoption is in the child's best interests;

c) have ensured that

(1) the persons, institutions and authorities whose consent for adoption, have been counselled as may be necessary and duly informed of the effects of their consent, in particular whether or not an adoption will result in the termination of the legal relationship between the child and his or her family of origin;

(2) such persons, institutions and authorities have given their consent freely in the required legal form, and

(3) the consents have not been induced by payment or compensation of any kind and have not been withdrawn; and

179

(4)the consent of the mother, where required, has been given only after the birth of the child; and

d) have ensured, having regard to the age and degree of maturity of the child, that

(1) he or she has been counseled and duly informed of the effects of the adoption and of his or her consent to the adoption, where such consent is required,

(2) consideration has been given to the child's wishes and opinions,

(3) the child's consent to the adoption, where such consent is required, has been given freely, in the required legal form, and expressed or evidenced in writing, and

(4) such consent has not been induced by payment or compensation of any kind.

Source: Hague Conference on Private International Law. "Hague Convention on Protection of Children and Co-Operation in Respect of Intercountry Adoptions." Available online. URL: http://adoption.state.gov/hague/overview/text.html. Accessed March 13, 2009.

International Labour Organization, Convention Concerning the Prohibition and Immediate Action for the Elimination of the Worst Forms of Child Labour (1999) (excerpt)

This convention seeks to eliminate the worst forms of child labor and sets forth definitions of those worst forms of labor, while recognizing, in its introductory section, the root causes of child labor.

Article 1

Each Member which ratifies this Convention shall take immediate and effective measures to secure the prohibition and elimination of the worst forms of child labour as a matter of urgency.

Article 2

For the purposes of this Convention, the term "child" shall apply to all persons under the age of 18.

Article 3

For the purposes of this Convention, the term "the worst forms of child labour" comprises:

all forms of slavery or practices similar to slavery, such as the sale and trafficking of children, debt bondage and serfdom and forced or compulsory labour, including forced or compulsory recruitment of children for use in armed conflict;

the use, procuring or offering of a child for prostitution, for the production of pornography or for pornographic performances;

the use, procuring or offering of a child for illicit activities, in particular for the production and trafficking of drugs as defined in the relevant international treaties;

work which, by its nature or the circumstances in which it is carried out, is likely to harm the health, safety or morals of children. . . .

Source: International Labour Organization. "ILO Convention 182, Convention Concerning the Prohibition and Immediate Action for the Elimination of the Worst Forms of Child Labour" (1999). Available online. URL: http://www.un.org/children/conflict/keydocuments/english/iloconvention1828.html. Accessed December 31, 2007.

United Nations Protocol to Prevent, Suppress and Punish Trafficking in Persons, Especially Women and Children, Supplementing the United Nations Convention against Transnational Crime (2000) (excerpt)

This is a foundational convention in the struggle against human trafficking. Defining trafficking in persons in words that have become the most commonly accepted definition, it commits its parties to criminalize trafficking within their borders, protect trafficking's victims, and work to prevent human trafficking.

Preamble

The States Parties to this Protocol,

Declaring that effective action to prevent and combat trafficking in persons, especially women and children, requires a comprehensive international approach in the countries of origin, transit and destination that includes measures to prevent such trafficking, to: punish the traffickers and to protect the victims of such trafficking, including by protecting their internationally recognized human rights,

Taking into account the fact that, despite the existence of a variety of international instruments containing rules and practical measures to combat the exploitation of persons, especially women and children, there is no universal instrument that addresses all aspects of trafficking in persons, . . .

Have agreed as follows:

Article 2
Statement of purpose

The purposes of this Protocol are:

(a) To prevent and combat trafficking in persons, paying particular attention to women and children;

(b) To protect and assist the victims of such trafficking, with full respect for their human rights; and

(c) To promote cooperation among States Parties in order to meet those objectives.

Article 3
Use of terms

For the purposes of this Protocol:

(a) "Trafficking in persons" shall mean the recruitment, transportation, transfer, harbouring or receipt of persons, by means of the threat or use of force or other forms of coercion, of abduction, of fraud, of deception, of the abuse of power or of a position of vulnerability or of the giving or receiving of payments or benefits to achieve the consent of a person having control over another person, for the purpose of exploitation. Exploitation shall include, at a minimum, the exploitation of the prostitution of others or other forms of sexual exploitation, forced labour or services, slavery or practices similar to slavery, servitude or the removal of organs;

(b) The consent of a victim of trafficking in persons to the intended exploitation set forth in subparagraph (a) of this article shall be irrelevant where any of the means set forth in subparagraph (a) have been used;

(c) The recruitment, transportation; transfer, harbouring or receipt of a child for the purpose of exploitation shall be considered "trafficking in persons" even if this does not involve any of the means set forth in subparagraph (a) of this article;

(d) "Child" shall mean any person under eighteen years of age.

United Nations Optional Protocol to the Convention on the Rights of the Child on the Sale of Children, Child Prostitution and Child Pornography (2000) (excerpt)

This protocol, as its title indicates, adds provisions to the Convention on the Rights of the Child (1989). In addition to prohibiting the commercial sexual exploitation of children, it raises concern about growing areas of exploitation, including sex tourism and Internet pornography.

Article 1

States Parties shall prohibit the sale of children, child prostitution and child pornography as provided for by the present Protocol.

Article 2

For the purposes of the present Protocol:

(a) Sale of children means any act or transaction whereby a child is transferred by any person or group of persons to another for remuneration or any other consideration;

(b) Child prostitution means the use of a child in sexual activities for remuneration or any other form of consideration;

(c) Child pornography means any representation, by whatever means, of a child engaged in real or simulated explicit sexual activities or any representation of the sexual parts of a child for primarily sexual purposes.

Article 3

1. Each State Party shall ensure that, as a minimum, the following acts and activities are fully covered under its criminal or penal law, whether such offences are committed domestically or transnational or on an individual or organized basis:

(a) In the context of sale of children as defined in article 2:

(i) Offering, delivering or accepting, by whatever means, a child for the purpose of:

a. Sexual exploitation of the child;

b. Transfer of organs of the child for profit;

c. Engagement of the child in forced labour;

(ii) Improperly inducing consent, as an intermediary, for the adoption of a child in violation of applicable international legal instruments on adoption;

(b) Offering, obtaining, procuring or providing a child for child prostitution, as defined in article 2;

(c) Producing, distributing, disseminating, importing, exporting, offering, selling or possessing for the above purposes child pornography as defined in article 2. . . .

Source: United Nations. "Optional Protocol to the Convention on the Rights of the Child on the Sale of Children, Child Prostitution and Child Pornography" (2000). Available online. URL: http://www.unhrchr.ch/html/menu2/6/crc/treaties/opsc.htm. Accessed December 31, 2007.

United Nations Optional Protocol to the Convention on the Rights of the Child on the Involvement of Children in Armed Conflicts (2000) (excerpt)

This protocol, which adds provisions to the Convention on the Rights of the Child (1989), is intended to eliminate the use of child soldiers. It prohibits compulsory recruitment of persons younger than 18 into the military or other armed groups and forbids their use in combat, among other measures.

The States Parties to the present Protocol,

. . . Noting that article 1 of the Convention on the Rights of the Child specifies that, for the purposes of that Convention, a child means every human being below the age of 18 years unless, under the law applicable to the child, majority is attained earlier, . . .

Have agreed as follows:

Article 1
States Parties shall take all feasible measures to ensure that members of their armed forces who have not attained the age of 18 years do not take a direct part in hostilities.

Article 2
States Parties shall ensure that persons who have not attained the age of 18 years are not compulsorily recruited into their armed forces.

Article 3
1. States Parties shall raise the minimum age for the voluntary recruitment of persons into their national armed forces from that set out in

article 38, paragraph 3, of the Convention on the Rights of the Child, taking account of the principles contained in that article and recognizing that under the Convention persons under 18 are entitled to special protection.

2. Each State Party shall deposit a binding declaration upon ratification of or accession to this Protocol that sets forth the minimum age at which it will permit voluntary recruitment into its national armed forces and a description of the safeguards that it has adopted to ensure that such recruitment is not forced or coerced.

3. States Parties that permit voluntary recruitment into their national armed forces under the age of 18 shall maintain safeguards to ensure, as a minimum, that:
    (a) Such recruitment is genuinely voluntary;
    (b) Such recruitment is done with the informed consent of the persons parents or legal guardians;
    (c) Such persons are fully informed of the duties involved in such military service;
    (d) Such persons provide reliable proof of age prior to acceptance into national military service.

4. Each State Party may strengthen its declaration at any time by notification to that effect addressed to the Secretary-General of the United Nations, who shall inform all States Parties. Such notification shall take effect on the date on which it is received by the Secretary-General.

5. The requirement to raise the age in paragraph 1 of the present article does not apply to schools operated by or under the control of the armed forces of the States Parties, in keeping with articles 28 and 29 of the Convention on the Rights of the Child.

Article 4

1. Armed groups that are distinct from the armed forces of a State should not, under any circumstances, recruit or use in hostilities persons under the age of 18 years.

2. States Parties shall take all feasible measures to prevent such recruitment and use, including the adoption of legal measures necessary to prohibit and criminalize such practices.

3. The application of the present article under this Protocol shall not affect the legal status of any party to an armed conflict.

Source: United Nations. "Optional Protocol to the Convention on the Rights of the Child on the Involvement of Children in Armed Conflicts" (2000). Available online. URL: http://www2.ohchr.org/english/law/pdf/crc-conflict.pdf. Accessed December 31, 2007.

United Nations Millennium Declaration (2000, excerpt)

This declaration was unanimously adopted by the leaders of 189 member nations. It pledges countries to eliminate extreme poverty and hunger, to achieve universal primary education, and to promote gender equality and empower women, among other goals, by 2015. In addressing these conditions, this declaration addresses several of the root causes of human trafficking.

19. We resolve further:

- To halve, by the year 2015, the proportion of the world's people whose income is less than one dollar a day and the proportion of people who suffer from hunger and, by the same date, to halve the proportion of people who are unable to reach or to afford safe drinking water.
- To ensure that, by the same date, children everywhere, boys and girls alike, will be able to complete a full course of primary schooling and that girls and boys will have equal access to all levels of education.
- By the same date, to have reduced maternal mortality by three quarters, and under-five child mortality by two thirds, of their current rates.
- To have, by then, halted, and begun to reverse, the spread of HIV/AIDS, the scourge of malaria and other major diseases that afflict humanity.
- To provide special assistance to children orphaned by HIV/AIDS.
- By 2020, to have achieved a significant improvement in the lives of at least 100 million slum dwellers as proposed in the "Cities Without Slums" initiative.

20. We also resolve:

- To promote gender equality and the empowerment of women as effective ways to combat poverty, hunger and disease and to stimulate development that is truly sustainable.

- To develop and implement strategies that give young people everywhere a real chance to find decent and productive work. . . .

Source: United Nations. "United Nations Millennium Declaration." Available online. URL: http://www.un.org/millennium/declaration/ares552e.htm. Accessed December 31, 2007.

INTERNATIONAL ACCOUNTS OF HUMAN TRAFFICKING

Victim Testimony and Reports (2005)

The following are selections from international victim testimony and description contained in the 2005 U.S. Trafficking in Persons Report.

CENTRAL AFRICA: Mary, a 16-year-old demobilized child soldier, forced to join an armed rebel group in central Africa, remembers: "I feel so bad about the things that I did. It disturbs me so much: that I inflicted death on other people. When I go home I must do some traditional rites because I have killed. I must perform these rites and cleanse myself. I still dream about the boy from my village whom I killed. I see him in my dreams, and he is talking to me, saying I killed him for nothing, and I am crying."

CAMBODIA: Neary grew up in rural Cambodia. Her parents died when she was a child, and, in an effort to give her a better life, her sister married her off when she was 17. Three months later they went to visit a fishing village. Her husband rented a room in what Neary thought was a guest house. But when she woke the next morning, her husband was gone. The owner of the house told her she had been sold by her husband for $300 and that she was actually in a brothel.

For five years, Neary was raped by five to seven men every day. In addition to brutal physical abuse, Neary was infected with HIV and contracted AIDS. The brothel threw her out when she became sick, and she eventually found her way to a local shelter. She died of HIV/AIDS at the age of 23.

ITALY: Viola, a young Albanian, was 13 when she started dating 21-year-old Dilin, who proposed to marry her, then move to Italy where he had cousins who could get him a job. Arriving in Italy, Viola's life changed forever. Dilin locked her in a hotel room and left her, never to be seen again. A group of men entered, and began to beat Viola. Then, each raped her. The leader informed Viola that Dilin had sold her and that she had to obey him or else

187

she would be killed. For seven days Viola was beaten and repeatedly raped. Viola was sold a second time to someone who beat her head so badly she was unable to see for two days. She was told if she didn't work as a prostitute, her mother and sister in Albania would be raped and killed. Viola was forced to submit to prostitution until police raided the brothel she was in. She was deported to Albania.

SINGAPORE: Karin, a young mother of two, was looking for a job in Sri Lanka when a man befriended her and convinced her that she could land a better job in Singapore as a waitress. He arranged and paid for her travel. A Sri Lankan woman met Karin upon arrival in Singapore, confiscated her passport, and took her to a hotel. The woman made it clear that Karin had to submit to prostitution to pay back the money it cost for her to be flown into Singapore. Karin was taken to an open space for sale in the sex market where she joined women from Indonesia, Thailand, India, and China to be inspected and purchased by men from Pakistan, India. China, Indonesia and Africa. The men would take the women to nearby hotels and rape them. Karin was forced to have sex with an average of 15 men a day or night. She developed a serious illness, and three months after her arrival was arrested by the Singaporean police during a raid on the brothel. She was deported to Sri Lanka.

Source: U.S. Department of State. "Trafficking in Persons Report, 2005," p. 21. Available online. URL: http://www. state.gov/documents/organization/47255.pdf. Accessed June 5, 2007.

Victim Testimony and Reports (2006)

The following are selections from international victim testimony and description contained in the 2006 U.S. Trafficking in Persons Report.

LIBERIA: A 13-year-old former child soldier from Liberia recounts; "They gave me pills that made me crazy. When the craziness got in my head, I beat people on their heads and hurt them until they bled. When the craziness got out of my head I felt guilty. If I remembered the person I went to them and apologized. If they did not accept my apology, I felt bad."

AFGHANISTAN: Naseema was forced by her mother into marriage at the age of four to a 30 year old neighbor in an Afghan village. At her husband's home, her father-in-law and 12 others in the family began torturing her. Her treatment included beatings and starvation, and she was forced to sleep outside in the cold with only a rug to protect her. Her abusers often used her as a human table, forcing her to lie on her stomach so they could cut their food on her bare back. At one point, her father-in-law locked her in a shed for two months and she was only allowed to leave once a day. The night before she escaped at the age of 12 in 2005, her father-in-law tied her hands together and poured scalding water over her head. She escaped the next day, fearing death at the hands of her husband's family, and was found by a rickshaw driver who took her to the hospital for treatment; it took over one month for her to heal from the various injuries inflicted upon her. She is now in a shelter and attending school.

ROMANIA: Maria, age 16, was tricked into traveling to Bucharest to find a job by a childhood friend. Unbeknownst to Maria, the friend had advertised in a Romanian port city that there was a "girl for sale." Maria was sold to a man who used her as a prostitute, along with an 11-year-old girl. For four months, she was forced to work as a street prostitute under the threat of beatings. She was fined, arrested, and interrogated numerous times by the police; however, her "protector" bribed the police, to release her, thus forcing her to prostitute again.

UGANDA: Michael was 15 when he was kidnapped by the Lord's Resistance Army (LRA) to serve as a combatant in the Ugandan insurgent force. During his forced service in the LRA, he was made to kill a boy who had tried to escape. He also watched another boy being hacked to death because he did not alert the guards when his friend successfully escaped.

Source: U.S. Department of State. "Trafficking in Persons Report, 2006," p. 20. Available online. URL: http://www. state.gov/documents/organization66086.pdf. Accessed June 5, 2007.

Victim Testimony and Reports (2007)

The following are selections from international victim testimony and description contained in the 2007 U.S. Trafficking in Persons Report.

Ko Aung said: "I was recruited by force, against my will. One evening while we were watching a video show in my village, three army sergeants came. They checked whether we had identification cards and asked if we wanted to join the army. We explained that we were underage and hadn't got identification cards. I said no and came back home that evening but an army recruitment unit arrived next morning at my village and demanded two new recruits. Those who could not pay 3000 kyats ($9) had to join the army, they said. My parents could not pay, and altogether 19 of us were recruited and sent to Mingladon [an army training center]."

Susie, 39-years-old, was in high spirits at the airport in Mombasa. She boarded a plane on her way to Germany to spend a three-month holiday, courtesy of her "boyfriend" who had lavished gifts on her. All hopes of an exciting, wonderful stay in a foreign land were shattered on arrival in Germany, when her boyfriend/trafficker confiscated her passport and denied her food for several days before informing her that she would work as a sex slave. She was raped repeatedly, beaten, and threatened with death. After enduring gross exploitation, Susie used a cell phone to call police.

Hanuel said: "I was sold to be the wife of a 47-year-old Chinese man who has no work skills and was very ill. My husband would hit me and say: 'You, do you have any idea how much I paid for you?' I am not the only North Korean woman in this area. As I was talking to some of the others, we came to realize that we have been sold into this kind of marriage."

At just 17-years-old, Maryam dreamed of a better future than her life in Kazakhstan. A man paid her parents $300 and forged a passport so that she could work in Russia as a shop assistant. When she arrived in Russia, the shop turned out to be a locked cell with barred windows and a metal door. After the armed guards told her she would be used as a prostitute, rather than a shop assistant, she said: "I refused by saying that they could do anything they want, but I wouldn't be a prostitute. I was punished for that. I was beaten up, raped, and starved. In five days I gave up."

"I was sold several times," she said. "I was living in a basement. There was always a huge line of clients and I couldn't service them all."

—Nadia, a 14-year-old Moldovan girl

Thirty-year-old Mara left her husband and two children in Ukraine to take a housekeeping job in Italy. Recruiters from an employment agency promised her a high salary. But once there, she was taken to a brothel where the owner said he had purchased her for several hundred dollars. He said she owed him money for the plane ticket. For nine months, Mara was controlled by this trafficker, who beat her when she refused a client. If a man complained about her, the brothel owner increased her debt. Mara was freed only when the Italian police raided the brothel. Charged with prostitution, she was deported to Ukraine.

Trying to support a nine-year-old daughter back home, Benito followed a brother who had found work at the brick kilns at Transcameta in the Brazilian Amazon. Promised adequate pay, he was deceived into working for an employer who did not pay him, but rather assigned him an ever growing debt for food and lodging costs not previously disclosed. He toiled six days a week and couldn't afford to leave, since he didn't have enough money to get back to his home 500 miles away. Benito and the other slave laborers were not paid anything for months. He was afraid he wouldn't see any wages at all if he left. Benito lived next to the brick kilns in a shack with no ventilation, running water, or electricity. He contracted malaria from the mosquitoes that swarmed the camp.

In December 2005, 25 Ukrainian victims were found on a Russian fishing boat in the Sea of Japan. Recruiters lured men, ages 18 to 50, from poor fishing communities on the Black Sea with promises of good pay for work aboard industrial fishing vessels. Once at sea, however, the men were forced at gunpoint to work extremely long days without pay. They were deprived of sleep and physically and psychologically abused. They were deprived of food and water if they refused to work and sometimes consumed crab bait, consisting of raw fish, sea water, and melted ice water to survive. Although the vessel served as a perfect prison, their passports were confiscated. The victims were found and rescued when a Russian Coast Guard crew boarded the vessel to search for illegal poached crabs. They found the victims exhausted and half-starved, locked in the ship's hold along with three tons of illegally poached crab.

Source: U.S. Department of State. "Trafficking in Persons Report, 2007," p. 17. Available online. URL: http://www. state.gov.documents/organization/82902.pdf. Accessed July 31, 2007.

Sex Slaves Returning Home Raise AIDS Risk, Study Says

This article describes the connection between sex trafficking and the spread of HIV/AIDS.

Adding another bleak dimension to the sordid world of sex slavery, young girls who have been trafficked abroad into prostitution are emerging as an AIDS risk factor in their home countries, according to a study being released today.

Girls who were forced into prostitution before age 15 and girls traded between brothels were particularly likely to be infected, the study found. . . .

Source: Donald D. G. McNeil, Jr. "Sex Slaves Returning Home Raise AIDS Risk, Study Says." *New York Times* (8/1/07).

NETHERLANDS

Article 273a Criminal Code

With passage of this national anti-trafficking legislation, Dutch law recognized trafficking forced labor as a form of modern-day slavery. (Earlier criminal codes had recognized only trafficking for sexual exploitation.)

Prior to 2005, only trafficking for sexual exploitation was recognized as human trafficking under Dutch law. The passage of this act broadened that definition to include forced labor and the involuntary harvesting of organs.

Article 273a (non-official, English translation of 1 January 2005)

1. Any person who:

(a) by force, violence or other act, by the threat of violence or other act, by extortion, fraud, deception or the misuse of authority arising from the actual state of affairs, by the misuse of a vulnerable position or by giving or receiving remuneration or benefits in order to obtain the consent of a person who has control over this other person recruits, transports, moves, accommodates or shelters another person, with the intention of exploiting this other person or removing his or her organs;

(b) recruits, transports, moves, accommodates or shelters a person with the intention of exploiting that other person or removing his or her organs, when that person has not yet reached the age of eighteen years;

(c) recruits, takes with him or abducts a person with the intention of inducing that person to make himself/herself available for performing sexual acts with or for a third party for remuneration in another country;

(d) forces or induces another person by the means referred to under (a) to make himself/herself available for performing work or services or making his/her organs available or takes any action in the circumstances referred to under (a) which he knows or may reasonably be expected to know will result in that other person making himself/herself available for performing labour or services or making his/her organs available;

(e) induces another person to make himself/herself available for performing sexual acts with or for a third party for remuneration or to make his/her organs available for remuneration or takes any action towards another person which he knows or may reasonably be expected to know that this will result in that other person making himself/herself available for performing these acts or making his/her organs available for remuneration, when that other person has not yet reached the age of eighteen years;

(f) wilfully profits from the exploitation of another person;

(g) wilfully profits from the removal of organs from another person, while he knows or may reasonably be expected to know that the organs of that person have been removed under the circumstances referred to under (a);

(h) wilfully profits from the sexual acts of another person with or for a third party for remuneration or the removal of that person's organs for remuneration, when this other person has not yet reached the age of eighteen years;

(i) forces or induces another person by the means referred to under (a) to provide him with the proceeds of that person's sexual acts with or for a third party or of the removal of that person's organs;

shall be guilty of trafficking in human beings. . . .

Source: Bureau Nationaal Rapporteur Mensenhandel. "Trafficking in Human Beings, Supplementary Figures: Fourth Report of the Dutch National Rapporteur" (2005), pp. 17–18, 39. Available online. URL: http://rechten.uvt. nl/victimology/national/NL-NRMEngels4.pdf. Accessed December 26, 2007.

Netherlands: Legalizing Brothels

In 1999, brothels were legalized in the Netherlands.

The lower house of Parliament voted to legalize brothels, saying regulation of the sex industry would help reduce trafficking in women, exploitation of minors and drug crimes. Prostitution is already legal but brothels are not. The measure now goes to the upper house, where it is expected to pass, becoming law on Jan. 1.

Source: New York Times (2/3/99).

UNODC Head Welcomes Dutch Campaign against Sexual Exploitation

In 2006, the Netherlands began a campaign to identify people trafficked into the country's sex industry.

The Executive Director of the United Nations *Office on Drugs and Crime* (UNODC), Antonio Maria Costa, welcomed the launch of a campaign against sexual exploitation in the Netherlands and said he hoped other countries would follow the Dutch example.

The campaign, which is being launched today by the Dutch Crimestoppers organization Meld Misdaad Anoniem and is financed by the Netherlands Ministry of Justice, will seek to identify possible victims of human trafficking who have been forced to work in the sex industry. Clients of prostitutes, local residents, shopkeepers and taxi-drivers will be encouraged to be aware of the warning signs and to pass on information.

"I welcome this initiative by the Netherlands and hope this campaign will lead to the rescue of victims," Mr. Costa said. "Victims of trafficking suffer the most cruel, degrading and violent treatment. I encourage people to support this important campaign and provide information to their local police or through the hotline. I hope other European countries will also do more to end sexual exploitation."

Source: UN Information Service, January 12, 2006. Available online. URL: http://www.unis.unvienna.org/unis/pressrls/2006/uniscp259.html. Accessed March 20, 2008.

Dutch Urge Clients to Report Forced Prostitution

This article provides details of the Netherlands's campaign to identify women trafficked into the country's sex industry.

The Netherlands launched a campaign on Thursday to fight forced prostitution by urging clients to alert police if they suspect women are being coerced into selling themselves.

Each year about 3,500 women are trafficked to the Netherlands to work in brothels or illegal escort agencies even though the Dutch have thousands of self-employed prostitutes and some of the most liberal sex laws in the world, research shows.

Billboard posters will be plastered around the country's red light districts, and flyers and magazine adverts will remind those who visit brothels or window-prostitutes that not all who work in the sex industry do so willingly. . . .

The posters depict a striking silhouette of a prostitute in spike-heeled knee-high boots, but the contours of her body form another silhouette of a man holding a gun to a woman's head.

The campaign to protect the forced prostitutes, who mainly come from eastern Europe with some from Asia, was launched by the Dutch justice ministry and the police.

Last year Dutch police received more than 600 tip-offs about women who may have been forced into prostitution, and 400 women contacted the Dutch foundation against female trafficking.

"A typical scenario is a woman leaves her country with someone she trusts, expecting to work in a bar or nightclub. But the person turns out to be a trafficker who sells her on to pimps in the Netherlands," a foundation spokeswoman said.

Source: Alexandra Hudson. Reuters (1/12/06).

Trafficked to the West

This article recounts the experience of a Lithuanian woman trafficked into the Netherlands's sex industry.

Last summer, she had been approached by a childhood friend, she told me.

He said he knew someone who was recruiting women to work as prostitutes in Holland.

Prostitution is illegal in Lithuania, but in Holland he said, she would make big money. Trusting him, she agreed.

Within weeks she arrived in Holland—only to find herself a prisoner in a brothel—sold by her friend to a Lithuanian gang.

For months she endured beatings, sexual abuse and a constant stream of clients.

She saw little of the money she had been promised. When she escaped back to Lithuania her childhood friend tipped off the gang members.

They beat her so badly, she almost died. Today she is in hiding, terrified that her attackers will return.

Source: Jill McGivering. BBC News (9/7/05). Available online. URL: http://news.bbc.co.uk/1/hi/programmes/from_our_own_correspondent/4663841.stm. Accessed March 20, 2008.

Canada Considers Further Legalizing Prostitution While Amsterdam Mayor Admits Legalization's Failure

In 2008, Amsterdam's mayor and law enforcement officers decried the increase of "modern slavery" in the wake of the Netherlands' legalization of brothels, while Canadian officials considered legalization of brothels in their own country.

A Liberal dominated government committee looking into prostitution is recommending the Canadian government legalize solicitation so that prostitutes may legally offer sex for money. Meanwhile the mayor of Amsterdam has for the first time admitted that the Dutch experiment to curb abuse by legalizing prostitution has failed miserably.

Police in Amsterdam's infamous red light district were quoted by Dutch media Friday as saying, "We are in the midst of modern slavery." Due to the legalization of prostitution in the Netherlands in 2000, police are hampered in confronting the horrors that are characteristic of the sex trade.

Even Amsterdam mayor Job Cohen, who as recently as four months ago was quoted in the media as praising the legalization of prostitution has been forced to admit the scheme's failure. "Almost five years after the lifting of the brothel ban, we have to acknowledge that the aims of the law have not been reached", said Cohen. . . .

Source: LifeSiteNews.com (10/5/05). Available online. URL: http://www.lifesite.net/ldn/2005/oct/05100508. html. Accessed February 6, 2008.

Mayor Unveils Plan to Clean Up Amsterdam's Red-Light District

In 1999, Amsterdam mayor Job Cohen, conceding that brothel legalization had increased the trafficking of women into the city's sex industry, announced plans to scale back the city's red-light district.

The mayor of Amsterdam announced plans on Monday to overhaul the city's red-light district, an area known for prostitution, sex shows and soft drugs.

Job Cohen said he doesn't want prostitution or drugs recriminalized, but would like to shut down the shops showcasing the prostitutes from behind glass windows.

He said a move in 2000 to legalize prostitution failed to curb gangsters running Amsterdam's sex trade.

Legalization "didn't bring us what we hoped and expected," he told reporters at the upscale Krasnapolsky Hotel on Dam Square, which backs onto the red-light district.

"We want in part to reverse it, especially with regard to the exploitation of women in the sex industry," he said.

Officials fear women are being forced into prostitution, something that legalization was supposed to prevent.

"We have seen in the last years that women trafficking has becoming more, so in this respect the legalizing of the prostitution didn't work out," Cohen said.

Source: Canadian Broadcast News (12/18/07). Available online. URL: http://www.cbc.ca/world/story/2007/12/17/ amsterdam-district.html?ref=rss. Accessed March 20, 2008.

NIGERIA

Trafficking in Persons (Prohibition) Law Enforcement and Administration Act (2003) (excerpts)

This law prohibited trafficking in Nigeria and established the National Agency for the Prohibition of Traffic in Persons and Other Related Matters (NAPTIP) to investigate and prosecute traffickers.

. . . 11-Any person who—

(a) exports from Nigeria to any place outside Nigeria any person under the age of eighteen years with intent that such person, or knowing it to be likely that such person will be forced or seduced into prostitution in that place, or

(b) imports into Nigeria from any place outside Nigeria, any person under the age of eighteen years with intent that may be, or knowing it to be likely that such person will be forced into prostitution any where in Nigeria, commits an offence and is liable on conviction to imprisonment for life.

12. Any person who—

(a) by the use of deception, coercion, debt bondage or any means whatsoever, induces any person under the age of eighteen years to go from one place to another to do any act with intent that such person may be, or knowing that it is likely that the person will be forced or seduced into illicit intercourse with another person, or

(b) in order to gratify the passions of another person, procures, entices or leads away, even with such person's consent, any person under the age of eighteen years, commits an offence and is liable on conviction to imprisonment for ten years without an option of fine.

13-(1) Any person who, having the custody, charge or care of any person under the age of eighteen years, causes or encourages the seduction, unlawful carnal knowledge or prostitution of, or the commission of an indecent assault upon any person, commits an offence and is liable on conviction to imprisonment for ten years.

(12) A person shall be deemed to have caused or encouraged the seduction, unlawful carnal knowledge, or prostitution of or the commission of indecent assaults upon any person who has been seduced, unlawfully carnally known, or indecently assaulted, or who has become a prostitute, if he knowingly allows such person to consort with, or to enter or continue in the employment of, any prostitute or person of known immoral character.

14-(1) Any person who procures a person who is under the age of eighteen years to have unlawful carnal knowledge with any other person or persons, either in Nigeria or any place outside Nigeria, commits an offence and shall be liable on conviction to imprisonment for ten years.

(2) Any person who procures any person under the age of eighteen years to—

(a) become a prostitute, either in Nigeria, or any place outside Nigeria,

(b) leave Nigeria with intent that such person may become a prostitute in any place outside Nigeria,

(c) leave such person's usual place of abode in Nigeria, with intent that such person engage in prostitution either in Nigeria or any place outside Nigeria, commits an offence and is liable on conviction to imprisonment for ten years.

15. Any person who—

(a) procures, uses or offers any person for prostitution, or the production of pornography, or for pornographic performance;

(b) procures, uses or offers any person for the production and trafficking in drugs;

(c) traffics any person for the purpose of forced or compulsory recruitment use in armed conflict commits an offence and is liable on conviction to imprisonment for fourteen years without an option of fine.

16. Any person who organizes or promotes foreign travels which promote prostitution of any person or encourages such activity commits an offence and is liable on conviction to imprisonment for ten years without an option of fine.

17. Any person who—

(a) conspires with another to induce any person under the age of eighteen years by means of any false pretence or other fraudulent means, permit any man to have unlawful carnal knowledge of such person commits an offence and is liable on conviction to imprisonment for five years;

(b) detains any person under the age of eighteen years against such person's will in or upon any premises for the purpose of being unlawfully carnally known by any man, whether a particular man or not, commits an offence and is liable on conviction to imprisonment for ten years.

18. Any person who—

(a) with threats or intimidation of any kind procures any person under the age of eighteen years, to have carnal connection with a man or an animal, either in Nigeria or any place outside Nigeria;

(b) under false pretence procures any person under the age of eighteen years to have carnal connection with a man within or outside Nigeria;

(c) administer to any person under the age of eighteen years, or causes any person under the age of eighteen years, to take any drug or any other thing with intent to, stupefy or over-power such person. In order to enable any man, whether a particular man or not, to have carnal knowledge of such person, commits an offence and is liable on conviction to imprisonment for ten years or a fine not exceeding N200,000.00.

19-(1) Any person who—

(a) takes or entices any person under eighteen years of age or any person of unsound mind out of the custody of the lawful guardian of such person without the consent of the guardian or conveys any such person beyond the limits of Nigeria without the consent of someone legally authorized to give consent to such removal, commits an offence and is liable on conviction to imprisonment for fourteen years without an option of fine;

(b) by force compels or any deceitful means induces any person to go from any place, commits an offence and is liable on conviction to imprisonment for ten years or to a fine not exceeding N200,000.00 or both;

(c) confines or detains another person in any place against his will or otherwise unlawfully deprive another person of his personal liberty, commits an offence and is liable on conviction to imprisonment for five years or to a fine of N100,000.00 or both;

(d) unlawfully takes an unmarried person under the age of eighteen years out of the custody or protection of such person's father or mother or other person having the lawful care or charge of such person and against the will of such father or mother or persons having lawful care or charge of such person, commits an offence and is liable on conviction to imprisonment for ten years without an option of fine; and

(e) with intent to deprive any parent, guardian, or other person who has the lawful care or charge of a person under the age of eighteen years, of the possession of such person forcibly or fraudulently takes or entices away, or detains the person, or receives or harbours the child, knowing the child to have been so taken or enticed away or detained, commits an offence, and is liable on conviction to imprisonment for fourteen years without an option of fine.

(2) Any person is deemed to detain any person in or upon any premises in paragraph (e) of subsection (1) of this section when the person is in or brought upon any such premises with a view to such person being so carnally known, or to detain such person in such premises with intent to compel or induce such person to remain in or upon the premises, he withholds from such person any wearing apparels, other property belonging to such persons or the person's traveling documents.

20. A person who kidnaps, abducts or by deceitful means lures any person away in order that such person may be killed for any purpose, commits an offence and is liable on conviction to imprisonment for life.

21. Any person who buys, sells, hires, lets or otherwise obtains possession or disposes of any person under the age of eighteen years with intent that such person be employed or used for immoral purposes or knowing it to be likely that such person will be employed or used for any such purposes, commits an offence and is liable on conviction to imprisonment for fourteen years without the option of a fine.

22. Any person who requires any other person, or permits any place outside Nigeria, to be used for forced labour commits an offence and is liable on conviction to imprisonment for five years or to a fine not exceeding N100,000.00 or to both fine and imprisonment.

23. Any person who imports, exports, removes, buys, sells, disposes, traffics or deals in any person as a slave. . . .

Source: Federal Republic of Nigeria, National Agency for the Prohibition of Traffic in Persons and Other Related Matters. "Trafficking in Persons (Prohibition) Law Enforcement and Administration Act, 2003." Available online. URL: http://www.naptip.gov.ng/pdf/naptiplawsigning.pdf. Accessed March 20, 2008.

The Lost Children of Nigeria's Sex Trade

In Nigeria, Voodoo priests are enlisted to perform ceremonies intended to silence trafficking victims.

"The witch doctor took some of my nails, and hair. He cut the heart of a chicken into small pieces and mixed it all into a potion with a local gin brew. I had to drink it," she whispered, "I was so frightened. I knew death would come if I betrayed the oath."

Rita, then 15, was told that she must never run away from her "sponsors" or go to the police, "if I did, the Gods would take advantage of me, or my parents," she said.

Her mother had taken Rita to the ceremony. After paying for her daughter to be taken to Europe for a "better life", she wanted to safeguard her investment. . . .

Traffickers promise parents that their girls will receive an education and good careers. It is traditional in Nigeria for offspring to be sent away to distant relatives for a better life, which makes the process seem to be more acceptable. Then the traffickers use the practices of black magic to control the children. . . .

Source: Jonathan Clayton. "The Lost Children of Nigeria's Sex Trade." *Times* (London, 4/5/04).

Nigeria's "Respectable" Slave Trade

In this article, a 15-year-old girl from Nigeria's Edo State describes the trafficking of some of her friends.

The Lagos middle class have a bountiful supply of house boys and house girls, brought from villages in the north by helpful aunts and uncles who pocket the cash and disappear.

No-one asks questions. No-one wants to know the answers.

For human trafficking is not something that happens on the criminal fringes of Nigerian society.

It is woven into the fabric of national life.

In Benin City, in the oil rich Edo state, east of Lagos, I met an articulate 15-year-old girl who said many of her friends had been trafficked.

"Their parents are involved," she said. "They say to the girls: 'Why don't you go with this man and work. We have no money, we have nothing to eat. You can send us money.' And so the girls go." . . .

Source: Allen Little. "Nigeria's 'Respectable' Slave Trade." BBC News (4/17/04). Available online. URL: http://news.bbc.co.uk/1/hi/programmes/from_our_own_correspondent/3632203.stm. Accessed February 2, 2008.

Nigeria: Dream of Freedom Turns to Prostitution Nightmare

Voodoo rituals intended to silence trafficking victims and induce compliance are often followed by long and dangerous journeys from Nigeria to Europe.

Valeria, who has spent time in Nigeria's Edo State, now works with victims of trafficking in Italy. She says traffickers often coerce victims by exploiting their belief in voodoo rituals.

"They often make a sachet with the girl's hair or underwear and even menstrual blood and they keep it," she said, "Girls truly believe that if they reveal the names of these people or don't pay them back, horrible things will happen to them and their families."

Merciless journey

Even before the girls arrive to discover the reality of their new life in Europe, they have often undergone excruciating journeys just to leave their home continent.

These days the high-priced voyage from West Africa to Europe is most often via the Sahara Desert, where it is easier for people to move about clandestinely with no papers.

"We walked for months," said Sharon, . . . who made what she called a "merciless journey" through the desert to reach the northern tip of Africa from which she could take a boat to Europe.

"Many people died. Sometimes we would drink our urine," she said shaking her head at the memory.

Source: UN Office for the Coordination of Human Affairs. "Nigeria: Dream of Freedom Turns into Prostitution Nightmare." (11/4/05). Available online. URL: http://irinnews.org/report.aspx?reportid=57008. Accessed February 24, 2008.

Interview Summary: A Fourteen-Year-Old Boy

The trafficking of Nigerian boys sometimes begins with the promise of a football career in Europe.

A fourteen-year-old boy is approached in Nigeria by a 'football agent', who promises him a great career and a contract with one of the European football clubs. After paying a significant fee, for which the boy's family has to borrow money, he is taken to the Netherlands. On arrival at Schiphol airport, the agent disappears and it becomes clear that nothing has been arranged. The boy is left to fend for himself and ends up in the illegal sector.

Source: Stichting Defense for Children International The Netherlands. "Investigating Exploitation: Research into Trafficking in Children in The Netherlands" (2005), p. 33. Available online. URL: http://polis.osce.org/library/f/2716/549/NGO-NLD-RPT-2716-EN-Investigating%20Exploitatio n.pdf. Accessed December 21, 2007.

Victim Testimony and Reports (2006)

The 2006 U.S. TIP Report contained several descriptions of trafficking cases involving Nigerian children, among others.

NIGER/MALI: The parents of 12-year-old Malik were convinced by a Koranic teacher—one of a revered group in Niger—that he would take the young boy to Mali, for further education. But once Malik and other Nigerien boys arrived in Mali from Niger, they were denied schooling and were forced by the teacher to beg in the streets for long hours to earn money for him. Malik eventually escaped. Strangers helped him return to his village in Niger where his family received him joyously after hearing of his ordeal.

NIGERIA/ITALY: Gloria was promised work in Rome in a fabric factory. Before leaving her native Nigeria, she underwent a voodoo ritual purportedly to oversee her safety in Italy and ensure her loyalty to her sponsor or "Madam." Upon arrival in Rome, Gloria was beaten by her Madam, who told her she would have to repay a huge trafficking debt through an estimated 4,000 acts of prostitution. Gloria received more beatings when she refused Madam's demands. She eventually acquiesced though she was then beaten for not earning enough money. When she became pregnant, Gloria was forced to have an abortion. She eventually found the courage to overcome the threats of voodoo reprisal and to escape to reclaim her life. She is now recovering in a shelter in Rome.

Source: U.S. Department of State. "Trafficking in Persons Report, 2006," p. 188. Available online. URL: http://www.state.gov/documents/organization66086.pdf. Accessed June 5, 2007.

Nigeria/United States

The 2007 U.S. TIP Report recounted the experience of a Nigerian girl trafficked to the United States.

14-year-old Jenny left her native Nigeria for the United States to work in the home of a couple, also originally from an African country. She thought she would be paid to look after their children, but the reality was very different. For five years Jenny was repeatedly raped by her employer and his wife physically assaulted her, sometimes with a cane, and on one occasion with a high-heeled shoe. Tipped off by a local NGO, law enforcement officials rescued Jenny and prosecuted the perpetrators.

Source: U.S. Department of State. "Trafficking in Persons Report: (2007)," p. 156. Available online. URL: http://www.state.gov.documents/organization/82902.pdf. Accessed July 31, 2007.

NAPTIP Raises Alarm over Babies' Sale

In 2008, the executive secretary of Nigeria's National Agency for the Prohibition of Traffic in Persons announced that baby-selling in Nigeria was occurring at an "unfortunate and alarming" rate.

The Executive Secretary of the National Agency for the Prohibition of Traffic in Persons (NAP-TIP), Mrs. Carol Ndaguba, has described the rate at which Nigerians sell their babies as "unfortunate and alarming".

According to a statement by NAPTIP's spokesman, Arinze Orakwue, Mrs. Ndaguba who decried this trend at the agency's first quarter programme review recently in Abuja, stated that an uglier dimension of enslavement has been introduced into the tragic scenario of traffic in persons in Nigeria.

She explained that various reports from the media and citizens on the sale of babies by hospitals, doctors, parents and illegal children homes prompted the agency to move against the trend.

"Reports from NAPTIP Zonal offices especially Enugu, indicted several homes and discovered camps where teenage mothers are kept until they deliver their babies whom these syndicates quietly sell for illegal adoption or rituals. However, NAPTIP is doing all it can to put an end to the ugly trend as we have placed our investigating officers in the zones on full alert," she said.

She blamed the increase in such acts on poverty and lack of social welfare and she called on state governments to sign the Child Rights Act and pursue the achievement of the actions enshrined in it.

"Children rights are human rights. Thus it is important that state governments show strong commitment towards poverty alleviation within their states. The simple fact that in this age and time, parents willingly dispose of their children as chattels shows a failure of our poverty alleviation efforts. We must move from mere promises to carrying out these actions."

She called on governors of various states to use the first ladies of their states to tackle issues relating to children and gender as these groups are very vulnerable in such situations.

Source: Atika Balal. "NAPTIP Raises Alarm over Babies' Sale." *Abuja Daily Trust* (2/07/08).

INDIA

The Immoral Traffic (Prevention) Act (1956) (excerpts)

Enacted when the Republic of India was in its seventh year, this act remains India's central anti-trafficking law. It defines trafficking solely in terms of trafficking for sexual exploitation.

3. Punishment for keeping a brothel or allowing premises to be used as a brothel.—(1) Any person who keeps or manages, or acts or assists in the keeping or management of, a brothel shall be punishable on first conviction with rigorous imprisonment for a term of not less than two years and which may extend to three years and also with fine which may extend to ten thousand rupees and in the event of a second or subsequent conviction, with rigorous imprisonment for a term which shall not be less than three years and which may extend to seven years and shall also be liable to fine which may extend to two lakh rupees . . .

5. Procuring, inducing or taking person for the sake of prostitution—(1) Any person who—

(a) procures or attempts to procure a person whether with or without his/her consent, for the purpose of prostitution; or

(b) induces a person to go from any place, with the intent that he/she may for the purpose of prostitution become the inmate of, or frequent, a brothel; or

(c) takes or attempts to take a person or causes a person to be taken, from one place to another with a view to his/her carrying on, or being brought up to carry on prostitution; or

(d) causes or induces a person to carry on prostitution;

shall be punishable on conviction with rigorous imprisonment for a term of not less than three years and not more than seven years and also with fine which may extend to two thousand rupees, and if any offence under this sub-section is committed against the will of any person, the punishment of imprisonment for a term of seven years shall extend to imprisonment for a term of fourteen years:

Provided that if the person in respect of whom an offence committed under this subsection, is a child, the punishment provided under this sub-section shall extend to rigorous imprisonment for a term of not less than seven years but may extend to life. . . .

Source: Republic of India. "The Immoral Traffic (Prevention) Act, 1956." Available online. URL: http://www.prsindia. org/docs/bills/1167469313/bill51_2007010251_Immoral_Traffic_Preventi on_Act1956.pdf. Accessed March 3, 2008.

The Bonded Labour System (Abolition) Act (1976) (excerpts)

This act abolished the legal recognition of India's bonded labor system.

Chapter II
Abolition of Bonded Labour System

4. Abolition of bonded labour system.—(1) On the commencement of this Act, the bonded labour system shall stand abolished and every bonded labourer shall, on such commencement, stand freed and discharged from any obligation to render any bonded labour.

(2) After the commencement of this Act, no person shall—
(a) make any advance under, or in pursuance of, the bonded labour system, or
(b) compel any person to render any bonded labour or other form of forced labour.

5. Agreement, custom, etc., to be void.—On the commencement of this Act, any custom or tradition or any contract, agreement or other instrument (whether entered into or executed before or after the commencement of this Act), by virtue of which any person, or any member of the family or dependant of such person, is required to do any work or render any service as a bonded labourer, shall be void and inoperative.

Chapter III
Extinguishments of Liability to Repay Bonded Debt

6. *Liability to repay bonded debt to stand extinguished.*—(1) On the commencement of this Act, every obligation of a bonded labourer to repay any bonded debt, or such part of any bonded debt as remains unsatisfied immediately before such commencement, shall be deemed to have been extinguished. . . .

Source: Republic of India. "The Bonded Labour System (Abolition) Act, 1976." Available online. URL: http://pb labour.gov.in/pdf/acts_rules/bonded_labour_system_abolition_act_1976.pdf. Accessed March 3, 2008.

The Child Labour (Abolition and Rehabilitation) Bill (2006) (excerpts)

This act expanded the list of occupations closed to children.

3. Notwithstanding anything contained in any other law for the time being in force, child labour in any form is hereby abolished.

4. The appropriate Government shall ensure that no person employs any child for performance of any of the following work, namely:—

(i) Domestic work;

(ii) Agricultural operations;

(iii) Construction activities and operations of transport industry;

(iv) Work in shop, factory, any establishment or organisation; and

(v) Manufacturing, trading or processing activity of any item.

Provided that any child may work at his own residence or perform any domestic work out of his volition.

5. The appropriate Government within its territorial jurisdiction shall ensure that no establishment sells or buys any product which has been manufactured or processed by any industrial establishment or factory employing child labour and it shall be the duty of every organisation to display in bold letters, at prominent location, in the organisation that it does not deal with any activity or product where child labour is involved.

Source: Republic of India. "The Child Labour (Abolition and Rehabilitation) Bill, 2006. Available online. URL: http://rajyasabha.nic.in/bills-ls-rs/2006/CVII_2006.pdf. Accessed March 14, 2008.

Ibrahimpur Journal; A Single-Minded Man Fights to Free India's Slaves

Kailash Satyarthi's work in India has resulted in the freeing of more than 40,000 bonded laborers in India.

The spare 15-year-old in a tattered shirt stood stiffly, shaking his head. "No," he said. "I don't know Bharat,"

Gently, Kailash Satyarthi placed his hand on the young man's shoulder and said: "Bharat is this country, where you live. Bharat is India."

Around Mr. Satyarthi and the 15-year-old, Bushan Lal, hovered a dozen other young men, some nodding in understanding, others wrestling with a new idea, the idea of India.

Mr Satyarthi explained: "These men have never seen a white person. They have never seen a newspaper. They have never heard of America. They don't know what money is. Some don't even know the name of their country. They were bonded laborers, people who have been in complete servitude."

Throughout India, bonded laborers toil, unpaid and ill treated, in what amounts to slavery in stone quarries, in brick kilns and yards, and in the rice paddies of central and southern India.

Bonded labor—the practice of engaging laborers without wages to pay off real or imagined debts—is against the law. But it persists despite court rulings, occasional police intervention and the work of people like Mr. Satyarthi, who works here at his center for bonded laborers 20 miles northeast of New Delhi.

<. . .>

Virtually all of India's bonded laborers are untouchables, who are at the bottom of the caste hierarchy. Some were born into their condition because their parents or grandparents were sold long before they were born. Others were lured into servitude by agents for quarry owners or brick kiln managers with promises of higher paving jobs than those they had. Still others fell into their position from the need to repay loans that

208

were readily given, but that can never be fully repaid. Once indentured, it is almost impossible to escape.

Source: Edward A. Gargan. "Ibrahimpur Journal; A Single-Minded Man Fights to Free India's Slaves." *New York Times* (6/4/92).

Children's Testimonies: Bonded Child Labor in India's Silk Industry

Here, two children describe their experience as bonded laborers in India's silk industry.

Before I came here I went to [a government] school, but after one year I withdrew from school because of a problem—my sister's illness. After my sister got sick, we took her to the hospital, but the doctor said we had to pay more money, so my parents bonded me for Rs. 1,700 [U.S.$35]. I was seven or eight years old.

I did winding [unwinding the cocoons], I didn't like to work, but I was forced to by my parents. They said I couldn't go to school but had to work. . . .

At 4:00 a.m. I got up and did silk winding. . . . I only went home once a week. I slept in the factory with two or three other children. We prepared our food there and slept in the space between the machines. The owner provided the rice and cut it from our wages—he would deduct the price. We cooked the rice ourselves. We worked twelve hours a day with one hour for rest. If I made a mistake—if I cut the thread—he would beat me. Sometimes [the owner] used vulgar language. Then he would give me more work.

—*"Yeramma S.," eleven-year-old girl, bonded at around age seven for Rs. 1,700 (U.S.$35) Karnataka, March 27, 2002*

<. . .>

My first loan was Rs. 6,000 [U.S.$125] from the first owner. Then we got another Rs. 1,000 [$21] from the second owner, and he paid the first owner. If I paid the loan back, then I wouldn't have to go to work. If there were no loan, I could stop working and go to the regular school. . . . Now we are unable to pay back the loan. My father is ill so we can't stop working. . . . I don't like the looms, but my parents ask me to go so I go, but I hadn't thought there would be this much pain in the work. . . . (There is no play time for me. If I have time, I will work in the house. . . . When I am not working in the loom I will do heavy housework. I will take the manure and work in the cattle farm.

—"Vimali T.," fifteen-year-old low-caste girl,
bonded to a loom owner for Rs. 8,000 ($167)
since age nine or ten, Kanchipuram, March 21, 2002.

Source: HRW. "Child Slaves Abandoned to India's Silk Industry" (press release). Available online. URL: http://www.hrw.org/press/2003/01/india-testimonies.htm. Accessed March 24, 2008.

India's Lost Girls

In India, the aborting of female fetuses is creating an artificially law ratio of females to males in many areas and contributing to an increase in the buying and selling of brides.

A marriage crisis is hitting thousands of men in parts of rural India which are running out of potential brides.

The traditional preference for boys instead of girls has led to widespread abuse of modern pre-natal scans.

The technology should protect the health of mother and baby.

But, wrongly used, it is a death sentence for unwanted girls.

The practice of determining the sex of a foetus and aborting girls is illegal, but widespread.

The worst affected states, such as Haryana and Punjab, now have some of the most skewed sex ratios in the world—and the proportion of baby girls is still falling.

Buying brides

A whole generation of young men is failing to find brides.

Many are now resorting to "buying" girls from poor communities outside the region to bear their children. . . .

In many clinics, the illegal and systematic abortion of girls is common practice.

In Punjab, special prayers of thanks greet the birth of a boy. Prejudice runs deep. Girls are born into silence. . . .

Source: Jill McGivering. "India's Lost Girls." BBC News (2/4/03). Available online. URL: http://news.bbc.co.uk/2.hi/south_asia/2723513.stm. Accessed March 24, 2008.

Why Did You Not Drown Me in a River?

Here, an Indian father describes the marriage of his 15-year-old daughter.

"We agreed to the marriage. They left the day after the wedding. We did not offer anything except food. They came prepared with the sari and everything. Tulie [age 15] cried at first but she seemed happy afterwards.

Two years ago, Tulie came on a visit with her husband. She had lost weight and looked very depressed. She had to serve a large family of in-laws. Her mother-in-law and her husband made her life very difficult. They beat her. She worked like a slave. She was not given time to eat or to rest. As she left she said: "Instead of marrying me, why did you not drown me in a river?" She cried the whole time. I felt sad but what could I do? How could I have kept my unmarried daughter in the house?

I cannot poison my daughters. If I send them away to survive, what is the problem? You don't know how troublesome and tormenting it is to keep an unmarried daughter in the house. Our community sent many girls to the West and we still do."

Source: Thérèse Blanchet. "Bangladesh Girls Sold as Wives in North India" (2003), p. 18. Available online. URL: http://www.aed-ccsg.org/resources/reports/UPMarriage.pdf. Accessed March 24, 2008.

They Could Not Talk to Their Own Mother

In the following, an Indian mother describes the sale of her daughters into marriage.

Last year, we gave the dalal who took our daughters 700 taka and, with my 21 year old daughter, I went. What I saw was appalling. My daughters were married to men who had been married before and had children from a previous wife. They had to work the land like Santal women. They were not given any consideration. My daughters could not spend any time with us. They are like slaves.

We were not allowed to go out and meet with other girls from our area who have been married there. We were kept in one room like prisoners. Food was brought to us but our daughters were kept away from us. We could not speak to them freely. In the end, we were told by their husbands: "Your daughters were sold to us for 40,000 taka. You need not come and visit them anymore. This damages our reputation." My son-in-law gave money to a man who took us back to the border.

People here know my daughters were married. After 18 years, I learned they have been sold. Now I know. They are like the cows one gets to plough the field. They get fed because they work and give birth to children. They could not talk to their own mother. They could not offer her a plate of food. If I had married my daughters to a beggar here, they would have been better off."

Source: Thérèse Blanchet. "Bangladesh Girls Sold as Wives in North India" (2003), pp. 15–16. Available online. URL: http://www.aed-ccsg.org/resources/reports/UPMarriage.pdf. Accessed March 24, 2008.

Human Trafficking Situation in India Grim

In 2005, an official from the U.S. Office to Monitor and Combat Trafficking in Persons described his findings in India.

Mark Taylor, senior coordinator of [reports for] the office [to Monitor and Combat Trafficking in Persons] and charged primarily with the preparation of the annual [Trafficking in Persons Report] was in Mumbai on Friday, as part of his visit to determine the situation in India.

In metros like Mumbai particularly, he said, there has been a marked shift over the last 4–5 years, in sex trafficking from areas like Kamathipura, the more conventional understanding of a brothel, to more mobile and unconventional populations like educated middle-class girls. . . .

He also spoke of the exploitative practices not normally considered as trafficking. On his visit this year to Tamil Nadu, Taylor got a first-hand insight into bonded labour in the rice mills of the state.

"Exploited persons and even law-enforcers in many cases are not yet aware that bonded labour amounts to trafficking and is an offence under Indian law." . . .

"The central government in New Delhi has not made sufficient efforts to use its national law enforcement agencies to investigate and prosecute inter-state and international trafficking," it added.

Another worrisome trend, said Taylor, was the growth of sex tourism in places like Goa and Pondicherry. . . .

Source: Times of India (2/4/05).

A Boy of 15 Years

The 2005 U.S. TIP Report contained this account of an Indian boy's trafficking into forced labor and his subsequent rescue.

Shadir, a boy of 15 years, was offered a job that included good clothes and an education; he accepted. Instead of being given a job, Shadir was sold to a slave trader who took him to a remote village in India to produce hand-woven carpets. He was frequently beaten. He worked 12 to 14 hours a day and he was poorly fed. One day, Shadir was rescued by a NGO working to combat slavery. It took several days for him to realize he was no longer enslaved. He returned to his village, was reunited with his mother, and resumed his schooling. Now Shadir warns fellow village children about the risks of becoming a child slave.

Source: U.S. Department of State. "Trafficking in Persons Report, 2005," p. 21. Available online. URL: http://www. state.gov/documents/organization/47255.pdf. Accessed June 5, 2007.

Bound by a Grandfather's Debt

The 2006 U.S. TIP Report contained this description of inherited debt bondage.

Raman was born at the same brick kiln site where his father and grandfather had worked their entire lives to pay off a debt incurred by his grandfather. For 15 years, Raman and his family earned three rupees (2 cents) per 80 kilo-gram bag of bricks to pay off the $450 advanced by the brick kiln manager. They were beaten with sticks and hit by the owner if they were not working hard enough or producing enough bricks. They could not leave, because the brick kiln owner threatened to hunt them down and beat them or bribe the police into arresting them. Sadly, Raman's story is not unusual for millions of low-caste laborers believed to be trapped in debt bondage in South Asia.

Source: U.S. Department of State. "Trafficking in Persons Report, 2006," p. 188. Available online. URL: http://www.state.gov/documents/organization66086.pdf. Accessed June 5, 2007.

India Sex Selection Doctor Jailed

This article describes a sting operation to uncover Indian doctors engaged in illegal ultrasounds to determine the sex of fetuses. It also examines the cultural preference for males and the resulting demand for sex-selective abortions.

A doctor in India and his assistant have been sentenced to two years in jail for revealing the sex of a female foetus and then agreeing to abort it.

This is the first time medical professionals have been jailed in such a case.

Under Indian laws, ultrasound tests on a pregnant woman to determine the gender of the foetus are illegal.

It has been estimated that 10m female foetuses may have been terminated in India in the past 20 years.

Dr Anil Sabhani and Kartar Singh were caught in a sting operation in the northern state of Haryana.

Government officials sent in three pregnant women as decoy patients to find out if the clinic would carry out abortions based on sex selection.

Audio and video evidence showed the doctor telling one woman that tests had revealed that she was carrying a "female foetus and it would be taken care of".

A cultural preference for sons over daughters has skewed India's sex ratio.

But convictions are rare due to lax and corrupt officials and the slow judicial system.

The government brought in laws 12 years ago to stop the practice of aborting female fetuses. . . .

The girl child has traditionally been considered inferior and a liability—a bride's dowry can cripple a poor family financially.

Source: "India Sex Selection Doctor Jailed." BBC News (3/29/06). Available online. URL: http://news.bbc.co.uk/2/hi/south_asia/4855682.stm. Accessed March 25, 2008.

Child Soldiers Being Used as Expendable Pawns in Armed Conflicts

The 2006 U.S. TIP Report contained this description of child soldiers in India.

In April 2007 the Chhattisgarh State Police ambushed a 12-member strong brigade of armed Naxalites (a group similar to the Maoists in Nepal) operating near Dhanora village. In the operation, the police arrested two girls, respectively aged 14 and 15 years old, who were wearing school uniforms and were armed with old 303 bore rifles. When questioned, the girls confessed that they had been picked up from school by the Naxalites, and given a few days' training on armed combat, before being sent out in the company of older members to fight against the State Police and the Salwa Judum, a State-sponsored private militia.

Elsewhere, in Chhattisgarh State's capital Raipur, five-year-old Saurabh reports for duty every day at the local police station and works as a boy police constable. Saurabh was employed by the State Police after his father was killed in an ambush by the Naxalites. Saurabh is not the only boy in the State Police. In nearby Korba Police Station, Manish Khoonte, a ten-year-old boy is employed as a police officer. Saurabh and Manish are paid US$ 57 per month by the State Government.

Source: U.S. Department of State. "Trafficking in Persons Report, 2006," p. 188. Available online. URL: http://www.state.gov/documents/organization66086.pdf. Accessed June 5, 2007.

When Aakesh Was Five

The 2007 U.S. TIP Report contained this account of Indian boys trafficked into forced labor.

When Aakesh was five years old, he was playing with friends in his village when some men drove into his village and asked the boys if they wanted to see a "video." The boys piled into the back of the vehicle and were driven 200 miles away. They were locked in a room for days without food and were beaten. The traffickers had abducted these vulnerable children so they could be forced to weave carpets. The boys were held captive for nine years. Two of Aakesh's friends didn't survive—one was shot while trying to escape and the other died from an untreated illness. The boys were 14 years old when they were rescued, barely able to speak. They were malnourished and wounded. . . .

Source: U.S. Department of State. "Trafficking in Persons Report: (2007)." Available online. URL: http://www. state.gov.documents/organization/82902.pdf. Accessed July 31, 2007.

Kidney Theft Ring Preys on India's Poorest Laborers

This article describes the operations of an organ trafficking ring in India.

As the anesthetic wore off, Naseem Mohammed said, he felt an acute pain in the lower left side of his abdomen. Fighting drowsiness, he fumbled beneath the unfamiliar folds of a green medical gown and traced his fingers over a bandage attached with surgical tape. An armed guard by the door told him that his kidney had been removed.

Mr. Mohammed was the last of about 500 Indians whose kidneys were removed by a team of doctors running an illegal transplant operation, supplying kidneys to rich Indians and foreigners, police officials said. A few hours after his operation last Thursday, the police raided the clinic and moved him to a government hospital.

Many of the donors were day laborers, like Mr. Mohammed, picked up from the streets with the offer of work, driven to a well-equipped private clinic, and duped or forced at gunpoint to undergo operations. Others were bicycle rickshaw drivers and impoverished farmers who were persuaded to sell their organs, which is illegal in India. . . .

Mr. Mohammed said he was driven four or five hours, to a secluded bungalow, where he was placed in a room with four other young men, under the watch of two armed guards.

"When I asked why I had been locked inside, the guards slapped me and said they would shoot me if I asked any more questions," Mr. Mohammed said, lying in a hospital bed, wrapped in an orange blanket, clenching his teeth and shutting his eyes in pain. He said the men were given food to cook and periodically nurses would take blood samples.

One by one, he said, they were taken away for operations.

"They told us not to speak to each other or we would pay with our lives," he said. "I was the last one to be taken." . . .

Source: Amelia Gentlemen. "Kidney Theft Ring Preys on India's Poorest Laborers." *New York Times* (1/30/08).

BELIZE

Trafficking in Persons (Prohibition) Act (2003, Summary)

Prior to passage of this act in 2003, Belize had no law that specifically addressed human trafficking.

The National Assembly has passed the Trafficking in Persons (Prohibition) Bill, 2003. The Bill seeks to give effect to and implement the Protocol to Prevent, Suppress and Punish Trafficking in Persons, especially women and children.

Belize is a party to the Protocol, which was adopted to supplement the United Nations Convention against Trans-national Organized Crime.

This Act creates, for the first time in Belizean law, the specific offences of trafficking in persons, as well as the offences of unlawfully withholding a person's identification papers in order to exploit the person, and transporting a person for the purpose of exploiting that person. There are also provisions for the court to order a trafficker to pay restitution to the victims and guidelines to be used by the court to determine the quantum of such restitution.

Source: Government of Belize. "Report on the Follow-up and Implementation of the Mandates of the Summit of the Americas Process, July 2005." Available online. URL: http://209.85.207.104/search?q=cache:pCkFfj8eMSgJ:www. summit-americas.org/Quebec-Foll ow%2520Up/National%2520Reports/2005/Belize%2520-%2520Report%25202005-Summit% 2520of%2520the%2520Americas.doc+belize+musa+human<0x00 2B>trafficking&hl=en&ct=clnk&cd=2 3&gl=us&clie nt=firefox-a. Accessed March 25, 2008.

Trafficking in Persons Seminar to Be Held (2004)

In 2004, the U.S. Department of Justice hosted a trafficking in persons seminar in Belize.

Police Investigators, Human Services Officers and Immigration Personnel are this week attending a four day Trafficking in Persons Seminar hosted by the U.S. Department of Justice. The Seminar began with a short Opening Ceremony at the Radisson Fort George Hotel, on Monday August 2nd with special remarks from United States Ambassador to Belize H.E. Russell Freeman.

The main objective of this seminar is to improve the techniques and efficiency of investigation and prosecution of Trafficking in Persons cases.

Presenters include Myesha Braden, Trial Attorney from the Child Exploitation and Obscenity Section of the U.S. Justice Department's Criminal Division; Lorna Grenadier, Victim/Witness Expert from the Civil Rights Division of the Justice Department; and F.B.I. Special Agent Terri Patterson.

The major areas being covered in the workshop are a broad introduction of Trafficking in Persons and relevant issues related to combating trafficking from a law enforcement perspective. The specialized audience will learn about the Prevention and Awareness of Trafficking in Persons and Implementing the New TIPS law with a victim perspective.

The Seminar ends on Thursday August 5th with the presentation of certificates to persons who attended.

Source: Government of Belize, Press Office. "Trafficking in Persons Seminar to Be Held." Available online. URL: http://www.governmentofbelize.gov.bz/press_release_details.php?pr_id=2739. Accessed March 25, 2008.

From the Belize Foreign Policy Yearbook (2004)

This government of Belize document describes Belize's response to its designation as a Tier 3 country in the U.S. 2003 TIP Report.

In June 2003, the Government of Belize became severely concerned when the USA State Department issued its 2003 Report on the Trafficking in Persons (TIP), which categorized Belize as a tier 3 country, i.e. one that is not making significant efforts to meet minimum standards to address the problem of trafficking in persons. Belize immediately expressed its disappointment with its ranking especially as it was the first time the country had been evaluated. Belize further expressed strong concerns with the methodology used in undertaking the report and on the lack of consultation with line Government Ministries.

The Government of Belize immediately responded by demonstrating the Government's commitment to fighting Trafficking in Persons. In June 2003,

Belize adopted comprehensive TIP legislation when it passed the Trafficking in Persons (Prohibition) Act. Belize promptly mobilized a Multi Agency National Task Force then chaired by the Chief Executive Officer in the Foreign Ministry, and now chaired by the Special Envoy for Gender, Children and HIV/AIDS.

As a direct result of the efforts of the National Task Force, the USA in September 2003 reviewed its previous categorization of Belize from a Tier 3 to a Tier 2 country, one which does not fully comply with the USA's Government minimum standards but which is making significant effort towards compliance.

Also in September 2003, Belize acceded to the United Nations Convention against Transnational Organized Crime and its Protocol to Prevent, Suppress and Punish Trafficking in Persons, especially Women and Children. . . .

Source: Government of Belize. "The Belize Foreign Policy Yearbook, 2004." Available online. URL: http//www.mfa.gov.bz/library/documents/yearbook_2004.pdf. Accessed March 25, 2008.

Human Trafficking: A New Form of Slavery in Belize

This article describes a seminar to train Belize's law enforcement and social services personnel to enforce Belize's 2003 anti-trafficking legislation.

"A new form of slavery" is how Director of Public Prosecutions Kirk Anderson characterised the situation of trafficking in persons in Belize.

He was speaking at a two-day training seminar to combat trafficking in persons at the Radisson Fort George Hotel in Belize City on April 14 and 15.

The event was designed to train personnel from several departments how to enforce the Trafficking Persons Prohibition Act, which Belize passed into law in 2003.

Some 70 participants attended the seminar among them Police and Immigration officials, magistrates, personnel of the Department of Human Services and the National Committee for Families and Children. "There are no elements to consider Belize as a major destination for traffickers, but the country is at high risk if preventative measures do not take place," concludes Juan Miguel Petit, a consultant commissioned by the Belize government to do an evaluation of trafficking in persons in Belize. Petit's report was presented along with his recommendations and conclusions during the seminar.

Source: "Human Trafficking: A New Form of Slavery in Belize." *Belize City Reporter* (4/22/05).

Belize Joins Anti-Human Trafficking Network

In 2006, Belize joined the Latin American Network.

Today Belize became the eight[h] member country of the Latin American Network, a regional effort to combat human trafficking, locate missing persons especially children and reunite them with their families. The web based initiative is a project funded by Save the Children Sweden and endorsed by the Organization of American States. . . .

Source: News 5 (4/26/06). Available online. URL: http://www.channel5belize.com/archive_news_cast.php?news_date=2006-04-26#a5. Accessed March 25, 2008.

Belize Not Doing Enough to Stop Human Trafficking

In 2006, Belize was again listed as a Tier 3 country.

Belize has been black listed by the U.S. State Department as one of the countries that is not doing enough to crack down on human trafficking.

The largest Caribbean island Cuba, is among the countries along with Venezuela, Saudi Arabia, Myanmar, Iran, Laos, North Korea, Sudan, Syria, Uzbekistan and Zimbabwe. . . .

Speaking with the media on Wednesday Prime Minister Said Musa questions the irony of Belize being on the list of smuggling nations along side Venezuela when only a few weeks ago Belize received a $25M loan from the same country.

The Embassy's Political Officer Brian DaRin, cautions that Belize's rank as tier 3 has absolutely nothing to do with its relationship with any other country. "It's solely about the action or in this case inaction of the government to crack down on human trafficking."

He adds, the Belize Immigration Department is tasked with releasing an annual report on trafficking in Belize and it should have been in December however, it was not done.

DaRin said immigration officials claim there have been raids on brothels but he's found no records from the police or social services interviews. . . .

Source: Ann-Marie Williams. "Belize Not Doing Enough to Stop Human Trafficking." *Belize City Reporter* (6/9/06).

U.S. Castigates Belize for Trafficking in Persons

This article discusses the reasons for Belize's Tier 3 designation in the 2006 U.S. TIP Report.

Belize is in bad books with the United States tonight following the State Department's annual investigation into worldwide human trafficking. According to a press release posted on the State Department's website, Belize, Iran, Syria, Zimbabwe, Uzbekistan and Laos are "not meeting minimum standards to fight trafficking in persons, a criminal practice". As a result, all three countries have been placed on a "Tier 3 list". That category is apparently "based more on the extent of the government's action or inaction to combat trafficking rather than the size of the problem, important though it is." . . .

Source: News 5 (6/6/06). Available online. URL: http://www.channel5belize.com/archive_news_cast.php?news_date=2006-06-06#a1. Accessed March 25, 2008.

Belize Placed on "Worst Offenders" Human Trafficking List

This article discuss the possibility of U.S. sanctions being imposed on Belize in consequence of its Tier 3 listing in 2006.

Belize has been added to a US blacklist of countries trafficking in people, a State Department report said Monday.

Iran, Syria, Zimbabwe, Uzbekistan, and Laos were also on the blacklist for the State Department's annual "Trafficking in Persons Report" which analyzed efforts in about 150 countries to combat trafficking for forced labour, prostitution, military service and other purposes.

The six countries join Venezuela, Saudi Arabia, North Korea, Sudan, Cuba and Myanmar among the "Tier 3" worst offenders of human trafficking who could face sanctions if they do not take immediate measures within 90 days. . . .

A key criteria of US law, which is used as a basis for the rankings, is protection of human trafficking victims.

"The law specifically says victims should not be punished for acts they commit after they've been trafficked, whether it's prostitution or anything else," said John Miller, a State Department advisor on efforts to stem the problem.

"We hope this situation will change in the next year," he said.

Source: P. Parameswaran. "Belize Placed on 'Worst Offenders' Human Trafficking List." Caribbean Net News (6/6/06). Available online. URL: http://www.caribbeannetnews.com/cgi-script/csArticles/articles/000018/001860. htm. Accessed March 24, 2008.

Extra House Businessman Busted on Alleged Human Trafficking

This article describes the use of forced labor in a Belize supermarket.

A Belize City businessman of Extra House supermarket was on Monday arraigned on charges of trafficking in human cargo, namely six counts of illegally holding the travel documents of six individuals of indian decent.

He's Jitendra Mortilal Chawla, 33, of Amara Avenue. He met bail of $5,000.00 and is scheduled to appear in court on Friday, July 7.

Chawla was picked up by police on Friday last, June 23 when they conducted a search at a warehouse at mile two on the Western Highway.

During the search police found a male person from India who told them Chawla took his travel documents.

When police raided Chawla's home they came across five more individuals, all of India who told the same story of having turned over their documents to their employer. . . .

There have been widespread reports of several Indian and Chinese businesses operating across the country known to bring these individuals in to work while witholding their travel documents.

Chawla's arrest this week comes almost three weeks after the United States government listed Belize as a Tier three country among other nations which are not doing enough to combat human trafficking.

Source: Angel Novelo. "Extra House Businessman Busted on Alleged Human Trafficking." *Belize City Reporter* (6/30/06).

Immigration Director's Cousin Arrested for Trafficking

In 2006, the cousin of Belize's director of immigration was arrested on charges of human trafficking.

As Belize continues to try to prove to the United States that we are taking measures to stop human trafficking, tonight there is word that a relative of the Director of Immigration has been arrested for the crime. On Friday, forty-two year old Amparo Zetina, the owner of the Caracol Bar was formally arraigned on one count of human trafficking. . .

According to officials from Human Services, Zetina was detained following a report by nineteen year old Guatemalan Amabilia Esquivel. Last Thursday, Esquivel went to the Corozal Police Station and told authorities that she had been attacked and beaten. During the course of an interview with the cops and human services, the authorities began to suspect that Esquivel was a victim of human trafficking. Esquivel's story is that her employer, Zetina, had initially hired her to work in a restaurant. But shortly after her arrival in Corozal, she was repeatedly asked to sexually satisfy male patrons at the Caracol Bar. Esquivel claims she said no to the requests, but that Zetina refused to pay her for her work. When she went to a friend to get help, Esquivel says she was ambushed and beaten by persons believed to be acting on her boss's behalf. . .

Source: News 5 (7/28/06). Available online. URL: http://www.channel5belize.com/archive_detail_story.php?story_id=16718. Accessed March 25, 2008.

Belize Gets Cracking on Human Trafficking

This article describes Belize's efforts to combat human trafficking in the wake of its 2006 designation as a Tier 3 country.

Belize is making a mighty effort to escape the stigma of a country which is soft on people traffickers.

Government has set up an anti-trafficking in Persons Committee to fight people trafficking, and this week the committee launched its first workshop for more than a hundred law enforcement officers and members of the social services sector at the UWI campus in Belize City.

Anita Zetina is the Chairman of this committee. She is also CEO at the Ministry of Human Development.

She explained that the workshop involves training people how to manage an Internet program to track down missing persons. . . .

Police Commissioner Gerald Westby, who spoke at the opening ceremony on Tuesday, said that trafficking in persons is a worldwide phenomenon, and authorities need to work harder to remove Belize from the Tier 3 black- list the United States government placed Belize on in June this year.

The US claims that Belize has failed to show evidence of significant law enforcement for victim protection.

The US has threaten to withdraw its aid programme.

Since then, police have arrested several suspects. He feels confident that convictions will follow.

Source: Angel Novelo. "Belize Gets Cracking on Human Trafficking." *Belize City Reporter* (8/4/06).

Organizations Team Up to Fight Trafficking in Persons

During the summer of 2006, efforts continued to address human trafficking in Belize.

Several organization have teamed up to fight trafficking in persons or human trafficking in Belize. Today those agencies began a two-day workshop to look closer at the problem. . . .

Source: "Organizations Team Up to Fight Trafficking in Persons." LOVE FM.COM (Radio Belize) (8/21/06). Available online. URL: http://www.lovefm.com/ndisplay.php?nid=4552. Accessed March 25, 2008.

Belize Finally Taken Off Tier 3 Human Trafficking List

In September 2006, Belize was removed from the U.S. list of Tier 3 countries.

The Musa administration is tonight breathing a sigh of relief following an announcement by the United States government that Belize has been removed from the list of Tier Three countries with regard to Human Trafficking. According to a press release issued by the Ministry of Foreign Affairs today, our new status means that the U.S. will "not impose sanctions or oppose any loan or utilization funds from multilateral agencies". This afternoon Minister of Human Development Sylvia Flores told us that while Belize acknowledges that human trafficking is a serious problem, there is only so much we can do with limited resources. . . .

Sylvia Flores

"Well certainly we provided the team with our plan of action and I think they may have been supervising what we were doing basically. And based on reports that they may have been gotten from some the agencies of government that we were trying to arrest some of the persons who were alleged to be trafficking in persons, so I believe whatever efforts that we were doing in the Ministry in collaboration with the Ministry of Home Affairs and Foreign Affairs, they were aware of all we were trying to do to address and arrest this problem. It is now to find the resources to be able to sustain what we are doing. It is important to note also that the problem might be bigger than we think it is, we don't know. We are trying to do our best as you recognize because our borders are porous. We are trying to do as much as we can with our limited resources, so we are hoping that they will understand that we are trying to do our best. There is so much that is beyond us at this time."

Source: News 5 (9/28/06). Available online. URL: http://channel5belize.com/archive_detail_story.php?story_id=17114. Accessed March 25, 2008.

Trafficking Policemen

In 2007, three police officers in Belize were charged with human trafficking.

Three officers—Police Constable (PC) #781 Lauren Flowers, 24, of Roaring Creek; PC #446 Allyson Muslar, 24, of #74 Eve Street in Belize City;

and PC Hersel Garcia, 29, of Lords Bank—have been caught on the wrong side of the law. They appeared today in the Belize City Magistrate's Court where they were read separate charges for human trafficking for sexually assaulting three females who had entered the country illegally.

The men, all represented in court by different attorneys—Dickie Bradley, Michael Peyrefitte and Linsbert Willis—were offered bail this evening, which they were able to meet. All bail offered was "house and lot" bail.

Today police held a press briefing at the Racoon Street Police Station at 10:00 a.m. to tell the media how they were able to make the first break in what they believe is a smuggling ring for illegal immigrants. Westby said that the police strongly believe that the men are a part of a bigger ring of international traffickers taking Central American immigrants through Belize to Mexico, from where they would then head on to the United States.

Commissioner of Police, Gerald Westby, told the media that he was certain that the group is very big, consisting of even Immigration officers. . . .

The policemen, along with the illegal immigrants, three of whom are minors, were taken to the Corozal Police Station. . . .

Source: Belize City Amandala (2/27/07).

Belize Tourism Industry Association [BTIA] Condemns Sexual Exploitation

In 2006, the Belize Tourism Industry Association (BTIA) implemented the code of conduct for the Protection of Children from Sexual Exploitation in Travel and Tourism. This 2007 article describes the code and BTIA's efforts to train those entrusted with its implementation.

Since the official launch of our "Code of Conduct for the Protection of Children from Sexual Exploitation in Travel and Tourism" on August 3rd, 2006, the BTIA has embarked on cross training programs in collaboration with ECPAT U.S.A. and our industry partners, The Belize Hotel Association, Belize Tourism Board, Belize National Tour Guides Association. Programme for Belize, and Rainforest Alliance.

As responsible tourism leaders, we implemented the Code of Conduct in Travel and Tourism. Consequently, we took the necessary actions.

1. To establish an ethical policy against commercial sexual exploitation of children

2. To educate and train the personnel in the country of origin and travel destinations

3. To introduce a clause in contracts with suppliers, stating the common repudiation of commercial sexual exploitation of children

4. To provide information to travelers by means of catalogues, brochures, etc

5. To provide information to local ?key persons?? at the destinations

6. To report annually

Maria Vega, Project Coordinator, explains that as the largest private sector tourism membership organization the BTIA is obliged to lead the way in protecting our children from sexual predators. We have pledged to continue our broad based trainings countrywide, and will work diligently to strengthen our networks. . . .

Source: Belize Tourism Industry Association, press release. "Belize Tourism Industry Association Condemns Sexual Exploitation" (4/20/07). Available online. URL: http://www.btia.org/news_industry_detail.php?release_id=313. Accessed March 25, 2008.

Human Trafficking Still a Problem

The 2007 U.S. TIP Report acknowledged that Belize had made "significant progress" in its efforts to combat human trafficking, but it also insisted that Belize needed to take additional measures.

The US State Department says four Caribbean countries have still not done enough to eliminate human trafficking.

In its 2007 Trafficking in Persons report, the State Department said Belize, Cuba, Guyana and Jamaica need to do more to combat human trafficking.

Last year Belize was harshly criticised by the US for not taking steps to end human trafficking, however, this year's report says Belmopan has made significant progress.

It credited the Said Musa government for increasing anti-trafficking training for law enforcement officials, and also improved protection services for victims.

"In February 2007 the government took a critical step to confront official trafficking-related corruption by arresting two police officers for human smuggling," the report said.

Despite this progress, Washington said more needs to be done for the government to advance its anti-trafficking goals.

The report also recommended that the Said Musa administration consider increasing penalties for sex trafficking and stepping up law enforcement efforts to investigate and prosecute traffickers. . . .

Source: "Human Trafficking Still a Problem." BBCCaribbean.com (6/13/07). Available online. URL: http://www. bbc.co.uk/caribbean/news/story/2007/06/070613_humantrafficking.shtml. Accessed March 25, 2008.

Anti-Trafficking in Persons Grant Award Ceremony

In October 2007, Belize received a grant of $BZ 160,000 from the United States, to be used in its efforts to combat human trafficking.

. . . It is my [U.S. ambassador Robert J. Dieter] pleasure to be here today to present a donation to Belize to help the country prevent human trafficking, protect victims, and prosecute offenders,

I am pleased announce that the United States will be providing Belize with more than $BZ 160,000 for assistance to Belize's anti-trafficking efforts. This funding, combined with the hard work and dedication of the Ministry of Human Development working together with the U.S. Embassy, is evidence of the prominent commitment of the United States to stand-by and support our partners to combat this modern form of human slavery. . . .

Source: Embassy of the United States, Belmopan, Belize, press release. "Anti-Trafficking in Persons Grant Award Ceremony, October 18, 2007." Available online. URL: http://belize.usembassy.gov/october_18.html. Accessed March 25, 2008.

PART III

Research Tools

6

~~~

How to Research
Human Trafficking

When undertaking any research project, it is important to distinguish between reliable and unreliable sources and to choose research strategies that will lead to as many reliable sources as possible. This can be particularly difficult when researching human trafficking. First, the activity is illegal and hidden, so even the most credible sources must sometimes extrapolate from what is seen and verified—usually through contact with legal authorities or aid workers—to estimate the true size and severity of the problem. This means that even the most credible sources cannot always provide the definitive answers desired.

Second, when a subject arouses the passion that human trafficking does, the surrounding commentary can contain inflated evidentiary claims. (Where a credible source on human trafficking will provide specific statistics only for *verified* incidents, i.e., the number of arrests and prosecutions in a given area, or the percentage of repatriated sex slaves testing positive for HIV/AIDS, and clearly estimate the full extent of modern slavery or categories such as sex trafficking and involuntary domestic servitude, an unreliable source may bolster calls for abolition or other redress with unsupported but seemingly certain statistics.) This means that all sources on human trafficking must be evaluated not in terms of intent—many unreliable sources are clearly well-intentioned—but for accuracy of information and a clear delineation between verified figures and best estimates. It is also necessary to evaluate the context in which figures are presented, as the purpose of a document may be served by a "best case" or "worst case" presentation. In discussing poverty as a root cause of trafficking, for example, one might examine various documents purporting to present a country's financial situation. Documents created to enlist charitable contributions might be biased toward a presentation of numbers that illustrate a country's continued shortcomings, while a document intended to illustrate progress toward meeting the UN Millennium

Development Goals, for example, might be biased toward a presentation of numbers that illustrate a country's progress.

Finally, an Internet search for information on human trafficking can lead to consumer-related sites; without the proper search terms, for example, an Internet search for information on forced marriage can lead to advertisements from and links to so-called mail-order bride companies. While such sites may document that there is, indeed, a consumer market for purchased wives, they are not otherwise, for obvious reasons, credible research sources. This chapter will help you to seek out information about human trafficking from sources known to be reliable and to adopt research strategies that will help you find and evaluate additional sources of information.

RESEARCHING CHATTEL SLAVERY
Primary Sources

Because chattel slavery was, for many years, a legally recognized system for the ownership of persons, those who practiced it did so openly. As a result, records of shipment, bill of sale, census tallies, and other records of ownership were carefully maintained. Many such records of chattel slavery in the United States have been digitized and are available in collections such as the slavery and abolition portion of the Smithsonian Institution's digital collection (http://civilwar.si.edu/resources_slavery.html), the digital collections at the New York Public Library's Schomburg Center for Research in Black Culture (www.nypl.org/research/sc/digital.html), and in the African-American Odyssey exhibition of the Library of Congress (http://lcweba.loc.gov/ammem.aaohtml). A search of newspapers from any year in which slavery was legally recognized will also provide documentation of chattel slavery activity, including advertisements for slave auctions or sales, rewards for the capture of runaway slaves, and the availability of slave collars and other instruments of punishment.

The autobiographical writings of formerly enslaved people, known as slave narratives or ex-slave narratives, are also excellent primary sources for information about chattel slavery. While many of these narratives were coauthored by whites or written by whites, perhaps with varying degrees of faithfulness, from the oral testimony of the formerly enslaved, they provide first-person testimony about life under chattel slavery. Sojourner Truth and Frederick Douglass, whose narratives are discussed in the Key Players section of this book, are but two of the approximately 6,000 formerly enslaved persons known to have left accounts of chattel slavery in the United States. "Documenting the American South," a digital library sponsored by the University Library of the University of North Carolina at Chapel Hill (doc.south.

unc.edu), has digitized all known narratives published in English by fugitive and former slaves prior to 1920. Other testimony of those who experienced chattel slavery firsthand was preserved in *Born in Slavery: Slave Narratives from the Federal Writers' Project, 1936–1938,* a Works Progress Administration project that led to the interviewing of more than 2,300 formerly enslaved persons and the photographing of 500 of them. Digitized versions of the original interviews, which were tape-recorded, are available at the Library of Congress. In 1988, the scholar and critic Henry Louis Gates, Jr., collected the works of 19th- and early 20th-century black women writers, including many formerly enslaved women, into a 30-volume set, The Schomburg Library of Nineteenth-Century Black Women Writers.

It is also possible to examine places where chattel slavery and abolitionist activities took place. The National Park Service (NPS) Aboard the Underground Railroad Web site provides a National Register of Historic Places travel itinerary associated with chattel slavery and abolition, particularly the Underground Railroad. The NPS also provides additional online resources about slavery (http://www.slaveryinamerica.org/resources/gw_npr.htm).

The African Burial Ground in New York City is a 6.6 acre site in Lower Manhattan. For 100 years (1690–1790) free and enslaved Africans were buried here. Once lost because of development, it was rediscovered in 1991 and is now administered by the NPS. It was declared a National Monument by George W. Bush in 2006 and includes an educational center.

Secondary Sources and Additional Information

There are many good secondary sources on chattel slavery. Susan Miers has been writing about the subject for more than two decades. Her books include *Britain and the Ending of the Slave Trade* and *Slavery in the Twentieth Century: The Evolution of a Global Problem.* In addition, she is an editor of *The End of Slavery in Africa* and the multivolume series, Women and Slavery. Milton Meltzer has also been writing about chattel slavery, among other issues, for more than 20 years. His books include *Slavery: A World History; and Black Americans: A History in Their Own Words, 1619–1983.* David Brion Davis, the director emeritus of the Gilder Lehrman Center for the Study of Slavery, Resistance, and Abolition at Yale University, is another writer whose work on chattel slavery spans two decades. His books include *AnteBellum American Culture: An Interpretive Anthology; Challenging the Boundaries of Slavery; Problems of Slavery in Western Culture; In the Image of God: Religion, Moral Values, and Our Heritage of Slavery;* and, most recently, *Inhuman Bondage: The Rise and Fall of Slavery in the New World.*

When undertaking a search for additional sources on chattel slavery, it is advisable to use the full phrase, chattel slavery to distinguish between it and modern slavery. In some cases, centuries-old traditions of slavery have continued without apparent change, despite the official outlawing of slavery in international and national law; information about this vestigial form of chattel slavery is generally classified under human trafficking or modern-day slavery.

MODERN-DAY SLAVERY
Primary Sources

Primary source materials for modern-day slavery include studies conducted by governments and international bodies, the reports of nongovernmental organizations (NGOs) working with rescued victims and in other capacities to combat human trafficking, newspaper accounts, documentary and investigative film footage, and the autobiographical writing of and interviews with formerly trafficked persons.

International bodies that issue or archive reports relevant to human trafficking include the following United Nations agencies:

International Labour Organization (ILO)

United Nations Children's Fund (UNICEF)

United Nations Office on Drugs and Crime (UNODC)

Examples of reports issued by these UN agencies include a report on the global patterns of human trafficking and reports on child marriage, child labor, and the use of child soldiers.

Regional economic and political unions of countries also work to address international issues such as human trafficking; their reports and/or summary documents will generally contain information about one or more of their member countries and a given issue, as well as an examination of the issue on a regionwide basis. Regional bodies include:

Association of Caribbean States

Association of Southeast Asian States

Economic Community of West African States

European Union

Organization of American States

The African Union

Reports issued by regional bodies include a study of human trafficking in three European Union member countries, while an example of regional cooperation on human trafficking includes the Economic Community of West African States' Plan of Action against Trafficking in Persons.

Individual countries also issue reports on human trafficking. One of the most important reports is the U.S. State Department's Trafficking in Persons Report (TIP Report). This annual report assesses up to 170 countries' records on human trafficking, including the extent of trafficking in and to the country, the particular forms of trafficking in each country, and each profiled country's efforts to end human trafficking within its borders. The reports also contain sections that focus on specific forms of modern slavery, such as child soldiers or involuntary domestic servitude, and excerpts from victims' statements. The U.S. Department of Justice also releases an annual report summarizing the United States's investigations and prosecutions of traffickers during each fiscal year. The U.S. Department of Health and Human Services, which has responsibility for verifying rescued trafficking victims and providing aftercare services, is also a good source of information about trafficking in the United States, as is the U.S. Immigration and Customs Enforcement, which, among other activities, investigates human trafficking through its Human Smuggling and Trafficking Unit.

Other countries also issue regular reports on human trafficking. The (Dutch) National Reporter on Human Trafficking, for example, presents regular reports on human trafficking in the Netherlands to the Dutch government. Moreover, many individual countries also issue reports on poverty and gender inequality, two of the root causes of human trafficking. The United Nations Millennium Declaration, adopted unanimously by all UN member nations in 2000, set forth an ambitious plan to eradicate the worst forms of poverty and eliminate other social ills by the year 2015. As part of working toward that goal, many member nations submit regular reports on poverty, health care, educational attainment levels, and other indicators of relative well-being within their countries. (The United Nations itself also issues an international overview of the same indicators.) Similarly, countries that are party to the Convention on the Elimination of All Forms of Discrimination against Women (CEDAW) are required to make regular reports to the United Nations about gender equality within their borders. While neither the Millennium Development Goals Progress Reports or the CEDAW-required reports are created to address human trafficking, they provide insight into trafficking's background conditions.

When reviewing the report of any international body or individual government, it is useful to also examine the media and NGO responses to those reports. NGOs working on the issue from a certain perspective may at times raise questions or concerns about government conclusions. Organizations working specifically on sex trafficking, for example, have at times raised questions about the United States. A TIP Report's favorable ranking of European countries with legal prostitution certainly suggests further areas of inquiry for a researcher. Additionally, some governments may present information in the best light possible, omit information that would be deemed derogatory, or occlude meaning with political speech. (See George Orwell's classic essay, "Politics and the English Language" [1946], for an excellent discussion of how language can be used to obscure rather than illuminate meaning, especially in political discourse.) For this reason, too, it is useful to examine the response to any given governmental report, as well as the report itself. With respect to the reports mandated for parties to the United Nations treaties, the United Nations accepts and archives so-called shadow reports filed by NGOs. These reports supplement—and sometimes dispute—information supplied by governments. An Internet search using the keywords "CEDAW" and "shadow report*" (the asterisk indicates a request for both "report" and "reports") will return links to NGO assessments of CEDAW-party governments' claims regarding their progress on gender equality.

NGOs also issue their own self-directed reports on human trafficking. To evaluate the credibility of an NGO, it is useful to consider whether it holds consultative status with United Nations Office on Drugs and Crime (UNODC). UNODC maintains a database of such organizations at www.unodc.org/unodc/en/ngos/NGO_Database.htm. It is also useful to note which NGOs have their research quoted in legitimate secondary sources or their leadership credited as experts by serious media outlets.

Media outlets are, themselves, sources of information on human trafficking. An Internet search of nationwide newspapers through the National Newspaper Index, a database available in many public and academic libraries, will return articles about human trafficking from the nation's newspapers, many of which can then be accessed either online or in library holdings. Alternatively, major newspapers such as the *New York Times* and the *Washington Post* can be searched individually, again, either online or in library holdings, for articles on modern slavery. The Human Trafficking Website, among other things, also provides links to newspaper articles, on a country-by-country basis, about modern slavery.

Documentary and investigative journalism programs also provide excellent primary-source information about human trafficking. *The Selling of Innocents* (1997) and *China's Stolen Children* (2008) are examples of excellent documentaries about modern slavery, while the *Dateline* episodes "Children for Sale" (NBC, 2005) and "Update, Victims of Child Sex Trade in Cambodia" (NBC, 2008) are examples of excellent investigative broadcast journalism on the subject; others are listed in the annotated bibliography of this book. As additional film footage of trafficking activity and its consequences become available in the future, media reviews will help the researcher to evaluate their merits.

Just as the autobiographical writings of former chattel slaves provided some of the strongest testimony against pre-20th-century slavery, the first-person accounts of former trafficking victims provide some of the strongest testimony against modern-day slavery. Such modern-day slave narratives include Ishmael Beah's *A Long Way Gone: Memoirs of a Boy Soldier,* Francis Bok's *Escape from Slavery: The True Story of My Ten Years in Captivity—and My Journey to Freedom in America* (2003), and Mukhtar Mai's *In the Name of Honor: A Memoir* (2006). In addition, Jesse Sage and Liora Kasten of the American Anti-Slavery Group have collected first-person accounts in *Enslaved: True Stories of Modern Day Slavery* (2006).

Secondary Sources

Because modern-day slavery is an issue that has surfaced fairly recently, the authors discussed here have not accumulated even two decades' worth of work and research on the subject. Rather, their books and articles provide accurate, valuable, and passionately delivered information about a still-emerging and still-growing problem. Kevin Bales's *Disposable People: New Slavery in the Global Economy* (revised edition, 2004) and *Understanding Global Slavery: A Reader* (2005), E. Benjamin Skinner's *A Crime So Monstrous: A Shocking Exposé of Modern-Day Slavery, Human Trafficking and Child Urban Markets* (2008), and John Bowe's *Nobodies: Modern American Slave Labor and the Dark Side of the New Global Economy* (2007) all examine multiple facets of modern-day slavery. Melissa Farley's *Prostitution and Trafficking in Nevada: Making the Connections* (2007), Victor Malarek's *The Natashas: Inside the Global Sex Trade* (2003), and Louisa Waugh's *Selling Olga: Stories of Human Trafficking* examine various aspects of sex trafficking. Nancy Scheper-Hughes, head of Organs Watch at the University of California, Berkeley, is currently the leading authority on trafficking for involuntary organ harvests; her papers "The Organ of Last Resort" and "The End of the Body: The Global Traffic in Organs or Transplant Surgery" are important sources of information on this form of human trafficking.

As additional secondary sources are made available it will be, again, important to evaluate the merits of the work. Media and scholarly reviews will help in this endeavor, as will the researcher's own evaluation of the authors' background and credentials. (Reviewing the above works, for example, one would find that Nancy Scheper-Hughes is professor and director of the doctoral program in critical studies of medicine, science, and the body at the University of California, Berkeley, as well as head of Organs Watch, and that Kevin Bales is both head of the well-respected NGO Free the Slaves and professor of sociology at Roehampton University, London, England.)

Remember that when searching for information on human trafficking in any format—books, articles, film, or government documents—Internet searches are likely to play a role. Many library card catalogs are now digitized and many a search for a film or newspaper article now begins on the Internet. While it can be a tremendous boon to have so very much information available from one's computer screen, the fact that so very much of that information is unfiltered—and, indeed, can be entirely bogus—can pose a problem to the researcher. Many academic and public libraries have subscriptions to online databases such as EBSCO Masterfile Index, JSTOR, Humanities Full-Text, or OmniFile Full-Text Mega; these and other databases your librarian may recommend can guide you to articles containing credible information, as will, again, a search through the online archives of a reputable newspaper or the Web site of an organization you have deemed to be trustworthy. If you decide to conduct an online search without first accessing one of these sites, the use of formal terminology, i.e., "sex tourism" rather than "sex tours" will help guide you toward reliable information.

7

Facts and Figures

HUMAN TRAFFICKING IN THE WORLD
1.1 Human Trafficking: Origin, Transit, and Destination Countries

INCIDENCE OF REPORTING OF ORIGIN COUNTRIES

VERY HIGH	HIGH	MEDIUM	LOW	VERY LOW
Albania	Armenia	Afghanistan	Argentina	Brunei
Belarus	Bangladesh	Algeria	Bhutan	Darussalam
Bulgaria	Benin	Angola	Botswana	Chad
China	Brazil	Azerbaijan	Burundi	Chile
Lithuania	Cambodia	Bosnia and	Canada	Costa Rica
Nigeria	Colombia	Herzegovina	Cape Verde	Egypt
Republic of	Czech	Burkina Faso	Democratic	Fiji
Moldova	Republic	Cameroon	Republic of	Jamaica
Romania	Dominican	Congo, Republic of	Congo	Macao,
Russian	Republic	Côte d'Ivoire	Djibouti	China SAR
Federation	Estonia	Croatia	Equatorial	Netherlands
Thailand	Georgia	Cuba	Guinea	Paraguay
Ukraine	Ghana	Democratic People's	Eritrea	Syrian Arab
	Guatemala	Republic of Korea	Gabon	Republic
	Hungary	Ecuador	Gambia	Uruguay
	India	El Salvador	Guinea	Yemen
	Kazakhstan	Ethiopia	Iran (Islamic	
	Lao People's	Haiti	Republic of)	
	Democratic	Honduras	Iraq	
	Republic	Hong Kong, China SAR	Jordan	
	Latvia	Indonesia	Lebanon	
	Mexico	Kenya	Lesotho	
	Morocco	Kosovo (Serbia and	Madagascar	
	Myanmar	Montenegro)	Maldives	

(continues)

INCIDENCE OF REPORTING OF ORIGIN COUNTRIES *(continued)*

VERY HIGH	HIGH	MEDIUM	LOW	VERY LOW
	Nepal	Kyrgyzstan	Nicaragua	
	Pakistan	Liberia	Panama	
	Philippines	Malawi	Rwanda	
	Poland	Malaysia	Republic of	
	Slovakia	Mali	Korea	
	Uzbekistan	Mozambique	Somalia	
	Vietnam	Niger	Sudan	
		Peru	Swaziland	
		Senegal	Tunisia	
		Serbia and	United States	
		Montenegro	of America	
		Sierra Leone	Zimbabwe	
		Singapore		
		Slovenia		
		South Africa		
		Sri Lanka		
		Macedonia		
		Taiwan		
		Tajikistan		
		Togo		
		Turkey		
		Turkmenistan		
		Uganda		
		United Republic of		
		Tanzania		
		Venezuela		
		Zambia		

INCIDENCE OF REPORTING OF TRANSIT COUNTRIES

VERY HIGH	HIGH	MEDIUM	LOW	VERY LOW
Albania	Belgium	Belarus	Algeria	Bahrain
Bulgaria	Bosnia and	Benin	Austria	Bangladesh
Hungary	Herzegovina	Burkina Faso	Azerbaijan	Belize
Italy	Czech	Canada	Botswana	Cambodia
Poland	Republic	Côte d'Ivoire	Brunei	Chad
Thailand	France	Croatia	Darussalam	China
	Germany	Cyprus	Cameroon	Colombia
	Greece	Egypt	Costa Rica	Dominica

VERY HIGH	HIGH	MEDIUM	LOW	VERY LOW
	Kosovo (Serbia and Montenegro) Myanmar Romania Serbia and Montenegro Slovakia Macedonia Turkey Ukraine	Gabon Georgia Hong Kong, China SAR India Kazakhstan Malaysia Mexico Netherlands Russian Federation Singapore South Africa Togo United Kingdom	Ghana Indonesia Lao People's Democratic Republic Latvia Lithuania Morocco New Zealand Nigeria Republic of Moldova Slovenia Spain Switzerland	El Salvador Equatorial Guinea Estonia Finland Guatemala Ireland Jamaica Japan Jordan Kyrgyzstan Lebanon Lesotho Malawi Mali Mozambique Nepal Niger Norway Pakistan Panama Philippines Saudi Arabia Republic of Korea Senegal Sweden United Republic of Tanzania Uruguay Vietnam Zambia Zimbabwe

INCIDENCE OF REPORTING OF DESTINATION COUNTRIES

VERY HIGH	HIGH	MEDIUM	LOW	VERY LOW
Belgium Germany Greece	Australia Austria Bosnia and	Albania Argentina Bahrain	Aruba Bangladesh Belize	Algeria Bhutan Brazil

(continues)

INCIDENCE OF REPORTING OF DESTINATION COUNTRIES *(continued)*

VERY HIGH	HIGH	MEDIUM	LOW	VERY LOW
Israel	Herzegovina	Benin	Brunei	Burundi Chad
Italy	Cambodia	Bulgaria	Darussalam	Chile
Japan	Canada	Burkina Faso	Congo,	Congo,
Nether-	China	Cameroon	Republic of	Democratic
lands	Cyprus	Cote d'Ivoire	Costa Rica	Republic of
Thailand	Czech Republic	Croatia	Ecuador	Djibouti
Turkey	Denmark	Curacao	Egypt	Dominica
United	France	Dominican	Haiti	Ethiopia
States of	Hong Kong,	Republic	Indonesia	Fiji
America	China SAR	El Salvador	Iraq	Gambia
	India	Equatorial	Ireland	Georgia
	Kosovo	Guinea	Kyrgyzstan	Honduras
	(Serbia and	Estonia	Lao People's	Jamaica
	Montenegro)	Finland	Democratic	Liberia
	Pakistan	Gabon	Republic	Malawi
	Poland	Ghana	Libyan Arab	Maldives
	Saudi Arabia	Guatemala	Jamahiriya	Morocco
	Spain	Hungary	Luxembourg	Mozambique
	Switzerland	Iceland	Mali	Republic of
	Taiwan	Iran (Islamic	Niger	Moldova
	United Arab	Republic of)	Oman	Senegal
	Emirates	Kazakhstan	Paraguay	Sierra Leone
	United	Kenya	Romania	Slovakia
	Kingdom	Kuwait	Slovenia	Sudan
		Latvia	Sri Lanka	Tajikistan
		Lebanon	Uganda	Trinidad and
		Lithuania	United	Tobago
		Macao, China SAR	Republic of	Zambia
		Malaysia	Tanzania	Zimbabwe
		Mexico	Uzbekistan	
		Myanmar	Yemen	
		New Zealand		
		Nigeria		
		Norway		
		Panama		
		Philippines		
		Portugal		
		Qatar		
		Republic of Korea		
		Russian		
		Federation		
		Serbia and		
		Montenegro		

VERY HIGH	HIGH	MEDIUM	LOW	VERY LOW
		Singapore South Africa Sweden Syrian Arab Republic Macedonia Togo Ukraine Venezuela Vietnam		

The United Nations classified countries as origin, transit, and/or destination countries for human traffickers and their victims. This list, released as part of a 2006 report, ranks countries according to activity reported in each category from 1996 to 2003.

Source: UNODC. "Trafficking in Persons: Global Patterns" (2006), pp. 18–20. Available online. URL: http://www.unodc.org/pdf/traffickinginpersons_report_2006ver2.pdf. Accessed March 12, 2009.

1.2 U.S. Trafficking in Persons Report, 2008 Tier Placements

TIER 1

Australia	Finland	Lithuania	Slovenia
Austria	France	Luxembourg	Spain
Belgium	Georgia	Macedonia	Sweden
Canada	Germany	Madagascar	Switzerland
Colombia	Hong Kong	Netherlands	United
Croatia	Hungary	New Zealand	Kingdom
Czech Republic	Italy	Norway	
Denmark	Korea, Rep. of	Poland	

TIER 2

Afghanistan	Ethiopia	Mali	Serbia
Angola	Ghana	Malta	Sierra Leone
Bangladesh	Greece	Mauritania	Singapore
Belarus	Honduras	Mauritius	Slovak Republic
Belize	Indonesia	Mexico	Suriname
Benin	Israel	Mongolia	Tanzania
Bolivia	Ireland	Morocco	Taiwan
Bosnia &	Jamaica	Nepal	Thailand
Herzegovina	Japan	Nicaragua	Timor-Leste
Brazil	Kazakhstan	Nigeria	Togo
Bulgaria	Kenya	Pakistan	Turkey
Burkina Faso	Kyrgyz Republic	Paraguay	Uganda
Cambodia	Laos	Peru	Ukraine
Chile	Latvia	Philippines	United Arab
Djibouti	Lebanon	Portugal	Emirates
Ecuador	Liberia	Romania	Uruguay
El Salvador	Macau	Rwanda	Vietnam
Estonia	Malawi	Senegal	Yemen

TIER 2 WATCH LIST

Argentina	Congo (DRC)	Guatemala	Panama
Armenia	Congo, Rep. of	Guinea	Russia
Azerbaijan	Costa Rica	Guinea-Bissau	South Africa
Albania	Cyprus	Guyana	Sri Lanka
Bahrain	Côte d'Ivoire	India	Tajikistan
Burundi	Dominican	Jordan	Tanzania
Cameroon	Republic	Libya	Venezuela
Central African	Egypt	Malaysia	Uzbekistan
Republic	Equatorial Guinea	Montenegro	Zambia
Chad	Gabon	Mozambique	Zimbabwe
China (PRC)	The Gambia	Niger	

Facts and Figures

TIER 3			
Algeria	Iran	Oman	Saudi Arabia
Burma	Kuwait	Papua	Sudan
Cuba	Moldova	New Guinea	Syria
Fiji	North Korea	Qatar	

The United States classifies countries according to their efforts to end human trafficking, with Tier 1 countries being the most favorable designation and Tier 3, the worst. This is the ranking as of 2008.

Source: U.S. Department of State. "Trafficking in Persons Report, 2008," p. 44. Available online. URL: http://www.state.gov/g/tip/rls/tiprpt/2008. Accessed March 11, 2009.

1.3 Trafficking in Persons Reports, 2001–2008 Tier Placement Histories: Netherlands, Nigeria, India, and Belize

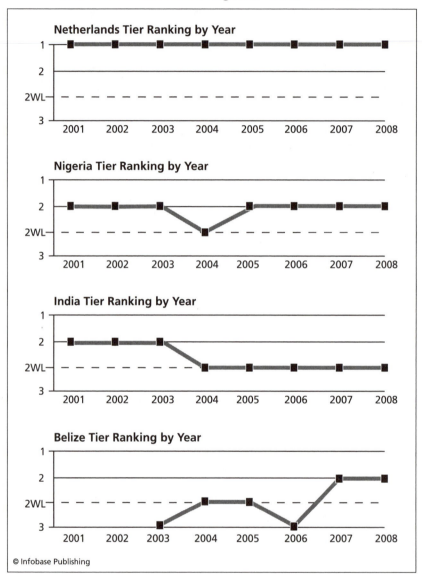

These graphs track the tier placement of Netherlands, Nigeria, India, and Belize in the U.S. Trafficking in Persons Reports from 2001 to 2008.

Source: U.S. Department of State. "Trafficking in Persons Report, 2008," pp. 71, 139, 191, 197. Available online. URL: http://www.state.gov/g/tip/rls/tiprpt/2008. Accessed March 11, 2009.

FIGHTING HUMAN TRAFFICKING

2.1 Parties to International Human Trafficking Documents

	United States	Netherlands	Nigeria	India	Belize
Protocol to Prevent, Suppress & Punish Trafficking in Persons	Signature and Ratification	Signature and Ratification	Signature and Ratification	Signature, No Ratification	Accession without Signature
ILO Convention 182, Elimination of the Worst Forms of Child Labour	Ratification	Ratification	Ratification	None	Ratification
Optional Protocol to the Convention on the Rights of the Child on the Sale of Children, Child Prostitutionand Child Pornography	Signature and Ratification	Signature and Ratification	Signature, No Ratification	Signature and Ratification	Signature and Ratification
Optional Protocol to the Convention on the Rights of the Child in Armed Conflict	Signature and Ratification	Signature, No Ratification	Signature, No Ratification	Signature and Ratification	Signature and Ratification
ILO Convention 29, Forced Labour	None	Ratification	Ratification	Ratification	Ratification
Hague Convention on the Protection of Children and Co-operation in Respect of Inter-Country Adoption	Ratification without Signature	Signature and Ratification	None	Signature and Ratification	Accession without Signature
ILO Convention 105, Abolition Of Forced Labour	Ratification	Ratification	Ratification	Ratification	Ratification
Hague Convention on the Protection of Children and Co-operation in Respect of Inter-Country Adoption	Ratification without Signature	Signature and Ratification	None	Signature and Ratification	Accession without Signature

This table indicates the actions taken and/or not taken by the United States, the Netherlands, Nigeria, India, and Belize with respect to international conventions and protocols that directly address modern-day slavery. Countries that have signed a convention are obligated to act in good faith to uphold the aims of that convention, but they are not legally bound by it. Countries that have ratified a convention are legally bound to abide by it.

Source: U.S. Department of State. "Trafficking in Persons Report, 2008," pp. 280-283. Available online. URL: http://www.state.gov/g/tip/rls/tiprpt/2008. Accessed March 12, 2009; Hague Conference on Private International Law. "Convention on Protection of Children and Co-operation in Respect of Intercountry Adoption." Available online. URL: http://www.hcch.net/index_en.php?act=conventions.text&cid=69. Accessed March 12, 2009.

2.2 Convention on the Elimination of All Forms of Discrimination against Women (CEDAW)

COUNTRY	SIGNATURE	RATIFICATION, ACCESSION, OR SUCCESSION	DECLARATIONS AND RESERVATIONS
United States	July 17, 1980	Not ratified	
Netherlands	July 17, 1980	July 23, 1991	Declaration: The Netherlands objects to the inclusion of paragraphs 10 and 11 in the Convention's preamble. These paragraphs refer, among other things, to colonialism and neo-colonialism.
Nigeria	April 24, 1984	June 13, 1985	
India	July 30, 1980	July 9, 1993	Declarations: Certain provisions will be enforced in "conformity with [India's] policy of non-interference in the personal affairs of any Community without its initiative and consent" and "though in principle [India] fully supports the principle of compulsory registration of marriages, it is not practical in a vast country like India with its variety of customs, religions and level of literacy." Reservations: India does not consider itself bound by Article 29, paragraph 1, which permits referral to the International Court of Justice if two State Parties cannot otherwise resolve a dispute.
Belize	March 7, 1990	May 16, 1990	

CEDAW, in addressing discrimination against women, addresses a root cause of human trafficking. This table reflects the actions taken and/or not taken by the United States, the Netherlands, Nigeria, India and Belize with respect to this convention. As discussed below table 2.1, countries that have signed a convention are obligated to act in good faith to uphold the aims of that convention, while countries that have ratified a convention are legally bound by it. Countries also become legally bound to a convention by accession or succession (legally succeeding a country that had earlier become party to a convention).

Source: United Nations. "Convention on the Elimination of All Forms of Discrimination against Women, State Parties." Available online. URL: http://www.un.org/womenwatch/daw/cedaw/states.htm. Accessed March 12, 2009.

GLOBAL MAPS AND ROUTES

3.1 Reported Human Trafficking: Main Origin, Transit, and Destination Countries[CS12]

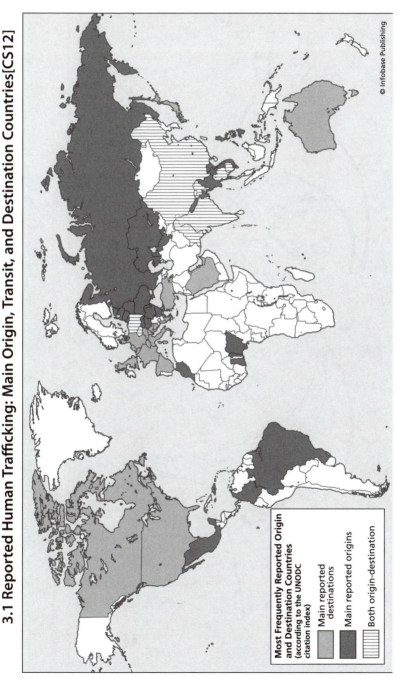

© Infobase Publishing

Most Frequently Reported Origin and Destination Countries (according to the UNODC citation index)

- Main reported destinations
- Main reported origins
- Both origin-destination

This map identifies the countries with the highest levels of human trafficking and categorizes those countries as origin, transit, and/or destination countries.

Source: UNDOC. "Trafficking in Persons: Global Patterns" (2006), pp. 17. Available online. URL: http://www.unodc.org/pdf/traffickinginpersons_report_2006ver2.pdf . Accessed March 12, 2009.

3.2 Global Human Trafficking Routes

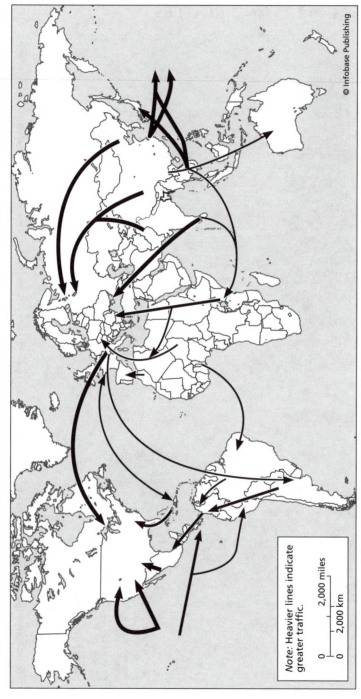

© Infobase Publishing

Note: Heavier lines indicate greater traffic.

0   2,000 miles
0   2,000 km

As this map illustrates, human trafficking victims are often transported very far from their countries of origin.

Source: International Organization for Migration. "Organized Crime Moves into Migrant Trafficking," Trafficking in Migrants, Quarterly Bulletin, no. 11 (June 1996): 2.

3.3 Child Marriage: Proportion of Women Aged 20–24 in Union by Age 18[CS13]

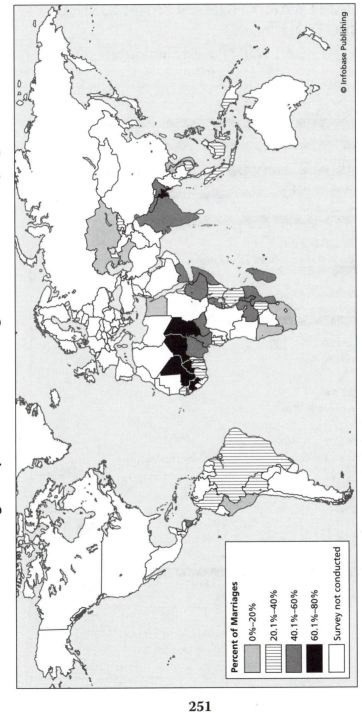

This map illustrates the prevalence of child marriage in many of the world's countries.

Source: UNICEF. "Early Marriage: A Harmful Traditional Practice" (2005), p. 3. Available online. URL: http://www.unicef.gr/pdfs/Early-Marriage.pdf. Accessed March 12, 2009.

INEQUALITY AND HUMAN TRAFFICKING CONNECTION

4.1 World Poverty Indicators
4.1 a

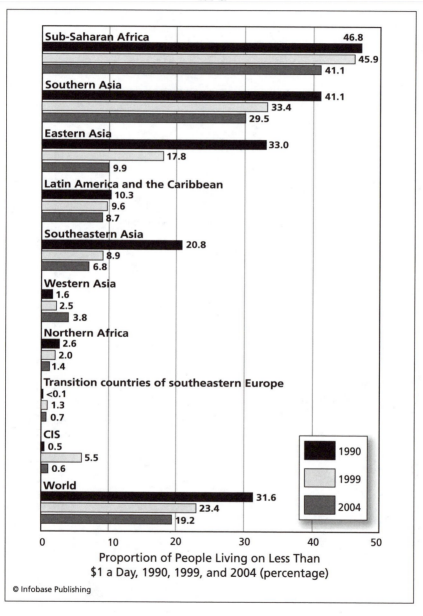

Sub-Saharan Africa
46.8
45.9
41.1

Southern Asia
41.1
33.4
29.5

Eastern Asia
33.0
17.8
9.9

Latin America and the Caribbean
10.3
9.6
8.7

Southeastern Asia
20.8
8.9
6.8

Western Asia
1.6
2.5
3.8

Northern Africa
2.6
2.0
1.4

Transition countries of southeastern Europe
<0.1
1.3
0.7

CIS
0.5
5.5
0.6

World
31.6
23.4
19.2

■ 1990
□ 1999
■ 2004

0   10   20   30   40   50

Proportion of People Living on Less Than
$1 a Day, 1990, 1999, and 2004 (percentage)

© Infobase Publishing

4.1 b

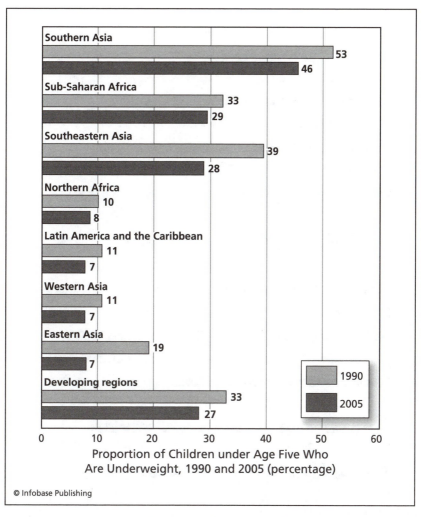

Proportion of Children under Age Five Who
Are Underweight, 1990 and 2005 (percentage)

© Infobase Publishing

Extreme poverty is a root cause of human trafficking. These graphs measure two important indicators of a country's poverty: (a) the percentage of people who live on less than $1.00 per day and (b) the percentage of children younger than five who are underweight.

Source: United Nations. "Millennium Development Goal Report, 2007," pp. 6 and 8. Available online. URL: http://www.un.org/millenniumgoals/pdf/mdg2007.pdf. Accessed March 12, 2009.

4.2 Global Primary and Secondary School Attendance
4.2 a

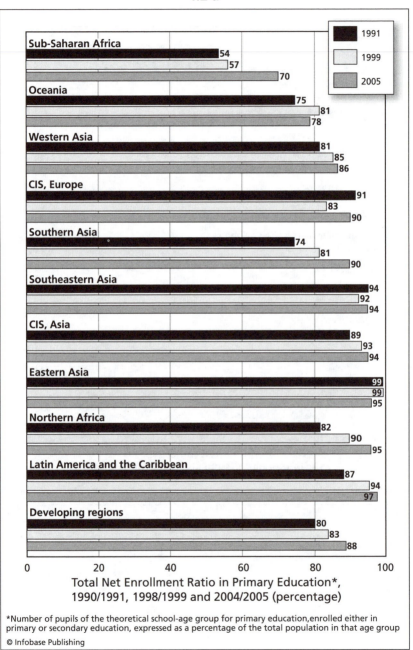

Total Net Enrollment Ratio in Primary Education*,
1990/1991, 1998/1999 and 2004/2005 (percentage)

*Number of pupils of the theoretical school-age group for primary education,enrolled either in
primary or secondary education, expressed as a percentage of the total population in that age group

© Infobase Publishing

4.2 b

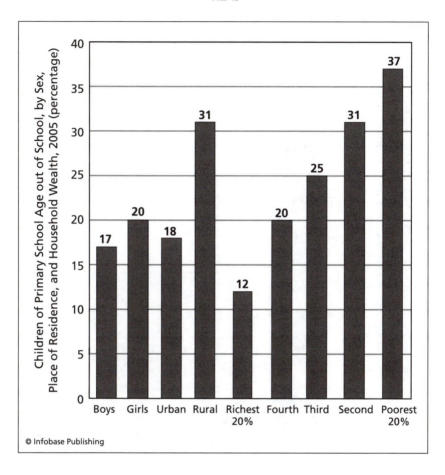

© Infobase Publishing

4.2 c

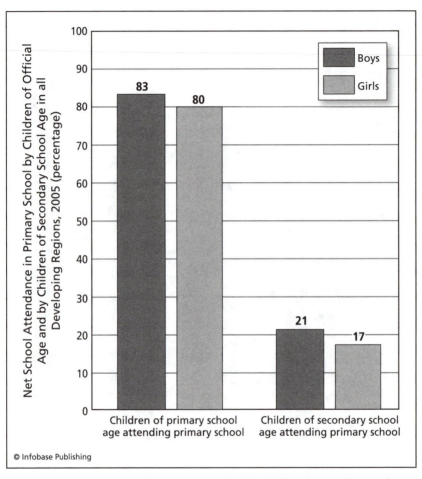

Lack of education and educational opportunities for one's children also contributes to human trafficking. These three graphs measure global school attendance.

Source: United Nations. "Millennium Development Goal Report, 2007," p. 10-11. Available online. URL: http://www.un.org/millenniumgoals/pdf/mdg2007.pdf. Accessed March 12, 2009.

4.3 Measures of Global Gender Inequality
4.3 a

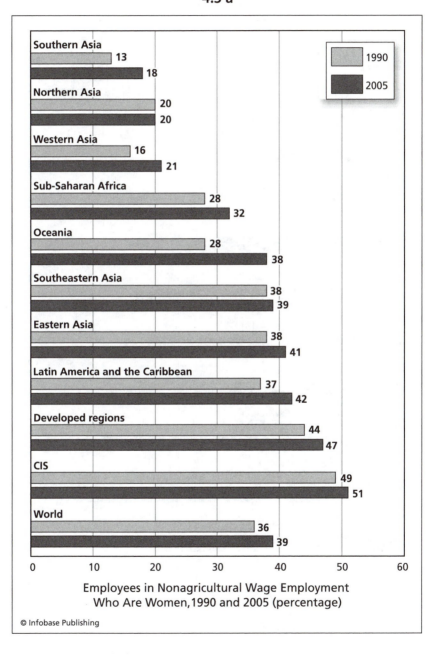

Employees in Nonagricultural Wage Employment
Who Are Women, 1990 and 2005 (percentage)

© Infobase Publishing

4.3 b

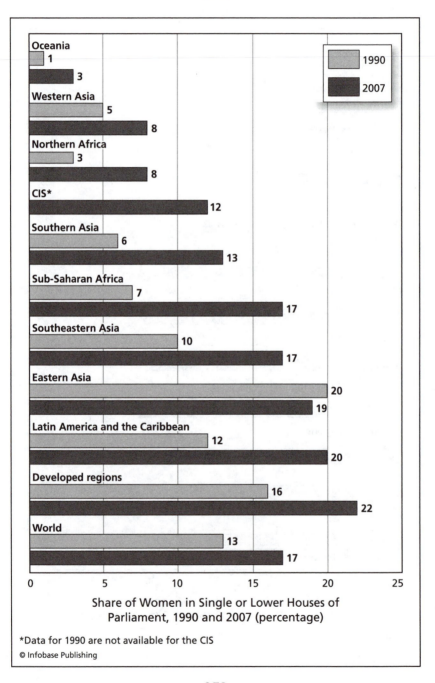

Share of Women in Single or Lower Houses of
Parliament, 1990 and 2007 (percentage)

1990

2007

Oceania
1
3

Western Asia
5
8

Northern Africa
3
8

CIS*
12

Southern Asia
6
13

Sub-Saharan Africa
7
17

Southeastern Asia
10
17

Eastern Asia
20
19

Latin America and the Caribbean
12
20

Developed regions
16
22

World
13
17

0   5   10   15   20   25

*Data for 1990 are not available for the CIS

© Infobase Publishing

4.3 c

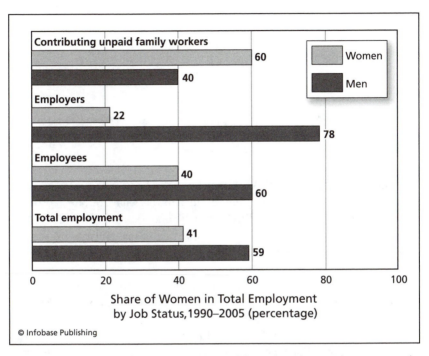

Gender inequality is also a root cause of human trafficking. These three graphs examine gender inequality by measuring women's participation in the workforce and in government.

Source: United Nations. "Millennium Development Goal Report, 2007," p. 12-13. Available online. URL: http://www.un.org/millenniumgoals/pdf/mdg2007.pdf. Accessed March 12, 2009.

8

Key Players A to Z

AMINA TITI ATIKU ABUBAKAR (1950–   )   Former second lady of the Federal Republic of Nigeria and the founder of the Nigerian NGO Women Trafficking and Child Labour Eradication Foundation (WOTCLEF), Chief (Mrs.) Amina Titi Atiku Abubakar was born in Lagos, Nigeria, on June 6, 1950. She was educated at Catholic girls' primary and high schools in Nigeria before attending Kaduna Polytechnic, from which she received a national diploma and a higher national diploma in catering and hotel management. She later studied hotel management at the Scuola International de Scienze Turitiche in Rome, Italy, under the sponsorship of the World Tourism Organisation and the Italian Ministry of Foreign Affairs. Following her graduation from Kaduna Polytechnic, Abubakar became a lecturer at that institution and married Alhaji Atiku Abubakar. Amina Titi Atiku Abubakar became second lady of Nigeria in 1999 when her husband became the country's vice president. Prompted by memories of her contact with Nigerian girls prostituted in Italy when she studied in Rome, Abubakar founded WOTCLEF in her husband's inaugural year. She continues to chair that organization and is one of the leading activists against human trafficking in Nigeria. Her book, *Educating the Nigerian Child* (written with Chris Chirwa), was published in 2005.

ESOHE AGHATISE (?–   )   Founder and executive director of Associazione Iroko Onlus, an NGO based in Turin, Italy, that assists Nigerian sex trafficking victims in both Turin and Nigeria. Aghatise is a lawyer with a master's degree in international economic and trade law from the University of Benin, Nigeria, and a doctorate in international economic and trade law from the Università Bocconi of Milan, Italy (1998). In addition to combating sex trafficking through her work as executive director of Iroko Onlus, Aghatise has published a number of articles exploring the link between prostitution and trafficking and produced *Viaggo di non Riturno* (Journey of No Return), a film about modern-day slavery. She was named one of eight "Heroes Acting to End Modern-Day Slavery" in the U.S. State Department's 2007 Trafficking in Persons Report (TIP Report).

AYAAN HIRSI ALI (1969–)   Author of *De Zoontesfabriek* (The Son Factory, 2002), *The Caged Virgin: An Emancipation Proclamation for Women and Islam* (2006), and a memoir, *Infidel* (2007), Ayann Hirsi Ali is a prominent and controversial critic of Islam's treatment of women. Born in Mogadishu, Somalia, on November 13, 1969, Ali entered the Netherlands in the early 1990s, claiming that she did so to escape an arranged marriage. She was awarded permanent residency and, later, Dutch citizenship. She earned a degree in political science at Leiden University and in 2003 was elected to the Dutch parliament, where she worked on legislation to strengthen the Dutch prohibition of female genital mutilation. In 2004, she and the filmmaker Theo van Gogh made a short film inspired by her second book, *The Caged Virgin*. Afterward, van Gogh was murdered by a Dutch-Moroccan man who claimed that the film was an insult to Islam; a note threatening Ali's life was left with van Gogh's body. In 2006, Ali resigned from the Dutch parliament amid allegations that she had not been fleeing a forced marriage when she entered the Netherlands and confirmation that she had deliberately not disclosed that she had not come to the Netherlands directly from Somalia. Although her Dutch citizenship has been revoked, she continues to live in the Netherlands as a permanent resident.

SARAH ANDERSON (?–)   A cofounder of the Break the Chain campaign, Anderson holds a B.A. in journalism from Northwestern University and a master's in international affairs from American University. She worked as an editor for the German national news agency Deutsche Presse-Agentur from 1988 to 1992 and as a consultant to USAID from 1989 to 1992. She is currently a fellow with the Institute of Policy Studies (her work at the institute led to the founding of Break the Chain) and a steering committee member of the Alliance for Responsible Trade.

MODUPE DEBBIE ARIYO (?–)   Founder and executive director of the UK–based NGO Africans Unite Against Child Abuse (AFRUCA), Ariyo holds a B.A. in French and education from the University of Benin, Nigeria, and a master's in urban policy from the University of North London. She had established DMA Consulting in London, England, when several well-publicized deaths of African children in England prompted her to found AFRUCA. In addition to her work at AFRUCA, Ariyo is a fellow of the School for Social Engineers and a board member of other NGOs related to human trafficking. She is a recipient of the Nigerian International Professional Network's Excellence in Humanitarian Work award.

KEVIN BALES (1952–   )   President and a cofounder of Free the Slaves and author of *Disposable People: New Slavery in the Global Economy* (2000; revised edition, 2004) and *Understanding Global Slavery* (2005), Bales was born on February 9, 1952, in Tulsa, Oklahoma. He holds a B.A. from the University of Oklahoma, an M.A. in sociology from the University of Mississippi, and a M.S. and a Ph.D. in economic history from the London School of Economics and Political Science. In addition to his work with Free the Slaves, Bales is a professor of sociology at Roehampton University, London, England.

ISHMAEL BEAH (1980–   )   Author of *A Long Way Gone: Memoirs of a Boy Soldier* (2007) and a leading voice against the use of child soldiers, Beah was born in 1980 in Sierra Leone. In 1994, after his village was raided and his parents killed, Beah became a child soldier with the Sierra Leone army. Beah was trained to kill the members of the rebel forces without remorse; his memoir presents a child's coerced military service filled with violence and atrocity. Beah was rescued by the United Nations in 1996 and sent to a rehabilitation camp. He was reunited with and adopted by an uncle; upon that uncle's death, he was adopted by an American woman who arranged for his immigration to the United States in 1998. He graduated from Oberlin College in 2004 and is currently a member of Human Rights Watch's children's rights division.

LUCAS BENITEZ (1976–   )   Farmworker and cofounder of the Coalition of Immokalee Workers (CIW), Benitez immigrated to the United States from Mexico at the age of 16. Benitez's experiences as a migrant worker in Florida's tomato fields prompted him to cofound CIW; working with that organization, he was instrumental in exposing two forced labor rings, in securing almost $100,000 in workers' back pay, and in winning a wage increase for migrant tomato pickers. Benitz was awarded the nonprofit group Do Something's BRICK award in 1999.

TAINA BIEN-AIMÉ (1958–   )   Attorney and the executive director of Equality Now, an international organization that pressures governments to end discrimination and violence against girls and women, including sex tourism and sex trafficking, Bien-Aimé holds a license in Political Science from the University of Geneva and the Graduate School of International Studies, Switzerland, and a J.D. from New York University. She practiced international corporate law at the New York City law firm of Cleary, Gottlieb, Steen & Hamilton from 1992 to 1996 and was Home Box Office's director of business affairs/film acquisitions from 1996 to 1999. In 2000, she became Equality Now's general counsel and in 2001 its executive director. Bien-Aimé was awarded a NOW-NYC Susan B. Anthony award for her "amazing efforts on behalf of women."

FRANCIS BOK (1979–)   Antislavery activist and the author of *Escape from Slavery* (2003), Bok was abducted from his village in southern Sudan when he was seven years old and forced to live in slavery in the northern Sudanese village of Kirio. He escaped after 10 years and in 1999 was granted UN refugee status. After being relocated to the United States, Bok studied at the Boston Evening Academy and became a speaker for the American Anti-Slavery Group. In 2000, he testified about his experiences before the Senate Committee on Foreign Relations, and in 2002 he was invited to return to Washington, D.C., for the signing of the Sudan Peace Act. Bok also carried the Olympic torch in 2002. He currently lives in Kansas and continues to travel across the country to speak against modern-day slavery.

GEORGE W. BUSH (1946–)   43rd president of the United States, George W. Bush was born on July 6, 1946, in New Haven, Connecticut, to Barbara Bush and George H. W. Bush, the 41st president of the United States. He holds a B.A. from Yale University (1968) and an M.B.A. from Harvard University (1975). Prior to entering politics, Bush served in the Texas Air National Guard, worked in the oil and gas industry, and was an owner and manager of the Texas Rangers baseball team. He was elected governor of Texas in 1994 and president of the United States in 2000. As president, George W. Bush signed the Trafficking Victims Protection Reauthorization Act (TVPRA) of 2003 and the TVPRA of 2005, thereby continuing the U.S. commitment to combating modern slavery that was formalized in the Victims of Trafficking and Violence Protection Act of 2000. (An act reauthorizing that legislation through 2011 is expected to reach his desk before the end of his term.) Since 2001, his administration has awarded more than $525 million to global anti-trafficking efforts.

KATHERINE CHON (1981–)   The president and cofounder of the Polaris Project, Chon was born in Kwangju, South Korea, and reared in Salem, New Hampshire. She received a B.S. in psychology from Brown University in 2002. While in her senior year at Brown, Chon and fellow student Derek Ellerman read about South Korean girls enslaved in prostitution and held in a massage parlor near Brown's campus; in response, the two seniors cofounded the Polaris Project to combat human trafficking and to assist its victims. Chon has testified before Congress and has received numerous awards in recognition of her work, including the Do Something's BRICK award (2005), Redbook Magazine's Strength and Spirit award (2006), and Running Start's Women to Watch award (2007).

WILLIAM JEFFERSON CLINTON (1946–)   Politician and 42nd president of the United States, Bill Clinton was born William Jefferson Blythe III on August 19, 1946, in Hope, Arkansas. His father had died several months before his birth; his mother remarried, and he took his stepfather's surname,

Clinton, when he was a teenager. He holds a B.S. in international affairs from Georgetown University (1968) and a J.D. from Yale University (1973); he also studied at Oxford University as a Rhodes Scholar. Prior to entering politics, Clinton taught law at the University of Arkansas. He was elected attorney general of Arkansas in 1976 and governor in 1978; defeated for reelection in 1980, he was again elected governor of Arkansas in 1982, a position he held for the next 10 years. He was elected president of the United States in 1992. As president, he supported and signed the Victims of Trafficking and Violence Protection Act of 2000.

JOB COHEN (1947–) Mayor of Amsterdam since 2001, Cohen was born in 1947 in Haarlem, the Netherlands. He studied in Haarlem and holds a law degree from the University of Groningen (1970). Before entering politics, he conducted research at Leiden University and taught at Maastricht University. He served as deputy minister for education in the cabinet of Dutch prime minister Ruud Lubbers in 1993; returning to academia the following year, he also remained a member of the Eerste Kamer, the Dutch upper house. He next served as deputy minister of justice in the cabinet of Dutch prime minister Wim Kok. Cohen became mayor of Amsterdam in 2001. In December 2008, he announced plans to reduce the size of Amsterdam's red light district and to raise the age for legal prostitution from 18 to 21, among other measures intended to combat sex trafficking in Amsterdam.

ANTONIO MARIA COSTA (1941–) Executive director of the Vienna-based UN Office of Drugs and Crime (UNODC), director-general of the United Nations office in Vienna, and an under secretary-general of the United Nations, Costa was born in Italy on June 16, 1941. He holds a degree in political science from the University of Turin (1963), a degree in mathematical economics from Moscow State University (1967), and a Ph.D. in economics from the University of California at Berkeley (1971). He began his career as a senior economist in the UN Department of International and Social Affairs in 1969 and was appointed under secretary-general at the Organization for Economic Cooperation and Development in 1983. In 1987, he became the European Union's director general for economics and finance and, in 1994, the European Bank for Reconstruction and Development's secretary general. He was appointed to head UNODC in May 2002. In that position, he oversees UNODC's Global Programme against Trafficking in Human Beings.

FREDERICK DOUGLASS (ca. 1817–1895) American abolitionist and author of *The Narrative of the Life of Frederick Douglass* (1845), Frederick Douglass was born Frederick Augustus Washington Baily in Maryland in or about February 1817 to an enslaved woman named Harriet Bailey. (He took the surname "Douglass" later in life.) Douglass was enslaved first on the Maryland plantation of Colonel Edward Lloyd, then in the Baltimore home of Mr. and Mrs. Hugh Auld, and ultimately in the Baltimore shipyards. He escaped to New York in 1838. He became a speaker for the Massachusetts Antislavery Society and, having learned to read from Mrs. Auld, wrote his autobiography. Upon publication of that autobiography, Douglass—a now-publicized fugitive slave—relocated to Britain to continue speaking for the abolitionist cause and to raise the funds necessary to purchase his freedom. He returned to the United States in 1847 and began publishing the abolitionist newspaper *North Star* in Rochester, New York. That newspaper would continue, with several name changes, until 1863, and it would be succeeded in 1870 by Douglass's Washington, D.C.–based *New National Era.* Douglass was a leading African-American voice both during the struggle for U.S. abolition and during Reconstruction. He died on February 20, 1895.

DEREK ELLERMAN (1978–) The interim executive director and cofounder of the Polaris Project. Ellerman holds a B.S. in cognitive neuroscience from Brown University (2002). Ellerman had returned to Brown University after founding the Providence-based Center for Police and Community (CPAC), a nonprofit organization addressing issues of police misconduct, when he and fellow student Katherine Chon read about South Korean girls enslaved in prostitution and held in a massage parlor near Brown's campus. In response, the two seniors cofounded the Polaris Project to combat human trafficking and to assist its victims. Ellerman was the organization's coexecutive director from 2002 to 2007 and currently serves as its interim executive director. In addition to his work with the Polaris Project, Ellerman has been the executive director of CPAC (1998–2002) and an adjunct professor at Trinity University (2005). He has testified before Congress and in 2004 was selected as a fellow with Ashoka Innovators for the Public.

ADI EZRONI (1978–) Celebrated Israeli actress and coproducer of *Holly,* a 2006 film about child sex tourism, Ezroni was born in a suburb of Tel Aviv, Israel, and was raised in Israel and New York. She studied at the Stella Adler Studio (2003–04) and holds a B.A. in psychology and political science from Tel Aviv University (2004). She also served as a medic instructor for the Israeli Defense Force (1997–99). While filming *Holly,* Ezroni and a coproducer, Guy Jacobson, were threatened with death and held hostage in Cambodia; their film was completed only under the protection of privately hired armed bodyguards. Ezroni and Jacobson were named 2008 TIP Report heroes by the U.S. State Department, which commended their courage and praised *Holly* as "one of the best researched narrative films on child sex tourism."

MELISSA FARLEY (1942–)   Founder of Prostitution Research & Education, editor of *Prostitution, Trafficking and Traumatic Stress* (2004) and author of *Prostitution and Trafficking in Nevada: Making the Connections* (2007) and more than 35 periodical publications on the subject of prostitution and/or trafficking. Farley holds a B.A. from Mills College (Oakland, California, 1964), an M.S. in clinical psychology from San Francisco University (1966), and a Ph.D. in counseling psychology from the University of Iowa (1973). An expert on prostitution and sex trafficking, she has been an expert witness in forensics examinations, an expert witness for prostituted women facing trial, and a featured speaker at more than three dozen conferences on prostitution and/or sex trafficking. She is an associate scholar with the Center for World Indigenous Studies.

RUCHIRA GUPTA (?–)   Investigative journalist, filmmaker, and a founder of India's Apne Aap, Gupta was first alerted to the plight of young trafficked women when she was on assignment in rural Nepal in 1994 and noticed that there seemed to be few young women or girls in the villages. She traced these missing girls and young women to India's brothels, and the resulting documentary, *The Selling of Innocents* (1997), won an Emmy for investigative journalism. The experience also prompted Gupta to found Apne Aap with 22 of the prostituted women who had been subjects in her film. In addition to offering direct assistance to women enslaved in prostitution through her work with Apne Aap, Gupta has worked with USAID to assist Bangladesh, Cambodia, Indonesia, and other Asian countries in their anti-trafficking efforts and with UNICEF to develop policies in Iran. She has addressed both the U.S. Senate and the UN General Assembly on behalf of sex trafficking victims.

GARY HAUGEN (1963–)   Founder, president, and CEO of International Justice Mission (IJM), Haugen holds a B.A. from Harvard University (1985) and J.D. from the University of Chicago Law School (1991). Prior to founding International Justice Mission, Haugen worked for the Lawyers Committee for Human Rights and for the U.S. Department of Justice. In 1994, he was the Officer-in-Charge of the UN's genocide investigation in Rwanda, an experience that prompted him to found IJM, a human rights organization that works, among other things, to combat human trafficking. Haugen is the author of *Good News About Injustice* (1999) and *Terrify No More* (2005).

NORMA HOTALING (1951–2008)   Founder and executive director of Standing Against Global Exploitation Project (SAGE) and a cofounder of San Francisco's First Offenders Prostitution Program (more informally known as the Johns' School). Hotaling held a B.S. in health education from San Francisco State University. Hotaling was herself a homeless prostitute and heroin addict who was ultimately jailed; after release from prison at age 38, she founded the SAGE Project to combat prostitution and the sexual exploitation of women. Hotaling died on December 16, 2008.

DONNA M. HUGHES (1954–   )   Professor and Eleanor M. and Oscar M. Carlson Endowed Chair of the Women's Studies Program at the University of Rhode Island and a leading researcher and expert on the international trafficking of women and children, Hughes holds a B.S. and M.S. in animal science and a Ph.D. in genetics from Pennsylvania State University. Prior to teaching at the University of Rhode Island, she was a lecturer at the University of Bradford, England. The institutions, organizations, and government agencies that have supported her research include the Association of American Colleges and Universities, the International Organization for Migration, the Coalition Against Trafficking in Women, the Council of Europe, the National Institute of Justice, the National Science Foundation, and the U.S. State Department. She has testified before the Czech parliament, the Russian Duma, the U.S. House International Foreign Relations Committee, and the U.S. Senate Foreign Relations Committee. Hughes is also one of the authors of the online *Factbook of Global Sexual Exploitation* (1999).

NOGI IMOUKHUEDE (?–   )   Imoukhuede is chairperson of Roots and Fruits Women's Farmers Society of Nigeria (RUFARM), a Nigerian NGO working to assist rural Nigerian women through a micro-loan program and other means, and a cofounder, with J. J. Owa, of Women's Rights Nigeria (a project of RUFARM). Imoukhuede received her education at the National University of Laos. In addition to serving as RUFARM's chairperson, she currently serves as the project co-coordinator and a lawyer for Women's Rights Nigeria. Imoukhuede's work addresses gender inequality, a root cause of the trafficking of women and girls in Nigeria.

GUY JACOBSON (1963–   )   Investment banker and coproducer of *Holly*, a 2006 film about child sex tourism, Jacobson holds a J.D. from University of California, Berkeley, School of Law (1993). The film grew out of Jacobson's experience in Phnom Penh, Cambodia, where girls he believed to be five or six years of age solicited him for prostitution and explained that they would be beaten for returning without money. While filming *Holly*, Jacobson and coproducer, Adi Ezroni, were threatened with death and held hostage in Cambodia for two weeks. Jacobson and Ezroni were named 2008 TIP Report heroes by the U.S. State Department, which commended their courage and praised *Holly* as "one of the best researched narrative films on child sex tourism."

VIPULA KADRI (?–2007)   Founder of Save the Children India (STCI), the Women's Institute for Social Education (WISE), and PRIDE India (a nutritional and health care organization), Kadri worked to address many social and justice issues in India, including human trafficking. She worked through organizations such as STCI, including its anti-trafficking campaign, to combat child trafficking in India, with large USAID–funded initiatives, and many small grassroots organizations all across India. Called "a pioneer in anti-human-trafficking in India" by Dr. P. M. Nair, project coordinator for the UNODC, she was also named a 2007 TIP Report hero by the U.S. State Department. She died unexpectedly on April 24, 2007. Her son-in-law Suniel Shetty, a well-known actor in India, as well as the rest of her family, have pledged to continue her work.

RAVI KANT (?–) Executive director of India's Shakti Vahini, an organization that addresses health and rights issues in India, including human trafficking, Kant is a law graduate of the Campus Law Centre, University of Delhi. He has lectured in India's police academies, filed successful public interest lawsuits on behalf of trafficking victims, and is a visiting, nonofficial member of India's Central Advisory Committee on Trafficking.

LIORA KASTEN (?–) Former director of the American Anti-Slavery Group (AASG) and currently a member of that organization's speakers' bureau. Kasten holds a M.A. in law and diplomacy from the Fletcher School, Graduate School of International Affairs, Tufts University (2008). She has traveled to India, southern Sudan, and Darfur on behalf of AASG and has participated in the organization's rescue missions. Kasten is the coeditor, with Jesse Sage, of *Enslaved: True Stories of Modern Slavery* (2008).

JOHN F. KENNEDY (1917–1963) The 35th president of the United States, John Fitzgerald Kennedy was born in Brookline, Massachusetts, on May 29, 1917. He received a B.S. from Harvard University in 1940. Prior to becoming president, Kennedy served in the U.S. Navy (1941–45), the U.S. House of Representatives (1947–52), and the U.S. Senate (1953–59). In 1961, he created USAID to coordinate the U.S.'s nonmilitary aid to foreign countries; that agency now plays a major role in assisting foreign countries with their anti-trafficking efforts, among other activities. Kennedy was assassinated on November 22, 1963.

HADIJATOU MANI KORAOU (ca. 1984–) The first former slave to sue a country for its failure to enforce its obligations under its own and international antislavery law, Koraou was born enslaved in Niger. Sold at age 12 against her mother's wishes, Karaou joined the household of El Had; Souleymane Naroua. While enslaved, she performed agricultural and household work; beginning at age 13, she was also subjected to sexual violence. She bore three of Naroua's children, two of whom survived infancy. When an NGO worker informed Naroua that slavery was illegal in Niger and that he could face penalties of up to 30 years' imprisonment, Naroua released Hadijatou from slavery. He refused to grant her liberty, however, claiming that she was his wife under Niger's customary law. Hadijatou brought her case to the local Tribunal Civil et Coutumier, which ruled that Hadijatou and Naroua were not married and that Hadijatou was free. When Naroua appealed, the Tribunal de Grand Instance found against her, ruling that "under Niger's customary law a slave girl is de facto married to her master once she is released."

In the course of subsequent appeals, Hadijatou married a man of her own choice. She was convicted of bigamy and sentenced to six months' imprisonment, along with her husband and her brother, who had consented to her marriage. Hadijatou, who served two months of her bigamy sentence, ultimately brought her case before the Economic Community of West African States (ECOWAS) Community Court of Justice in Niamey. In a landmark decision that establishes precedent for all 15 ECOWAS member states, Niger was found guilty of violating its own and international antislavery law and of gender discrimination (Niger's customary law was found to discriminate against women). While others have sued individuals involved in their enslavement, Hadijatou Mani Koraou is the first former slave to have sued a county for its action or inaction regarding slavery within its borders.

MARK P. LAGON (1964–   )   The current ambassador-at-large for modern slavery, director of the Office to Monitor and Combat Trafficking in Persons (TIP Office), and a senior adviser to the secretary of state, Lagon holds a B.A. from Harvard University and a Ph.D. from Georgetown University. Prior to assuming the position of ambassador-at-large in 2007, Lagon was a senior analyst (1995–98) and deputy staff director (1997–98) of the House Republican Policy Committee; a fellow at the Project for the New American Century (1998–99); a senior Republican staff member of the Senate Foreign Relations Committee (1999–2002); a member of the secretary of state's policy planning staff (2002–04); and deputy assistant secretary of state for international organization affairs (2004–07). As director of the TIP Office, Lagon oversees and coordinates the U.S. response to domestic and international human trafficking.

ABRAHAM LINCOLN (1809–1865)   The 16th president of the United States, Abraham Lincoln was born on February 12, 1809, in Hodgenville, Hardin County, Kentucky. He received a basic early education in a log schoolhouse and later, having relocated to Illinois, studied law with the encouragement of Springfield lawyer and Whig Party official John Todd Stuart. In September 1836, Lincoln passed the bar and was admitted to practice law in Illinois. Prior to becoming president, Lincoln served in the Black Hawk War (1832), as

postmaster of New Salem, Illinois (1833–36), for four terms in the Illinois legislature (1835–40), and for one term in the U.S. Congress (1847–49), maintaining
his law practice throughout most of these years. Lincoln's 1858 campaign for
the U.S. Senate was unsuccessful, but his debates with the prevailing candidate,
Stephen A. Douglas, brought Lincoln to national attention. He was elected
president in 1860 and won reelection in 1864. During the conduct of the Civil
War, Lincoln issued the Emancipation Proclamation, which freed forever those
enslaved by states in rebellion against the United States. Lincoln was shot by an
assassin on April 14, 1865, and died on April 15, 1865.

RACHEL LLOYD (1976–) Born in England, Rachel Lloyd holds a B.A.
in Psychology from Marymount Manhattan College and a Masters in applied
urban anthropology from the City College of New York. As a 13-year-old
girl in England, Lloyd dropped out of school to help support her alcoholic
mother. After a short time spent working in factories and restaurants, Lloyd
became enmeshed in prostitution, first in England and then in Germany. By
the time she was 17, she had been raped, had survived a murder attempt by
her pimp, and had tried three times to kill herself. She found assistance in
a German church and eventually emigrated to the United States where she
completed her education and began to work with women incarcerated at
Riker's Island for prostitution. Realizing that there were minor girls among
them, she founded Girls Educational and Mentoring Services (GEMS) in
1999 to rescue girls and young women from commercial sexual exploitation.
Her awards include the Reebok Human Rights Award and the North Star
Fund's Frederick Douglass Award, among others.

BENE MADUNAGU (?–) Cofounder, with Grace Osakue, of Girls'
Power Initiative (GPI) Nigeria, a skill, rights, and sex education program for
Nigerian girls. Madunagu is the general coordinator of Development Alternatives with Women for a New Era (DAWN), an organization dedicated to
achieving gender justice, democracy, and economic justice in Nigeria. Madunagu works to, among other things, address gender inequality as a factor
in the trafficking of women and girls in Nigeria. She received a MacArthur
Foundation Fund for Leadership Development award in 1995.

MUKHTAR MAI (Mukhtaran Bibi) (ca. 1972–) First Pakistani woman
to successfully bring a lawsuit against men who participated in a vengeance
rape. Mai was born about 1972 in Meerwala, Punjab, Pakistan. She received
little education and reached adulthood without learning to read. At 16, she
entered an arranged marriage that ended three years later. In 2002, when
Mai was about 30 years old, she was gang raped in a tribal court–sanctioned
punishment for her younger brother's alleged crime of having been in the

company of an unrelated woman. (Mai's family contended that the story of the young boy's crime was fabricated to cover up the fact that he himself had been sexually assaulted by men in the unrelated woman's family; the men have since been convicted of sodomy.) Rather than commit suicide after the rape, as is common in Pakistan after such an attack, Mai took her attackers to Pakistan's courts. At the end of a three-year legal battle, four men were convicted of the rape and two of facilitating it. In 2005, Mai received Glamour magazine's Woman of the Year award. She has since established a school in Meerwala, where she both works as an administrator and takes classes in reading and writing alongside the other students. In 2009, she married Nasir Abbas Gabol, a constable whom she met while he was charged with protecting her from death threats. Her marriage was hailed as yet another instance in which Mai (who became known as Mukhtaran Bibi upon marriage) has defied her society's stigma against rape victims. Mai's memoir, *In the Name of Honor* (written with Marie-Therese Cuny), was published in 2006.

JOHN R. MILLER (1938–) Former ambassador-at-large for modern slavery, director of the Office to Monitor and Combat Trafficking in Persons (TIP Office), and a senior adviser to the secretary of state, Miller was born on May 23, 1938, in New York City. He holds a B.A. from Bucknell University (1959), an M.A. from Yale University (1964), and an LL.B. from Yale University Law School (1964). Prior to becoming ambassador-at-large and director of the TIP Office, Miller served in the U.S. Army (1961) and Army Reserves (1961–68), as assistant attorney general of the State of Washington (1965–68), as member and president of the Seattle City Council (1972–80), and as a member of the House of Representatives (1985–93). He also practiced law in Seattle and was an adjunct professor at the University of Puget Sound. As director of the TIP office, Miller oversaw and coordinated the U.S. response to domestic and international human trafficking. He continues to work to keep the issue of modern slavery before the public.

JESSICA NEUWIRTH (1961–) A cofounder and president of Equality Now, an international organization that pressures governments to end discrimination and violence against girls and women, including sex tourism and sex trafficking, Neuwirth holds a J.D. from Harvard Law School (1985). She worked for Amnesty International from 1985 to 1990, and then as an associate at the international law firm of Claery, Gottlieb, Steen & Hamilton. She has also worked with the United Nations, both as an attorney in the Office of Legal Affairs and as an expert consultant on issues of sexual violence to the International Criminal Tribunal for Rwanda. Among other Rwandan cases, she worked on the case of Jean-Paul Akayesu, which resulted in a 1998 landmark decision recognizing rape as a form of genocide. She founded Equality Now in 1992.

BISI OLATERU-OLABEGI (?–)   Founder of the Women's Consortium of Nigeria (WOCON), Olateru-Olabegi holds an LL.B. from the University of Ife, Nigeria (1975). Prior to founding WOCON in 1995, she founded the law firm of Bisi Olateru-Olabegi & Associates in Lagos, Nigeria, and was a solicitor and advocate of Nigeria's Supreme Court. She also served as president of the Nigerian chapter of the International Federation of Women Lawyers. In 1996, Olateru-Olabegi helped to prepare a study on the trafficking of Nigerian women and girls for the UN Special Rapporteur on Violence against Women. She is currently the head of WOCON's management team, as well as head of the organization's three state offices in Enugu, Laos, and Ogun states. Olateru-Olabegi and WOCON work for women's rights and for an end to human trafficking.

JEFFREY D. SACHS (1945–)   Economist, *Time* magazine's 100 most influential people in 2004, and author of *Common Wealth: Economics for a Crowded Planet* (2008) and *The End of Poverty: Economic Possibilities for Our Time*, among other books, Sachs was born in Detroit, Michigan, in 1945. He holds a B.A. from Harvard College (1976) and an M.A. (1978) and Ph.D. (1980) from Harvard University. He became an assistant professor in 1980, an associate professor in 1982, and a full professor in 1983, all at Harvard University. Director of the Harvard Institute for International Development from 1995 to 1999 and director of the Center for International Development, Harvard, from 1999 to 2002, Sachs is currently a professor of sustainable development and of health policy and management at Columbia University and director of Columbia University's Earth Institute. He also served as the director of the UN Millennium Project, as special adviser to Secretary-General Kofi Annan, and as chairman of the World Health Organization's Commission on Macroeconomics and Health. His recent work suggests that extreme poverty—the poverty experienced by people who live on one dollar or less each day—could be eliminated if the world's developed countries donated 0.7 percent of their GNP to be invested in poorer countries' education, family planning, health, nutrition, environmental and biodiversity conservation, and infrastructure. Such investment, Sachs believes, would raise the income of the world's poorest people to up to two dollars per day, an increase that would allow them to engage in economic activity and pull themselves further out of poverty. His work is particularly relevant to the UN Millennium Development Goal of halving extreme poverty by 2015 and of reducing poverty's role in human trafficking.

KAILASH SATYARTHI (1954–)   Founder and chairman of the Global March Against Child Labor, cofounder of the South Asian Coalition on Child Servitude (SACCS), and chairman of the Global Campaign for Education,

Satyarthi was born in Vidisha, Madhya Pradesh, India, in 1953. Satyarthi's work with SACCS has included the forcible freeing of more than 40,000 bonded laborers and the establishment of the "Bal Mitra Gram" program to help individual villages eradicate child labor. He also created the Rugmark program to certify Indian-made rugs as free of child labor. Satyarthi has received numerous awards, including the Robert F. Kennedy Human Rights award (1995), the Friedrich Ebert Stiftung International Human Rights award (1999), and the Raoul Wallenberg Human Rights award (2002). He was named a 2007 TIP Report Hero by the U.S. State Department.

NANCY SCHEPER-HUGHES (1944–) Cofounder and co–project director of Organs Watch and professor and director of the doctoral program in critical studies of medicine, science, and the body at the University of California, Berkeley, Scheper-Hughes was born in New York State on September 25, 1944. She holds a B.A. (1970) and a Ph.D. (1976), both from the University of California, Berkeley. At Organs Watch, she works to research and prevent human rights violations related to the harvesting of organs for transplant, including human trafficking for involuntary organ harvesting. She was a member of the Bellagio Task Force on Organ Transplant (1996–98) and coauthor of the first Task Force Report on trafficking in human organs (1977). In 2007, Scheper-Hughes received the Berkeley William Sloane Coffin Award for moral leadership.

HANS STÜCKELBERGER (1930–) International president and a cofounder of Christian Solidarity International (CSI), Stückelberger was born in Schiers, Switzerland. CSI is a faith-based human rights organization that, among other initiatives, works to combat human trafficking. Under Stückelberger's leadership, CSI's anti-trafficking program includes the use of donated funds to redeem, or purchase, enslaved persons, thus securing their freedom. While this form of direct action is controversial—its critics believe the practice increases the demand for trafficked persons—Stüuckelberger adamantly defends the practice.

SOJOURNER TRUTH (ca. 1797–1883) An abolitionist and women's rights activist, Truth was born Isabella Baumfree to enslaved parents in Ulster County, New York, in or around 1797. She was sold at about age nine to John Nealy, then to an owner in Kingston, New York, and, ultimately, to John J. Dumont, owner of a plantation near Kingston. Truth was married to a man named Thomas who was also enslaved to Dumont; the couple had five children, most of whom were sold away from them. Truth escaped from Dumont without Thomas in 1826, the year before New York State was scheduled to emancipate slaves born prior to 1799 (the last category of slaves to be freed in New York). With the help of Quaker sympathizers, she later sued successfully for the return of her youngest son, Peter, who had been illegally sold to an Alabama resident. She became known as a powerful preacher and took the name Sojourner Truth in 1843. Truth became a prominent speaker on the abolitionist lecture circuit in the late 1840s. After the Thirteenth Amendment abolished slavery throughout the United States, Truth—a women's rights activist as well as an abolitionist—refused to support the Fourteenth Amendment since it extended suffrage to black men while leaving women without the vote. Her work on behalf of the enslaved continued beyond the abolition of slavery: Beginning in 1864, she worked with the Freedmen's Bureau, the Freedmen's Relief Association, and the Freedmen's Hospital to assist the newly freed, many of whom were impoverished and unemployed. Without success, she also petitioned Congress to grant federal lands in the West to freed people. Her autobiography, *The Narrative of Sojourner Truth* (written with Olive Gilbert), was privately printed in 1850. Sojourner Truth died on November 26, 1883.

HARRIET TUBMAN (ca. 1820–1913)   Scout, spy, nurse, women's suffrage supporter, abolitionist, and conductor on the Underground Railroad, Harriet Tubman was born Araminta Ross to enslaved parents in Dorchester County, Maryland, in or about 1820. During childhood, she adopted the name Harriet. She married John Tubman in 1844 and escaped to Philadelphia alone in 1849. She made 19 or 20 returns to the South to free approximately 300 enslaved people, including her parents, her sister and her children (scheduled for auction at the time of their rescue), and her six brothers and their families. (Tubman's husband died in the South in 1867.) The Fugitive Slave Law in 1850 encouraged the capture of any escaped slave and Tubman's particular capture was further encouraged by rewards that began at $12,000 and, by 1858, reached $40,000, but Tubman was never captured. During the Civil War, Tubman served as a nurse, spy, and scout, famously leading Colonel James Montgomery in the Combahee River expedition of June 1863. After the Civil War, she was an active participant in the women's suffrage movement and a founder of the National Association of Colored Women (1896). In 1903, she deeded her home to the African Methodist Episcopal Church for the founding of the Harriet Tubman Home for the Aged and Indigent Colored People. Harriet Tubman died on March 10, 1913, in the home for the aged that bore her name.

WILLIAM WILBERFORCE (1759–1833)   English abolitionist, dedicated to fighting slavery in Great Britain and its colonies, Wilberforce was born in Hull, England, on August 24, 1759. He studied at St John's College, Cambridge. In 1790, he was elected to the House of Commons, where he renewed and deepened a friendship with Prime Minister William Pitt. Wilberforce began campaigning within the House of Commons to abolish the British slave trade in 1798. In 1807, with the support of Pitt and others, an Act for the Abolition of the Slave Trade was passed in Parliament, and the trading of slaves in the British Empire was outlawed. In 1823 Wilberforce and others founded the Anti-slavery Society to work for a total abolition of slavery itself. In 1833, Parliament passed the Slavery Abolition Act, making slavery illegal throughout the British Empire. Wilberforce died on July 29, 1833.

MUHAMMAD YUNUS (1940–) Nobel laureate, economist, and founder and managing director of the micro-credit Grameen Bank, Yunus was born in Chittagong, Bangladesh, on June 28, 1940. He holds a B.A. (1960) and an M.A. (1961) in economics from Dhaka University and a Ph.D. in economics from Vanderbilt University (1969). Prior to founding Grameen Bank, he was an assistant professor of economics at Middle Tennessee State University and a professor of economics at Chittagong University. His proposal that banks lend poor people loans as small as $27 to fund small-business start-ups was spurned, and he began making and guaranteeing such small loans himself. Grameen Bank, which translates as "Bank of the Villages" in the Bengali language, was founded in 1983. By 2006, Grameen Bank had made approximately $5 billion in what are now known as micro-loans to approximately 6.6 million people in about 70 villages, with a default rate of only 1.5 percent. The program has had tremendous success in helping people out of poverty and, since 97 percent of its loan recipients are female, tremendous success in empowering women, thus combating two root causes of human trafficking. Yunus's other initiatives to aid Bangladesh include Grameen Telecom, which provides mobile phone service to the country's rural areas, and Grameen Shakti ("energy"), which makes solar panels and other alternative energy technologies available in Bangladesh. Yunus and Grameen Bank were corecipients of the Nobel Peace Prize in 2006, and Yunus won the James C. Morgan Global Humanitarian award in 2008.

9

Organizations and Agencies

Africans Unite Against Child Abuse (AFRUCA)
URL: http://www.afruca.org
Unit 3D/F Leroy House
436 Essex Road
London N13QP
United Kingdom
Phone: (011-44-20) 7704 2261
Fax: (011-44-20) 7704 2266

Founded by Debbie Ariyo in 1981, AFRUCA is an organization dedicated to protecting the rights and welfare of the African child in the United Kingdom. Its efforts against trafficking have included a 2003 "Denouncing the Better Life Syndrome" media and seminar campaign in Nigeria, a 2007 international conference entitled "Trafficking of African Children to the U.K.: Addressing the Supply and Demand Nexus," and a child trafficking awareness video. AFRUCA also offers assistance to survivors of child trafficking in the United Kingdom.

American Anti-Slavery Group (AASG)
URL: http://www.iabolish.org
198 Tremont Street #421
Boston, MA 02116
USA
Phone: 1-800-884-0719, (617) 426-8161
Fax: (270) 964-2716
E-mail: action@iabolish.org

Founded by Dr. Charles Jacob in 1994, AASG maintains a Bearing Witness Program to support trafficking survivors in their work against slavery, as well as a national speakers bureau. Among other direct aid activities, AASG partners with Christian Solidarity International to purchase the freedom of enslaved people; it also provides educational and other support to the newly freed.

Anti-Slavery International (ASI)
URL: http://www.antislavery.org
Thomas Clarkson House
The Stableyard
Broomgrove Road
London SW9 9TL
United Kingdom
Phone: (011-44-20) 7501 8920
Fax: (011-44-20) 7738 4110
E-mail: info@antislavery.org

Established in 1839, Anti-Slavery International is the oldest human rights organization in the world. Its efforts to end modern-day slavery include research and documentation, the lobbying of governments and international agencies, and educating the public, among other measures. Since 1991, it has also given an annual antislavery award to highlight an individual or other organization's courage and leadership in the fight against human trafficking.

Apne Aap
URL: http://www.apneaap.org
Himadri Building
22, Ballygunge Park Road
Kolkata - 700 019 India
Phone: (011-91-33) 228-12-955/228-34-354
E-mail: apneaap2003@rediffmail.com

Founded by journalist and documentary filmmaker Ruchira Gupta and 22 prostituted women in 1998, Apne Aap ("self-help" in Hindi) is dedicated to the prostituted women's "aim . . . to lead the end of their own exploitation and prevent their sisters from being exploited through sex trafficking." In addition to working to end modern-day slavery, the group runs soup kitchens and other assistance programs for women in prostitution and their children.

Bonded Labour in the Netherlands (BLinN)
URL: http://www.blinn.nl/?c=home&lang=gb
BLin-N — Humanitas / Novib
Postbus 71
1000 AB Amsterdam

The Netherlands
Phone: (001-31-20) 523 1100
Fax: (001-31-20) 622 73 67
E-mail: info@blinn.nl

A program established by Humanitas and Oxfam Novib, BLinN assists trafficking victims rescued in the Netherlands, including foreign nationals who may remain in the Netherlands for several years while their traffickers are prosecuted.

Break the Chain Campaign
URL: http://btcc.ips-dc.org/index.htm
P.O. Box 34123
Washington, D.C. 20043
Phone: (202) 234-9382
Fax: (202) 387-7915
E-mail: joy@ips-dc.org

Founded in 1997 as the Campaign for Migrant Domestic Workers by Sarah Anderson and Martha Honey, the Break the Chain Campaign, as the organization was renamed in 2003, works to end involuntary servitude and other abuse of live-in domestic workers in the Washington, D.C., area. It offers direct assistance to victims, educational outreach to the public, and technical assistance to law enforcement and other public service personnel, among other activities.

Bureau Nationaal Rapporteur Mensenhandel
(National Reporter on Human Trafficking)
URL: http://english.bnrm.nl
Postbus 20301
2500 EH Den Haag
The Netherlands
Phone: (011-31-70) 370 45 14
Fax: (011-31-70) 370 45 37
E-mail: g.baboeram@minjus.nl

The Bureau Nationaal Rapporteur Mensenhandel is responsible for ascertaining and monitoring the size of the Netherlands's trafficking problem, reporting on the effectiveness and consequences of existing anti-trafficking policies in the Netherlands, and making suggestions for improvements in those policies.

Children of the Night
URL: http://www.childrenofthenight.org

14530 Sylvan Street
Van Nuys, California 91411
USA
Phone (Hotline): (800) 551-1300
Phone (Main): (818) 908-4474
Fax: (818) 908-1468
E-mail: llee@childrenofthenight.org

Founded in 1979, Children of the Night is an American organization working nationwide to rescue and assist prostituted children, a mission that includes advocating the rescue rather than the criminalization of prostituted minors. They work with and are assisted by law enforcement personnel in many major American cities, including Anaheim, Hollywood, Las Vegas, Miami, New York, Phoenix, Santa Ana, San Diego, and Seattle.

Christian Solidarity International (CSI)
URL: http://www.csi-int.org
Zelglistrasse 64
P.O. Box 70
CH-8122 Binz (ZH)
Switzerland
Phone: (011-41-44) 982 33 33
Fax: (011-41-44) 982 33 34
E-mail: info@csi-int.org

Founded in 1977 by Rev. Hans Stückelberger, the Swiss-based CSI is an international anti-trafficking organization with national committees, including one in the United States. CSI—inspired by Christian scripture and in support of the Universal Declaration of Human Rights's religious freedom clause—is dedicated to the rescue and education of enslaved people. Among other activities, it engages in the purchasing of enslaved people to secure their freedom.

Coalition Against Trafficking in Women (CATW)—International
URL: http://www.catwinternational.org/
International Secretariat
Brussels, Belgium
Fax: (011-32-2) 344 2003
E-mail: brussels@cawinternational.org

Founded in 1988, CATW works to end the sexual exploitation of women. Among the first NGOs to target human trafficking and, in particular, sex trafficking, CATW was awarded Category II Consultative Status with the United

Nations Economic and Social Council just one year after its founding. It conducts research into the scope and effects of sex trafficking and other forms of sexual exploitation and has provided expert testimony to national congresses and other governing bodies, among other activities.

Coalition of Immokalee Workers (CIW)
URL: http://www.ciw-online.org
P.O. Box 603
USA
Immokalee, FL 34143
Phone: (239) 657-8311
Fax: (239) 257-5055
E-mail: workers @ciw-online.org

Founded in 1993, CIW works to improve the working conditions of Florida's agricultural workers, including the elimination of modern-day slavery in the U.S. fast-food supply. Among its accomplishments are recent agreements—following a nationwide antislavery campaign and boycotts—with Taco Bell and McDonald's. Pursuant to these agreements, Taco Bell and McDonald's will require a 1 cent per pound increase in the wages paid to tomato pickers and monitor the working conditions of their subcontractors' employees. As this is written, CIW is trying to reach a similar agreement with Burger King.

1979 Convention on the Elimination of All Forms of Discrimination
against Women (CEDAW)
URL: http://www.un.org/daw
2 UN Plaza
DC2-12th floor
New York, NY 10017
USA
Fax: (212) 963-3463
E-mail: daw@un.org

Created in 1982, CEDAW is responsible for monitoring women's progress in countries that have ratified or acceded to the 1979 United Nations Convention on Elimination of All Forms of Discrimination against Women. State parties to the convention are obligated to provide a report of the status of women within their country, as well as their plans for improvement, every four years. CEDAW is composed of 23 experts on women's issues from various countries, each of whom serves a four-year term.

COördinatiecentrum MENSenHAndel (COMENSHA)
URL: http://www.mensenzijngeenhandelswaar.nl

Founded as Stichting Tegen Vrouwenhandel (Foundation against Trafficking in Women, Netherlands), this organization was renamed COördinatiecentrum MENSenHAndel (COMENSHA) in 2007 (the name change was made to acknowledges that both men and women are trafficked). COMENSHA is the organization responsible for registering victims of trafficking in the Netherlands, arranging services for trafficking survivors, and providing a centralized repository for legislative and other information, among other functions.

Covenant House International
URL: http://www.covenanthouse.org
5 Penn Plaza
New York, NY 10001
USA
Phone: (212) 727-4000

Growing out of the work of Father Frank Ritter and others with New York City's homeless youths in the late 1960s and formally incorporated with Father Ritter as its first executive director in 1972, Covenant House International now works in 21 cities in the United States and Central and South America to shelter and aid "homeless, runaway and throwaway youth." It has created an informational CD-ROM "Human Trafficking Resources Disk," and its members staffed the U.S. Trafficking Hotline during its first year of operation. (Father Ritter stepped down as Covenant House's executive director in 1990 amid allegations of sexual and financial misconduct. The board subsequently initiated a series of reforms and was returned to the National Charities Information Bureau's approved list in 1992, after an absence of two years.)

End Child Prostitution, Child Pornography and Trafficking in Children for Sexual Purposes (ECPAT)
URL: http://www.ecpat.net
328/1 Phayathai Road
Rachathewi, Bangkok
Thailand 10400
Phone: (011-66-2) 215 3388
Fax: (011-66-2) 215 8272

Envisioned in 1990 as a three-year regional campaign against the commercial sexual exploitation of children in Asia, ECPAT is now a global network whose members and partner groups work in more than 70 countries to end the sexual exploitation of children. Among other activities, ECPAT co-organized a World Congress against the Commercial Exploitation of Children (1996) in Stockholm, Sweden, and a Second World Congress against the Commercial Sexual Exploitation of Children (2001) in Yokohama, Japan. An NGO with special consultative status with the United Nations Economic and Social Council, EPCAT has prepared a number of reports on child sex exploitation in various countries.

Equality Now
URL: http://www.equalitynow.org
PO Box 20646
Columbus Circle Station
New York, NY 10023
USA
Fax: (212) 586-1611
E-mail: info@equalitynow.org

Founded in 1992, Equality Now is a human rights organization working for an end to violence and discrimination against women, including an end to human trafficking. Among other activities, it brought more than 50 organizations together to form the New York State Anti-Trafficking Coalition, which was instrumental in the passage of New York State's 2007 anti-trafficking legislation. It has also established the Fund for Grassroots Activism to End Sex Trafficking, which helps to fund grassroots and local anti-trafficking efforts around the world.

Fair Trade Federation (FTF)
URL: http://www.fairtradefederation.org/ht/d/Home/pid/175
Hecker Center, Suite 107
3025 Fourth Street NE
Washington, DC 20017-1102
USA
Phone: (202) 636-3547
Fax: (202) 636-3549

Incorporated as the North American Alternative Trade Organization in 1994, and renamed in 1995, the Fair Trade Federation works with U.S. and international businesses and nonprofit organizations to assure that their business practices embody fair trade practices. An FTF fair trade logo on consumer goods indicates that the producer has undergone a rigorous screening process that assures, among many other things, that slave labor was not a part of a good's growth or production.

Free the Slaves (FTS)
URL: http://www.freetheslaves.net/NETCOMMUNITY/
Page.aspx?pid=183&srcid=-2
514 10th Street NW, 7th Floor
Washington DC 20004
USA
Phone: (202) 638-1865
E-mail: info@freetheslaves.net

Inspired by Kevin Bales's book *Disposable People,* Jolene Smith and Peggy Callahan joined Bales in establishing Free the Slaves in 2000. The stated mission of Free the Slaves is "to end slavery worldwide." It works toward that end by training antislavery workers to rescue enslaved persons, by educating the destination-country public about modern-day slavery, by lobbying businesses to eliminate slave labor in their supply chains, and by helping to strengthen local economic and other origin-country structures to reduce pull factors, among other things. It also provides housing, food, educational, medical, and other assistance to the people it rescues, to "help them *stay* free."

Girls Educational and Mentoring Services (GEMS)
URL: http://www.gems-girls.org
Phone: (212) 926-8089
E-mail: info@gems-girls.org

Founded in 1999 by Rachel Lloyd, GEMS is a New York State survivor-led organization dedicated to assisting girls and young women who have been exploited in the commercial sex trades and to ending the commercial sexual exploitation of children. GEMS helps girls and women aged 12 to 21 to escape the commercial sex trades and to envision and create new lives for themselves. GEMS views minors in the commercial sex trades as trafficked persons and also works to change public policy that, among other things, frequently classifies prostituted American children as criminals rather than as victims. GEMS was instrumental in New York State's passage in 2008 of the Safe Harbor for Exploited Youth Act, the first state law in the country to recognize minors in the sex trades as victims of sexual exploitation.

Girls' Power Initiative (GPI)
URL: http://www.gpinigeria.org/crossrivercentre
44 Ekpo Abasi Street
P.O. Box 3663
UNICAL Post Office, Calabar
Nigeria

Phone: (011-234-80) 33 57 895
Fax: (011-234-87) 23 62 98
E-mail: gpicalabar@gpinigeria.org

Founded in 1993 by Grace Osakue and Bene Madunagu, GPI works to provide Nigerian girls with rights education, skills training, and other resources to aid in their growth "into self-actualized young women." Among the activities it offers to and on behalf of adolescent girls are school outreach programs, career development tours, and writing and editorial opportunities. It also provides empowerment coaching that includes assistance in "saying NO, when you mean NO," a process that GPI describes as "involv[ing] courage, strength and conviction based on accurate information and analysis of life realities" in Nigeria.

Global Alliance Against Traffic in Women (GAATW)
URL: http://www.gaatw.net
191/1 Sivalai Condominium
Soi 33, Itsaraphap Road
Bangkok-yai
Bangkok 10600
Thailand
Phone: (011-66-2) 864 1427/8
Fax: (011-66-2) 864 1637

Founded in 1994 in Chiang Mai, GAATW is an alliance of NGOs from around the world dedicated to protecting migrant women's human rights, including the elimination of human trafficking. In addition to supporting effective anti-trafficking strategies, GAATW has also criticized what it sees as the negative consequences of anti-trafficking policies. Its 2007 report, "Collateral Damage: The Impact of Anti-Trafficking Measures on Human Rights around the World," for example, expressed concern that, among other things, "Some anti-trafficking measures involve forms of restrictions on individual rights, notably on freedom of movement . . . when trafficked persons are confined . . . ostensibly for their own good, or teenagers are instructed not to leave their own village to look for work elsewhere, for fear that they might be trafficked."

Human Rights Watch (HRW)
URL: http://www.hrw.org
350 Fifth Avenue, 34th Floor
New York, NY 10118-3299
USA
Phone: (212) 290-4700

Fax: (212) 736-1300
E-mail: hrwnyc@hrw.org

Founded in 1978 as Helsinki Watch to monitor Soviet bloc countries following the signing of the Helsinki Accord, Human Rights Watch, as the organization was renamed in 1988, the New York–based Human Rights Watch now monitors and reports on the developing human rights records of more than 70 countries. Its Campaign against the Trafficking of Women and Girls has issued reports on trafficking in Japan, Greece, China, Bosnia and Herzegovina, Uganda, Togo, Saudi Arabia, and Malaysia, among other countries. HRW is also conducting a Stop Child Trafficking in West Africa.

IFAT: The International Fair Trade Association
URL: http://www.ifat.org/index.php
Prijssestraat 24
4101 CR Culemborg
The Netherlands
Tel.: (011-31-345) 53 59 14
Fax: (011-31-847) 47 44 01

An organization of international fair trade associations, IFAT holds regional conferences and biennial international conferences to assist its member organizations in establishing fair trade principles and in encouraging the adoption of those principles in their home countries.

International Justice Mission (IJM)
URL: http://www.ijm.org
P.O. Box 58147
Washington, DC 20037
USA
Phone: (703) 465-5495
Fax: (703) 465-5499
E-mail: contact@ijm.org

Founded in 1997 by Gary Haugen, IJM is a United States–based organization that works through the court systems in Asian, African, and Latin American countries to apply national laws against human rights abuses, including human trafficking. In addition to securing the legal release of trafficking and other victims—sometimes with information gathered by IJM workers who infiltrate brothels and other trafficking establishments—and the punishment of human rights abusers, IJM provides victim aftercare services and works to strengthen public justice systems in the countries it serves. While IJM is based in the United States, it hires most of its staff in the countries where its work is carried out.

International Labour Organization (ILO)
URL: http://www.ilo.org
4, route des Morillons
CH-1211 Genève 22
Switzerland
Phone: (011-41-22) 799 6111
Fax: (011-41-22) 798 8685
E-mail: ilo@ilo.org

Founded in 1919 following the end of World War I in the belief that only "decent treatment of working people" would lead to lasting world peace, the ILO became a specialized agency of the United Nations in 1949. As the agency responsible for the formulation and oversight of international labor relations, the ILO is at the forefront of efforts to end forced labor. Three of its conventions—No. 182, Elimination of the Worst Forms of Child Labour; No. 29, on Forced Labour; and No. 105, Abolition of Forced Labor—are central to international law on human trafficking. Its International Programme on Child Labour was created in 1992 to focus specifically on the eradication of child labor.

International Organization for Migration (IOM)
URL: http://www.iom.int/jahia/Jahia/lang/en/pid/1
17, route des Morillons
CH-1211 Geneva 19
Switzerland
Phone: (011-41-22) 717 9111
Fax: (011-41-22) 798 6150
E-mail: hg@iom.int

Founded in 1951, IOM is an intergovernmental organization of 122 member states (including the United States) devoted to "humane and orderly migration for the benefit of all." In 1994, the IOM began its countertrafficking efforts, which have been devoted to the prevention of trafficking and the protection of trafficking survivors, including assistance with repatriation or resettlement in the destination country or a third country, depending upon the victim's wishes. IOM has established projects and informational prevention campaigns in approximately 85 countries, including South Africa, where its public service announcement that was run on the country's television stations throughout 2008 won an award. In addition to conducting educational outreach and providing direct assistance to trafficking survivors, IOM conducts research on human trafficking, with particular focus on trafficking routes and the participation of organized crime, among other areas.

National Agency for the Prohibition of Trafficking in Persons and Other Related Matters (NAPTIP)
URL: http://www.naptip.gov.ng
P.M.B. 5161
Wuse, Abuja
Nigeria
Phone: (011-234-9) 413-1969
Phone (Hotline) (011-234-9) 413-2797
E-mail info@naptic.gov.ng

Established in 2003, NAPTIP is the agency responsible for addressing human trafficking in Nigeria, including the coordination of all human trafficking legislation, the creation and implementation of witness protection systems, the investigation and prosecution of traffickers, and the rehabilitation of trafficking survivors, among other activities mandated by the UN Protocol and Nigeria's Trafficking in Persons (Prohibition) Law Enforcement and Administration Act of 2003.

National Campaign on Dalit Human Rights (NCDHR)
National Secretariat
8/1, 2nd Floor, South Patel Nagar
New Delhi, India 110008
Phone: (011-91-11) 25842249
Fax: (011-91-11) 25842250
E-mail: ncdhr@vsnl.net

Established in 1998 as India celebrated the 50th anniversary of its independence from Great Britain and the United Nations marked the 50th anniversary of the Universal Declaration of Human Rights, NCDHR works to end caste-based discrimination and, particularly, the practices associated with untouchability in India. In addressing these issues, NCDHR addresses a root cause of human trafficking in India. NCDHR describes its campaign as "an expression of Hope as well as Anguish: Hope that we Dalits can re-establish our lost humanity, dignity, and security of life; Hope that we Dalits have the power for achieving justice, equality, and dignity regardless of caste, gender, religion, race, or ethnicity."

Organs Watch
URL: http://sunsite.berkeley.edu/biotech/organswatch

c/o Dept. of Anthropology
University of California, Berkeley
232 Kroeber Hall
Berkeley, CA 94720
USA
E-mail: orgwatch@uclink4.berkeley.edu

Established in 1999 at the University of California, Berkeley, by medical anthropologist Nancy Scheper-Hughes and others, Organs Watch is dedicated to investigating "the social and economic context of organ transplantation, focusing on the human rights implications of the desperate, world-wide, search for organs."

Physicians for Human Rights (PHR)
URL: http://physiciansforhumanrights.org
2 Arrow Street, Suite 301
Cambridge, MA 02138
USA
Phone: (617) 301-4200
Fax: (617) 301-4250

Founded in 1986, PHR was a corecipient of the Nobel Peace Prize for its efforts to promote the health of people throughout the world by working to secure worldwide human rights. PHR's physicians, nurses, and other health-care specialists travel to the world's wars and AIDS-ravaged areas, as well to prisons and other sites within the United States to investigate and document the negative physical effects of human rights violations. PHR has issued a number of reports documenting the individual and public-health consequences of human trafficking and has given testimony before Congress, including testimony in 2003 before the U.S. House International Relations Committee about the association between sex trafficking and the spread of HIV/AIDS.

Polaris Project
URL: http://www.polarisproject.org
P.O. Box 77892
Washington, DC 20013
USA
Phone: Tel: 202-745-1001
Fax: 202-745-1119
E-mail: Info@PolarisProject.org

Founded in 2002 by Katherine Chon and Derek Ellerman, then seniors at Brown University, the Polaris Project was named for Polaris, the North Star, so important to those who once fled chattel slavery in the United States. With five offices in the United States and Japan, the Polaris Project emphasizes grassroots community action that includes identifying and reaching out to victims, providing aftercare for rescued victims, and advocating for legislative and policy improvements. Since January 2008, it has operated the U.S. Trafficking Hotline.

Red Latinoamericanos Desaparecidos
(Latin American Network for Missing Persons)
URL: http://www.latinoamericanosdesaparecidos.org/index_en.html

Established in 2002, the Latin American Network for Missing Persons is an Internet-based organization devoted to locating Latin Americans who have disappeared during armed conflict, hurricanes, voluntary migration, and as a result of human trafficking. It has received more than 3.1 million requests for assistance since its inception.

SAGE Project, Inc.
1385 Mission Street, Suite 300
San Francisco, CA 94103
USA
Phone: (415) 905-5050
Fax: (415) 554-1914
E-mail: info@sagef.org

Founded in 1992 by Norma Hotaling, herself a survivor of addiction, homelessness, and prostitution, the Sage Project (Standing against Global Exploitation) is a San Francisco organization that works locally to end commercial sexual exploitation and to improve the lives of its victims and survivors. Among other initiatives, SAGE works toward a policy of prosecuting the purchasers of sex services rather than the prosecution of prostitutes and works with local law enforcement to change the definition and perception of a "child prostitute" to that of a commercially exploited child.

Salvation Army International
URL: http://www.salvationarmy.org/ihq/www_sa.nsf
International Headquarters
101 Queen Victoria Street
London EC4P 4EP
England
Phone: (011-44-20) 7332 0101
Fax: (011-44-20) 7236 4681

Founded in England in 1852 by William Booth, Salvation Army International is a religious and charitable organization with offices in many of the world's countries, including the United States. In addition to its other charitable and aid endeavors, Salvation Army International works against sex trafficking. Internationally, the Salvation Army has established a safe house in Malawi, explored income-producing projects for women in Zimbabwe, and organized a "Not for Sale" Sunday awareness campaign in the U.K.'s churches, among other efforts. In the United States, the Salvation Army currently leads the Initiative against Sexual Trafficking, a coalition of faith-based assistance and advocacy organizations working to end human trafficking and provide services to its victims. It has also produced a training manual for social workers and others who work with trafficking survivors and maintains a resource list on its Web site, including Emergency Response to Suspected Trafficking Cases, A two-page document available at http://www.salvationarmyusa.org/usn/www_usn.nsf/vw-sublinks/FEA3C28E98F1CD6B85256 F65006A722B?openDocument. It walks individuals through the factual and safety considerations that arise when a case of trafficking is discovered and outlines the steps an individual can take to begin governmental intervention.

Shakti Vahini
URL: http://www.shaktivahini.org
307, Indraprastha Colony
Sector 30-33, Faridabad
Haryana 121008
India
Phone (office): (011-91-129) 22 58 111, (011-91-129) 32 05 245
Phone (mobile): (011-91-931) 25 99 210

Based in India's Haryana State, Shakti Vahini is an NGO dedicated to promoting human rights in India through legal action, lobbying, public awareness campaigns, and protests and mass mobilizations, among other means. It has conducted extensive research into human trafficking and its root causes in India, including research on bonded labor, forced marriage, and female foeticide. In 2004, the organization also released a Trafficking in India Report that examined each of India's states and ranked them in five tiers according to the presence of human trafficking in each state.

Social Alert International
URL: http://www.socialalert.org/k/index.
php?option=com_frontpage&Itemid=1
Chaussée de Haecht, 579
1031 Brussels

Belgium
Phone: (011-32-2) 246 36 94
Fax: (011-32-2) 246 30 10

Created in 1997, Social Alert International is an international coalition of organizations dedicated to the protection of economic, social, and cultural rights. It works toward the recognition of workers' rights by researching and documenting abuses in various parts of the world and by issuing and publicizing denunciations of those who violate workers' rights, among other measures. In 2007, Social Alert International launched its Decent Work, Decent Life campaign to assist enslaved workers and others exploited in the informal economy and to demonstrate to governments and the international community that "Decent Work is the only sustainable way out of poverty. . . ."

Sunlaap
URL: http://www.sunlaapindia.org
38B Mananirban Road
Kolkata—700 029
India
Phone: (011-91-33) 2702 1287
Fax: (011-91-33) 2465 3395
E-mail: sunlaap@vsnl.net

Founded in 1987, Sunlaap's ultimate goal is to end the social imbalances that result in sex discrimination and violence against women and children. It works to end the sex trafficking of women and children, while also offering support services to the children of prostituted women. Among its initiatives are four shelter and training facilities for minor girls rescued from India's brothels, both girls who were sexually exploited and girls whose prostituted mothers have placed their daughters in Sunlaap's care. With partner community-based organizations, Sunlaap is also conducting a public awareness campaign about violence and abuse issues, including internal and transnational trafficking.

United Nations Children's Fund (UNICEF)
URL: http://www.unicef.org/index.php
UNICEF House
3 United Nations Plaza
New York, New York 10017
USA
Phone: (212) 686-5522
Fax: (212) 779-1679
E-mail: information@unicefusa.org

291

Recipient of the 1965 Nobel Peace Prize, UNICEF was established by the United Nations in 1946 to provide direct aid to European children confronting disease and starvation following World War II; it was made a permanent part of the United Nations in 1953. UNICEF works worldwide to improve the health and welfare of children and, guided by the United Nations Convention on the Rights of the Child, to protect the rights of children. Its efforts against trafficking include research into various forms of child trafficking, including child marriage. The UNICEF Innocenti Research Center (IRC), established in 1988, works "to respond to the evolving needs of children and to develop a new global ethic for children"; in April 2008, IRC held consultations with child trafficking experts to help lay the groundwork for the November 2008 World Conference III against the Sexual Exploitation of Children and Adolescents.

United Nations Educational, Scientific and Cultural Organization (UNESCO)
URL: http://www.unesco.org
7, place de Fontenoy
75352 Paris 07 SP
France
Phone: (011-33-1) 45 68 10 00
Fax: (011-33-1) 45 67 16 90
E-mail: bpi@unesco.org

Founded in November 1945, UNESCO is an agency of the United Nations dedicated to promoting international cooperation in the areas of culture, communications, education, and social and natural science. With respect to human trafficking, UNESCO's Project to Fight Human Trafficking in Africa is working in pilot countries Benin, Lesotho, Mozambique, Nigeria, South Africa, and Togo to find "more effective and culturally appropriate policy-making to fight the trafficking of women and children." It is also working to assist countries in their attempts to meet the Millennium Development Goals and, in so doing, works to address root causes of trafficking.

United Nations Global Initiative to Fight Human Trafficking (UN.GIFT)
URL: http://www.ungift.org/index.php
United Nations Office on Drugs and Crime
P.O. Box 500
1400 Vienna
Austria
Phone: (011-43-1) 26060 0
E-mail: UN.GIFT@unvienna.org

Created under the auspices of the UN Office on Drugs and Crime with financial support from the United Arab Emirates, UN.GIFT brings together a number of transnational organizations—the International Labour Organization, the Organization for Migration, the United Nations Children's Fund, and the Organization for Security and Co-operation in Europe (OSCE)—as well as the United Nations High Commissioner for Human Rights, to provide a coordinated, global strategy to end human trafficking. Toward that end, UN.GIFT is working to identify the best practices in the struggle against human trafficking and to make this information available to law enforcement agencies. It also encourages and supports anti-trafficking partnerships and action among those in academia, business, government, the media, and the public, among other initiatives.

United Nations Office on Drugs and Crime (UNODC),
Global Programme against Trafficking in Human Beings (GPAT)
URL: http://www.unodc.org/unodc/en/human-trafficking/index.html
P.O. Box 500
1400 Vienna
Austria
Phone: (011-43-1) 26060 5687
Fax: (011-43-1) 26060 5983
E-mail: ahu@unodc.org

The only United Nations program to have a criminal justice mandate, GPAT is the United Nations Office on Drugs and Crime's anti-trafficking unit. It assists countries in drafting or revising anti-trafficking legislation and trains individual nations' law enforcement and other relevant personnel to better combat human trafficking. GPAT also helps countries to produce trafficking-prevention public service announcements and to create victim and witness protection policies, among other activities.

United States Agency for International Development (USAID)
URL: http://www.usaid.gov/index.html
Information Center
United States Agency for International Development
Ronald Reagan Building
Washington, D.C. 20523-0016
USA
Phone: (202) 712-4320
Fax: (202) 216-3524

Created by President John F. Kennedy in 1961 to coordinate U.S. nonmilitary foreign assistance programs pursuant to the 1961 Foreign Assistance Act,

USAID provides direct assistance to developing countries, including assistance with anti-trafficking efforts.

United States Department of Health and Services (HHS), Campaign to Rescue and Restore Victims of Human Trafficking
URL: http://www.afc.hhs.gov/trafficking
Administration for Children and Families
370 L'Enfant Promenade S.W
Washington, D.C. 20447
USA
Phone (Hotline): (888) 373-7888

HHS is responsible for certifying rescued or escaped persons as trafficking victims eligible for a special visa and U.S. government services such as temporary housing, legal, and educational assistance. HHS also sponsors and funds the Trafficking Information and Referral Hotline at 1-888-373-7888 (staffed by Covenant House) for victims of trafficking or people who believe they may have come in contact with a trafficked person. Operators at the hotline will help to assess the immediate safety of the victim and help to coordinate the appropriate governmental and nongovernmental response.

United States Department of Justice
URL: http://www.usdoj.gov
950 Pennsylvania Avenue NW
Washington, DC 20530-001
USA
Phone: (202) 514-2000
E-mail: askDOJ@usdoj.gov

Established by Congress in 1870 (and preceded by the part-time Office of the Attorney General), the Department of Justice is the department responsible for the administration and enforcement of federal law. As such, it investigates and prosecutes violations of the Thirteenth Amendment to the Constitution and the Victims of Trafficking and Violence Protection Act of 2000, among other violations of federal law.

United States Department of State
URL: http://www.state.gov
2201 C Street NW
Washington, DC 20520
USA
Phone: (202) 647-4000

The Department of State is responsible for the conduct of U.S. foreign relations and diplomacy. It is headed by the Secretary of State, who is required to submit an annual Trafficking in Persons Report to the U.S. Congress. The Department's Office to Monitor and Combat Trafficking in Persons coordinates the United States' domestic and international efforts to end human trafficking, including the funding of global projects.

United States Immigration and Customs Enforcement (ICE)
URL: http://www.ice.gov/
Phone (Hotline): (866) DHS-2ICE (866-347-2423)

A part of the U.S. Department of Homeland Security since passage of the 2002 Homeland Security Act, ICE is responsible for securing the U.S. border and issues of economic, infrastructure, and transportation security. With respect to human trafficking, the ICE conducts Operation Predator, an investigative program intended to combat sex crimes against children, and administers the Civil Asset Forfeiture Reform Act (CAFRA), the law that mandates governmental seizure of property used in smuggling or harboring aliens, including property used in human trafficking. ICE works with domestic and international NGOs to disseminate information about special visas and other immigration protections available to trafficking victims in the United States.

Veilige Haven (Safe Haven)
URL: http://www.veilige-haven.nl
Amsterdam
The Netherlands
Phone: (001-31-20) 573 94 01
E-mail: info@veilie-haven.nl

A collaborative initiative of several service organizations, Veilige Haven is a drop-in support center for gay, lesbian, bisexual, and transgendered youths in Amsterdam, particularly immigrant Muslim youths of Antillean, Moroccan, Surinamese, and Turkish descent whose sexual orientation is not heterosexual and who may, among other difficulties, be at risk for sexual exploitation.

Women's Consortium of Nigeria (WOCON)
URL: http://www.wocononline.org
P.O. Box 54627
Ikoyi, Logos
Nigeria

Phone: (011-234-1) 26 35 300
Fax: (011-234-1) 26 35 331
E-mail: info@wocononline.org

Founded in 1995 by Bisi Olateru-Olabegi, WOCON is a coalition of organizations working for women's rights in Nigeria, including their right to be free from human trafficking. Among other activities, WOCON conducts research on trafficking in Nigeria, produces videos and other materials for use in public awareness campaigns, and coordinates services for trafficked girls returned from Italy.

Women's Rights Watch Nigeria
URL: http://www.rufarm.kabissa.org/index.htm
E-mail: nogiede@yahoo.com/nogi@rufarm.kabissa.org

Founded by Noi Imoukhuede and J. J. Owa as a project of Roots and Fruits Women's Farmers Society of Nigeria (RUFARM), Women's Rights Watch Nigeria works to eliminate the violations of women's rights in Nigeria, including violations inflicted in the name of tradition, such as forced childhood marriages. It has conducted national and international petition drives and maintains an active legal services clinic, among other initiatives.

Women Trafficking and Child Labour Eradication Foundation
(WOTCLEF)
URL: http://www.wotclef.org
Plot 306, Gabes Street, Wuse Zone 2
Abuja, FTC
Nigeria

Founded in 1999 by Amina Titi Atiku Abubakar, wife of then vice president of the Republic of Nigeria, WOTCLEF is an NGO dedicated to ending the trafficking of Nigerian persons, especially women and children. It offers financial assistance to keep children in school, thereby reducing one incentive to accept traffickers' fraudulent offers; runs public awareness campaigns; provides aftercare and legal services to trafficking survivors; and lobbies for the government's adoption of best practices to prevent trafficking, among other initiatives. WOTCLEF has recently also opened a Florida office in the United States to address the origin-country causes of human trafficking.

10

Annotated Bibliography

This annotated bibliography will direct you to articles, books, Internet documents, and other sources of information relevant to human trafficking. These suggested sources are divided into the following categories:

Belize

Chattel Slavery

Child Marriage, Forced Marriage, and Council-Ordered Punishment Rapes/Marriages

Child Soldiers

Forced Labor

India

Involuntary Domestic Servitude

Netherlands

Nigeria

Poverty

Scope and Magnitude of Human Trafficking

Sex Tourism

Sex Trafficking

Trafficking for Involuntary Organ Harvests

Trafficking in Infants

United States

Entries within each category are divided by type of reference work: books, articles, Web sites, and film/video/TV. In some cases, a reference contains information about more than one category; in such cases, it has been placed in the most relevant category. (Each reference appears only once.)

BELIZE

Web Sites

Government of Belize, Ministry of National Development. "First Millennium Development Goals Report" (2004). Available online. URL: http://www.undg.org/index.cfm?P=87&f-B. Accessed January 10, 2008. This report, which outlines Belize's progress in meeting the UN's Millennium Development Goals, provides detailed information about poverty, education, and gender equality in Belize.

Petit, Juan Miguel. "Trafficking in Persons in Belize. Preliminary Report: November 2004." Available online. URL: http://www.oas.org.atip/Belize/BELIZE-%20Petit.pdf. Accessed February 19, 2008. This report, commissioned by Belize following its listing as a Tier 3 country in the U.S.'s 2002 Trafficking in Persons Report, outlines the state of trafficking in Belize at the beginning of the millennium, as well as risk factors for an increase in trafficking and steps the government might take to reduce modern-day slavery in Belize.

U.S. Department of State. "Country Reports on Human Rights Practices, 2002: Belize." Released 2003. Available online. URL: http://www.state.gov/g/drl/rls/hrrpt/2002/18320.htm. Accessed March 4, 2008. This report on Belize's human rights practices was issued in 2003, the year Belize was first named as a Tier 3 country with respect to human trafficking.

———. "Country Reports on Human Rights Practices, 2005: Belize." Released 2006. Available online. URL: http://www.state.goav/g/rls/hrrpt/2005/61716.htm. Accessed March 4, 2008. This report focused on Belize's human rights practices in 2005, a year in which Belize earned a Tier 2 Watch List ranking with respect to human trafficking.

———. "Country Reports on Human Rights Practices, 2006: Belize." Released 2007. Available online. URL: http://www.state.gov/g/drl/rls/hrrpt/2006/78880.htm. Accessed March 4, 2008. This report focused on Belize's human rights practices in 2006, a year in which Belize was listed, for the second time, as a Tier 3 country with respect to human trafficking.

CHATTEL SLAVERY

Web Sites

Library of Congress. African-American Odyssey. Available online. URL: http://lcweb2.loc.gov/ammen/aaohtm. Accessed October 27, 2008. This is a digitized collection of records of chattel slavery.

New York Public Library's Schomburg Center for Research in Black Culture. Digital Collections. Available online. URL: http://www.nypl.org/research/sc/digital.html. Accessed October 27, 2008. Among the Schomburg Center's collections are digitized records of chattel slavery.

Smithsonian Institution. Digital Collection, Civil War/Slavery and Abolition. Available online. URL: http://civilwar.si.edu/resources_slavery.html. Accessed October 27, 2008. This is digitized collection of records of chattel slavery.

Annotated Bibliography

Books

Engerman, Stanley, Seymour Drescher, and Robert Paquette, eds. *Slavery.* Oxford: Oxford University Press, 2001. This book brings together writings and documents from classical times to 1997 regarding various aspects of chattel slavery.

Meltzer, Milton. *Slavery: A World History,* updated ed. New York: Da Capo Press, Inc. This book follows the history of slavery from its earliest traces in Mesopotamia (now Iraq) of 10,000 years ago through its continuation today.

Miers, Suzanne. *Slavery in the Twentieth Century.* New York: Altamira Press, 2003. This book begins with an overview of the 19th-century abolitionist movement and continues with an examination of chattel slavery's legal persistence through the second half of the 20th century. It concludes with an overview of modern-day slavery.

Walvin, James. *Atlas of Slavery.* Harlow, England: Pearson Longman, 2006. This atlas provides a historical and geographic view of chattel slavery though maps illustrating slave-holding territories, routes, and emancipations, beginning with a map of ancient Greece and continuing through the 19th-centrury slave trade in the Indian Ocean. Stalin's relocations of Soviet peoples, the Russian gulag, and the Holocaust are treated as modern examples of slavery and illustrated in additional maps. (Human trafficking is not addressed.)

Wright, John. *The Trans-Saharan Slave Trade.* New York: Routledge, 2007. This book explores the trans-Saharan chattel slave trade from the seventh century to the 20th century.

Television/Film/Video

Amazing Grace. Directed by Michael Apted, written by Steven Knight. 117 minutes. 2006. Distributed by Samuel Goldwyn Company, Domestic Theatrical Distributor Momentum Pictures Limited, et al. This film dramatizes the struggle of William Wilberforce to end chattel slavery in Great Britain.

Amistad. Directed by Stephen Speilberg, written by David Franzoni. 152 minutes. 1997. Distributed by DreamWorks SKG. This film dramatizes the 1839 mutiny of enslaved Africans bound for America aboard the slave ship *Amistad,* as well as the ensuing legal battle for their freedom.

Roots. Directed by Marvin J. Chomsky, John Eman, et al., written by Alex Haley (book), William Blinn (adaptation and screenplay), et al. 573 minutes (miniseries). 1977. David L. Wolper Productions. This miniseries, which was based on Alex Haley's 1976 best-selling novel *Roots: The Saga of an American Family,* dramatizes the multigenerational struggle of a family based on Haley's own, from enslavement in Africa to ultimate liberation in the United States. (Two copyright infringement suits were brought against Haley following the publication of *Roots;* one was dismissed and the other, involving claims over a brief passage, was settled.)

Traces of the Trade: A Story from the Deep North. Directed and produced by Katrina Browne and written by Katrina Browne and Alla Kovan. Ebb Pod Productions. 86 minutes. 2008. In this documentary, a Rhode Island family explores the slave-trading past of their ancestors and, in so doing, exposes the slave-trading role played by America's northern states, even after the ostensible end of chattel slavery in the North.

CHILD MARRIAGE, FORCED MARRIAGE, AND COUNCIL-ORDERED PUNISHMENT RAPES/ MARRIAGES

Books

Ali, Ayaan Hirsi. *Infidel.* New York: Free Press, 2007. This memoir traces the coming of age of Ayaan Hirsi Ali, a Somali-born Muslim woman now living in the Netherlands, through her escape from a forced marriage to her emergence as a controversial advocate of Muslim women's rights, while also outlining her view of those rights. (Allegations have been made that Ali did not flee an arranged marriage.)

Mai, Mukhtar. *In the Name of Honor: A Memoir.* Linda Coverdale, Trans. New York: Atria, 2006. In this book, Mukhtar Mai tells of suffering a gang rape in 2002, a rape that was ordered by her Pakistani village tribal council in punishment for her 12-year-old brother's alleged unsanctioned relationship with a woman; her refusal to exile herself or commit suicide in the aftermath of the gang rape; her successful lawsuit before Pakistan's supreme court; and the Pakistani girls' school she has since established.

Articles

Crossette, Barbara. "U.N. Agency Sets Its Sights on Curbing Child Marriage." *New York Times* (3/8/01). This article describes the consequences of child marriage and the UN's efforts to end the tradition.

LaFraniere, Sharon. "Nightmare for African Women: Birthing Injury and Little Help." *New York Times* (9/28/05). This article provides information about prevalence and consequences of fistula injuries in Africa, as well as the efforts of physicians to increase the number of fistula repair surgeries.

———. "Forced to Marry Before Puberty, African Girls Pay Lasting Price." *New York Times* (11/27/05). This article describes the realities faced by young married girls in Africa. It includes interviews with a number of these married girls.

Web Sites

Equality Now. "The Willingness of 'Mail-Order Bride' Companies to Provide Services to Violent Men." Available online. URL: http://www.equalitynow.org/reports/mailorderbride.pdf. Accessed August 10, 2008. This report examines the abusive environment faced by many so-called mail-order brides and the complicity of agencies placing them into mail-order marriages.

"Fistula Women." BBC World Service. Available online (audio and text). URL: http://www.bbc.co.uk/worldservice/sci_tech/highlights/010321_hospital.shtml. Accessed June 19, 2008. This article provides information about the causes and consequences of obstetric fistula and the efforts of physicians in Ethiopia's Fistula Hospital to repair a significant number of the injuries.

"Infants Saved from Wedlock to Landlord's Son." *Daily Times* (Pakistan, 7/19/06). Available online. URL: http://www.dailytimes.com.pk/default.asp?page=20060719story_19-7-2006_pg7_26. Accessed October 8, 2007. This article documents a Pakistani village council's order that two infant girls be married in compensation for their father's unpaid debt and the subsequent arrest of the men involved in this now outlawed practice.

Wilkinson, Isambard. "Blood Debt Women Offered Up for Rape." Telegraph.Co.UK (9/11/05). Available online. URL: http://www.telegraph.co.uk/news/worldnews/asia/pakistan/1503645/Blood-debt-women-offere d-up-for-rape.html. Accessed June 22, 2008. This article documents a Pakistani village council's order that five women be "abducted, raped or killed" for their defiance of their village council–ordered marriages in compensation for a relative's crime.

UNICEF. "Early Marriage: A Harmful Traditional Practice" (2005). Available online. URL: http://www.unicef.org/publications/index_26024.html. Accessed November 2, 2007. This UNICEF report examines the cultural context and consequences of early marriage, and especially the consequences for girls.

United Nations Population Fund's Campaign to End Fistula. Available online. URL: http://www.endfistula.org. Accessed June 30, 2008. This Web site provides links to information about fistula and efforts to eradicate it. It also contains interviews with survivors of the injury.

Film/Video/TV

Blind Mountain. Written, produced, and directed by Li Yang. 97 minutes, Released by Kino International, 2007. (In Mandarin, with English subtitles.) In this film, which premiered at the Cannes Film Festival in May 2007, Huang Lu plays Bai Zuemei, a Chinese college student deceived into a forced marriage.

Child Marriage. Neeraj Kumar, director, producer, and writer. 86 minutes. This award-winning documentary examines arranged child marriage among various castes in India's Haryana and Rajasthan states, providing footage of these weddings and examining arguments both from those who oppose the practice and those who believe it is in the best interest of the children concerned.

CHILD SOLDIERS

Books

Beah, Ishmael. *A Long Way Gone: Memoirs of a Boy Soldier.* New York: Farrar, Straus & Giroux, 2007. This memoir provides a first-person account of the author's induction into armed conflict in Sierra Leone at age 13, the violence he subsequently engaged in and endured, and his ultimate rescue and healing.

Web Sites

Human Rights Watch. "Children in the Ranks: The Maoists' Use of Child Soldiers in Nepal" (2007). Available online. URL: www.hrw.org/reports/2007/nepal0207. Accessed November 5, 2007. This Human Rights Watch report documents the Maoist's use of children as soldiers in Nepal.

———. "Complicit in Crime: State Collusion in Abductions and Child Recruitment by the Karuna Group" (2007). Available online. URL: http://www.hrw.org/reports/

2007/srilanka0107/. Accessed November 5, 2007. This Human Rights Watch report documents the Karuna group's use of children as soldiers in Sri Lanka.

———. "Early to War: Child Soldiers in the Chad Conflict" (2007). Available online. URL: http://hrw.org/reports/2007/chad0707webwcover.pdf. Accessed October 19, 2007. This Human Rights Watch report documents the use of children as soldiers in Chad.

———. "Facts about Child Soldiers." Available online. URL: http://www.hrw.org/campaigns/crp/fact_sheet.html. Accessed December 1, 2007. This Human Rights Watch fact sheet provides information about the worldwide use of children as soldiers.

Film/Video/TV

Public Broadcasting System. "Wide Angle: Lord's Children." This episode of Wide Angle examines the efforts to rehabilitate three children who served as soldiers under Lord's Resistance Army leader Joseph Kony. The full episode and other relevant information is available online. URL: http://www.pbs.org/wnet/wideangle/episodes/lords-children/introduction/1769/. Accessed August 14, 2008.

Soldier Child. Directed and written by Neil Abramson. Palomar Pictures. 75 minutes. 1998. This documentary examines the violence perpetrated by more than 12,000 child soldiers in Uganda and the Ugandan efforts to rehabilitate these children.

FORCED LABOR

Web Sites

Human Rights Watch. "Contemporary Forms of Slavery in Pakistan" (1995). Available online. URL: http://www.hrw.org/reports/pdfs/c/crd/pakistan957.pdf. Accessed November 19, 2007. This Human Rights Watch report provides a close examination of forced labor in Pakistan, including a close examination of forced labor in Pakistan's agricultural industry, carpet-weaving factories, and brick kilns.

International Labour Organization. "A Global Alliance against Forced Labour: Global Report under the Follow-up to the ILO Declaration on Fundamental Principles and Rights at Work, 2005." Available online. URL: http://www.ilo.org/dyn/declaris/DECLARATIONWEB.DOWNLOAD_BLOB?Var_DocumentID=5059w. Accessed December 1, 2007. This ILO global report on forced labor analyzes current trends and root causes, giving particularly close analysis to forced labor in South Asia, Latin America, and Africa.

Nathan, Debbie. "Oversexed." *The Nation* (8/29/05). Available online. URL: http://www.thenation.com/doc/20050829/Nathan. Accessed December 1, 2007. In this article (available as an Internet document), Nathan argues that while sex trafficking receives more attention from the media, forced labor is, indeed, an even greater problem.

Books

Bok, Francis, with Edward Tivnan. *Escape from Slavery: The True Story of My Ten Years in Captivity—and My Journey to Freedom in America.* New York: St. Martin's Press,

2003. In this book, Francis Bok details his enslavement in Sudan at the age of seven, his escape at 17, and his emergence as an antislavery activist in the United States.

Fuentes, Annette, and Barbara Ehrenreich. *Women in the Global Factory.* Boston: South End Press, nd. This 64-page pamphlet, based on the authors' 1981 article in *Ms.* magazine, examines the exploitation of women and girls in the world's factories and includes a chapter on trafficking in women.

Ross, Robert J. S. *Slaves to Fashion: Poverty and Abuse in the New Sweatshops.* Ann Arbor: University of Michigan Press, 2004. This book chronicles the history of sweatshops and examines the conditions prevalent in today's sweatshops, including modern-day slavery.

Film/Video/TV

The Sugar Babies: The Plight of the Children of Agricultural Workers in the Sugar Industry of the Dominican Republic. Directed and written by Amy Serrano. Siren Studios. 95 minutes. 2007. This documentary exposes the exploitation, including human trafficking, of Haitian-descended sugar cane workers and their children in the Dominican Republic.

INDIA
Web Sites

Asian Legal Resource Centre. "India: Child Soldiers Being Used as Expendable Pawns in Armed Conflicts (A Written Statement Submitted by the Asian Legal Resource Center to the 6th Session of the UN Human Rights Council)." Available online. URL: http://www.alrc.net/doc/mainfile.php/alrc_statements/442. Accessed February 14, 2008. This document detailing the use of child soldiers by both government and insurgent forces in India is the text of a written statement supplied by the Asian Legal Resource Centre to the 6th session of the UN Human Rights Commission in September 2007.

End Child Prostitution, Child Pornography and Trafficking of Children for Sexual Purposes. "Global Monitoring: Report on the Status of Action against Commercial Sexual Exploitation of Children, India" (2006). Available online. URL: http://www.childtrafficking.com/Docs/ecpat_india_0870.pdf. Accessed January 3, 2008. This report by ECPAT examines the scope and nature of commercial sexual exploitation of children in India, as well as efforts to combat that exploitation.

Human Rights Watch and Center for Human Rights and Global Justice, NYU School of Law. "Hidden Apartheid: Caste Discrimination against India's 'Untouchables' (Shadow Report to the UN Committee on the Elimination of Racial Discrimination)." Available online. URL: http://www.hrw.org/reports/2007/india0207/india0207webwcover.pdf. Accessed February 6, 2008. This report examines the status of Dalits ("Untouchables") in India and makes recommendations for ending discrimination against them.

Human Rights Watch, Children's Rights Project. "The Small Hands of Slavery: Bonded Child Labor in India." Available online. URL: http://www.hrw.org/reports/pdfs/c/

crd/india969.pdf. Accessed June 2, 2008. This report examines bonded child labor in India's silver, carpet-weaving, silk, leather, and other industries, while also examining the cultural and legal context for this exploitation and making recommendations to combat it.

International Institute for Population Sciences and Macro International. "National Family Health Survey (NFHS-3), 2005-06: India." Available online. URL: http://www.measuredhs.com/pubs/pdf/FRIND3/00FrontMatter00.pdf. Accessed January 3, 2008. This report provides a detailed examination of individual and family life in India, including details regarding nutrition, maternal and child health, and educational attainment.

Save the Children. "Child Domestic Work: A Violation of Human Rights: Report on the Legal Position of Child Domestic Workers in India." Available online. URL: http://www.savethechildren.in/india/key_sectors/LegalprovisionsinIndiaforCDW.pdf. Accessed January 7, 2008. This report examines child domestic workers in India in the context of domestic and international law and makes recommendations to better protect India's children.

Shakti Vahini. "Female Foeticide, Coerced Marriage & Bonded Labour in Haryana and Punjab; a Situational Report" (2003). Available online. URL: http://www.ungift.org/pdf/situational_report.pdf. Accessed January 17, 2008. This report provides a close examination of coerced marriage and bonded labor in two Indian states, as well as an examination of women's gender inequality and the practice of female foeticide in India.

———. "Trafficking in India Report—2004." Available online. URL: http://www.crin.org/docs/traffickingreport.pdf. Accessed January 17, 2008. This report, which examines human trafficking in each of India's states, was praised by the U.S. Department of State as providing a comprehensive "Trafficking in Persons Report" for that country.

U.S. Department of State. "Country Reports on Human Rights Practices, 2005: India." Released March 2006. Available online. URL: http://www.state.gov/g/drl/rls/hrrpt/2005/61707.htm. Accessed January 16, 2008. This report presents the U.S. assessment of India's human rights practices in the year 2004, including with regard to human trafficking.

———. "Country Reports on Human Rights Practices, 2006: India." Released March 2007. Available online. URL: http://www.state.gov/g/drl/rls/hrrpt/2006/78871.htm. Accessed January 16, 2008. This report presents the U.S. assessment of India's human rights practices in the year 2005, including with regard to human trafficking.

INVOLUNTARY DOMESTIC SERVITUDE
Books

Ehrenreich, Barbara, and Arlie Russell Hochschild. *Global Woman: Nannies, Maids, and Sex Workers in the New Economy.* New York: Metropolitan Books, 2002. This examination of the migration and abuse of women from developing countries includes chapters on Thai children sold into brothels and sex tourism, as well as a chapter on involuntary domestic servitude.

Web Sites

Social Alert. "Invisible Servitude: An In-Depth Study on Domestic Workers in the World" (2000). Available online. URL: http://www.socialalert.org/k/index.php?option=com_content&task=view&lang =fr&id=94. Accessed February 29, 2008. This report examines the working conditions and abuse, including involuntary domestic servitude, of domestic workers throughout the world. Particular attention is devoted to domestic workers in Africa, Asia, Europe, and Latin America.

NETHERLANDS
Web Sites

Bureau Nationaal Rapporteur Mensenhandel. "Trafficking in Human Beings, Supplementary Figures: Fourth Report of the Dutch National Rapporteur" (2005). Available online. URL: http://rechten.uvt.nl/victimology/national/NL-NRMEngels4.pdf. Accessed December 26, 2007. This is the Dutch Rapporteur's most recent report to be translated into English. (The Dutch Rapporteur is the agency responsible for monitoring human trafficking in the Netherlands.) The report gives detailed information regarding trafficking investigations, victims, and prosecutions in the Netherlands.

Commission of the European Communities, DG Justice & Home Affairs. "Research Based on Case Studies of Victims of Trafficking in Human Beings in 3 EU Member States, i.e., Belgium, Italy, and the Netherlands" (2003). Available online. URL: http://www.ontheroadonlus.it/rootdown/RapIppocra.pdf. Accessed January 12, 2008. This report presents the Commission of the European Communities' findings on human trafficking in three EU countries, including the Netherlands. The commission's investigation included the scope of trafficking, the relevant legal framework, and the rescue and prosecution efforts in each of the countries studied.

End Child Prostitution, Child Pornography and Trafficking of Children for Sexual Purposes. "Global Monitoring: Report on the Status of Action against Commercial Sexual Exploitation of Children, The Netherlands" (2006). Available online. URL: http://www.ecpat.nl/ariadne/loader.php/en/ecpat/documenten/Global_Monitoring Report_-NET HERLANDS.pdf/. Accessed January 2, 2008. This report examines child sex trafficking in the Netherlands and that country's efforts to combat it.

Netherlands Ministry of Foreign Affairs. "Dutch Policy on Prostitution: Questions and Answers, 2005." Available online. URL: http://www.prostitutionprocon.org/pdf/netherlands/pdf. Accessed December 26, 2007. This presentation of the official Dutch position on prostitution does not reflect the restrictions announced in December 2007 by the mayor of Amsterdam, but it nonetheless provides a good overview of Dutch policy regarding prostitution.

Stichting Defense for Children International the Netherlands. "Investigating Exploitation: Research into Trafficking in Children in the Netherlands" (2005). Available online. URL: http://polis.osce.org/library/f/2716/549/NGO-NLD-RPT-2716-EN-Investigating%20Exploitatio n.pdf. Accessed December 21, 2007. This report examines the trafficking of children within and into the Netherlands for purposes of commercial sexual exploitation and various forms of forced labor. It also examines the relevant legal framework in the Netherlands and makes recommendations to better combat child trafficking.

NIGERIA
Web Sites

Federal Republic of Nigeria, National Population Commission. "Nigeria Demographic and Health Survey, 2003." Available online. URL: http://www.measuredhs.com/pubs/pdf/FR148/00FrontMatter.pdf. Accessed January 10, 2008. This survey, conducted by the Nigerian Population Commission, provides extensive information about the daily lives of Nigeria's people, including information about women's participation in marital decision-making (broken down by the female's age at marriage and other factors), educational attainment, and media access.

Federal Republic of Nigeria. "Millennium Development Goals Report, 2004." Available online. URL: http://www.undoc.org/index.cfm?P=87&f=N. Accessed February 4, 2008. This report, which assesses Nigeria's progress in meeting the UN's Millennium Development Goals, provides detailed information about educational attainment, gender equity, and poverty, among other societal factors in Nigeria.

Fetuga, Bonale M., Fidelis O. Njokama, and Abediyi O. Olowu. "Prevalence, Types and Demographic Features of Child Labour Among School Children in Nigeria." Available online. URL: http://www.biomedcentral.com/content/pdf/1472-698X-5-2.pdf. Accessed February 10, 2008. This study examines child labor in Nigeria, especially among children who work while enrolled in school.

International Fund for Agricultural Development. "Enabling the Rural Poor to Overcome Poverty in Nigeria." Available online. URL: http://www.ifad.org/operations/projects/regions/PA/factsheets/ng.pdf. Accessed February 1, 2008. This report examines the causes and consequences of rural poverty in Nigeria, and it assesses initiatives to improve the living standards of Nigeria's rural people.

International Labour Organization. "Review of Legislation and Policies in Nigeria on Human Trafficking and Forced Labour" (2006). Available online. URL: http://se2.isn.ch/serviceengine/FileContent?serviceID=RESSpecNet&fileid=4C9F2FBB-ABEC-1C5E-E147-2047D0E7EFEC&lng=en. Accessed December 20, 2007. This report examines the scope and nature of human trafficking in Nigeria, especially trafficking for forced labor; reviews the pertinent legislation; lists and describes the trafficking cases prosecuted in Nigeria; and makes recommendations for better addressing the issue.

International Labour Organization/International Programme on the Elimination of Child Labour. "Combating Trafficking in Children for Labour Exploitation in West and Central Africa." Available online. URL: http://portal.unesco.org/shs/en/files/3602/10718321711ilochildtrafficking.pdf/ilochildtrafficking.pdf. Accessed January 20, 2008. This report provides a synthesis of studies on trafficking in children in Benin, Burkina Faso, Cameroon, Côte d'Ivoire, Gambia, Ghana, Mali, Niger, Nigeria, and Togo.

Network Against Human Trafficking in West Africa. "Country Reports: Nigeria." Available online. URL: http://nahtiwa.virtualactivism.net/countryreports.htm. Accessed

February 1, 2008. This country report on Nigeria focuses exclusively on the issue of human trafficking in Nigeria.

Nwogu, Vicky. "Trafficking of Persons to Europe: The Perspective of Nigeria as a Sending Country." Available online. URL: http://www.nuoveschiavitu.it/ns/doc_leggi/relazione_nigeria.doc. Accessed January 11, 2008. This paper, presented at the 2005 AIS and OIKOS conference entitled "Trafficking and Migration: A Human Rights Approach," examines the causes and types of human trafficking in Nigeria and offers recommendations to better combat trafficking in Nigeria.

Population Council. "The Experience of Married Adolescent Girls in Northern Nigeria" (2007). Available online. URL: http://www.popcouncil.org/pdfs/Nigeria_MarriedAdol.pdf. Accessed January 2, 2008. This report is an in-depth examination of the lives of young married girls in Nigeria.

———. "Child Marriage Briefing: Nigeria." Available online. URL: http://www.popcouncil.org/pdfs/briefingsheets/NIGERIA.pdf. Accessed December 18, 2007. This briefing gives an overview of child marriage in Nigeria and, in particular, the marriage of minor females and the negative consequences of such marriages for these girls.

UNESCO. "Policy Paper No. 14.2(E), Human Trafficking in Nigeria: Root Causes and Recommendations" (2006). Available online. URL: http://unesdoc.unesco.org/images/0014/001478/147844E.pdf. Accessed December 17, 2007. This report examines the cultural context and root causes of human trafficking in Nigeria, assesses the relevant legal and legislative framework, and makes recommendations to better combat human trafficking in Nigeria.

United Nations. "Press Briefing: Press Conference on UNFPA Project to Treat Obstetric Fistula in Nigeria." Available online. URL: http://www.un.org/News/briefings/docs/2005/UNFPA_Briefing_050222.doc.htm. Accessed February 1, 2008. This press release describes the UN's 2005 "Fistula Fortnight," a volunteer effort of international medical personnel to treat as many of Nigeria's estimated 400,000 to 800,000 fistula victims as possible within a two-week period and, simultaneously, to train Nigerian surgeons, nurses, and social workers to assist the Nigerian women who are living with this child-bearing injury.

United Nations Information Service. "Significant Progress in the Fight Against Trafficking in Human Beings in West African Sates." Available online. URL: http://www.unis.unvienna.org/unis/pressrels/2001/cp400.html. Accessed February 20, 2008. This United Nations Information Service press release outlines the 2001 agreement among the Economic Community of West African States member states (Benin, Burkina Faso, Cap Verde, Côte d'Ivoire, Gambia, Ghana, Guinea, Guinea-Bissau, Liberia, Mali, Niger, Senegal, Sierra Leone, Togo, and Nigeria) to work together to combat transnational human trafficking.

United Nations Office for the Coordination of Human Affairs, Integrated Regional Information Networks. "Nigeria: Dream of Freedom Turns to Prostitution Nightmare." Available online. URL: http://www.irinnews.org/report.aspx?reportid=57008. Accessed: February 2, 2007. This article examines the lives of Nigerian girls prostituted in Italy.

United Nations Office on Drugs and Crime. "Measures to Combat Trafficking in Human Beings in Benin, Nigeria and Togo" (2006). Available online. URL: http://www.

unodc.org/documents/human-trafficking/ht_research_report_nigeria.pdf. Accessed December 17, 2007. This report examines the nature and extent of human trafficking in Benin, Nigeria, and Togo and assesses each country's efforts to combat trafficking.

POVERTY

Books

Sachs, Jeffrey D. *The End of Poverty.* New York: Penguin Group, 2006. In this book, Jeffrey Sachs—a leading economist and special adviser to UN Secretary-General Kofi Annan during Annan's term—examines global poverty and outlines a plan to eradicate it.

Singer, Peter. *The Life You Can Save.* New York: Random House, 2009. In this book, the philosopher Peter Singer—named one of the "100 Most Influential People in the World" by Time magazine—seeks to define the leading of an ethical life as one that includes doing what one can to end world poverty. In addition, he evaluates the large and small actions that individuals in wealthy nations can take to aid the poor and provides a suggested "sliding scale" for giving according to means. Most important, he makes the case that individuals in wealthy nations actually have the ability to end extreme poverty in the world.

Yunus, Muhammad. *Banker to the Poor: Micro-Lending and the Battle against World Poverty.* New York: Public Affairs, 2003. In this book, Muhammad Yunis—the creator of the micro-lending business model and winner of the 2006 Nobel Peace Prize—explains how and why micro-lending works.

———. *Creating a World without Poverty.* New York: Perseus Publishing, 2007. In this book, Yunus discusses the possibility of competitive markets aiding in the eradication of poverty and also profiles a number of companies that are already working in this manner.

Web Sites

United Nations. "The Millennium Development Goals Report" (2007). Available online. URL: http://www.un.org/millenniumgoals/pdf/mdg2007.pdf. Accessed December 1, 2007. This report provides detailed information about poverty, educational, and gender-equity measures in UN member countries.

———. "UN Millennium Development Goals." Available online. URL: http://www.un.org/millenniumgoals/. Accessed June 2, 2008. This Web site provides information about the United Nations's Millennium Development Goals and the progress of nations in meeting them by the target date of 2015.

The World Bank. "PovertyNet." Available online. URL: http://web.worldbank.org/WBSITE/EXTERNAL/TOPICS/EXTPOVERTY/0,,menuPK:3369 98~pagePK:149018 ~piPK:149093~theSitePK:336992,00.html. Accessed June 2, 2008. This World Bank Web site provides information and analysis regarding global poverty, including a poverty impact analysis database, a poverty mapping site, videos, and links to recent news on global poverty.

SCOPE AND MAGNITUDE OF INTERNATIONAL HUMAN TRAFFICKING

Books

Bales, Kevin. *Disposable People: New Slavery in the Global Economy*. Revised Edition. Berkeley: University of California Press, 2004. This book, a revised edition of a book first published in 2000, gives a complete overview of the nature of modern-day slavery and examines the forms it takes in Thailand, Mauritania, Brazil, Pakistan, and India. Its final chapter offers suggestions for individuals who wish to combat human trafficking.

———. *Understanding Global Slavery: A Reader*. Berkeley: University of California Press, 2005. In this book, Kevin Bales examines the factors that cause and sustain global human trafficking.

Sage, Jesse, and Liora Kasten, eds. *Enslaved: True Stories of Modern Day Slavery*. New York: Palgrave Macmillan, 2006. This book provides an overview of modern-day slavery; first-person accounts of victims trafficked in or to the United States, Sudan, Lebanon, Egypt, China, and Belarus; a first-person account of a former slaveholder in Mauritania; and an epilogue entitled "Where You Come In," addressed to those wishing to combat human trafficking.

Savona, Ernesto Ugo. *Measuring Human Trafficking: Complexities and Pitfalls*. New York: Springer-Verlag New York, LLC, 2007. This book, which examines the different definitions of human trafficking and the different estimates of trafficking victims, argues for an improved monitoring and measuring protocol for modern slavery.

Skinner, E. Benjamin. *A Crime So Monstrous: A Shocking Exposé of Modern-Day Slavery, Human Trafficking and Child Urban Markets*. New York: The Free Press, 2008. In this book, E. Benjamin Skinner describes what he witnessed in four years of on-the-ground research into human trafficking on five continents, including interviews with presently and formerly enslaved persons, slave traders and slaveholders, and today's abolitionists.

Articles

"Slavery by Any Other Name." *Economist* (1/6/97), 42. In just under three pages, "Slavery by Any Other Name" outlines the 1997 evidence that "slavery is entrenched in Asia, Africa, and Latin America."

Web Sites

Free the Slaves. "What's the Story." Available online. URL: http://www.freetheslaves. Accessed July 31, 2007. This Web site provides a video of interviews with rescued trafficking victims and experts in the field, an interactive map detailing human trafficking activity, and other resources.

International Organization for Migration. "Protection Schemes for Victims of Trafficking in Selected EU Member Countries, Candidate and Third Countries" (2003). Available online. URL: http://www.iom.hu/PDFs/Protection%20Schemes%20for

%20VoT%20in%20EU%20Candidate%20and%20Third%20Countries.pdf. Accessed June 7, 2008. This report explores the "human rights imperative" in ending human trafficking and the evolving international definitions of human trafficking, provides case studies of human trafficking in Albania, Austria, Belgium, Czech Republic, Germany, Hungary, Italy, the Netherlands, Spain, and Ukraine, evaluates the efforts of EU member countries' anti-trafficking initiatives, and makes recommendations to better combat modern-day slavery.

McGill International Law Society. "Conference on Human Trafficking in Canada" (March 20, 2006). Available online. URL: http://mils.mcgill.ca/resources/Human_ Trafficking.pdf. Accessed October 1, 2007. This summary of the 2006 Conference on Human Trafficking in Canada includes the observations of individual members of the Royal Canadian Mounted Police as well as an overview of the scope and magnitude of human trafficking in Canada and an evaluation of the country's efforts to combat it.

UNESCO. "Trafficking Statistics Project." Available online. URL: http://www.unescobkk. org/index.php?id=1022. Accessed August 10, 2007. This UN project, available for access online, compiles the trafficking estimates of various governments and organizations, offers comparisons of these frequently differing estimates, and maintains a human trafficking bibliography.

United Nations Department of Peacekeeping Operations. "Human Trafficking and United Nations Peacekeeping DPKO Policy Paper" (March 2004). Available online. URL: http://www.un.org/womenwatch/news/documents/DPKOHumanTraf-fickingPolicy03-2004.pdf. Accessed March 29, 2008. This UN Department of Peacekeeping Operations (DPKO) policy paper was formulated in response to "allegations and incidences of [UN] peacekeeper involvement with trafficking." It addresses those allegations and incidences and sets forth policies intended to prevent future trafficking involvement and activity among UN peacekeepers.

UNODC. "Trafficking in Persons: Global Patterns" (2006). Available online. URL: http://www.unodc.org/pdf/traffickinginpersons_report_2006-04.pdf. Accessed June 6, 2006. This UNODC report examines the reported regional flow of human trafficking in Africa, Asia, Europe, the Commonwealth of Independent States, the Americas, and Oceania, identifies the world's origin, transit, and destination countries for human trafficking victims, and analyzes global patterns related to human trafficking, including the involvement of organized crime.

SEX TOURISM

Web Sites

"Child Sex Tourism Raises Its Head in India." Indo-Asian News Service, October 14, 2007. Available online. URL: http://sify.com/news/fullstory.php?id=14542872. Accessed October 16, 2007. This news article examines the emergence of child sex tourism in India.

Ferreira, Emsie. "South Africa Child Sex: Child Sex Trafficking Rising in South Africa as Poverty Spreads: Survey." Agence France-Presse (11/22/00). Available online. URL: http://www.aegis.com/news/afp/2000/AF001165.html. Accessed June 20, 2008. This news article describes the rise of child sex trafficking in South Africa and, particularly, the use of children in South Africa's sex tourism trade.

United Nations. "Press Conference on Human Trafficking and Sex Tourism" (October 21, 2004). Available online. URL: http://www.un.org/News/briefings/docs/2004/Martin_Press_Cfc_041020.doc.htm. This press release provides information about the prevalence of sex tourism in various countries and the efforts of the United States to address it.

Film/Video/TV

NBC. "Children for Sale." In this 2005 episode of *Dateline*, Chris Hansen goes undercover to expose sex tourism in Cambodia and, in the process, documents the rescue of a number of enslaved young girls. The episode resulted in the arrest of an American physician traveling in Cambodia as a sex tourist.

———. "Update, Child Victims of Sex Trade in Cambodia." In this 2008 episode of *Dateline*, Chris Hansen visits with girls rescued from sex slavery during his investigative reporting in 2005. This episode reviews the original 2005 reporting and examines efforts to heal and educate the young girls.

SEX TRAFFICKING
Books

Farley, Melissa, ed. New York: The Haworth Maltreatment & Trauma Press, 2003. Co-published simultaneously as the *Journal of Trauma Practice* (vol. 2, nos. 3, 4 2003), this book brings together papers written on prostitution and trafficking by physicians, psychiatrists, lawyers, sociologists, professors, and activists. Among other things, the book contains clinical evaluations and documentation of posttraumatic stress order among women prostituted in nine countries; an examination of the relationship between prostitution and trafficking; a close examination of the trafficking of women and children from Mexico to the United States; the argument against legalizing prostitution; and a section entitled "Healing from Prostitution and Trafficking."

Malarek, Victor. *The Natashas: Inside the Global Sex Trade.* New York: Arcade Publishing, 2003. This book examines the growing global trade in young women from eastern Europe and the countries that were formerly part of the Soviet Union, as well as the official corruption that facilitates sex trafficking in and from these countries.

Waugh, Louisa. *Selling Olga: Stories of Human Trafficking.* London: Orion Books, 2008. This book examines the global trade in women, particularly the trafficking of eastern European women for sexual exploitation, which is illuminated with close attention to the experience of an eastern European woman named Olga. *Selling Olga* also includes a discussion of trafficking in women for forced labor.

Web Sites

Balkan Human Rights Web Pages. "A Form of Slavery: Trafficking in Women in OSCE Member States: Country Report (2000)." Available online. URL: http://www. greekhelsinki.gr/english/reports/ihf-wit-july-2000.html. This Web site provides links to country reports on trafficking in women in a number of OSCE (Organization for Security and Co-Operation in Europe) member states, namely Albania, Bosnia, Bulgaria, Croatia, Greece, Kosovo, Macedonia, Montenegro, Romania, Serbia, Slovenia, and Turkey.

Hughes, Donna M., Laura Joy Sporcic, Nadine Z. Mendelsohn, Vanessa Chirgwin, The Coalition against Trafficking in Women. "The Factbook on Global Sexual Exploitation" (1999). Available online. URL: http://www.uri.edu/artsci/wms/ hughes/factbook.htm. Accessed February 19, 2008. This online factbook about sex trafficking compiles statistics and other information available as of 1999 from NGO, government, and media sources. It is divided into sections by country.

Socialsyrelsen. "Prostitution in Sweden" (2003). Available online: URL: http://www. socialstyrelsen.se/NR/rdonlyres/A688D624-4505-431F-A9CF-DCD7C12D0539/2 719/200413128.pdf. Accessed June 20, 2008. This report analyzes prostitution in Sweden, including the voluntary and involuntary entrance of women and girls into prostitution, and the effect of Sweden's 1999 law criminalizing the purchasing of sex.

U.S. Department of Health and Human Services. "Sex Trafficking Fact Sheet." Available online. URL: http://www.acf.hhs.gov/trafficking/about/fact_sex.pdf. Accessed June 15, 2008. This two-page fact sheet defines human trafficking, summarizes the methods by which victims are deceived, outlines the various forms of slavery endured by those trafficked for sexual exploitation, and discusses the assistance available to sex-trafficking victims.

U.S. Department of State. "The Link between Prostitution and Sex Trafficking." Available online. URL: http://www.state.gov/r/pa/ei/rls/38790.htm. Accessed June 15, 2008. This State Department publication examines the evidence that "Prostitution and related activities—including pimping and patronizing or maintaining brothels—fuel the growth of modern-day slavery by providing a facade behind which traffickers for sexual exploitation operate."

Film/Video/TV

Eastern Promises. Directed by David Cronenberg, written by Stephen Knight (screenplay). 100 minutes, 2007. This film dramatizes Russian organized crime's involvement in human trafficking for sexual exploitation through the story of a young woman who dies in childbirth but leaves behind a diary.

Human Trafficking. Directed by Christian Duguay. Lifetime TV miniseries, 2005. This miniseries, which focuses exclusively on trafficking for commercial sexual exploitation, dramatizes the representative experiences of three female victims and the efforts of immigration officers to secure their rescue.

Selling of Innocents. 57 minutes, 1997. Directed by Ruchira Gupta, produced by Simcha Jacobovici. This documentary examines the trafficking of women and girls from Nepal to Mumbai (formerly Bombay), India. It won an Emmy for investigative journalism.

Trade. Directed by Marco Kreuzpaintner, written by Jose Rivera (screenplay) and Peter Landesman (story). 120 minutes, 2007. This film, based on a *New York Times* article by Peter Landesman, dramatizes the kidnapping by sex traffickers of a 13-year-old Mexican girl, her subsequent enslavement in the U.S. sex trade, and the efforts of her 17-year-old brother to rescue her.

TRAFFICKING FOR INVOLUNTARY ORGAN HARVESTS

Articles

Gentlemen, Amelia. "Kidney Theft Ring Preys on India's Poorest Laborers." *New York Times* (1/30/08). This article provides information about a case involving the involuntary harvesting of organs in India.

"India: Kidney Ring Suspect Arrested." *New York Times* (2/8/08). This article reports on an arrest made in India's January 2008 organ harvesting case and provides additional details about that case.

"Top Transplant Surgeons Involved in Organ Trafficking, Expert Says." *International Herald Tribune* (2/14/08). This article examines the growth in organ trafficking and interviews a leading activist in the field who asserts that top surgeons around the world are complicit in the trade.

Web Sites

McBroom, Patricia. "An 'Organs Watch' to Track Global Traffic in Human Organs Opens Mon., Nov. 8, at UC Berkeley" (11/3/99). University of California, Berkeley. Available online. URL: http://berkeley.edu/news/media/releases/99legacy/11-03-1999b. html. Accessed February 16, 2008. This news release provides information about a University of California at Berkeley project created to monitor global trafficking in organs.

Scheper-Hughes, Nancy. "The Organ of Last Resort." Available online. URL: http://www. unesco.org/courier/2001_07/uk/doss34.htm. Accessed April 20, 2008. This article discusses organ harvesting and what has become known as medical tourism, including a discussion of contributory factors.

———. "The End of the Body: The Global Traffic in Organs for Transplant Surgery." Available online. URL: http://sunsite.berkeley.edu/biotech/organswatch/pages/cadraft. html. Accessed August 11, 2008. This article documents trafficking for involuntary organ harvesting and other forms of coerced donation. It also examines the commodification of the body and so-called organ tourism's movement of organs "from South to North, from third world to first world, from poor to rich bodies, from black and brown to white bodies . . ." and other patterns of exploitation.

TRAFFICKING IN INFANTS
Web Sites

"53 Babies Found, 110 Suspects Arrested for Baby Trafficking Case." *People's Daily* (10/8/04). Available online. URL: http://english.peopledaily.com.cn/200410/08/ eng20041008_159275.html. Accessed October 4, 2007. This article provides information about infants sold in China and the arrests of those involved in their trafficking.

"Gang Trafficking Over 60 Babies Cracked." China Economic Net (9/9/07). Available online. URL: http://en.ce.cn/National/Local/200709/08/t20070908_12834260. shtml. Accessed September 14, 2007. This article provides information about arrests made in a Chinese infant trafficking group and the rescue of infants in their custody.

Kitsantonis, Niki, and Matthew Brunwasser. "Baby Trafficking Is Thriving in Greece." *International Herald Tribune* (12/18/06). Available online: URL: http://www.iht. com/articles/2006/12/18/news/babies.php. Accessed October 20, 2007. This article provides information about the selling of infants in Greece, and especially the sale of Bulgarian Roma infants to Greek nationals. The views of those who do and do not consider these sales to be trafficking are presented.

Plovdiv, Nicola Smith. "Revealed: Bulgaria's Baby Traders." *Sunday Times* (10/1/06). Available online. URL: http://www.timesonline.co.uk/tol/news/world/article656620.ece. Accessed October 2, 2007. This article was written by a reporter who posed as a prospective purchaser of a Bulgarian Roma infant. It includes interviews with women who were deceived and/or forced into relinquishing their infants, as well as interviews with an immigration official and a public prosecutor.

UNICEF Innocenti Research Center. "Chinese Woman Sentenced to Death over Baby Trafficking" (5/14/04). Available online: URL: http://www.childtrafficking.org/cgi-bin/ct/main.sql?ID=702&file=view_document.sql< 0x0026>TITLE=-1&AUTHOR =-1&THESAURO=-1&ORGANIZATION=-1&TYPE_DOC=-1&TOPIC=-1&GEOG=-1&YEAR=-1&LISTA=No&COUNTRY=-1&FULL_DETAIL=YES. Accessed September 20, 2007. This article provides information about a case of trafficking in infants in China and the sentencing of a woman convicted in that case.

———. Child Trafficking Research Hub. Available only online. URL: http://www.childtrafficking.org/eng/database.html. Accessed October 4, 2007. This Web site provides links to documents and news on child trafficking, including information on trafficking in infants, when the search keywords "baby trafficking" are entered.

Film/Video/TV

China's Stolen Children. Kate Bewett and Brian Woods, producers; Jezza Neumann, director. 2008. This documentary, filmed undercover, examines trafficking in infants and children in China. It was winner of Best International Current Affairs Programme at the Royal Television Society Awards (2008), Broadcast Awards 2008 Winner, and the official selection of the 2008 Human Rights Watch Film Festival.

UNITED STATES
Books

Bowe, John. *Nobodies: Modern American Slave Labor and the Dark Side of the New Global Economy.* New York: Random House, 2007. This book examines modern-day slavery in the United States, with close attention to cases in Florida, Oklahoma, and Saipan (part of the Northern Mariana Islands, a commonwealth in political union with the United States).

Farley, Melissa. *Prostitution and Trafficking in Nevada: Making the Connections.* San Francisco: Prostitution Research & Education, 2007. *Prostitution and Trafficking in Nevada* examines legal and illegal prostitution in Nevada; the abuses suffered by women in prostitution; the presence of trafficked women in both legal and illegal prostitution; the evidence that prostitution—and especially legal prostitution—increases the number of trafficked women; and the evidence that the open, unchallenged presence of prostitution—whether legal or illegal—increases the rape rates for other women in the geographic vicinity.

Zhang, Sheldon Z. *Smuggling and Trafficking in Human Beings: All Roads Lead to America.* Westport, Conn.: Greenwood Publishing Group, 2007. This book examines human trafficking and consensual smuggling into and within the United States, the overlap between the two, and the United States's efforts to combat trafficking.

Articles

Greenhouse, Stephen. "Migrant-Camp Operators Face Forced Labor Charges." *New York Times* (6/21/02). This article provides information about 40 Mexican workers enslaved near Buffalo, New York, and the arrests of those who held them in modern-day slavery.

Hakim, Danny, and Nicholas Confessore. "Albany Agrees on Law against Sexual and Labor Trafficking." *New York Times* (5/17/07). This article provides information about legislation passed in New York State in 2007 to combat human trafficking.

Herbert, Bob. "The Wrong Target." *New York Times* (2/19/08.) This op-ed column discusses the forced prostitution of a 13-year-old girl in New York City and the customary treatment of child prostitutes as criminals rather than as victims.

Kilgannon, Corey. "N.Y. Couple Convicted in Slave Case." *New York Times* (12/17/07). This article documents the conviction of a couple charged with forced labor and other charges in one of the most high-profile human trafficking cases of 2007.

Landesman, Peter. "The Girls Next Door." *New York Times* (1/25/05). This article—which was the basis for the Lifetime film *Human Trafficking* (discussed in the Sex Trafficking section of this bibliography)—chronicles the lives of young girls trafficked into the New York metropolitan area for commercial sexual exploitation.

Miller, John R. "The Justice Department, Blind to Slavery." *New York Times* (7/11/08). In this op-ed piece, Miller, a former U.S. ambassador at large on modern-day slavery, criticizes the U.S. Justice Department's opposition to a 2008 proposed bill intended to strengthen the United State's ability to combat human trafficking.

Sontag, Deborah. "7 Arrested in Abuse of Deaf Immigrants." *New York Times* (7/1/97). This article documents the arrests of those who trafficked deaf immigrants into forced begging (a form of forced labor) on New York City's subways.

Vitello, Paul. "From Stand in Long Island Slavery Case, a Snapshot of a Hidden U.S. Problem." *New York Times* (12/3/07). In this article, Paul Vitello reviews a 2007 case of involuntary servitude in New York and examines the prevalence of involuntary servitude in the United States.

Web Sites

Arizona State University, Department of English. "The AntiSlavery Literature Project." Available online. URL: http://antislavery.eserver.org. Accessed May 20, 2008. This project, based in Arizona State University's Department of English and Iowa State University's Department of English's E-Server, is working to make the American literary history of slavery available online. The texts currently available include poetry, prose fiction, travel accounts, slave narratives, tracts, and treatises, among other primary source documents from America's slaveholding past, as well as a collection of contemporary global slave narratives, curated by Free the Slaves' Kevin Bales and Zoe Todd.

California Alliance to Combat Trafficking and Slavery Task Force. "Human Trafficking in California" (2007). Available online. URL: http://safestate.org/documents/HT_Final_Report_ADA.pdf. Accessed November 15, 2007. This report examines the scope and nature of human trafficking in California and California's efforts to assist victims and prosecute traffickers. It also makes recommendations for California to better combat trafficking in the state.

Coalition against Trafficking in Women. "Sex Trafficking of Women in the United States: International and Domestic Trends" (2001). Available online. URL: http://action.web.ca/home/catw/attach/sex_traff_us.pdf. Accessed June 30, 2008. This study examines the trafficking of international and U.S. women for sexual exploitation in the United States. It includes interviews with survivors of sex trafficking in the United States.

End Child Prostitution, Child Pornography, and Trafficking of Children for Sexual Purposes. "Report on the Status of Action against Commercial Sexual Exploitation of Children: United States of America" (2006). Available online. URL: http://www.ecpat.net/eng/A4A_2005/PDF/Americas/Global_Monitoring_Report-USA.pdf. Accessed June 20, 2008. This report examines the sex trafficking of children in the United States.

Free the Slaves and Human Rights Center, University of California, Berkeley. "Hidden Slaves: Forced Labor in the United States" (2004). Available online: URL: http://www.hrcberkeley.org/download/hiddenslaves_report.pdf. Accessed November 8, 2007. This report examines forced labor in the United States's agricultural and textile industries and in its commercial sex trade; the United States's legal response to forced labor and the actual implementation and enforcement of U.S. anti-trafficking legislation; and the health consequences of forced labor and services available to victims. It also assesses lessons learned thus far and makes recommendations for the United States to better combat modern-day slavery.

Annotated Bibliography

Human Rights Watch. "Hidden in the Home: Abuse of Domestic Workers with Special Visas in the United States" (2001). Available online. URL: http://www.hrw.org/reports/2001/usadom/. Accessed June 30, 2008. This report examines the abuse, including human trafficking, of the domestic workers of foreign diplomats, the heads of international corporations and institutions, and others with special visas that permit them to enter the United States with their personal staffs and forbid those staff members from working for anyone but that employer while in the United States.

"India Escapes U.S. List of Worst Human Traffickers." CNN.com (6/13/07). Available online. URL: http://www.cnn.com/2007/US/06/12/human.trafficking/index.html. Accessed April 27, 2008. This article documents the placement of India and other countries on the United States's 2007 Trafficking in Persons Report.

Miller, John R. "Call it Slavery." Available online. URL: http://www.wilsoncenter.org/index.cfm?fuseaction=wq.essay&essay_id=459603. Accessed July 25, 2008. In this essay, Miller, a former U.S. ambassador-at-large on modern slavery, outlines the nature and magnitude of modern-day slavery, explores parallels between the 19th-century and modern-day abolitionist movements, and examines the means by which modern-day slavery can be fought.

Richard, Amy O'Neill. "International Trafficking in Women to the United States: A Contemporary Manifestation of Slavery and Organized Crime" (1999). Available online. URL: http://www.cia.gov/library/center-for-the-study-of-intelligence/csi-publications/books-and-mon ographs/trafficking.pdf. Accessed June 30, 2008. This study examines the trafficking of women and girls to the United States, the forms of exploitation faced by these trafficking victims, and the involvement of organized crime in modern-day slavery.

Sharifi, Solmaz. "Modern Abolitionists at the U.S. State Department: How the U.S. Government Fights Human Trafficking." Available online. URL: http://www.cia.gov/library/center-for-the-study-of-intelligence/csi-publications/books-and-mon ographs/trafficking.pdf. Accessed June 30, 2008. This article, adapted from an article that first appeared in *Slate* magazine, outlines the efforts of the U.S. State Department to combat human trafficking.

U.S. Department of Justice. "Attorney General's Annual Report to Congress on U.S. Government Activities to Combat Trafficking in Persons, Fiscal Year 2006." Available online. URL: http://www.usdoj.gov/ag/annualreports/tr2006/agreporthuman trafficing2006.pdf. Accessed November 26, 2007. This report outlines the Department of Justice's fiscal year 2006 prosecutions of traffickers and other measures taken that year to combat modern-day slavery.

———. "Bureau of Justice Statistics: Federal Prosecution of Human Trafficking, 2001–2005." Available online. URL: http://www.ojp.usdoj.gov/bjs/pub/pdf/fpht05.pdf. Accessed July 3, 2008. This report provides a statistical analysis of the Department of Justice's prosecutions of traffickers from 2001 to 2005.

———. "Fact Sheet: PROTECT Act." Available online. URL: http://www.usdoj.gov/opa/pr/2003/April/03_ag_266.htm. Accessed December 22, 2007. This fact sheet outlines the provisions of the Prosecutorial Remedies and Other Tools to End the Exploitation of Children Today, also known as the PROTECT Act.

——. Press Release. "Six Indicted in Conspiracy for Trafficking and Holding Migrant Workers in Conditions of Forced Labor in Western New York" (6/19/02). Available online. URL: http://www.usdoj.gov/opa/pr/2002/June/02_crt_360.htm. Accessed July 3, 2008. This press release provides information on indictments in connection with the enslaving of Mexican immigrants in a work camp near Buffalo, New York.

——. "Report to Congress from Attorney General John Ashcroft on U.S. Efforts to Combat Trafficking in Persons in Fiscal Year 2003." Available online. URL: http://www.usdoj.gov/ag/050104agreporttocongresstvprav10.pdf. Accessed November 26, 2007. This report outlines the prosecutions and other initiatives taken by the U.S. Department of Justice to combat modern-day slavery in the fiscal year 2003.

——. "Report on Activities to Combat Human Trafficking, Fiscal Years 2001–2005." Available online. URL: http://www.usdoj.gov/crt/crim/trafficking_report_2006.pdf. Accessed July 3, 2008. This report describes the investigations, prosecutions, and other anti-trafficking initiatives of the U.S. Department of Justice between 2001 and 2005.

——. "Report to Congress from Attorney General John Ashcroft on U.S. Efforts to Combat Trafficking in Persons in Fiscal Year 2003." Available online. URL: http://www.usdoj.gov/ag/050104agreporttocongresstvprav10.pdf. Accessed November 26, 2007. This report summarizes the United States's efforts to combat human trafficking in the fiscal year 2003, including investigations and prosecutions of traffickers, international anti-trafficking grants, domestic and international anti-trafficking training assistance, and immigration and other assistance rendered to trafficking victims in the United States.

——. "Report to Congress from Attorney General Alberto R. Gonzales on U.S. Efforts to Combat Trafficking in Persons in Fiscal Year 2004." Available online. URL: http://www.usdoj.gov/ag/annualreports/tr2004/agreporthumantrafficing.pdf. Accessed July 5, 2008. This report summarizes the United States's efforts to combat human trafficking in the fiscal year 2004, including investigations and prosecutions of traffickers, international anti-trafficking grants, domestic and international anti-trafficking training assistance, and immigration and other assistance rendered to trafficking victims in the United States.

U.S. Department of State. "Anti-Trafficking Programs Awarded in Fiscal Year 2007." Available online. URL: http://www.state.gov/g/tip/rls/rpt/97990.htm. Accessed July 6, 2008. This Web document lists the international anti-trafficking programs that received U.S. funding in fiscal year 2007.

——. "The Facts about Child Sex Tourism." Available online. URL: http://www.state.gov/g/tip/rls/fs/2005/51351.htm. Accessed July 7, 2008. This U.S. Department of State fact sheet defines child sex tourism (CTS), outlines international law regarding CTS, summarizes U.S. governmental efforts to combat the crime, and suggests ways for governments and U.S. citizens and businesses to help eradicate this form of modern-day slavery.

——. "Fighting Human Trafficking Inside the United States." Available online. URL: http://www.america.gov/st/washfile-english/2004/May/20040512092435A

JesroM0.8681147.html. Accessed July 7, 2008. This U.S. Department of State fact sheet outlines U.S. efforts to combat human trafficking and provides contact information for the various U.S. agencies involved in that effort.

———. "Trafficking in Persons Report, 2001." Available online. URL: http://www.state. gov/documents/organization/4107.pdf. Accessed July 7, 2008. The U.S. Trafficking in Persons Reports are issued annually, as mandated by the Victims of Trafficking and Violence Protection Act of 2000. These reports provide an overview of international modern-day slavery and a close examination of modern-day slavery in individual countries. They also rank countries from Tier 1 (best effort to combat trafficking) to Tier 3 (least effort to combat trafficking). This report was the first "Trafficking in Persons Report" to be issued by the U.S. Department of State.

———. "Trafficking in Persons Report, 2002." Available online. URL: http://www.state. gov/g/tip/rls/tiprpt/2002/. Accessed July 7, 2008. This is the second "Trafficking in Persons Report" to be issued by the U.S. Department of State. This was the last year in which Tier 3 countries did not face sanctions.

———. "Trafficking in Persons Report, 2003." Available online. URL: http://www.state. gov/g/tip/rls/tiprpt/2003/. Accessed July 7, 2008. This is the third "Trafficking in Persons Report" to be issued by the U.S. Department of State. For the first time, the report's Tier 3 countries faced possible U.S. sanctions.

———. "Trafficking in Persons Report, 2004." Available online. URL: http://www.state. gov/g/tip/rls/tiprpt/2004/. Accessed July 7, 2008. This is the fourth "Trafficking in Persons Report" to be issued by the U.S. Department of State. The first report to be issued after the Trafficking Victims Protection Reauthorization Act of 2003, it introduces a special "Watch List" category for countries deemed to require special scrutiny in the year following the report's release.

———. "Trafficking in Persons Report, 2005." Available online. URL: http://www.state. gov/g/tip/rls/tiprpt/2005/. Accessed July 7, 2008. This is the fifth "Trafficking in Persons Report" to be issued by the U.S. Department of State. This report's introduction discusses child sex tourism, the link between prostitution and trafficking, the involvement of soldiers in sex trafficking, bonded labor, the escalation of trafficking in the aftermath of natural disasters, and child soldiers, among other aspects of modern-day slavery.

———. "Trafficking in Persons Report, 2006." Available online. URL: http://www.state. gov/g/tip/rls/tiprpt/2006/. This is the sixth "Trafficking in Persons Report" to be issued by the U.S. Department of State. It includes a special focus on slave labor, sexual slavery, the intersection of caste and slavery in South Asia, unaccompanied minors and trafficking, and child soldiers in Burma, among other aspects of modern slavery.

———. "Trafficking in Persons Report, 2007." Available online. URL: http://www.state. gov/documents/organization/82902.pdf. Accessed July 31, 2007. This report provides specific information on involuntary servitude (including an examination of involuntary servitude in diplomatic residences), brokered and forced marriages, especially among Asian women, the forced labor of children in West Africa's cocoa industry, and modern-day slavery in Burma, among other examples of human trafficking. This is also the first report to include an assessment of the United States's role in trafficking and its efforts to abolish slavery within its borders.

———. "Trafficking in Persons Report, 2008." Available online. URL: http://www.state. gov/g/tip/rls/tiprpt/2008. Accessed October 27, 2008. This report is, as this is written, the most recent Trafficking in Persons Report to be released by the U.S. Department of State. The most extensive Trafficking Report to date, it reviews 170 countries for evidence of trafficking and efforts to combat it. It also focuses on the involvement of international peacekeepers in modern-day slavery, women's role in human trafficking, and the failure of legalized prostitution to reduce trafficking.

The White House. "Fact Sheet: Operation Predator." Available online. URL: http://www. whitehouse.gov/news/releases/2004/07/20040707-10.html. Accessed July 20, 2008. This White House Fact Sheet provides information on child sexual exploitation and "Operation Predator," an initiative of the U.S. Department of Homeland Security/U.S. Immigration and Customs Enforcement to expand the investigation and prosecution of those who sexually exploit children.

———. "Office to Monitor and Combat Trafficking in Persons." Available online. URL: http://www.state.gov/g/tip/. Accessed June 30, 2008. This Web site provides links to human trafficking fact sheets, a list of United States–funded anti-trafficking programs, a human trafficking photo gallery, information on reporting suspected trafficking victims, and the U.S. Trafficking in Persons reports, among other resources.

Film/Video/TV

Holly. Guy Moshe, director. Guy Moshe and Guy Jacobson, writers. 114 minutes. 2006. This film dramatizes the story of an American dealer in stolen artifacts and his attempt to rescue a child sex slave in Cambodia.

Very Young Girls. David Schisgall, director. 83 minutes. 2007. This documentary explores prostitution in the United States, making special note of the fact that the average age of entry into prostitution is 13 and interviews teenage victims and survivors of commercial child exploitation.

Chronology

1502

- First known enslaved African person is sent to the New World.

1807

- Great Britain bans the Atlantic slave trade throughout its empire.

1808

- The United States bans the slave trade, without changing the status of those already enslaved in the United States.

1820

- The United States passes legislation categorizing slave trading as piracy and making it punishable by death.

1833

- Slavery is made illegal throughout the British Empire.

1839

- Anti-Slavery International is founded (Britain).

1852

- The Salvation Army International is founded (Britain).

1863

- President Abraham Lincoln issues the Emancipation Proclamation, freeing all slaves held in the Confederate states.

1865

- The Thirteenth Amendment abolishes slavery throughout the United States.

1874

- The so-called Padrone statute is passed in the United States to prevent the use of boys being used without pay as "beggars, bootblacks, or street musicians" on the streets of American cities.

1888

- Brazil becomes the last of the Atlantic slave-trade countries to abolish slavery.

1910

- The Mann Act, also known as "The White Slave Act" (United States).

1919

- The International Labour Organization is founded (Switzerland).

1926

- League of Nations Slavery Convention.

1929

- Child Marriage Restraint Act set age of consent at 14 for girls and 18 for males. (India).

1930

- International Labour Organization Convention 29, Concerning Forced Labour.

1935

- National Labor Relations Act (United States).

1938

- Fair Labor Standards Act (United States).

1945

- United Nations Educational, Scientific, and Cultural Organization (UNESCO) is founded.

1946

- The United Nations Children's Fund (UNICEF) is founded.

1948

- United Nations Universal Declaration of Human Rights.
- United Nations Convention for the Suppression of the Traffic in Persons and of the Exploitation of the Prostitution of Others.

1949

- An amendment to the Child Marriage Restraint Act raises the age of consent for girls to 15, while leaving the age of consent at 18 for boys (India).

1951

- The International Organization for Migration is founded (Switzerland).

1952

- Qatar abolishes chattel slavery.

1953

- The United Nations adopts the demised League of Nations's 1926 Slavery Convention with several amendments.

1955

- Civil Rights Act is passed in India. Among other things, it made the practice of untouchability a punishable offense.

1956

- United Nations Supplemental Convention (No. 105) on the Abolition of Slavery, the Slave Trade, and Institutions and Practices Similar to Slavery.
- Prevention of Immoral Traffic Act (India).

1957

- International Labour Organization Abolition of Forced Labour Convention.

1961

- Dowry Prohibition Act, amended in 1984 and 1986 (India).
- United States Agency for International Development is created.

1965

- United Nations Convention on the Elimination of All Forms of Racial Discrimination.

1970

- Oman abolishes chattel slavery.

1972

- Covenant House International is formally incorporated (United States).

1976

- Bonded Labour System (Abolition) Act (India).

1977

- Christian Solidarity International is founded (Switzerland).

1978

- An amendment to the Child Marriage Restraint Act raises the age of consent to 18 for girls and 21 for boys (India).
- The organization now known as Human Rights Watch is founded (United States).

1979

- United Nations Convention on the Elimination of All Forms of Discrimination against Women.
- Children of the Night is founded (United States).

1980

- Mauritania outlaws slavery for the third time and becomes the last country to prohibit chattel slavery.

1981

- Indecent Representation of Women (Prohibition) Act (IRWPA) (India).
- Africans Unite Against Child Abuse is founded (England).

1983

- Migrant Seasonal Worker Act, revised 1986 and 1995 (United States).

1986

- Child Labour (Prohibition and Regulation) Act (India).
- Physicians for Human Rights is founded (United States).

1987

- Sunlaap is founded (India).

1988

- The Coalition against Trafficking in Women is founded (Belgium).

1989

- The Scheduled Caste and the Scheduled Tribes (Prevention of Atrocities) Act (India) prohibits the committing of atrocities against aboriginal and lower caste persons.

1990

- End Child Prostitution, Child Pornography, and Trafficking in Children for Sexual Purposes is founded (Thailand).

Chronology

1992 '

- Bonded Labor System (Abolition) Act (Pakistan).
- The SAGE Project (the Standing against Global Exploitation Project) is founded (United States).
- Equality Now is founded (United States).

1993

- The Coalition of Immokalee Workers is founded (United States).
- Girls' Power Initiative is founded (Nigeria).
- The Hague Convention on the Protection of Children and Co-operation in Respect of Inter-Country Adoption is concluded.

1994

- Prohibition of Sex Selection Act, also known as the Pre-Natal Diagnostic Techniques Act (India).
- Transplantation of Human Organs Act (India) prohibits the payment for human organs, among other things.
- American Anti-Slavery Group is founded.
- The organization now known as the Fair Trade Federation is founded (United States).
- The Global Alliance against Traffic in Women is founded (Thailand).

1996

- First World Congress against the Sexual Exploitation of Children and Adolescents is held in Stockholm, Sweden.

1997

- The Campaign for Migrant Domestic Workers is founded; it is later renamed the Break the Chain Campaign (United States).
- The International Justice Mission is founded (United States).
- Social Alert International is created (Belgium).

1998

- Apne Aap is founded (India).
- The National Campaign on Dalit Human Rights is established (India).

1999

- International Labour Organization Convention 182, Convention Concerning the Prohibition and Immediate Action for the Elimination of the Worst Forms of Child Labour.

- Organs Watch is established (United States).
- Women Trafficking and Child Labour Eradication Foundation is founded (Nigeria).
- The International Criminal Court is established.

2000

- United Nations Protocol to Prevent, Suppress and Punish Trafficking in Persons, Especially Women and Children.
- United Nations Optional Protocol to the Convention on the Rights of the Child on the Sale of Children, Child Prostitution and Child Pornography.
- United Nations Optional Protocol on the Rights of the Child in Armed Conflict.
- United Nations Millennium Declaration.
- Trafficking Victims Protection Act (United States).
- The Bureau of the Dutch Rapporteur on Trafficking in Human Beings is established.
- The Netherlands legalizes brothels.
- Juvenile Justice (Care and Protection of Children) Act, revised 2006 (India).
- Free the Slaves is founded (United States).

2001

- The U.S. Department of State issues the first Trafficking in Persons Report.
- The Second World Congress against the Sexual Exploitation of Children and Adolescents is held in Yokohama, Japan.
- The Economic Community of West African States' Declaration on the Fight against Trafficking in Persons.
- The Economic Community of West African States' Initial Plan of Action against Trafficking in Persons (2002–03).

2002

- South Asian Association for Regional Cooperation Convention on Trafficking.
- The Polaris Project is founded (United States).
- Red Latinoamericanos Desaparecidos (Latin American Network for Missing Persons) is established.

2003

- Prosecutorial Remedies and other Tools to End the Exploitation of Children Today Act (United States).
- Trafficking in Persons Law Enforcement and Administration Act (Nigeria).
- National Agency for the Prohibition of Trafficking in Persons established (Nigeria).

- Child Rights Act (Nigeria).
- "Operation Predator" is launched in the United States.
- Goa Children's Act (India) eliminates bail and increases fines and jail terms for those convicted of exploiting children in sex tourism.

2005

- Hindu Succession Act gives equal inheritance rights to Buddhist, Hindu, Jain, and Sikh women, including married daughters.
- The Netherlands's Criminal Code is amended to include forced labor as well as sex trafficking.
- *Vani* marriages (also called *swara* or *sang-chati* marriages) are outlawed in Pakistan.

2007

- New York State passes one of the toughest and most comprehensive state anti-trafficking laws in the United States.
- Amsterdam's mayor, Job Cohen, implements a plan to begin closing down the city's "window brothels" and other restriction on prostitution, saying that the Netherlands's legalization of brothels in 2000 had increased sex trafficking and the presence of organized crime.

2008

- The Third World Congress against the Sexual Exploitation of Children and Adolescents is held in Brazil.
- New York State passes the Safe Harbor for Exploited Youth Act and becomes the first state in the country to treat prostituted minors as victims rather than as criminals.
- A regional court convicts Niger of failure to prevent slavery and orders immediate steps to uphold its obligations under international treaties. The decision sets a precedent that will be applicable in all member states of the Economic Community of West African States.
- The Community Court of Justice of the Economic Community of West African States rules, in *Hadijatou Mani Koraou v. the Republic of Niger*, that Niger is guilty of gender discrimination and of failing to prevent slavery. This is the first time that a formerly enslaved person has sued a country for its action or inaction regarding slavery within its borders.

2009

- Congolese warlord Thomas Lubanga is brought to trial in the International Criminal Court on charges of using child soldiers. (As this is written, the case, *Prosecutor v. Thomas Lubanga Dyilois*, is in progress, and no verdict has been rendered.)

Glossary

amniocentesis   a prenatal test generally used to determine the genetic health of a fetus but also sometimes used to determine the sex of the fetus with an intent to abort a fetus of a particular sex (usually female).

Caesarian section/C-section   the surgical delivery of a child through an incision in the mother's abdomen.

chattel slavery   the legally recognized ownership of persons.

child labor   the use of minors in the workplace under terms considered inappropriate for children. These terms can include work during school or overly long hours, work in dangerous occupations, or any entry into the workplace prior to a specified age.

child marriage   according to international law, the marriage of a person before age 18.

child sex tourism   The traveling of persons to engage in commercial sex acts with children.

child soldier   according to international law, a soldier younger than 18.

coercion   according to the U.S. Department of State, "(a) threats of serious harm to or physical restraint against any person; (b) any scheme, plan or pattern intended to cause a person to believe that failure to perform an act would result in serious harm to or physical restraint against any person; or (c) the abuse or threatened abuse of the legal process."

commercial sex act   according to the U.S. Department of State, "any sex act on account of which anything of value is given to or received by any person."

convention   a legally binding international agreement, used synonymously with "treaty" and "covenant."

covenant   a legally binding international agreement, used synonymously with "convention" and "treaty."

Dalit   in India, the caste formerly known as the "untouchables."

debt bondage   According to the U.S. Department of State, "the status or condition of a debtor arising from a pledge by the debtor of his or her personal services or those of a person under his or her control as a security for debt, if the value of those services as reasonably assessed is not applied toward the liquidation of the debt or the length and nature of those services are not respectively limited and defined."

declaration   a document that sets forth certain agreed-upon principles, objectives, or standards, but one that is not legally binding.

dowry   monies paid by a bride's family to the groom's family upon a marriage.

fair trade   a designation certifying that a particular good is produced using fair labor standards, it also certifies that slave labor has not been used in a good's production.

female foeticide   the selective aborting of female fetuses for purposes of sex selection.

female infanticide   the killing of female infants, particularly when done so because the infants are female.

fistula   *see* OBSTETRIC FISTULA.

forced labor   the use of force, fraud, or coercion to enslave a person in non-sexual work.

forced marriage   according to international law, a marriage in which one or both parties has no meaningful right of refusal.

human trafficking   used interchangeably with "trafficking in persons" and "modern or modern-day slavery," human trafficking is the enslavement of persons without the support of law.

involuntary servitude   according to the U.S. Department of State, this "includes a condition of servitude by means of (a) any scheme, plan, or pattern intended to cause a person to believe that, if the person did not enter into or continue in such condition that person or another person would suffer serious harm or physical restraint; or (b) the abuse or threatened abuse of the legal process."

micro-loan/micro-lending   loans made in small dollar amounts to impoverished people.

modern or modern-day slavery   used interchangeably with "trafficking in persons" and "human trafficking," modern or modern-day slavery is the enslavement of persons without the support of law.

nongovernmental organization (NGO)   organizations formed and operating outside of governments.

obstetric fistula   an injury sustained during childbirth that results in a tear between a woman's bladder and/or rectum and her vagina. The child of such a delivery is generally stillborn, and the woman loses control of her bowel and/or bladder.

pedophile   one who has sexual relations with a child.

redemption/redeem   to purchase the freedom of an enslaved person.

red-light district   an area where the sex trades are openly conducted.

remittance   monies sent by expatriates to family members or others who remain in the expatriates' homelands.

sang-chati **marriage**   also known as *vani* or *swara* marriages, *sang-chati* marriages are tribal-council-ordered marriages in which a female from one family is awarded to another family in compensation for a crime committed by a man in the female's family.

severe form of trafficking   according to the U.S. Trafficking Victims Protection Act, "(a) sex trafficking in which the person induced to perform such an act has not attained 18 years of age; or (b) the recruitment, harboring, transportation, provision, or obtaining of a person for labor or services, through the use of force, fraud, or coercion for the purpose of subjection to involuntary servitude, peonage, debt bondage, or slavery."

sex tourism   the traveling of persons to engage in commercial sex acts.

sex trafficking   according to the U.S. Department of State, "the recruitment, harboring, transportation, provision, or obtaining of a person for the purpose of a commercial sex act.

swara **marriage**   also known as *vani* or *sang-chati* marriages, *swara* marriages are tribal-council-ordered marriages in which a female from one family is awarded to another family in compensation for a crime committed by a man in the female's family.

trafficking in persons   used interchangeably with "modern or modern-day slavery" and "human trafficking," trafficking in persons is the enslavement of persons without the support of law.

transplant tourism   the traveling of persons to receive transplant surgeries in countries not their own.

treaty   a legally binding international agreement, used synonymously with "convention" and "covenant."

T-Visa   a visa made available by the U.S. government to verified victims of human trafficking in the U.S.

vani **marriage**   also known as *swara* or *sang-chati* marriages, *vani* marriages are tribal-council-ordered marriages in which a female from one family is awarded to another family in compensation for a crime committed by a man in the female's family.

Index

Page numbers in **boldface** indicate major treatment of a subject. Page numbers followed by *c* indicate chronology entries. Page numbers followed by *f* indicate figures. Page numbers followed by *g* indicate glossary entries. Page numbers followed by *m* indicate maps.

involuntary domestic
servitude **19**
economic
motivations of
consumer 27
France 32
India 93, 98–99
Nigeria 79, 83
United States 45,
49–50, 148–157
involuntary servitude
(term) 329g
IOM. *See* International
Organization for
Migration
IPEC (ILO/International
Programme on the
Elimination of Child
Labour) 78
IRWPA (Indecent
Representation of
Women [Prohibition]
Act, India) 324c
Islam 84, 88–89
Italy 77, 80

J

Jacobson, Guy 267b
jirga 14
Johnson, Chris 58
Juvenile Justice (Care
and Protection of
Children) Act (India)
326c

K

Kadri, Vipula 267b–
268b

Kant, Ravi 268b
Kasten, Liora 268b
Kazakhstan 12
Kennedy, John F. 268b
Khatun, Meena 94–95
kidnapping 70
kidney scouts 100–101
"Kidney Theft Ring
Preys on India's
Poorest Laborers"
(Amelia Gentlemen,
New York Times)
216–217
Kloudas, Spyridon 17
Koraou, Hadijatou Mani
32–33, 268b–269b
Kristof, Nicholas D.
94–95
Kumar, Amit 100, 101

L

labor contractors 50–51
Lagon, Mark P. 60, 269b
"Leader of New
York–Connecticut
Sex-Trafficking Ring
Pleads Guilty" (PR
Newswire) 161
League of Nations
Convention to
Suppress the Slave
Trade and Slavery. *See*
Slavery Convention
legalized prostitution
70–74, 89–90, 326c,
327c
Lewis, Gary 94
licensing, of brothels 73

Lincoln, Abraham 132,
269b–270b, 321c
Lloyd, Rachel 57, 270b
loans 20
Lord's Resistance Army
(LRA) 22
"The Lost Children of
Nigeria's Sex Trade"
(Jonathan Clayton,
Times, London) 201
"lover boys" 10, 12, 70,
71, 75
LRA (Lord's Resistance
Army) 22
Lubanga, Thomas 32,
326c

M

Madunagu, Bene 270b
Mai, Mukhtar 270b–
271b
malams 88
Mann Act 55, 133–134,
322c
manufacturing 99.
See also sweatshop
manufacturing
maps and routes
249m–251m
marriage
arranged 14–15, 81,
97–98
brokered 16, 25, 93
child 81–82, 87,
96–98, 102, 251m,
328g
early 14–16, 81–82,
96, 108